Meaning and Interpretation of Music in Cinema

MUSICAL MEANING AND INTERPRETATION
Robert S. Hatten, editor

DAVID NEUMEYER

Meaning and Interpretation of Music in Cinema

with contributions by James Buhler

INDIANA UNIVERSITY PRESS

Bloomington & Indianapolis

This book is a publication of

Indiana University Press
Office of Scholarly Publishing
Herman B Wells Library 350
1320 East 10th Street
Bloomington, Indiana 47405 USA

iupress.indiana.edu

The paper used in this publication meets the minimum requirements
of the American National Standard for Information Sciences—
Permanence of Paper for Printed Library Materials, ANSI Z39.48–1992.

Manufactured in the United States of America

Library of Congress Cataloging-in-Publication Data

Neumeyer, David.
  Meaning and interpretation of music in cinema / David
Neumeyer ; with contributions by James Buhler.
    pages cm. — (Musical meaning and interpretation)
    Includes bibliographical references and index.
    ISBN 978-0-253-01642-3 (cl : alk. paper) — ISBN 978-0-253-
01649-2 (pb : alk. paper) — ISBN 978-0-253-01651-5 (eb) 1. Motion
picture music—Analysis, appreciation. 2. Motion picture music—
History and criticism. I. Buhler, James, 1964– II. Title.
    ML2075.N48 2015
    781.5'42—dc23
                                                        2014047475

1 2 3 4 5   20 19 18 17 16 15

For Laura, who was named after the film;

Kat, who at five was already her own producer;

Dana, who wrote her own script;

and in memory of Livonia Warren McCallum,
who was the model for Princess Glory
in Gulliver's Travels *(1939).*

Contents

Preface

This book continues along a path I started down more than two decades ago: a synthesis of the methods and priorities of film studies and music studies. That is hardly a novelty in the present day, I am pleased to report, as the literature of film music studies continues to grow in both quantity and quality. Technological advances have certainly contributed enormously to these gains—over the past decade, the visual has become ever more a routine part of daily activity and has moved ever more firmly to the forefront of cultural attention—but progress has also come with the inevitable shifts of focus and priority that accompany generational change.

Readers who know my earlier work—a significant portion of it written in coauthorship with James Buhler—will expect to find that the text-object for study is the sound track, not the music track within it. That expectation will certainly be fulfilled here, but this volume is distinguished from my previous publications in that I posit a framework based on the priority of speech (dialogue) and then explore its implications for the analysis and interpretation of music in film. The voice is the place where film studies and (film) music studies meet: the voice—having its source in an agent—guarantees the priority of the image and narrative at the same time that it forces attention to sound and the image/sound dialectic basic to the cinema.

Organization

The book's seven chapters are gathered in three parts. The first of these is titled "Meaning and Interpretation" and moves about among issues and questions for film music analysis and film style in relation to sound. Chapter 1 lays out the ideological and methodological ground. The study of narrative sound film concerns itself with the two components of the film (sound and image) and their interplay with narrative; music is one component of the sound track. I argue that the sound track has a "natural" hierarchy in which speech has priority. "Natural" is in scare quotes here because I accept its status *a priori* without adding any specific cognitive or evolutionary arguments.[1] At the same time, the *mise-en-bande* (integrated or multiplane sound track; Altman 2000, 341), with its complex and historically contingent interplay of music, dialogue, ambient sound, effects, and silences, can be interpreted as a kind of musical composition, and aural analysis can then be brought to bear on the sound track as a whole, its relation to the image, and its contribution to narrative. The distinction between music *for* film (understood semiautonomously) and music *in* film (understood as an element of the sound track) is central (Altman 2000, 340). In the final section, three case studies of characteristic scenes with music from *To Have and Have Not* (1944) provide illustrations of the chapter's main points.

Chapter 2 continues the methodological work, first in the form of a discussion of an audiovisual analytic heuristic outlined by Michel Chion (1994, 189; 2003, 263), then in terms of a set of binary oppositions understood as the basis of film music's narrative functions. These five binaries are the familiar diegetic/nondiegetic, along with foreground/background, clarity/fidelity, synchronization/counterpoint, and empathy/anempathy. The internal dialectic of each of these functions and their interactions is construed in terms of a "fantastical gap" or complex field lying between oppositions (Stilwell 2007, 184). Examples include scenes from *The Big Sleep* (1946), *North by Northwest* (1959), *Casablanca* (1943),[2] *M* (1931), *Written on the Wind* (1957), and *Prénom Carmen* (1983). The final section of the chapter begins with discussion of the correlations of diegetic/nondiegetic and onscreen/offscreen. Apart from their joining in song performance, music and voice come most closely together in the several modes of the acoustic and the acousmatic. After an excursus on presence/absence, an opposition even more fundamental than the five binaries, the discussion leads to a summary example for the chapter's presentation: the opening sequences from *Rebecca* (1940).

Parts 2 and 3 continue the work by extended example. They are in effect mirrors of each other, though both are devoted to close reading: part 2 offers an extended reading of music in a single film, *Casablanca*, and part 3 looks at a variety of (mostly) recent films that make use of two compositions by J. S. Bach: the C Major Prelude from *The Well-Tempered Clavier*, Book I, and the very closely related prelude from the Cello Suite in G Major. The original plan for part 3 was to focus entirely on the C Major Prelude, but because the number of films in which it appears is not large, I was obliged to add the G Major Prelude, which has come into increasing favor with filmmakers over the past twenty-five years.

The notion of the sound track as musical composition receives its most extended treatment in chapter 3. James Buhler and I particularly emphasize the impact on interpretation of the concept of acoustic stylization, the recognition that sound tracks, like image tracks, are not merely "recorded" but edited, constructed. In chapter 4, a very detailed analysis of one scene—when Rick and Ilsa first meet in his café—brings with it a return to the central issues of vococentrism, which are worked out here in the form of questions for interpretation. Chapter 5, then, looks at the filmic contexts of that reunion scene: the two later confrontations between Rick and Ilsa, for which the underscore composer, Max Steiner, reworked and developed the same music. To close, we return to the theme of acoustic stylization with a reading of the film's airport finale.

Musical topics and their transformations (as troping, or the creative juxtaposition of topics [Hatten 2004, 2–3]) come into the foreground in part 3. Earlier, the chapters of part 2 had particularly emphasized two of the three principles from chapter 1: music *in* film, or the priority of the sound track over its individual components; and the sound track as constructed, or the priority of clarity over fidelity. In part 3, the issue of music *for* and music *in* film receives some further consideration, but the third principle is the real focus of attention: the omnivorous appetite of the music track, or the functional equivalence of musical styles and topics. Depending on tempo in performance, the C Major and G Major Preludes are an instance of either the étude or the pastoral topic. The étude includes the pedagogical, the perpetual motion or kinetic, and the virtuosic. The pastoral ranges from the historical pastoral mode, representing leisurely pleasure in the outdoors, to the religious pastoral. I argue that the audiovisual combination inevitably involves a troping effect on preexisting music, in line with Michel Chion's insistence that image and sound will always affect ("add value" to) one another: that is to say, any music in film is film music, but any film will also change the musics it incorporates.

Background

In mid-2009, at about the time I finished a final editing pass for our textbook, *Hearing the Movies: Music and Sound in Film History,* my colleague and frequent coauthor, James Buhler, urged me to collect our several cowritten research articles—which had appeared in a variety of venues—and publish them as an essay anthology. Shortly thereafter, Robert Hatten discussed with me the possibility of a monograph for his series Musical Meaning and Interpretation, published by Indiana University Press. As this series represents a creative intersection between music theory, musical semiotics, and music historical studies, it promised to be a particularly congenial home for our work, which has been concerned with negotiating a productive space for film music studies between the disciplines of music studies and film studies. I set out to write a volume that would summarize but also considerably expand on arguments that I have made or that Jim and I have collectively made elsewhere, drawing in citations to the burgeoning literature in film music studies, as well.

The book as it stands maintains that overall strategy, but it is the product of a somewhat more complex process of textual collation and creation. Chapter 1, by and large, summarizes arguments I have been making for many years, with the exception of my more recent concept of "vococentric cinema," developed in a closely related series of conference papers I presented in 2006 and 2007 (the reading of a scene from *The Big Sleep* in chapter 2 is also based on those papers).[3] With the exception of some material in the section on *Rebecca* (1940) in chapter 2 and a few isolated short texts identified in the notes, these papers and all remaining material have not been previously published. The majority of chapter 3 is a lightly edited version of those sections in a published article for which James Buhler is the principal author (Neumeyer and Buhler 2005). The detailed description of character action and events in the reunion scene from *Casablanca* in chapter 4 is also his work (from an unpublished text), as is the more theoretical material on vococentrism in the same place. I am grateful for his permission to include those contributions here.

As to the broad argument of the book: The insistence on the sound track—not the music track—as the object of study is a position that Jim and I share. The radicalization of that claim to include the notion of a vococentric cinema, however, is my own, though the reader will certainly recognize the seeds of it in the work of Chion.

Acknowledgments

The reader will now understand why my first, and happy, obligation is to thank James Buhler. In addition to contributing a substantial amount of material, he was willing to take time out to read and comment on the draft texts for parts 1 and 2. I am also grateful to Jim for the chapters he contributed to a volume I recently edited: *The Oxford Handbook of Film Music Studies;* these survey film theory since roughly 1945 and connect it to music and the sound track. I have drawn on his explanations at several points here. Quite apart from arguments or texts, everywhere in the book his influence will be apparent, as we have gradually developed over the years a common viewpoint about the nature and priorities of film music studies. The path to that result might be best characterized as my initially pointing the way (in the late 1980s), Jim's taking that path, and dragging me along after. That is to say, his commitment to film music studies as an interdisciplinary field (rather than a sideshow in twentieth-century music studies)—and his gaining command of the necessary literatures—definitely preceded mine, and I have learned a great deal from him, then and since.

It is also a pleasure to thank Robert Hatten for his enthusiastic early interest in the project and his guidance throughout its several stages, from proposal, writing, and editing to production. His careful editing of the entire manuscript has made it a much better book. And I am delighted that, between the signing of the original contract and the completion of the manuscript, Robert became our colleague in the Sarah and Ernest Butler School of Music, The University of Texas at Austin. At Indiana University Press, I thank Raina Polivka, music, film, and humanities editor; Jenna Whittaker, assistant sponsoring editor; Naz Pantaloni, Jacobs School of Music librarian and copyright consultant to the press; Nancy Lightfoot, production coordinator; and Mary M. Hill, copyeditor. The index was prepared by Martin L. White.

I have drawn on work with two other coauthors. Laura Neumeyer wrote the interesting parts in what is otherwise a densely theoretical article on Barthes, the photograph, and the moving image (Neumeyer and Neumeyer 2007); some material from that article, substantially revised, reappears here in chapter 1. Nathan Platte's thorough and clearly written study of the score materials and music production process greatly enhanced our jointly written volume on *Rebecca* for the Scarecrow Film Score Guides series (Neumeyer and Platte 2012); the case study in chapter 2's section on the acousmêtre is developed from that book.

Over the past twenty-five years, I have carried out research in a number of archives, most extensively in these: MGM and Warner Bros. Collections, Doheny

Library, University of Southern California; Franz Waxman Collection, Special Collections, Ahern Library, Syracuse University; Republic Pictures and Max Steiner Collections, Special Collections, Harold B. Lee Library, Brigham Young University; and the David O. Selznick Collection, Harry Ransom Humanities Research Center, The University of Texas at Austin. I am grateful to these institutions for making these important archives available to researchers and to the archivists and their assistants for helping to make my visits both pleasant and productive.

I am also happy to acknowledge Joel Love, a recent doctoral graduate in music composition at The University of Texas at Austin. Joel did the digital engraving of musical examples for this volume, including the complex reductions and linear analysis graphs, and did so with skill and efficiency—and, beyond that, with informed interest in the topic. In addition, he did several transcriptions of audio from sound tracks. Joel also offered insights into jazz influences and film-scoring practices in *Sunset Boulevard* (1950) in connection with an analysis that I reluctantly decided to delete from the final version of the manuscript.

Christopher Husted carried out research for me relating to *Girl of the Golden West* and *Casablanca* using archive collections stored at the University of Southern California and in the Los Angeles local office of the American Federation of Musicians. He also created some of the preliminary versions of the music examples.

It is appropriate to acknowledge the leadership and ongoing support of film music studies by three UT Austin administrators: Douglas Dempster, dean of the College of Fine Arts; Robert Freeman, former dean of the college; and B. Glenn Chandler, former director of the School of Music. In addition, I thank Douglas Dempster and Glenn Chandler for their support of the school's Center for American Music.

I am indebted to Douglas Dempster for publication support supplied from College of Fine Arts funds and to the President's Office of The University of Texas at Austin for a publication subvention grant. Support from these sources has allowed me to use a considerably larger number of musical examples, screen stills, and figures than would otherwise have been possible.

The Office of the Vice President for Research, The University of Texas at Austin, awarded two special research grants and a research leave appointment (fall 2011) that provided the time to complete the first draft manuscript. I am especially grateful to David Bordwell, emeritus professor of communication arts, University of Wisconsin–Madison, for his role as an external referee in securing that leave.

Finally, I acknowledge the following individuals and organizations for their permission to reproduce more extended excerpts from copyrighted material: Warner/Chappell (through Alfred Music, Inc.: Troy Schreck, contract and licensing administrator) for cue 4,7 (reunion scene) from Max Steiner's music to *Casablanca;* Faber Music for European rights to the same; Indiana University Press for a figure and table from Raymond Bellour, *The Analysis of Film* (2000) and for a figure from an article of mine in *Wagner and Cinema,* edited by Jeongwon Joe and Sander Gilman (2009); Breitkopf & Härtel for score citations from Suite no. 2 by Johann Adam Reincken (in *Sämtliche Werke für Klavier/Cembalo,* edited by Klaus Beckmann [1982]); and Michael L. Klein for his assistance with our efforts to contact the copyright holder of an article by James Buhler and myself from *Interdisciplinary Studies in Musicology 5* (Poznan, 2005).

Part I

Meaning and Interpretation

1 Music in the Vococentric Cinema

A simple, typical example of sound practice in the Hollywood studio era (roughly 1930–60) may be found in a few moments from *The Dark Corner* (1946), an A-level *film noir* obviously meant as a stand-alone sequel to *Laura* (1944). An evening party at the lavish home of Hardy Cathcart (Clifton Webb) includes a dance sequence that begins with a straight-on view of members of Eddie Heywood's band (figure 1.1a), followed by a pan across the dancing couples to Cathcart and his wife, Mari (Cathy Downs, figure 1.1b). The sound level of the band is maintained during the pan but drops a little as Webb's voice enters at the original, higher sound level; the band is now offscreen and in the sonic background. The couple, in medium shot, are seen at a very modest angle (to emphasize the dance), but on the reverse to Mari (figure 1.1c), a standard shot / reverse shot with an eyeline match is used, confirming the priority (and, with the tighter framing, also the privacy) of their conversation.[1] The backgrounding of the music serves narrative clarity and happens in collusion with the camera: the pan charts distance covered, but no attention is paid to a drop in volume for the physical circumstances of the room (in other words, the band actually *should* be louder as Cathcart and Mari talk). Music begins as performance, but it leads before long to the voice.[2]

The work presented in this book is grounded in two assertions: the integrated sound track is basic, and the cinema is vococentric. These are elaborated as three general principles, the first of which recognizes that the sound track is the film's audio system and asserts that, as such, the sound track has priority over any of its individual elements. The second acknowledges that the sound track is constructed—the overriding priority in the classical system being narrative clarity, not acoustic fidelity—and it is hierarchical, with the voice (speech, dialogue) at the top, music and sound effects below.[3] The third follows directly from the second: film music is stylistically plural. It is in fact any music used in a film; that is, no special status is given to symphonic underscore.[4]

The three principles will be familiar to those who know my published work over the past decade or more, including texts coauthored with James Buhler. In the present volume, however, I have radicalized my position through a claim that the narrative sound film is vococentric. In a sense, the claim of vococentrism is simply a restatement of the first two principles above: if the sound track as a whole is the proper object of study, then analysis and criticism must always take into account—begin from—the internal sound track hierarchy. I will seek to convince

Figure 1.1, a–c. *The Dark Corner* (1946), dance (at about 21:20): (a) music played by Eddie Heywood's band; (b) initial view of Hardy and Mari Cathcart; (c) second view. Screen stills.

the reader—as I am myself convinced—that, reductive as this model may appear, it yields results that are truer to film as an art. Furthermore, it is both richer and more nuanced with respect to music than the all-too-common approach in which film is seen as a backdrop for interpretation of its music. Analysis and interpretation are also greatly enriched by the recognition that, although the sound track as a whole has priority, its internal hierarchy guarantees a dialectic among its elements. As we shall see, the fact that the sound cinema is vococentric does not mean the hierarchy is mechanically expressed in every filmic situation. The voice (as speech) is the benchmark, but other elements, and especially music, often compete with it. Beyond that, I will argue that two basic structures—of action (agency in the image) and of speech (agency in the sound track)—give rise to the basic formal units of spectacle and dialogue.

This Book's Title, Part 1: Meaning, Interpretation

In order to position the kind of work that arises from the three principles outlined above in relation to the critical practices of the music studies discipline, it will be useful to examine the four keywords in this book's title.[5] The first of them, "meaning," may be defined as whatever arises from acts of interpretation as they operate on cinematic texts or, more specifically for my purpose here, on cinematic texts as read in terms of the musical component of their sound tracks. Making sense of that definition, however, requires a comparable definition of "interpretation," preferably of course one that does not collapse into the circular by including the word "meaning." I respect the distinction between meaning and interpretation implied by the title of this Indiana University Press book series—one would not need both of them if the two terms were really pretty much the same (as many of us came to assume for a while in the 1980s, when terms like "narrative," "interpretation," "criticism," and the like were expanding dramatically, seeming to co-opt whole fields in a rush to the multidisciplinary). The paired words in the series title suggest that "meaning" is better defined as what arises from the effects generated by texts, which for most films (like most literature) very particularly means narrative effects. "Interpretation," on the other hand, is a handy umbrella term for critical practices, that is to say, what it is we do with—or how it is that we respond to—the effects that texts generate.

The two terms as defined here align well with Robert Hatten's "historical meanings" (or "stylistic knowledge") and "hermeneutic inquiry" as they are expressed in the following passage from his book *Interpreting Musical Gestures, Topics, and Tropes*: "We maintain that the 'aesthetic' is no illusion, . . . that we still have access to *relatively objective* (by which I mean *intersubjectively defensible*) historical meanings—both at the general level of style (which can be *reconstructed* to a degree that the evidence will allow) and at the more detailed level of a work (which must be interpreted not only from stylistic knowledge but also through hermeneutic inquiry)" (2004, 6; emphasis in the original). David Bordwell makes a similar distinction based more directly on disciplinary practices and in a negative formulation that reflects his pessimistic view of the state of film studies in the 1980s: "Interpretation of individual films can be fruitfully renewed by a historical scholarship that seeks out the concrete and unfamiliar conditions under which all sorts of meaning are made. Further, interpretation should not overwhelm analysis of form and style; the critic should not strive to reduce every effect to the conventions of interpretive reason" (1989, 273).[6]

The distinction between meaning and interpretation is connected to a historical trajectory beginning with nineteenth-century critics, commentators, and historians who gave priority to the author, often radically in the notion of the genius and masterwork. This view began to be contested as early as the 1890s and was under siege by the 1930s, by which time priority was shifting to the text, specifically the text as system (whether construed as organic or mechanical). Early structuralist models and the interpretive practices exemplified in literary studies by the New Critics represent this phase well. By the late 1960s, the opposition closed system / infinite meaning began to shift criticism into its poststructuralist phase, and with that change attention swiftly moved away from the text to the reader (or viewer, audio-viewer [Chion 1994, xxv], critic), most directly through interpretive models of deconstruction in literary studies (eventually imported into music, as well) and reader-response theory, but also through cognitivist analytical models, most prominently for music studies through Lerdahl and Jackendoff's (1983) generative theory of tonal music and for film studies through Bordwell's (1985) narrative theory. Only in recent decades has the balance been righted somewhat because of attention given to empirical audience-response research (Bordwell 2008, 20).[7]

This author-text-reader tricolon is simply a historically mapped version of a model of communication dating to the 1920s and closely linked to information theory (Shannon and Weaver), to linguistics (Jakobson's six communication functions), and through linguistics to literary theory and interpretation (cited in Cobley 2008, 15). The literature on these issues is very large indeed—almost all of literary theory over the past fifty years and a significant part of film theory from the 1960s through at least the mid-1990s is fundamentally concerned with it—and each of the positions has its strong, sometimes strident, advocates. I do not argue that any should be privileged; in practice, they obviously can, as Jakobson's model already made clear (the "poetic" function, for example, simply gives priority to experience of the text, etc.).[8] Instead, I assert that the interpreter must always be clear in locating the focus and—the harder part—be willing to acknowledge its limitations. Bias toward the author is always in danger of collapsing into the hagiographic (and becomes indistinguishable from promotion or marketing). Bias toward the text too readily turns formalistic (tending to praise complexity for its own sake). And, finally, bias toward the reader-critic can, paradoxically, be merely willful, even when it is plainly constrained by the conventionalized patterns of interpretive rhetoric, whether or not tied to a more or less fully articulated ideology.

Without making particular theoretical or ideological claims, then, I find that separating textual effects from interpretive practices—at least provisionally—

has greater heuristic value for the study of films, and sound and music as integrated within them, than does insisting that they cannot or should not be separated. In any case, this separation results in selective emphases, not a brick wall, and it creates priorities for interpretation, not an unbridgeable ideological divide (unless the critic chooses to foreground one, of course). Bordwell helpfully separates what he calls "comprehension" from "interpretation": under each heading he includes two types of meanings that the reader or viewer might construct. Under "comprehension" fall referential meanings and explicit meanings. Referential meanings are those that attempt to make sense of the diegetic world and character actions, whereas explicit meanings try to reconstruct the film's (author's) goals and intentions based on what is directly presented. Under "interpretation" are implicit meanings and symptomatic meanings. Implicit meanings go a step further than explicit meanings, to the abstract level of thematic statements, whereas symptomatic meanings assume a critical stance in the sense of "reading against the grain," assuming a fissure between a film's presentation and themes, and its underlying ideology (Bordwell 1989, 8–18).

Bordwell, however, also says one should not "assume that the four sorts of meanings constitute levels which the critic must traverse in a given sequence. . . . There is evidence [for example] that whereas beginning interpreters of poetry do read referentially and have trouble making the thematic leap, skilled interpreters try out implicit meanings from the start and often neglect the 'literal' level, or summon it up only to help the interpretation along" (1989, 11). Given that it can require some effort to pay specific attention to music and its effects, however, the literature has profited from careful descriptions, that is, attention to referential and explicit meanings that include music and sound. Robynn Stilwell uses such examples in the context of her theoretical construction of the diegetic/nondiegetic pair, the opposition that has come under criticism repeatedly since it was clearly formulated in relation to film music by Claudia Gorbman (1987).[9] Stilwell argues against abandoning or radically reconceiving the opposition: "Because the border between diegetic and nondiegetic is crossed so often does not invalidate the separation. If anything, it calls attention to the act of crossing and therefore reinforces difference" (2007, 184). It should be noted that Stilwell's argument is consistent with Gorbman's original description: "Significantly, the only element of filmic discourse that appears extensively in nondiegetic as well as diegetic contexts, and often freely crosses the boundary line in between, is music. Once we understand the flexibility that music enjoys with respect to the film's diegesis, we begin to recognize how many different kinds of functions it can have: temporal, spatial, dramatic, structural, denotative, connotative—both in the diachronic flow of a film and at various interpretive levels simultaneously" (1987, 22). What Stilwell calls the "fantastical gap" is a "border region," "a transformative space, a superposition, a transition between stable states" (2007, 200). Presumably because her essay is concerned with filling out the definition of the "fantastical gap," her examples tend to concern themselves with Bordwell's level of "comprehension" rather than "interpretation." We will look briefly at her discussion of the main-title sequence from the Jane and Anna Campion film *Holy Smoke* (1999).

Among the powers of the "fantastical gap" is the ability to flip a "default" cluster of terms that associates underscore with empathy and subjectivity (as in "point-of-view music," where we effectively "hear" a character's emotions) and source or diegetic music with anempathy (emotional neutrality or indifference) and objectivity (as, for instance, in the dance scene from *The Dark Corner* discussed above: the music is simply expected in that real-life situation). "Holly Holy," a song by Neil Diamond, frames the main-title sequence of *Holy Smoke*. As such it acts as a "simple, extended sound advance, a transition from nondiegetic to diegetic," a design that is "technically unexceptional" for historical-statistical reasons: "Many films begin with credit music that is full sounding and apparently nondiegetic but 'shrinks' to the diegetic space of the first postcredit scene." What does require explanation (Stilwell's "A closer look, however, reveals . . .") is the reversal of functional roles: "Relative objectivity in the nondiegetic [gives way] to relative subjectivity in the diegetic" (Stilwell 2007, 197)—that is, what is at first just a song for the conventional formal frame of the main-title sequence becomes closely linked with Ruth's (Kate Winslet's) response to the cult's partying ritual (that is to say, Ruth of the film becomes associated with Holly of the song). The remainder of Stilwell's analysis is a detailed explication of this process, beginning from a thematic linking of song and film. The song "is clearly about a search for meaning and redemption, reflecting Ruth's search for 'the real stuff' in India," a search that leads her to join a cult, which she has effectively already done by the time the song is over. First attracted by "a happy group of young, mostly European women in Indian dress" (figure 1.2a–b), Ruth follows them to a multistory building. She reaches the roof to find the cult members eating, talking, and dancing (figure 1.2c). "The transition from nondiegetic to diegetic takes place slowly, in an almost dreamlike fashion. . . . It is only [during subsequent nighttime shots] at the peak of the music, the drive to the recapitulation of the chorus from the bridge, that the visuals . . . and the music coincide [we see dancers shouting words in time to the music], confirming that it is indeed, or has become, diegetic. This creates a sense of arrival, of the completion that Ruth will find here" (197–98).

Stilwell's description, then, reads explicit meanings that include music, as if to answer the question "Why did the directors use this song for the opening?" and makes use of referential meanings as needed. In the limited context of this example, that would be enough, but interpretation clearly guides the reading. From the observation that the design used here is unusual (and the implicit assumption that establishing sequences often provide significant information about the film that follows) comes the thematic statement about this opening in relation to Ruth's life goals. Stilwell's analysis is obviously text centered, as befits the goal of her essay. It would have been author centered if used in a critical appreciation of Campion's career. It would have been viewer/reader centered if it was the background for an exploration of responses to this opening, plausible "hermeneutic windows" (Kramer 1990, 9–10) being a moment of stylistic excess near the begin-

music
angelo badalamenti

Figure 1.2, a–c. *Holy Smoke* (1999), main title sequence; music by Neil
Diamond, "Holly Holy." Screen stills.

ning (the nondiegetic status of the music is disturbed when we see a close-up of hands as Ruth and her friend ride a crowded train and we hear the audience clapping in the sound track) or, in the final moments of synchronization, the curious fact that we see only men (and them not too well) in the darkness.

An extension to Bordwell's third category, symptomatic meanings, would have led well outside the scene to a cultural, political, or religious critique of cults or of the parallelisms the Campions establish between Ruth's joining the cult and her parents' attempts to stop her (through the person of cult deprogrammer PJ Waters [Harvey Keitel]). In the following comment from his review of this film, the late Roger Ebert stops just short of this step, inviting his readers to take it for themselves: "Ruth comes onscreen as one kind of person—dreamy, escapist, a volunteer for mind-controlling beliefs—and then turns into an articulate spokeswoman for Jane and Anna Campion's ideas. . . . It's difficult to see how the Ruth at the end of the film could have fallen under the sway of the guru at the beginning. Not many radical feminists seek out male gurus in patriarchal cultures" (2000).

Finally, I should emphasize that one is certainly not obliged to go through each of Bordwell's four meaning categories in order (as if in some repetition of an evolutionary succession). Any experienced scholar will freely combine them in a way that serves the point of the argument. Among many examples in the recent literature, I would point to Catherine Haworth's (2012) excellent study of music and gender relations in B-level *films noirs* from the 1940s. Haworth's larger argument is clearly focused on symptomatic meanings: she summarizes one film, *Stranger on the Third Floor* (1940), by saying that "despite [the male lead's] relatively unusual presentation as hero and the positive aspects of [the female lead's] construction as female detective, the film uses their romantic relationship primarily as a means of diminishing [her] agency and reinforcing [his] narrative dominance" (553). Within this context of patriarchy, "music and sound can . . . be read as reinforcing his dominance for much of the film, despite his increasingly fragile mental state and incarceration in its latter stages" (555). Serving this argument, however, are detailed analytical descriptions along with thematic statements and careful style-historical generalizations.

This Book's Title, Part 2: Cinema, Music

Continuing with examination of the book's title, I will skip to the last of the four keywords, "cinema." By this I mean the practices of feature film production, postproduction, distribution, and exhibition, the body of texts that arise from those practices, and the cultures associated with both practices and texts, along with the meanings circulated by them. In this volume I concern myself with the narrative feature film, but without prejudice toward other genres (such as the live or animated short, the experimental or avant-garde film, or the documentary), toward other audiovisual media (such as television or digital platforms), or toward other aesthetic or entertainment forms that rely on reproduced sound (such as radio or the varieties of portable music players). The narrative feature film has overwhelmingly been the object of case studies and the source of examples in the film literature and in the more specialized film music literature. Furthermore, the great majority of films discussed have been American. Although these biases are rapidly diminishing—a change for the good—they do suit my own repertorial interest in early film. My research has been primarily concerned with the era of the classical sound film (roughly 1930–70) and, even there, more closely with the first two decades—that is, with the transition decade (1926–35) up to the first years of serious competitive pressure from television around 1950. My exploration of more recent films in the two chapters of part 3 is a nod in a different direction, but beyond that I wish to emphasize that my usual repertorial preferences do not reflect those I necessarily advocate for others, nor do they reflect present trends. The current literature is in fact increasingly concerned with much more recent cinema, including transnational cinema, television, and internet-based media, while at the same time demonstrating a dramatically improved and deepened scholarship on pre-sound-era film practices.

Finally, then, "music." Unlike "cinema," which I limit pragmatically, I construe "music" in a very broad sense. As the third of my general principles listed above has it, any music used in a film is film music. And, furthermore, any music used in the context of film exhibition (as in new performances with silent films) or other creative adaptation is also film music. With this, I allow no bias toward repertoires or functional types, toward classical music as opposed to popular musics (or high art over low), composed over stock, symphonic underscore over diegetic performances, complex over simple, ambiguous against overdetermined, or understated as opposed to spectacular. (Note, in this connection, that neither of my examples so far—from *The Dark Corner* and *Holy Smoke*—has involved symphonic underscore, the easiest type to affiliate with concert music.) Even now, music remains one element of the sound track, despite the sudden and radical upsurge in nuance and complexity that became possible with the introduction of Dolby noise reduction in the 1970s and that kick-started the modern practices of sound design. In the context of a feature film's sound track, music most often works in one or more of three ways: (1) referentially (supplying or reinforcing identifying markers of time, place, social status, ethnicity, etc.); (2) expressively (as a marker of emotion); (3) motivically (that is, in the manner of the motif in literature or motive in music, supplying recurring elements that help to clarify the processes of narrative comprehension).[10]

Apart from the issue of narrative functions, the (sometimes radical) juxtaposition or intermingling of musical styles in film—beginning in fact before the sound era in silent film exhibition practices, and also found in early radio and early television—has only recently begun prompting different, less nostalgia-prone historical narratives of twentieth-century music, which even at this late date seem not able to escape the bounds of Romantic conceptions of classical music's special moral authority. This is a large subject, of course, worthy of a volume to itself.[11] I approach it only indirectly here through repertoire choice (that is to say, by not privileging older musics) but, more importantly, through a historical account that gives a central place to the influence of technology in the progress of the arts over the past century.

The Vococentric Cinema

In his discussion of sound track hierarchy—the idea that the voice has priority—Michel Chion quotes Alfred Hitchcock's statement that "the position of the face determines the shot composition," and then, as Chion puts it, "I had only to transpose this lucid remark to the aural register: the first thing people hear is the voice." The sound cinema is vococentric: "The voice hierarchizes everything around it" (1994, 6), and it is the technical and aesthetic practices of sound design itself that guarantee this hierarchy. By "sound design" here I mean not just the present-day common meaning—post-1970 practices that grew out of stereo multitrack recording—but also the invention and consolidation of the continuous-level sound track in the 1930s. As Rick Altman, McGraw Jones, and Sonia Tatroe describe it, the development of this model, which was not complete until nearly a decade after the appearance of the first sound feature films, originated in competition for priority in the sound track among various traditions ("live vs. recorded music, ex cathedra lectures vs. situated dialogue, narrative sound effects vs. vaudevillesque comic effects") and, for each, a corresponding "group of workers, a set of economic commitments, and a body of beliefs regarding the value of a particular sound strategy" (Altman 2000, 357). The compromise that was worked out—"the new overdetermined, multiplexed *mise-en-bande*"—solved a central problem for speech, scale matching, because "a nearly continuous but back-grounded effects track" anchored the sound/image relation in ambient sound, and thus the voice could always be foregrounded. This "foregrounded but intermittent dialogue track" was supported by nondiegetic music whose "variations in volume . . . provide[d] continuous commentary, while making way for narratively important dialogue" (358).[12] Diegetic music, of course, could serve the same role in some circumstances, as we saw in the dance scene from *The Dark Corner.*

It is Chion who reminds us that the continuous-level sound track is not a unitary sound track, and for a simple reason: "Sound in film is voco- and verbocentric, above all, because human beings in their habitual behavior are as well" (1994, 6). "Vococentric" refers to the priority of the voice, "verbocentric" to the priority of the text, particularly of course the text of speech (Chion 2009, 73). "Vococentric" also includes what I will call the grain of the voice (its sound and texture), where "verbocentric" would also include text presented directly on-screen, in signs, letter inserts, and so on. In the classical model, narrative-image-sound may be a set of relations, but it is first of all a hierarchy. Narrative unfolded by images—the fundamental property of a film—is supported by sound: most directly (and one can argue necessarily) by speech, more indirectly (and one can argue incidentally) by music and effects. Or, as one early film music theorist, Leonid Sabaneev, put it: "It should always be remembered, as a first principle of the aesthetics of music in the cinema, that [narrative] logic requires music to give way to dialogue" (quoted in Gorbman 1987, 77). All this means that the "base option" in sound track analysis is to position music in relation to the voice.

Incongruous though it might seem at first, the cinema hierarchy and the idea of the vococentric cinema can be supported by Carolyn Abbate's notion of music as "sticky," which she offers in the context of an extended critique of nineteenth-century ideas of absolute music and their persistence into the present, not only in the sense of the autonomous artwork but also in the notion of music's transcendent powers. "One might say that music is stickier and less important than the romantics—including the many still with us—want to imagine." Abbate, however, does not so much replace these ideas as merge them: "[Music] is at once ineffable *and* sticky; that is its fundamental incongruity. Words stick to it. . . . Images and corporeal gestures stick as well." When Abbate then says that "physical grounding and visual symbolism and verbal content change musical sounds by recommending how they are to be understood" (2004, 523–24; emphasis in original), she is restating what Chion identifies as "added value," a cognition-based "audiovisual contract" under which image and sound mutually influence each other (1994, 5; 2009, 212–14).

Abbate's notion of "stickiness" is a somewhat broader version of Edward T. Cone's notion of appropriation: "Music does not express emotions but appropriates them" (quoted in Cook 1998, 96). Cook's own theory of musical multimedia qualifies this idea by limiting it functionally—that is, not *every* combination of music and text, for example, is going to be meaningful (96–97)—and by insisting on an ongoing, dynamic interaction (not a static combination). This "reciprocal transfer of attributes that gives rise to a meaning constructed, not just reproduced, by multimedia" (97) is equivalent to the relationship between sound and image in Chion's audiovisual contract.[13]

I will adopt Abbate's term to suggest that narrative reference impedes or slows down the diachronic flow of music in time. Music that is "stuck" to organized meaning pays homage to the vococentric nature of cinema. The more music participates in supporting, advancing, or commenting on narrative, the more it loses the integrity of its diachronic flow.[14] With respect to analysis and interpretation, this means being wary of hearing films too strongly in terms of music. One must try not to exaggerate music's role, try not to reinstate the old mysteries and powers to which Abbate refers. Claiming film music for a discipline by constructing interpretations of implicit meanings grounded in the idea that music is "equal" to the image, or "agential," will only work if one also acknowledges the limitations of the contexts in which such claims can be made, or, to put it another way, if one acknowledges the limitations imposed by an inevitably distorted mode of viewing and hearing a film. This is, of course, simply another way of putting the point that our priority should be music *in* film, not music *for* film (Altman 2000, 340).

By developing a series of oppositions as a cluster (several binaries where the terms on each side are linked), I will connect Abbate's music stickiness to Roland Barthes's conception of the relation of film and photograph. The binary pair *studium/punctum* is the central construct in Barthes's last book, *Camera Lucida,* which, like most of his late publications (including the better-known *Pleasure of the Text* and *A Lover's Discourse*), is at a counterpole to his early establishment and promulgation of a scientific semiology. Still, a consistent thread may readily be perceived throughout his career, most obvious early in the *Mythologies* and still at the heart of the argument in *Camera Lucida.* This unifying element is the opposition of bourgeois illusion to the reality of subjective experience, of desire. In other words, the *studium/punctum* pair in *Camera Lucida* is closely related to the more familiar *plaisir/jouissance* (pleasure/bliss) from *The Pleasure of the Text* and *lisible/scriptible* (readerly/writerly) from *S/Z.* The still photograph facilitates his concern with a simple, austere opposition between what he calls *studium* and *punctum,* between "ordinary" or organizing cognition and the raw perception excited by anomalies. The *studium* is the mechanism of bourgeois illusion with respect to the photograph: the search for order, for clarity, for unity in the photograph's theme, depiction, and design, all of these as mediated through cultural codes. The *punctum,* on the other hand, is transgressive, accidental, and disruptive: an element that "sticks out," that forces attention to immediate experience and abandons the orderly in the effort to reach that experience. Or, as Laura Mulvey puts it, "the *studium* belongs to the photographer; the *punctum* to the viewer" (2006, 62). The eye moves across a photograph—as it must constantly do or else lose focus. As Bordwell explains:

> All humans use their eyes to search their environment. Because only a narrow region of our eye's anatomy, the fovea, possesses critical focus, the eyes move to let the fovea attend to items of interest. Sometimes the eyes track slowly moving objects via smooth pursuit movements; more often, three or four times per second, our eyes jump from spot to spot in what are called saccades. Saccades sample the environment, bringing features into sharp focus for only about a quarter of a second. If the item is worth studying, microsaccades or flicks shift the fovea slightly over the target. The process of visual search is active, fast, and indebted to our biological heritage. (2005, 38–39)

In this context of eye motion, the *punctum* becomes a moment of attention, an unusual point of interest that stops the eye. The very attention creates a discrepancy, a gap, whose resolution might be systematic—that is, part of the process of interpretation, of making narrative sense out of the photograph—or might fail: the discrepancy may never resolve entirely and therefore will at the very least force us to keep in mind always the constructedness, the artifice, the myth-making of a photograph's aesthetic order (and, by extension, of a dominant culture).[15]

Through these steps, then, we can easily align *studium/punctum* with movement and stasis and, through them, with film and photography. At one point about midway through *Camera Lucida,* Barthes briefly considers the distinction between the photograph and film and asks, "Do I add to the images in movies? I don't think so; I don't have time: in front of the screen, I am not free to shut my eyes; otherwise, opening them again I would not discover the same image; I am constrained to a continuous voracity; a host of other qualities, but not *pensiveness*" (1981, 55; emphasis in original). This *pensiveness* is the fixed attention aroused by the *punctum,* in contrast to the always active contemplation of the *studium*. Thus, we have:

studium	*punctum*
motion	stasis
film	photography

Camera Lucida was published just after Barthes's death in 1980. Three years later, Raymond Bellour challenged Barthes's negative conclusion by invoking the photographic insert: "Creating a distance, another time, the photograph permits me to reflect on cinema. Permits me, that is, to reflect that I am at the cinema" (1987, 7). "In this, the photograph . . . make[s] the spectator of cinema, this hurried spectator, [into] a pensive one as well" (10). In other words, the disruptive element of the insert does have the potential to "stop" the film, even if the result (in classical cinema, at any rate) is unlikely to go beyond a momentary awareness of a film's constructedness (before it rushes on): or the pair active-flow-of-narrative against static-insert. As Bellour puts it, "The presence of the photograph, diverse, diffuse, ambiguous, thus has the effect of uncoupling the spectator from the image, even if only slightly, even if only by virtue of the extra fascination it holds. It pulls the spectator out of . . . the ordinary imaginary of the cinema" (10). Recently, Robert Ray has extended this sense of stopping, or being fascinated, to the institution of film studies as a discipline. Commenting on a striking but apparently unmotivated shot of Greta Garbo in *Grand Hotel* (1932), he says that it poses a challenge: "What can we say that will do it justice? The movies, of course, are full of such moments, and the discipline of film studies arose, at least in part, to explain them" (Ray 2008, xii).

The pair *studium/punctum* is matched to motion/static (that is, the moving, analyzing eye versus the staring, fascinated eye), to Bellour's transposition to film/photography, and, through his example, to active-flow-of-narrative/static-insert.[16] We then easily add speech/text-on-screen and, having ventured into the sound track, move on to define music flowing-in-time as a term. But then what is opposed to it? A film is like music; the film "stops" in the photographic insert—can music "stop" likewise? Although there are a number of ways this can happen (long-held notes, for example), it is especially—or perhaps most distinctively—in reaching for language (associative themes, perhaps also topics) that music becomes static (synchronic rather than diachronic), and thus arises the final term: "music 'stopped' by narrative reference." Like the insert in the image track, a topical reference or motivic recall in the music element of the sound track particularly pulls the audio-viewer out of the diachronic flow.[17]

To complete the cluster, I repeat the pair film/photography and place the three pairs discussed just above:

film	photography
active-flow-of-narrative	static-insert
speech	text-on-screen
music-flowing-in-time	music-stopped-by-narrative-reference

An archetypical example of the *punctum* involving music may be found at the end of *The Iron Lady* (2011), the recent biopic of Margaret Thatcher in which Meryl Streep does her utmost to top Helen Mirren's extraordinary depiction of another British public figure, Queen Elizabeth II (*The Queen*, 2006). The film has been criticized for dwelling overmuch on Mrs. Thatcher's final years, for depicting her as suffering from Alzheimer's disease (a notion that has been strongly disputed), and, perhaps most importantly, for failing to forward a distinct point of view about the famous prime minister's life and career (Ebert 2012). Indeed, the filmmakers have gone to the opposite extreme: they have used a common design that is tailor-made to invoke empathy—an elderly person looking back over her life in a series of flashbacks—and they have stoked it further by making the framing story hallucinations of her dead husband as she belatedly cleans out his clothes and other effects. In the film's final moments, Streep is shown in medium close-up as she washes teacups (at about 1:38:00). She is looking out a window (we do not see the frame); offscreen sounds from outdoors (children playing, then birds, a motorbike, and finally the children again) emphasize her isolation; the look on her face is an odd mixture of the self-satisfied, the vacant, and the contemplative (as we know that she has finally reconciled herself to her husband's death, the film's main plotline). She turns to leave the kitchen, and, just as she reaches the open doorway, the C Major Prelude from J. S. Bach's *Well-Tempered Clavier*, Book I, starts (as do superimposed credits, a name at a time, beginning of course with Streep herself). Daniel Barenboim's rather perky performance confirms Thatcher's newly positive mood and even hints at an improved sense of health, as do Streep's actions as she first looks down the stairwell, then taps the stair's corner post, and finally walks off in a decided manner to the right, going out of sight. The music continues for nearly another minute, as we see the empty kitchen in continued daylight, then dark in late evening, followed by a fade to black, during which the music finishes (at 1:40:06). Barenboim adds a gratuitous mordent to the third note from the end (sixteenth-note E4), and this odd figure, combined with the completely blackened screen, stops the film dead in its tracks. A musician cannot ignore it, but I suspect that others will hear it, too, since the composition is so well-known. I will not attempt an interpretation here, the point being simply that this tiny gesture pulls the audio-viewer abruptly into asking questions about the film, perhaps starting first with "Why do we hear that music (Bach; *that* Bach)?" In the event, the ensuing end credits seem more than usually detached from the film that precedes them.[18]

A similar but more problematic example involving music—one that not only disrupts attention but actually interferes with narrative comprehension—may be found in an early *film noir* from Twentieth Century-Fox, *I Wake Up Screaming* (1941). Like *The Dark Corner*, this film concerns the tragic outcome of obsessive love, but here it is the investigating detective (played by Laird Cregar) who is the one with the obsession. Victor Mature (as Frankie) is a promoter who heartlessly manufactures a career for a waitress as the result of a wager with two friends, then finds himself framed for her murder, and eventually works his way out of trouble with the help of the victim's sister (played by Betty Grable). The main-title music is Alfred Newman's lyrical theme from *Street Scene* (1931), a *Rhapsody in Blue* sound-alike that was used repeatedly to open Fox films in this period (it appears in *The Dark Corner,* too).[19] Although it could reasonably invoke the urban for contemporaneous audiences, the lushness of the melody and its setting fail to telegraph anything like the grit, darkness, or murder one typically associates with *film noir.* In *I Wake Up Screaming* the problem is compounded by the frequent use of short quotations of this theme, alternating with "Over the Rainbow." The latter is very disconcerting for a modern audience, but it was not for audiences in 1941, since neither *The Wizard of Oz* nor the song had acquired its current iconic status. What *are* disconcerting for any sympathetic viewer are the repeated intrusions of fragments of the two tunes at a sound level equal to speech, such that they appear to insist, almost in random alternation, on urbanity ("Street Scene") and hopeful normality ("Over the Rainbow").

A more complex and apposite example of the treatment of music can be found in *M* (1931), Fritz Lang's first sound film, which has justly been celebrated in all its aspects, from production values to story, acting, and the rich variety of scenes and styles. Brophy is typical in his praise but worth quoting here because of the specific attention he gives to sound: "For a film made so near to the technological advent of sound in the cinema, *M* bears a sophistication in its sound design unmatched by other 'psycho' films of its time as well as many made since. The film is highly designed in its visuals and gesturally ornate in its camera work, and the sound to *M* shares similar weight in its formalist expression and poetic symbolism" (2004, 158). Music, though by no means a major factor in the film except as motif (during the first half only of its one-hour, eleven-minute duration), is often mentioned because it provides an important plot device. Through a whistled tune, a blind beggar identifies the murderer everyone has been searching for (see nos. 8a and 8b in figure 1.3). That tune is the theme of "In the Hall of the Mountain King," the finale of Edvard Grieg's first *Peer Gynt Suite,* a clever choice on Lang's part because it would have been very familiar to his audience as one of the most commonly used music cues from the concert repertory during the silent era. It appears, for example, in Erno Rapée's collection *Motion Picture Moods* (published by Schirmer in 1924) under the heading "Sea and Storm," but it was also commonly used as an *agitato-misterioso* (Rapée's *Encyclopedia* of 1925 lists it under "Northern/Storm-Misterioso" and also under "Mysterioso-Heavy"). The only music we hear in M is made either by humans whistling or by a hurdy-gurdy, which at first wheezes and also whistles too as another beggar winds it up.[20] Inspector Lohmann whistles a tune himself at one point, but most of the whistling is done by the murderer, Hans Beckert (Peter Lorre)—or, rather, appears to be done by Beckert: Lorre was not able to achieve "the particular off-key tone that Lang required," and so the director did the whistling for him (Thomas

2012, 37). Thomas notes that the commonly related story about Lorre's inability to whistle at all was invented by Lang.

We hear the tune eight times (see collated screen stills in figure 1.3): (1) at 6:55, a minute after we first see Beckert, as a shadow, he whistles the first phrase twice with his back to the camera; (2) at 10:00, after Elsie Beckmann's murder is discovered, Beckert whistles, with erratic rhythm, while he writes a letter to a newspaper; (3) and (4) at 53:36, after he sees another potential victim (we see him purse his lips, as if whistling) and at 53:50, offscreen, as if continuing; (5) through (7) at 55:08, after the girl escapes and he goes to a café to collect himself, at 56:06 again, then at 56:25 as he leaves the café; (8) at 57:33, offscreen, as we see the blind beggar, then diminishing in volume when the beggar asks a comrade to look down the street at a man walking away and then excitedly tells him to pursue the man. Of the fifth through seventh instances above, Daniel Goldmark and his co-editors say that "just this once [the whistling] does not seem to be coming from Beckert's lips, though it could hardly be coming from anywhere else" (2007, 1). As the list shows, we do not see his face during the first two instances, we do see him purse his lips for the third instance, but the fourth is offscreen. As no. 5 in figure 1.3 plainly shows, Lorre does purse his lips in the café. There is no reason to believe that, even when he balls his fists on his ears (no. 6b), the music suddenly "becomes uncanny, disembodied." Given its topical associations from silent-era performance practice, "In the Hall of the Mountain King" was *always* uncanny. And certainly there is no reason to suppose that one should make a leap to a reading of symptomatic meanings, a music scholar's vision of film, according to which music is both special and equal, a world where films are really about music (Goldmark, Kramer, and Leppert 2007, 3–6).[21]

Whistling by the murderer, police whistles, a sharp whistling by one of the beggars when Beckert is spotted—these are the film's large articulations (sync points on a grand scale; Chion 1994, 190; 2009, 263–77, 469), and they divide the film into two parts very effectively because they are absent from the second half.[22] "In the Hall of the Mountain King" is rarely as loud as other whistling, which is placed forward in the mix, but then so are the voices—the whistled sounds stand out only by their harshness and high pitch. The sound track is richly varied—sometimes silent, sometimes direct recorded with effects clearly heard, but at other times with effects suppressed. Overall, *M* is a remarkable "talkie," a film dominated by speech.

The treatment of the title song from *Written on the Wind* (1957) offers a subtler example that is also more typical of classical Hollywood practice. None of the widescreen melodramas on which Douglas Sirk's reputation was built in the 1950s can be described as romance or comedy (that is, films with happy endings), but *Written on the Wind* is particularly relentless in its devastating characterizations and in the havoc the four principals wreak, not only on themselves, but on others around them. Siblings Kyle (Robert Stack) and Marylee (Dorothy Malone) taunt each other. Mitch (Rock Hudson) resists the long-term understanding of Marylee and her father, owner of the Hadley Oil Company (played by Robert Keith), that Mitch will marry her. Lucy (Lauren Bacall) cannot quite contain her own interest

Figure 1.3. *M* (1931), "In the Hall of the Mountain King." Screen stills collated with cue numbers.

in Mitch despite the devastating consequences for her spouse, Kyle, and the father does not relinquish his long-standing attitude favoring Mitch over his own son. There is, nevertheless, a certain harsh logic in the outcome: Kyle and his father lie dead, Mitch and Lucy drive off together,[23] and Marylee is left on her own to run the company—for which, we suspect, from the final shot of her through her father's office window, she may well have the right temperament.

Written on the Wind is a sumptuous film with richly designed interiors, bright sports cars, and a local gas-station restaurant both roomy and appropriately seedy. It is also a film with as good a monaural sound track as has ever been made. The hierarchy of elements is traditional, however: the voice is strongly foregrounded, with a volume and resonance equal to the oversize images of the characters on the wide screen. Effects are by no means absent, but with the exception of automobile sounds, which become an aural hook that solidifies the motif of the sports car being driven too fast, effects stay in the background. According to the timings on the studio cue sheet, music is present for forty-eight minutes and forty seconds of the film's ninety-nine-minute runtime. The majority of that is Frank Skinner's underscore, which the sound editor has placed very carefully in the mix, just high enough to be heard and make its contributions, but not so high as to intrude on the voice. Some of what I identify as underscore is composed of song arrangements by the composer and his brother Al that are used as music for onscreen dancing (and therefore mixed higher) but without any real concession to diegetic plausibility.

There are two exceptions to this inventory of the music in the underscore. The first is the theme song, which was written by Victor Young, with lyrics by Sammy Cahn, and the second is "Temptation," by Arthur Freed and Nacio Herb Brown, a hit in the early 1930s thanks to Bing Crosby's rendition of it as a sultry ballad. I will discuss them in reverse order here. "Temptation" is not only a famous moment but also the film's most prominent sync point, or audiovisual accent.[24] The sinuous legato of the tune is clear, but the arrangement is exaggeratedly Latin, played very loud on a phonograph in Marylee's room (we see her turn the player on). Despite the unequivocal diegetic status of the music, volume level and sound characteristics are completely unrealistic. Marylee, in a flowing red dress, dances wildly to the record, and when the film cuts downstairs to Mitch and her father, we can still hear the music, now diegetically much more plausible as loud music being played upstairs. The crux of the narrative is here and in the immediate aftermath, as her father dies of a heart attack while climbing the stairs to confront her. *Written on the Wind* is not subtle, and neither are its musics.

At the beginning of the film, we first hear loud car sounds, then *agitato* underscore, and finally The Four Aces' title-song performance, which blends into and moves out of the music track cleanly. A relatively early example of a device that became a cliché in both film and television by the 1960s, the song is sung through the main-title sequence. Its lyrics and their setting, however, are jarring. Lines about infidelity and inconstancy are set with no hint of irony to a slow and sentimental love ballad. Skinner subsequently inserts this theme song smoothly into his underscore: it reappears seven times in the course of the film, including the

Figure 1.4, a–c. *Written on the Wind* (1957), images associated with the first statements of the theme song. Screen stills.

end credits. The sum of these later cues is eight minutes, twenty-six seconds. The film's first eight cues are as follows. (Titles and timings are taken from the studio cue sheet; entrance and end timings are from the Criterion DVD, and sums do not quite match the cue sheet timings.)

Reel 1
1. Prologue—(duration 0:51); music in at DVD timing 0:10, with automobile noise throughout; segue to
2. Main Title ("Written On The Wind")—(duration 1:37); music in at 1:03, minimal effects under it; song finishes at 2:32 and is replaced by wind
3. Display—(duration 0:55); music in at 2:53, segue to
4. "Written On The Wind"—(duration 0:10); music out at 4:06 under dialogue

Reel 2
5. "Written On The Wind"—(duration 0:10); music in at 9:29, repeated notes only as introduction to cue 6; segue to
6. Abduction from [Club] "21"—(duration 1:34); slow foxtrot (?) in thirty-two-bar binary form, closed in E♭; segue to
7. "Written On The Wind"—(duration 0:12); as if coda to cue 6, repeated notes at first, then theme song first phrase; segue to
8. Abduction from [Club] "21"—(duration 0:10); tag leading off tonic $^6_4$ chord to a C♭ first inversion as ending stinger; music out at 11:37, followed by airplane noise

In the deliberately excessive manner of the Sirk melodrama, the song's opening lines about infidelity are heard against a sustained shot of Mitch in medium close-up with Lucy lying on a bed in the background (see figure 1.4a). Adding to the effect is one of Sirk's stylized figures: characters contained and isolated by window frames. Lucy is the wife of Kyle—a principal point of tension throughout the film is Mitch's interest in but principled refusal to pursue Lucy, while at the same time he firmly rejects Marylee. A compressed version of events seen more fully later in the film culminates just after the singers finish: a shot is heard, and Kyle emerges from the house, falls, and dies. Barely a minute later, and thus early in the long flashback that takes up the majority of the film, the repeated notes that open the theme song are heard in the underscore as Lucy and Mitch first meet (cue 4). This is brief and so subtle that it can easily be missed: only the affect (tempo, orchestration) is suggestive. The music here sounds like an extended introduction to a song performance, but no song ensues. Cue 5 does pick up on this idea as the repeated notes now introduce a thirty-two-bar slow foxtrot (cue 6), which is heard against conversation between Kyle and Lucy as they head to and arrive at the airport. They board Kyle's private plane to find Mitch already there (his role, we learn, is to look after Kyle). Kyle had hoped to be alone, but he laughs it off (figure 1.4b). The repeated notes reappear as the motive for the coda to the foxtrot, but when Mitch and Lucy speak alone (figure 1.4c), the first phrase of the theme song clearly emerges. Brief as it is, this statement has been prepared well by the composer of the underscore, and it "speaks" to the situation as effectively as either image or speech, interrupting both to remind us of the main-title sequence.

"Realism"/Spectacle: On Music's Place

The title song for *Written on the Wind* and Dorothy Malone's dance to "Temptation" push the envelope of music's orderly participation in the voice-dominated model of what I will call a "constructed realism" below. Quite a different model was proposed in the early sound film era. Following post–World War I French aesthetic priorities, Virgil Thomson and others promoted the idea of a "neutral background music, a *senza espressione* style that throws whatever is seen against it into high relief" (1981, 156). Aaron Copland, who had also been trained in Paris, said much the same thing (1957, 257). In the classical synchronized cinema, onscreen space and diegetic place are made to coincide so that the character or object appears naturally unified, the representation of an organic body, whatever sort of world that body may seem to occupy. The background, by contrast, defines that world and need not be synchronized even when it is motivated. Traditional nondiegetic music does not usually seem problematic despite its apparent lack of motivation: its indifference to acoustical fidelity is unmarked, since music, when treated this way, can be understood as a stylized background—like stylized sets or lighting.

Though he promoted a neutral underscore, Thomson certainly did grasp the character and effect of a foregrounded music, in particular a foregrounded nondiegetic music. He says, for example, that the quotation of familiar melodies (or familiar musical topics) "to accentuate or to comment [on] a situation is of course an old and very useful device," but when foregrounded, "the music becomes more than tune. It *speaks* its name. It is present on the stage" (Thomson 1933, 190–91; my emphasis). Referring to a specific example from the early sound era—an extended passage from Wagner's *Tristan und Isolde* in *L'âge d'or* (1930)—Thomson says that "it does not express the drama that is taking place. [Instead,] it is there as an actor or a chorus calling attention to what is not taking place, or rather to what is taking place in a very different way from that depicted by the music" (191).[25] Copland makes the same point, but he invokes narrative rather than actorial qualities: "Music serves the screen . . . [by] underlining psychological refinements—the unspoken thoughts of a character or the unseen implications of a situation. Music can play upon the emotions of the spectator, sometimes counterpointing the thing seen with an aural image that implies the contrary" (1957, 256–57).

To be sure, music as spectacle—in performance, in action, and as mute emotion—can take priority over the voice, but these instances also belong to the silent film. What was truly new about music in the sound film was the practice of dialogue underscoring, and it is a matter of simple statistics that dialogue underscoring far outweighs music's other uses in the sheer number of minutes of screen time allotted to it. But the problem remained, as Jean Mitry's critical remarks make clear: "Film music following the role established for it in the silent era is silly and useless. The tiresome orchestrations supposed to bring out the highlights in the drama and create an apparently essential atmosphere are more of a hindrance than a help. A film can quite easily dispense with [such] acoustic adornments" ([1963] 1990, 249). Mitry's dismissal may seem extreme, but it was an entirely reasonable response in the context of a vococentric film cognition and the environment of the classical, continuous-level sound track. Music needs the voice—or to put it another way, music needs the hierarchy of sound and links to image and narration guaranteed by the voice. Speech mediates for a music that, except in performance and perhaps in spectacle and in mute emotion, really has no place in the cinema except by the historical coincidence of certain theatrical conventions (Neumeyer 2000a, 9–13).[26] Recall too that, for Altman, Tatroe, and Jones, the significant historical event was the development of background sound, in relation to which a distinct and effective role for nondiegetic music could be found. It was not merely the continuation of a theatrical tradition that guaranteed music's role but also a number of technological improvements during the transition years. What music *did* contribute was some of the elements of stylization that were required if the talking film was to be construed as something other than a recording of the world. The principle of psychological realism governing narrative film requires such stratification—that is to say, the audio-viewer must be given a means to discern that the world depicted is not simply what is seen and heard but something more or other than what it appears to be.[27]

The role of nondiegetic music in the sound film is easy to misunderstand. Amy Herzog, for example, offers a clear and concise summary of Claudia Gorbman's concept of music as "unheard": "Nondiegetic scores typically map themselves onto the rhythm of the image, supporting the flow of narrative action without interrupting it. . . . Music stabilizes the image and secures meaning while remaining as unobtrusive as possible." Then, as did a good many other authors after Gorbman's book was published in 1987, Herzog sets up an opposition, saying that "there are many instances, however, when this hierarchy is inverted and music serves as the dominant force in the work, creating a musical moment. Certain film scores refuse to remain subservient to the image and achieve a dramatic presence." The anthropomorphism is telling: "Scores refuse . . . and achieve" (Herzog 2010, 6). Herzog is giving us the language of resistance, of transgression and emergence. Gorbman's phrase "unheard melodies," however, refers more generally to music's status in sound track synchronization, not subservience in the terms that Herzog reads it.[28] *All* elements of a filmic system, not just music, are subservient to narrative in the classical feature film, a model that, despite technological and stylistic change, persists in its basic outlines into the present day. Underscore music can, and frequently does, "achieve a dramatic presence" in the context of highly synchronized filmic situations, as we just saw above in *Written on the Wind* and as multiple examples from *Gone with the Wind, Dark Victory* (both 1939), *Spirit of St. Louis* (1957), *Ben Hur* (1959), *Star Wars* (1977), and many, many other films will further attest.

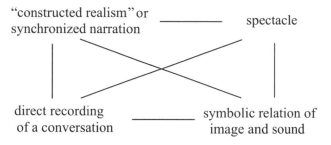

Figure 1.5. Relations of the vococentric model and spectacle, along with their negations.

We can make better sense of music's role by reading an opposition between spectacle and the "constructed realism" of synchronization. In order to sort the several relations involved, I have positioned the pair in a square of logical oppositions (also known as a semiotic square or a Greimassian square; see figure 1.5).[29] By convention, the initial term (at the upper left) is the unmarked term in a binary pair: here, it is the default state of the sound film. The objective of synchronized narration that closely ties image and sound is to give the impression of a physical world in which subject-agents can move—thus, the phrase "constructed realism," which can be taken as synonymous with "psychological realism," although it emphasizes a different aspect of the model. The hierarchies of sound in such a world are those of the world we know: they are vococentric.

In relation to synchronization, spectacle, at the upper right of figure 1.5, is marked as both atypical and expressive, as centered on the body rather than on the voice. Synchronization and the sound track hierarchy appropriate to it are actively opposed by the "unreal construction" of spectacle. Here, "unreal" means the "artificiality" or "atypicality" of a musical or pantomimic performance against, say, the everyday realism of a conversation between two people. The emphasis has changed to the "construction," what we are presented, what we see, and therefore the term used is "spectacle," an alternative to cause-and-effect-based narrative. Dances, games, chases, parades, and other scenes of action generally belong to this category. The sound track hierarchy is indeed flipped: music and effects are assumed, as is the voice acting as musical instrument in song, but the speaking voice tends to be minimized, unsynchronized, or absent.[30]

The opposition of synchronized realism and spectacle is fundamental to the treatment of sound, including music. The early film musicals, such as *The Broadway Melody* (1929), gave that opposition to us in stark form, as they often consisted entirely of talking alternating with singing, a combination of "talkie" and vaudeville revue. Many low-budget westerns in the 1930s and 1940s were built similarly, alternating dialogue and action scenes (travel, chases, or shootouts). The singing cowboy films of Gene Autry, Roy Rogers, and others were only slightly more complex in that they added singing to the list of action scenes. In the dance and conversation sequence from *The Dark Corner* discussed earlier, we have both functions on a small scale: the band (performance, spectacle, the eye and ear focus on them regardless of anything else that might happen, the film "stops" for them) and the "constructed realism" of the dancing couple's conversation.

As with its other extreme elements, the "Temptation" scene in *Written on the Wind* radically emphasizes the realism/spectacle opposition in a visually stark "upstairs/downstairs" construction. Marylee has gone to her room upstairs, while Mitch and her father continue to talk in his study downstairs. Cutting back and forth between the rooms is not smoothed over by the sound track. Instead, the audio-viewer lurches from one to the other, from the loud spectacle of the dance to the men's conversation, which seems almost suppressed by the noise.

I should note here that the opposition speech/spectacle or voice/action does not contradict David Bordwell's assertion that spectacle and action forward narrative (Bordwell and Thompson 2011, 122–25) and therefore that "the distinction between action and story [is] untenable" (122). The terms of an aesthetic that places narrative clarity first must inevitably require that action, too, serves narrative—or, to put it another way, will continually encourage the viewer to impute narrative significance to what he or she sees and hears. In this section and in figure 1.5, I am concerned with a more basic level, with characteristic qualities or gestures of a scene or sequence regardless of (or, before considering) a narrative context. Similarly, figure 1.5 is not intended to contradict Adrienne McLean's (1993) excellent study of female musical and dance performance in *films noirs*. Her argument is that, beyond the potential of such spectacles to forward narrative (as with Bordwell), they can be sites of empowerment as well.

Each term in the initial pair of figure 1.5 necessarily generates its negation or contrary. These are to be understood not actively as forming additional oppositions (except between themselves) but passively as an undermining—a kind of logical shadow—or at most passive-aggressively as a rejection or repudiation. The negation of "constructed realism" at the lower right of figure 1.5 is the Eisensteinian montage, which ignores or rejects synchronization in order to highlight symbolic relations of sound and image. It is also the contrary aesthetic of Adorno and Eisler, which calls on music to break the synchronization in order to open the way for ideological critique of the image. Although Adorno and Eisler's model is often presented as an alternative to the standard practices of classical Hollywood, figure 1.5 suggests that it is properly understood as a repudiation.

The expression of a negation to the initial term also creates an opposition between the two terms at the right side of the square, indicated by the vertical line drawn between them in figure 1.5.[31] In both cases the orienting power of the voice is undermined or minimized, but spectacle focuses on the events—especially actions of human bodies (also including human-controlled animals or machines)—whereas its opposing term insists on imposing on the image (less often sound) an independent level of symbolic meanings. The opposition between spectacle and "counterpoint" highlights two different ways of conceiving a nonrealist aesthetic.

The logical constraints are tightest with the final term, which is both the negation of spectacle and another oppositional term for both the first and third terms—though in different ways, of course. The negation of the "unreal construction" of spectacle, at least, is both simple and obvious: the radical rejection of the stylization of performance and of a flipped sound hierarchy can be found in a direct-recorded conversation. See the lower left of figure 1.5, where it is understood as a stationary camera and an unedited image track. In the classical cinema, ironically, the precision of postproduction dubbing was so great that, in order to emphasize the realism, one would be obliged to add the kind of random effects and background speech events characteristic of truly direct-recorded sound.[32] The opposition between "counterpoint" and direct-recorded conversation pits realist and nonrealist concepts against one another, a conflict of aesthetic priorities. Similarly, the opposition between direct recording and synchronization puts what one might call an ultrarealist aesthetic against the "constructed realism" of continuity editing.

The division between voice-centered "constructed realism" and visual or action-centered spectacle is essential to the sound cinema as it developed in the studio era. The next section turns to music in relation to ideas of narrative, first with respect to autonomous concert music, then to music in an audiovisual context.

Narrative and Music: Two Paths

Echoing the parallel historical paths of music performed in the context of dance, theater, or ritual, on the one hand, and music performed in salon or concert, on the other hand, there have been two main approaches to the relationship of music and narrative. In the nineteenth century, the genres involved took on an oppositional character, even became the objects of dialectical struggle: sonata versus song, symphony versus opera. But it was exactly in the midst of this, inspired (or driven) by the Romantic fascination with literary subjectivity, that a notion of a specifically musical narrativity arose—that is, a potential for an understanding of narrative process in supposedly nonnarrative or "absolute" music. The "sonata as novel" was a concept that derived from changes in social and commercial status. The recital or concert had become a significant public venue in the wake of the radical democratizing changes and rise of the middle class; and the sonata was the largest and most serious of the several categories of sheet music text-commodities. Theorizing about the nature and possibility of narrative in music, however, is a largely twentieth-century phenomenon, a varied collection of latter-day responses to a wall separating "absolute" and "program" music that was thicker and more unyielding in the Modernist era than it had ever been in the previous century.[33]

We would expect Arnold Schoenberg to have a more nuanced view of an absolute/program music divide, given the importance of vocal music in his early career, and indeed he does say that "drama and poetry are greatly inspiring to a composer." In his account, by the early nineteenth century, "extramusical tendencies, such as poetic and dramatic subjects, emotions, [and] actions . . . had become influential, . . . tendencies [that] caused changes in every feature of the musical substance." Even if these changes might "be debatable aesthetically," they "resulted in great developments. In descriptive music the background, the action, the mood, and the other features of the drama, poem, or story become incorporated as constituent and formative factors in the musical structure." Nevertheless, he is uneasy that the constraints of working to text force the musical materials to give up some of their native character, which could otherwise "develop in a direction different from that in which a text forces it," and he warns that the foregrounding of texts can hide weaknesses in a melody (Schoenberg 1969, 76).[34]

The situation, then, is essentially this: in concert music, the question of narrativity is open, disputed, but of interest to those who are uncomfortable with the simple formalism or austere idealism of music as sonic pattern (of the sort propounded by Stravinsky), on the one hand, and to those who wish to avoid constant recourse to contextualizing (or subjectivizing) social, historical, or ideological factors, on the other hand. In music for singing, for the theater, dance, or film, however, there really is no question: different degrees of narrativity are assumed, either transferred onto the music by textual, actional, or scenic elements or understood as the product of an integration of music and other elements.

As Byron Almén points out, a central theoretical issue has been the degree of alignment between musical narrative and explanations of literary narrative (2008, 11–12). The greater the alignment—made appealing by motifs as actors or formal designs as plot archetypes—the more the temptation to find equivalents for narrators, causal relations, and so on. Arguing against such alignments are principally "the absence of referentiality in music, a subject-predicate relationship, a narrator, and a past tense" (11). Almén proposes that we regard literary narrative as a particular instance of a broader category that would establish "a set of foundational principles common to all narrative media" and at the same time permit "principles unique to each medium" (12).

The situation for music in film will be more complicated than simply assuming narrativity because film is audiovisual—only one possible instance of the combination of music with the visual. It is certainly true that structuralist literary theory (Gérard Genette) and semiology (Roland Barthes) provided a foundation for analysis and interpretation of films in work by Christian Metz, Raymond Bellour, Seymour Chatman, and others, including, for film music, Claudia Gorbman.[35] On the other hand, whenever music's own properties—its "music-ness"—come forward, then the internal hierarchy that assumes priority in an ultimately text-based (if visually presented) narrative threatens to come unglued, and the same kinds of questions asked of narrative in concert music can intrude, albeit never to the same extent, as the images do not disappear or disintegrate into willful associations. In this respect, music is unique: it is very difficult, even in the context of spectacle, for any visual elements to separate themselves from narrative processes. Even sound effects, for example, in a loud car race or air or space battle, are not exempt, except that, when pressed into the foreground, they can tie themselves as much or more to music-like patterning and processes as to narrative.[36]

The distinction between routine and focused attention that is at the core of Barthes's *studium/punctum* pair has practical consequences for the study of film and film music. As Robert Ray puts it, the "invisible style" that characterized classical Hollywood and that "succeeded so well in effacing itself in strong narratives [means] that detecting its workings requires concentration. We can observe its procedures most effectively in short sequences from movies that we know well enough to be able momentarily to suspend our normal interest in the story line" (1985, 45). The goal of this "invisible style," which was based on the technique called "continuity editing" codified in the early 1920s (synonymous with film editing ever since), was to cover over the inevitable spatial and temporal discontinuities required of efficient dramatic narration. In the classical model, music participates fully in realizing the "invisible style," actively suppressing its (admittedly conventional) continuities for the sake of aiding and abetting the construction and maintenance of an apparent physical space and apparent temporal integrity. This is at the heart of Gorbman's phrase "unheard melodies," the idea that music's first allegiance is to narrative, and in this sense it subordinates itself to the image—or, strictly speaking, to the narrative system. "Unheard," as I noted above, has nothing to do with whether or not music is foregrounded.

Earlier also I quoted Ray's observation that film studies arose partly in order to provide explanations for unusual or difficult moments in films. Ray goes on to say that the "task has proved more difficult than it once appeared: 'The movies are difficult to explain,' Christian Metz once admitted in his famous epigram, 'because they are easy to understand'" (2008, xii). For Metz, the dilemma was one that is very familiar to music studies scholars as well: how to study an artwork, through whatever interpretive bias—descriptive, thematic reading, ideological critique—without losing the sense of pleasure that brought one to the work in the first place. In the end, Metz became pessimistic about the chance of success. In this connection, Ray also cites Theodor Adorno's dismissal of Walter Benjamin's notion of a detail-driven historical method: "Your study is located at the crossroads of magic and positivism. That spot is bewitched. Only theory could break the spell" (xiv). In this quote Ray can find both a definition of cinema ("the crossroads of magic and positivism") and a concise expression of that outcome Metz came to lament (the need to "break the spell").

Robert Scholes (1982) comes at the problem from a different direction, with the viewpoint of the literary scholar. For him, Metz's strategy of semiotic analysis is well grounded, but the ontological status of film as enactment (representation) poses a significant problem. Going back to an ancient distinction derived from Aristotle's *Poetics,* Scholes sets the novel and the film against one another, the former representing storytelling (language, speech), the other mimesis (enactment). In this view, the novel is especially good at telling richly contextualized stories but struggles at representation, at scene setting and description, while film does the reverse: it is efficient at showing but struggles with conceptualization.

"Film, because it excels all other narrative media in its rendition of material objects and the actions of creatures, is the closest to actuality, to undifferentiated thoughtless experience" (72)—that is to say, as Metz lamented, movies "are easy to understand." Laura Mulvey makes the same point with "the photograph cannot generalize" (2006, 10). Therefore, film must work to "achieve some level of reflection, of conceptualization, in order to reach its optimum condition as narrative" (Scholes 1982, 72).

Invoking a familiar semiotic model, Scholes describes a continuum of increasing specificity and rigor, where *narration* is a simple recounting, as if in conversation; *narrative* implies a greater organization of material; and *story* has still more organization, casting narrative in a distinct form for which readers/listeners have "a certain set of expectations about its expressive patterning and its semantic content" (1982, 60). Regardless of place on this continuum (and irrespective of whether Scholes's terms are the best ones), a reader responds through an interactive process Scholes calls "narrativity": "A fiction . . . guides us as our own active narrativity seeks to complete the process that will achieve a story" (60). The analytical heuristic a reader uses in engaging this narrativity is simple: construction of a temporal sequence and reading of cause-and-effect relationships within that sequence (62–63).[37] In the sound film, continuity editing assists the audio-viewer most consistently and reliably, and the voice not only adds additional information but also confirms the image track. The most efficient schemata are those in which voice and image editing are closely synchronized, as in a shot / reverse shot sequence, or else carefully distinguished, as in voice-over narration. Visual spectacle, on the other hand, is generally inefficient at forwarding narrative.

As I argued earlier, music largely mimics the voice's functions in the three categories of referential, expressive, and motivic. All of these might be understood, in a given scene or moment, as supplying information not available in the image or as narrowing possible interpretations by redundancy (a kind of focusing). When music is foregrounded, whether through continuous presence or prominence, it takes on a role like that of a voice-over narrator. Performance, as an audiovisual spectacle, is notably inefficient with respect to narrativity but can make up for it in intensity or memorability—or it can be undermined through backgrounding or through narrative intrusion (one or both of these happens to every one of the dozen musical performances in *Casablanca,* for example).

With respect to music's potential role in the sound track, then, I disagree with Gorbman's assertion that "the nondiegetic voiceover is perceived as a narrative intrusion, and music is not" (1987, 3). Certainly the nondiegetic voice-over is readily understood as a "narrative intrusion," but I would argue that *anything* understood clearly to be in the nondiegetic register has that potential, including music (Neumeyer and Buhler 1994, 379; see also Davison 2004, 34–35). Both music and voice can occupy that vague territory of the nondiegetic where they are generally understood to be part of the filmic discourse (as if commentary by the filmic narrator), but they always also hold the potential to facilitate the in-

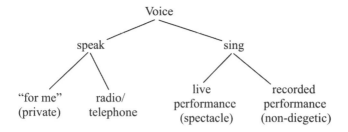

Figure 1.6. Categories of the voice in cinema.

tervention of an extrafilmic narrator. Granted, music's narrational address remains more implicit than that of the voice-over, which most often belongs to one of the characters. Nondiegetic music that draws attention to itself, on the other hand, moves decisively toward the role of the filmic narrator, tries to set itself up in the role of a voice, an impossible task without singing, of course, but also the source of nondiegetic music's curiously subversive power: the voice that cannot be a voice speaking a well-defined body of codes that cannot be a language.

Finally, then, the ontological status of the sound track guarantees that it always has the potential for narration or commentary; its hierarchy guarantees that priority goes to the voice (and that music mimics the voice's functions and modes);[38] and its flexibility guarantees a variety of effects, ranging from informational speech to emotionally charged speech, the contrapuntal speech of excited or lively conversation, the articulating or interruptive functions of effects, neutral music (whether diegetic or nondiegetic), and foregrounded music whose topics or other associations or references highlight music's discursive capacities.

The admittedly reductive scheme in figure 1.6 seeks to get at the nested hierarchy of the several characteristic (that is, most likely) states of the voice in cinema. From this, the reader will also surely deduce that my definition of "voice" is similarly reductive, nothing more than "human speech in the sound track." This is sufficient for my purpose here, which is the parsing of the sound track in preparation for analysis and interpretation. Of course, since the voice (speech) is the privileged meeting place of image and sound in the sound film, definitions of voice and the scope and direction of arguments vary widely in the literature.[39] As figure 1.6 has it, the voice of friendly or intimate conversation, as we have seen, is the default mode in sound cinema. (I have not included the public voice of medium long shots or outdoor conversation, mainly because there is very often a discrepancy between the image and aural perspective. Indeed, more likely is the close-miked "voice in the ear," the aural analogue to an extreme close-up.) Against this we measure the distanced voice of radio or telephone, which cannot overcome its technological mediation (as understood in relation to the diegesis, of course). Singing, likewise, can be separated into live and recorded, present and distanced. Each, however, has a clear weakness (again in relation to the diegetic).

A live performance always has the potential to shift attention from the music, from the singing, toward spectacle, toward *looking* at the singer. A recorded performance, on the other hand, threatens to lose its hold on the diegetic and slip into the nondiegetic realm.

Three Sequences from *To Have and Have Not* (1944)

The three readings in this section illustrate the fundamental ways in which music is incorporated into the classical model of film narration. Two of these we have already encountered—diegetic performance in the scene from *The Dark Corner* and the formal frame as a main-title sequence in *Holy Smoke*—and the third has been mentioned: underscore of dialogue or action (in the case of the third example below, it will be both at once).

To Have and Have Not is among several stand-alone sequels produced by Warner Bros. in an effort to cash in on the extraordinary and largely unexpected success of *Casablanca*—others include *Passage to Marseille* (1944), *The Mask of Dimitrios* (1944), *The Conspirators* (1944), and *Hotel Berlin* (1945).[40] All of these films reprise roles for some subset of the *Casablanca* cast. Sydney Greenstreet and Peter Lorre star in *The Mask of Dimitrios,* for instance. Humphrey Bogart appeared in the turgid *Passage to Marseille* earlier in the year. *To Have and Have Not* redeemed that miscue handsomely, thanks to strong performances by Bogart and also by newcomers Lauren Bacall and Hoagy Carmichael. Although Carmichael had been writing songs for films since 1932, *To Have and Have Not* was his first significant acting role, and it appears to have come about from the coincidence that the film's director, Howard Hawks, and Carmichael were neighbors and their wives became friends (McCarthy 1997, 368; also Sudhalter 2002, 234).

The plot is for the most part *Casablanca* on a smaller canvas: Bogart's Harry Morgan is the same politically disinterested individualist caught in a repressive system (here it is the Vichy government on the Caribbean island of Martinique) who nevertheless aids a Resistance fighter and his wife. Carmichael and the Hôtel Marquis, run by "Frenchy" (Marcel Dalio, the croupier Emil from *Casablanca*), stand in for Sam and Rick's Café Américain, and corrupt policemen stand in for the Nazis. Lauren Bacall's Slim, on the other hand, is nothing like Ingrid Bergman's Ilsa Lund. Slim (whose proper name is Marie) is an anti-Ilsa, unattached, opportunistic, and mainly concerned with ways to make money, not in order to follow a cause but simply to get back home after an interrupted trip from South America has left her stranded. Slim is far more like Harry (whom she calls "Steve") than she is like the idealistic heroine of *Casablanca,* and she is also viewed by Harry in quite a different way, "as a potential partner [rather] than a potential threat" to the relationship represented in a traditional patriarchal marriage (Wexman 1993, 25; the reference is actually to *The Big Sleep,* but the description fits *To Have and Have Not* just as well). And, on a more personal level, Bacall "played her role [as the wisecracking, aggressive woman] to perfection, evoking from Bogart an emotional depth that he had not previously displayed on-screen—not even opposite Bergman" (Schatz 1997, 220).

Table 1.1. *To Have and Have Not* (1945), music cue list

#	Reel/title	By	When	Notes
	REEL 1			
1-2	a. To Have and Have Not b. Native Street	Waxman	0:00	Very short break between the two
	REEL 2			
3	Martinique segue to:	Carmichael	In 11:37; out 12:44	Still outdoors as dialogue stops. Music offscreen—all of it; song finishes; segue
4	"Baltimore Oriole"	Carmichael and Webster	Brief clapping then in; out 14:02	Offscreen—all, even when Bogart and Bacall go upstairs; continues, then goes out after door closes (song doesn't finish)
5	"Am I Blue?"	Akst and Clarke	14:40–16:16	Briefly offscreen, then we see Carmichael for the first time; brief clapping, Carmichael names next song, then segue
6	"Limehouse Blues"	Braham-Furber	16:28–17:32 song ends, clapping	Play of onscreen/offscreen as Bogart and Bacall go upstairs
	REEL 3			
7	a. "Baltimore Oriole" b. The Shot	a. Carmichael b. William Lava	In 22:40, out with gunshots at 24:36; (b) out 25:53	Offscreen first (heard downstairs)
8	"Mammy Jinny's Jubilee"	Muir and Gilbert	25:30 – 25:55	Carmichael plays piano; fast, as if to bring people back
9	"Flower Song"	Gustav Lange	25:58 – 26:09	Short—a joke allusion, as a man is dead
	REEL 4			
10	a. "Jungle Chant" b. Sangmele [sic] dance	Carmichael Carmichael	32:55–34:08	In native club: apparently just one tune; (a) is intro offscreen, then (b) partly onscreen

Table 1.1. *continued*

#	Reel/title	By	When	Notes
11	"The Rhumba Jumps"	Carmichael and Mercer	34:25–35:14	In native club still; band starts up again, first offscreen then on; out with fade (song doesn't finish)
	REEL 5			
12	"Baltimore Oriole"	Carmichael; developed by Waxman?	In 37:15 as he walks across hall; out 40:10	Nondiegetic orchestra—too large to be Cricket's band, and music is too complex. Near the end of their long conversation
	REEL 6			
13–18	"How Little We Know"	Carmichael and Mercer	In 45:58 with dissolve to hotel; out 48:50	As if writing song, Carmichael/Bacall alone at first; then Carmichael sings; Bogart enters; Carmichael keeps playing afterward; break between 17 and 18; 18 is whistle (hum?) by Bogart on the boat
	REEL 7			
19	a. "At Sea" segue to: b. "Behold How Beautiful"	Waxman; Carmichael and Adams	In 54:10 with fog; out 1:00:35 with dissolve to hotel	Dramatic music for sea trip; (b) Bacall sings with Carmichael and three sailors
20	"Behold How Beautiful"	Carmichael	See 19b; out 1:03:38	Carmichael offscreen whistling; three sailors still
	REEL 9			
21	"Hong Kong Blues"	Carmichael	In 1:20:00 with scene change; out 1:22:30	Onscreen performance
22	Piano chords	—		

REEL 10

23	"How Little We Know"	Carmichael	1:27:48	Bacall hums (preparing for performance)
24	Orchestra tuning	—	1:28:35	Off- then onscreen
25	"How Little We Know"	Carmichael	1:29:00–1:30:35	Bacall sings with band
26	"Behold How Beautiful"	Carmichael	1:30:45	Offscreen; others upstairs

REEL 11

27	"Am I Blue?"	Akst; developed by Waxman?	1:31:50; song ends, clapping at 1:34:00, then the shot, and segue to 28a	Orchestral version, elaborate. Tune clearly heard when the door is opened. Action contrasts with music (anempathetic or neutral)
28	a. "Baltimore Oriole" b. "Martinique" c. "Cricket He No Solid" d. "How Little We Know"	a.–d. Carmichael	(a) to (b) time lapse and change of music 1:36:10; same for (c) at 1:36:36; 1:38:24 clear segue to (d)	They go downstairs, parallel to early scene (door closing upstairs; music continues downstairs while villains (corrupt policemen) are tied up
29	"How Little We Know"	Carmichael; developed by Waxman?	Ending	As they go downstairs to leave; just a short orchestral ending using "How Little"

Sources: From a copy in the Franz Waxman Collection, Syracuse University. Some of the information in the first three columns comes from a studio cue sheet dated 31 October 1944.

A summary of the music in *To Have and Have Not* appears in table 1.1, from which one can see that the film has a large number of diegetic performances (on the model of the first act of *Casablanca*) but surprisingly little underscore (in which it differs substantively from *Casablanca,* where orchestral underscore is the dominant element in the music track after the first act).[41] The cues discussed below are nos. 1–2, 5, and 19a—the establishing sequence, a song performance, and a nighttime action scene with underscoring, respectively.

Establishing Sequence

The elements of film narrative are space, time, and agency, in that order. A film has to position characters in a (presumed) physical space before they can act as agents, before they can move the story forward through their actions. As in any type of narrative, "Hollywood's strategies (formal and thematic) consistently urged the spectator to merge" with the principal characters, the actors and agents of the story, but an "illusion of reality depended on a far more substantial identification with the film's whole diegesis, that nonexistent, fictional space fabricated out of temporal and spatial fragments" (Ray 1985, 38).

To Have and Have Not opens with credits shown against the background of a globe, a painting on which we see the easternmost Caribbean island chain in the foreground and the Gulf of Mexico at the horizon. The camera moves in near the end of the credits sequence to pinpoint, then identify, the capital of Martinique (see figure 1.7a). This final image is, for our purpose here, shot 1, the typical landscape/cityscape of an establishing shot. Cut to a wharf crowded with people going about their business. Despite all the activity, especially in the foreground, the camera picks out and follows one person (Bogart) who walks across the scene from upper right to lower left (figure 1.7b, from shot 2; cut to shot 3, figure 1.7c). When he stops at the official's kiosk, he says an emphatic "Morning," which prompts an almost simultaneous cut to a two-shot of the official and Bogart, at which point the former also speaks (shot 3, figure 1.7d). Music, which has been continuous since the studio logo at the beginning of the film, had started to drop in volume near the end of shot 1, drops further during shot 2, and goes out three seconds into shot 3 on a single held note in the clarinets.

When the physical environment is introduced, onscreen and offscreen spaces are defined, and with them a diegesis (world) that includes, most importantly for our purpose, the potential for sound. Space and an airy medium are the basic requirements for sound. Thus, the story might start with the identification of an agent (Bogart) in shot 3, but the sound track is already actuated in shot 1, whether or not we in fact hear anything at that time. Rick Altman (2008, 15–16) argues that we recognize the basic distinction between levels (narrator and narration) at the moment when we realize that the process of what he calls "following" has kicked in (in this case, when we realize the camera is picking Bogart out from the crowd), and only then has a diegesis arisen. The physical space suggested by the images is insufficient on its own: narrative is not merely driven but is in fact created by agency.[42] I would counter that the camera has already done some of the

Figure 1.7, a–d. *To Have and Have Not*, establishing sequence. (a) Fort de France, painting at 1:20; (b) wharf, with Humphrey Bogart walking at 1:25; (c) Bogart reaches the official's kiosk at 1:32; (d) two-shot that immediately follows at 1:33. Screen stills.

work. The map shown during the main-title sequence effectively "creates" the narrator's depicted world for us, especially as that world becomes more and more specific (from world to Caribbean, then to Fort de France).

Altman argues that narrative amounts to "characters acting" and that the basic device by which the camera clarifies agency is through what he calls "following" individuals onscreen: "The process of following . . . highlights character and narrator, diegesis and narration. It is precisely this simultaneous emphasis on two different levels that constitutes narrative" (2008, 16). I would add that the first principle of classical film narration is clarity, not accuracy of representation (recall that clarity is the core of the second of my three general principles from early in this chapter). The elements that realize clarity of narrative presentation in film have come to be known collectively as the "classical style," which, as Bordwell insists, should not be understood as "an iron rule" that is universally enforceable "but [rather] a set of principled options, adaptable to different situations" (284; as this suggests, "classical style" is not restricted to studio-era sound films).[43] Ambiguity is hardly banished but can be understood in a functional opposition to clarity that by no means rules out a perceivable dialectical relationship. For Altman, time and story space only emerge when a character-agent is identified (followed). As my reading of the opening of To Have and Have Not suggests, I would order the sequence differently: space appears in the image first, then time emerges thanks to the persistence of that space; with those two comes the possibility of sound; finally, then, may appear a significant character, an agent. In the classical style, all the elements come together (storytelling begins, in Altman's terms) when the character speaks—when Bogart says "Morning." Films can—and do—open in many different ways, but all are read in terms of—or, when appropriate, can be said to struggle against—a formal frame that establishes a diegesis and leads to the synchronized sound of some agent's voice.

Sound often helps at this juncture because accompanying music will fade and speech or some sound effect will take over. The former is linked retrospectively to the narrator level and speech or effect to the diegesis or narration level, as in the move from shot 2 to shot 3. Although this is certainly an obvious and unimpeachable tie between sound and narrative levels, the distinction in fact is typically made earlier, as here at the moment of shot 1, when the visual and the aural—or image and sound (specifically, music)—represent the narrative levels to the audio-viewer as diegetic and nondiegetic, respectively.

Diegetic space, in other words, can be established and levels of narration opened by nothing more than the juxtaposition of image and sound, regardless of the latter's point of origin (if any). The diegetic is the register of the story world and its actors or agents. The nondiegetic is the register of the narration or the narrator. Both are necessary to establish and maintain a world of psychological realism. From this simple structure flow infinite possibilities for the crafting and presentation of narrative.[44]

In this opening sequence, for example, music moves fluidly from one to the other of the two states I described above. At first it is a performance, a vestige of

Figure 1.8. *To Have and Have Not,* Waxman's main-title cue, ending. Three-stave reduction. (From a copy of the piano/conductor score in the Franz Waxman Collection, Syracuse University.)

silent-film-era programs in the high-end picture palaces, here a miniature over-ture accompanied by images closely synchronized only once—at the main title itself. The very retreat of this music into the background is a narrative signal ("Now it is time to pay attention to the image"), as is its slowing down and clear-ing out of content to just a held note (as if "I now cede the sound track to speech: listen"). And as music falls, speech rises in a coordinated pattern. Like music, the speech (or other vocal noises) of actors may range from those associated with everyday activities and social interactions to the sound film's characteristic high-lighting (presence or "for-me-ness" [Altman 1992, 250]) of one or more princi-pals in a scene. In the opening moments of *To Have and Have Not,* what might easily have been the generic speech of the crowd on the wharf is offered as the briefly foregrounded noise of the footfalls of two boys as they run toward and past the camera. This is followed perhaps two seconds later by a single footfall (Bogart) on the same wood-plank stair and then, at the same interval, by the highlighted speech of Bogart and the official.

The simplicity of design in this sequence owes a great deal to the production methods and priorities of the classical Hollywood model, which emphasized clarity and often used overdetermination (redundancy) to achieve it (an idea par-ticularly emphasized by Raymond Bellour in an early analysis that I will discuss in detail in the opening section of chapter 2). As an establishing scene, however, it is quite short, but that is because it is in fact only the first of three parts in a longer opening scene that continues with Bogart's walking to the wharf's edge, where his boat is tied, and finally into town to the hotel where much of the film's action will take place.

The materials of the music itself emphasize topical clarity, with fragments of stern fanfares and an evocation of the generic exotic, a rhythmic, vaguely "na-

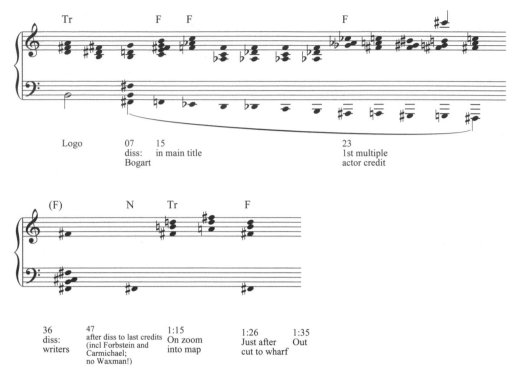

Figure 1.9. *To Have and Have Not,* main-title cue. Sketch. Tr = parallel triad figure; F = fanfare; N = "native" music. (Based on a copy of the piano/conductor score in the Franz Waxman Collection, Syracuse University.)

tive" music, in this instance against a static pitch design, an unusual device for a main-title cue where it is not essentially a song statement.[45] The composer, Franz Waxman, succeeds in establishing a clear but never precisely defined tonality. The bass progression consists of an opening B followed by a chromatic progression through an octave F♯2–F♯1, after which the final note persists to the end through pedal points and sustained upper voice and as bass of an ostinato (see figure 1.8). Above this, various sonorities support a series of punctuation-relaxation gestures, only occasionally as consonance-dissonance pairs, more often as defined by *sforzandi* and sudden *tutti* blasts. We are told in no uncertain terms that this will be a "heavy" dramatic action film. (The term "heavy" is drawn from the music vocabulary of the silent era, where "light," "neutral," and "heavy" signified expressive levels for many topical categories. Thus, a "light andante" might be a whimsical accompaniment to lovers' conversation, whereas "heavy andante" might be used for the tragic scene of a mother's loss.)[46]

Short and constantly shifting as it is, Waxman's main-title cue is surprisingly organized, not only tonally (at least in its bass-directedness and long static ending) but also motivically—see the sketch in figure 1.9. The series of parallel major triads ("Tr" in the figure) heard against the studio logo appear again near the end, now as a series of minor triads (with one concession: what would be a D minor triad becomes D major to fit the ostinato below it). The initial statement of the fanfare figure ("F") in trombones and horns (starting on F♯) is answered immediately by one a tritone away in the trumpets, a traditional symbol of the grotesque that is ironically undone by the harmony, whose intense dissonance over the F♯ statement suddenly resolves to an F minor triad, resulting in the only bit of traditional (if still chromatic) functional progression in the entire main-title cue. A few seconds later, the tritone is "fixed" to the fifth, C♯, in a *fortissimo tutti*. The original level, F♯, returns at the end (during shots 2 and 3) against the bass ostinato of the "native" music ("N").[47]

Whether the rounding off in the return of the parallel triads and the fanfare is meant motivically or topically or is simply a device of composition—a reference to the beginning as a means of ending, a cadence in a situation where no other means of articulating an ending is handy—is impossible to decide. This suggests that the relation of music's narrative functions in film and its "music-ness" will not always (or perhaps not even often) be that of simple opposition. In this instance, as in the vast majority of cases, even into the present day, a composer's original underscore is an aural trace of his or her response to the film print. That trace can be obscured by limits posed by director instructions, mixing changes, and the presence of other sound track elements, but, surprisingly perhaps, composers generally had more freedom during the studio era than they often did later on, and, as here, the formal framing cues of main titles and end credits minimized the external interference.[48] It is only to be expected that a composer's response would be capable of extending to the familiar materials of note writing, pitch, and form design—of charting a movement back from the aesthetic to the poietic, in Jean-Jacques Nattiez's terms (1990, 11–12).

And how does a music-heavy sequence like this confirm the notion of a vococentric cinema? It occupies the place of the theatrical formal frame and thus has the double function of simply announcing the event to follow (one of the roles of the fanfare) and also of telling the audio-viewer something about that film. Both "announcing" and "telling" are functions of a narrator. By fulfilling that role, the orchestral music positions itself firmly within the level of the extradiegetic (that is, nondiegetic). In other words, the music works to forge a clear distinction between levels, creating the possibility—the expectation—that a diegetic world will follow, and it can then confirm the "reality" of that diegesis by ceding place to speech and agency when Bogart says "Morning" and the official responds.

"Am I Blue?"

Cue no. 5 (see again the cue list in table 1.1) lasts just under two minutes. The lead-in to this performance offers a clear illustration of the multiplane, constant-level sound track: dialogue gives way to effects-like crowd noise at the same vol-

Figure 1.10. *To Have and Have Not,* Hoagy Carmichael and Lauren Bacall performing "Am I Blue?" Carmichael's first appearance onscreen. Screen still.

ume, then to music. This passing of the aural baton is standard procedure, to be sure, but in this instance the constant level also finally integrates characters and environment (the space of the hotel), in particular Hoagy Carmichael, who has been heard playing twice earlier (see cues 3 and 4) but only now appears onscreen (see figure 1.10). In both earlier instances, the music served both topical and spatial functions: identifying the hotel/club environment and extending offscreen space, first to include it (as Bogart approaches from outside; figure 1.11a) and then to remind us of it (connecting to the more neutral space of the hotel's upper floor; figure 1.11b).

Cricket, Carmichael's character, plays a short introduction and then sings the chorus from "Am I Blue?," a song originally heard in the 1929 Warner Bros. musical *On with the Show!* The band gradually joins in as the chorus proceeds. As it ends, Slim approaches the piano, Cricket tells her to "take over," and they shift back to the bridge with Slim singing, after which Cricket joins Slim to sing the reprise.[49]

The scene is just slightly more complex than the close synchronization of musical form and editing suggests. A dissolve from the previous scene reveals Harry sitting at a table in the cramped lobby-bar-café area of the hotel's main floor. The piano intro starts offscreen, then in quick succession: (1) a long shot of the band and nearby guests, many of them crowded around and behind the piano,

Figure 1.11, a–b. *To Have and Have Not,* (a) Bogart and client approach the Hotel Marquis; (b) in Bogart's room upstairs. Music is heard offscreen in both instances. Screen stills.

as Cricket continues to play; (2) cut to a nearby table where Slim sits with a man obviously interested in her; (3) a closer shot of Cricket, who begins to sing. As he goes through the song's A phrases, Slim tries to get Harry's attention (cutaways from the band to his table). The end of the performance is clearly the end of the scene: the hotel manager approaches Harry's table and talks about a group of men who want to hire his boat in order to help a Resistance fighter escape from the island, returning the focus of the narrative to the action of the previous scene.

If, as Chion claims, attention by habit goes to the voice and its source, then the embodied singing voice, perhaps paradoxically, would be the best cinematic instantiation of music: music centered in the body of a character-agent.[50] But the pairing is hardly perfect from a narrative point of view. In this instance, the song's lyrics permit only a few rather obtuse references to a romantic relationship that Slim would apparently like to establish with Harry but that is not advancing. The ambiguity is increased by the fact that previous scenes, although they have provided motivation for Slim's interest, have not offered much of a reason to take it as seriously as the film is suggesting here. The camera editing is designed to give priority to the band and its performance throughout, making the cutaways to Bogart's table clumsy.[51] And, finally, Cricket's naming of the song before the performance and additional comments during the song as he tells Slim to take over signal the fragility of lyrical singing, which always threatens to collapse back into the realism of everyday speech.[52]

"At Sea"

As I noted earlier, the music of *To Have and Have Not* is dominated by performances. The only orchestral underscore cues are the main title (1–2) and numbers 7b, 19a, and 29. Cue 7b is an action cue, mixed low under effects during the scene in which police chase Resistance fighters; 29 is a very short end-title cue.[53]

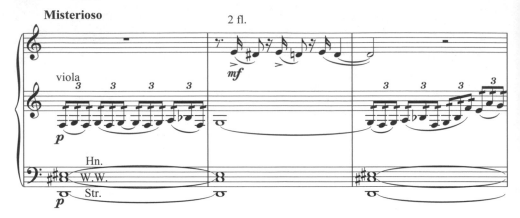

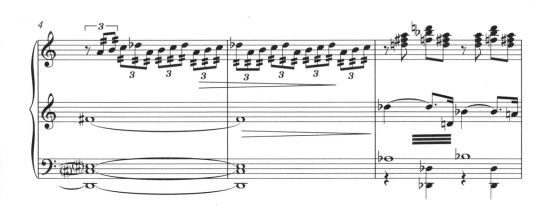

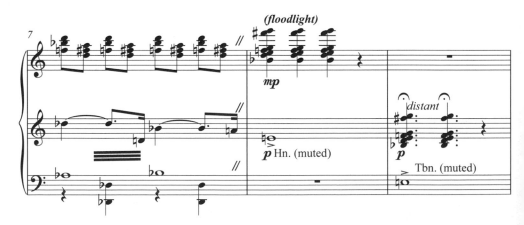

Figure 1.12. *To Have and Have Not,* "At Sea," Unit 2. Three-stave reduction. (Based on a copy of the piano/conductor score in the Franz Waxman Collection, Syracuse University.)

Figure 1.13. *To Have and Have Not,* "At Sea," Units 3, 4, and beginning of 5. Sketch. (Based on a copy of the piano/conductor score in the Franz Waxman Collection, Syracuse University.)

Waxman's "At Sea" (19a), on the other hand, is a continuous musical accompaniment to an extended sequence that alternates action and conversation. In this sense, it represents both basic types of symphonic underscore: music to accompany action and to underscore dialogue.

The sequence begins several minutes earlier (at 50:20) as Harry leaves port. The boat noise effect is strong throughout, dipping only slightly for conversation after Eddie (Walter Brennan), who was hiding below, emerges. A time lapse on a cut brings us to fog and night (at 51:30), with a long shot of the boat, then a cut to the cabin. A longer conversation ensues, with sound managed the same way as before. Eddie finally goes below, and another cut brings back the long shot / cabin pair (54:09), and at this point the music starts (Unit 2 of the sequence; see figure 1.12). The underscore follows a pattern throughout: some musical mimesis (in the familiar manner of text painting) accompanies or alternates with punctuating figures that draw attention to characters, objects, and action. At the outset of figure 1.12, the mysterious and vague murmuring of fog, boat, and nighttime in bar 1 is followed by the contrasting alert of accented notes (half steps set against the first bar's whole steps, all over a remarkably dissonant low-register chord). In Unit 3 (see figure 1.13), the music of the opening returns while Harry and Eddie

Music in the Vococentric Cinema 45

Figure 1.14. *To Have and Have Not,* "At Sea," Unit 6. Sketch. (Based on a copy of the piano/conductor score in the Franz Waxman Collection, Syracuse University.)

talk, and only after that (at 0:58 of the cue) does the long shot of the boat return. The fanfare theme from the main title, clearly intimated in bars 6–8, returns in a clear and strong presentation on the same F♯ position we heard it over fifty minutes earlier. The same basic pattern continues through Unit 4, where the conversation is between Harry and de Bursac, the Resistance fighter; Unit 5, which leads up to the encounter with the patrol boat; and Unit 6, the escape and subsequent transfer of de Bursac and his wife to a rowboat (see figure 1.14).

The multiplane sound track is in force throughout. Only once does the volume level break appreciably, and that is strongly motivated: Harry tells everyone to be quiet so that he can listen for the sound of the patrol boat's engine. The engine noise—the only effect we hear other than gunshots—rises and falls according to circumstance or in deference to dialogue and music. The music works similarly in relation to dialogue and significant moments of engine noise (such as the long shots of the boat). The music establishes its own layers: the mimetic "waves" in bar 1 over the growling dissonance that is an obvious analogue to the engine noise (that is, the chord mediates between the music and effects here, enabling them to merge at times, an important feature of this cue)—see also the opening of Unit 4 and the appearance of the patrol boat (bar 66 of the score). In and around the effects and music/effects, image-reinforcing or image-enhancing figures alternate with associative melodic fragments, especially the fanfare (bar 6, at 0:58, and after 1:56) but also two subtle references to "La Marseillaise" (at 1:26 and again after 4:43), both at moments calling attention to de Bursac's role as Resistance fighter. Waxman cites not the familiar figures of the tune but the melancholy ending of the internal phrase immediately preceding the final call to arms: "While peace and liberty lie bleeding" (see figure 1.15a–b).

The whole of cue 19a is extraordinarily dissonant and tonally uncertain. Both dramatic dissonance and tonal wandering are common enough in music for action scenes, particularly those involving struggle, but Waxman takes the dissonance up a notch beyond what his Warner Bros. colleague Max Steiner might have done in a similar situation. Note, for example, that the opening bar's D minor scale figures over its tonic D are answered by D♯; later (at 0:41) that answer

Figure 1.15. (a) internal phrase from "La Marseillaise"; (b) quotation in *To Have and Have Not,* "At Sea." (Figure 1.15b from a copy of the piano/conductor score in the Franz Waxman Collection, Syracuse University.)

Figure 1.16. *To Have and Have Not,* "At Sea," all. Reduced sketch. S = sea theme; F = fanfare; M = "La Marseillaise." (Based on a copy of the piano/conductor score in the Franz Waxman Collection, Syracuse University.)

becomes F♯ in anticipation of the fanfare's appearance over a B minor $^6_4$ (at 0:58). The tonal design does not offer much with which to define a coherent process, but its largest outline is clear enough (see figure 1.16): bass D in Unit 2 moves to F♯ after Unit 3 starts; the process is repeated as departure in Unit 4 and return to F♯ (and B minor) in Unit 5; then departure again but returning to G♯ at the end of Unit 5; and a final departure-return pair in Unit 6, again settling on G♯. Waxman could easily have returned to F♯ instead—in line with the pitch design he used in the main-title cue—but in this case he had a reason to shift the bass up a step: on the cut to the hotel (and just overlapping the final bass notes of the orchestral cue) we hear Cricket (offscreen) playing an intro to "Behold How Beautiful" in A♭ major.

Conclusion: Image/Action; Sound/Speech

What can we make of the music for "At Sea"? It is exactly the kind of writing that Gorbman is referring to in the following (though she generalizes to "film music"): "To judge film music as one judges 'pure' music is to ignore its status as a part of the collaboration that is the film. Ultimately it is the narrative context, the interrelations between music and the rest of the film's system, that determines the effectiveness of film music" (1987, 12). And of course I should add to "narrative context" the hierarchical and dialectical nature of the sound track itself.[54] In describing the competing conceptions of sound space during the early years of the sound film, James Lastra (2000, 180–82) invokes a distinction between film sound as mechanical and as representational. Both of these characterizations rest on metaphors, extensions of the eye and of writing, respectively, and are functionally expressed in film through the pair fidelity/clarity—or, more fully, acoustic fidelity and narrative clarity. In the one instance, it is as if the viewer is present in the sound space (otherwise, "fidelity" would have no meaning). In the other instance, the viewer is being shown a space (a diegesis) whose sound characteristics are managed (and vary) according to the needs of the presentation.[55] The sound film, however, does not necessarily abandon fidelity—instead, it becomes a stylistic choice. For that reason, I will present clarity/fidelity as an opposition in chapter 2, but it is, at bottom, false, because a fidelity that is constructed, however clear, is always at the service of narrative clarity. In the image, a constructed fidelity is best realized through action (the still image may be or become spectacle, but it raises questions that can only be answered through action or speech). In the sound track, the constructed fidelity of synchronized speech accomplishes the same task (unanchored sound may be aural design, but it raises questions about the relation of the sound and the image).

The establishing sequence in *To Have and Have Not* is strongly teleological: its goal is Bogart's voice, the word "Morning." By contrast, "Am I Blue?" as a musical performance erases the distinction between music and speech; as spectacle, it forces the narrative to hunt for ways to circumvent it. In the sequence with orchestral underscore, "At Sea," the recurrent, prosaic voice of Bogart anchors the action (so to speak), which might otherwise have been rendered quite effectively mute (though not silent). Pleasure in the experience of the establishing sequence comes in part from the ease of following its three distinct strands, two in the image (credits, background images) and one in the sound track (the main-title cue), in part from the expressive tension between the narratively static formal frame with the inexorable sweep into the first scene. The pleasure of a song performance embedded in a film centers on the paradox of the artificiality of this "perfect union" of music and speech. The ocean sequence forwards narrative with spectacle, and it offers by far the most complex interplay of sound track elements in the film. Even there, speech is still the benchmark—indeed, Bogart's lines are almost all commands—but the sound track dialectic is in full play.

2   Tools for Analysis and Interpretation

"In actual movies, for real spectators, there are not *all the sounds including the human voice. There are voices, and then everything else.* In other words, in every audio mix, the presence of a human voice instantly sets up a hierarchy of perception" (Chion 1999, 5; emphasis in original). The reader may well still wonder whether my insistence on vococentrism in the sound film is not overly reductive, whether the sound track hierarchy—Chion's "hierarchy of perception"—constrains and so threatens to impoverish interpretation. Early in chapter 1, I responded to this concern by noting the richness of the sound track's internal dialectic, which was certainly on display in the three scenes from *To Have and Have Not* that were discussed at the end of that chapter. Here, I will add two additional points.

First, as the words "real spectators," "instantly," and "perception" in the quote above suggest, the sound track hierarchy is grounded in human cognition.[1] As Chion notes later on (1999, 81), even in recent decades industry professionals continue to resist directors' creative attempts to underplay or mix down dialogue. Such misgivings surely are as much a result of culture as they are of cognition, but whatever an optimal balance between the two might be, it is clear that the vococentric cinema not only was a model for the studio era but also serves as such for the present and recent past. James Lastra reminds us that "as filmmakers gradually solved their conflicts and agreed upon a new and flexible set of formal strategies, they established the basic norms of sound and image that persist in large part today, shaping our own technologically mediated experience of the world" (2000, 10).

Second, I will again invoke Robert Scholes's distinction between novel and film: if the novel must work hard to show, the film must work hard to mean. In other words, the need for conceptualization is great, and thus there is more than normal heuristic value in theoretical work, models, frameworks, hierarchies, and other such constructs. So long as one is aware of the limitations of these devices, interpretation is thereby enabled and nurtured, and a focus on music or even effects is not overly constrained but is properly contextualized in the audio-viewer's experience.

The two central constructs developed from the three principles in chapter 1 were that analysis is grounded in the hierarchical and dialectic nature of the sound track and that interpretation is grounded in the distinction between music *for* film and music *in* film. In the present chapter, I largely assume that distinction while filling out details of the sound track's internal dialectic through an analytical heuristic designed by Chion and through a set of interrelated oppositions that I call the "five binaries" and that have traditionally supported readings of film music in relation to narrative.

Chion's Audiovisual Analysis Model and Music

As I noted in chapter 1, the basic strategy of an interpretive routine begins with close attention to something in the film, whether obvious (foregrounded), disruptive (Barthes's *punctum,* Ray's "difficult moment," Kramer's "hermeneutic window"), or not obvious (lost amid the vast amount of information that a film puts forward to a viewer, especially a gap in the overall narrative or inadequacy in character representation or motivation). Although its goals are considerably broader, the audiovisual analysis heuristic that Michel Chion sets up in chapter 10 of *Audio-Vision* can also work very effectively in service of this strategy with respect to sound. His model is almost entirely restricted to description (Bordwell's referential and explicit meanings) but leads directly into interpretation.[2] Four stages are worked through in order. Drawing on verbs used by Chion (1994, 189–92), I will label these "Itemize," "Characterize," "Locate sync points," and "Compare sound and image."

"Itemize" and "Characterize" may be taken together: in a second pass through the model (1994, 205–12), Chion gathers them under the heading "Locating the dominants." Itemizing the sound track elements, as the verb suggests, is intended to be pure description: what is present and when. The result is an inventory, a list similar in detail to a shot list. It will, however, also include an evaluation of the relative foregrounding of each of the three sound track elements (speech, music, effects) and therefore a limited degree of interpretation. The second stage, characterizing sound quality and consistency, refines this last step: it involves analysis of the interaction and balance of sound elements. (Do they tend to merge or stay distinct? How much reverberation is involved? Is there any masking of sounds that appear in the same register?) Even from these initial steps, it should be clear that Chion's objective in constructing his method of audiovisual analysis is to force the listener-analyst to pay attention to all sound elements equally, including the one most commonly neglected in the classical sound film: sound effects.

The third stage, which I characterize with the phrase "Locate sync points," is concerned with what Chion calls "audiovisual phrasing."[3] This is something of a leap beyond the previous cataloging of the first two stages with respect to level (size of unit) and degree of interpretation. One can itemize and characterize any arbitrary segment of a film's sound track, but audiovisual phrasing properly applies at the level of the scene and above. (See also chapter 3, where James Buhler applies this idea to the entirety of *Casablanca.*) Chion's own definition of audiovisual phrasing is vague: "Everything in a film sequence that concerns the organization of time and rhythm, including breathing, the timing of salient elements, punctuation, rests, temporal crystallizations" (2009, 469). In practice, audiovisual phrasing applies to both the third and fourth stages of analysis. In the former case, one is still separating out the sound track as if it were a musical composition; in the latter, the rhythms of sync points are studied in conjunction with the image track.

With my fourth stage, "Compare sound and image," I capture Chion's "Narrative analysis/comparison" from his second pass. Apparently another large step beyond the previous tasks, this fourth stage actually involves several tasks, including some further cataloging, all of them keyed to "comparison," and all of them, frankly, self-evident. One such task considers pacing through a comparison of the rhythms of image and sound: Do they match? Do they not? In both cases, what is accomplished or attempted by that mode? Another is a cataloging of materials and their degree of definition (for example, precise sound versus unfocused image; Chion 1994, 190). Still another is whether sound and image complement or contradict one another with respect to narrative information. In a scene from *Casablanca* (to be discussed in a later section of this chapter), the apparently primary narrative event is the arrival of Ilsa Lund and Victor Laszlo at Rick's Café Américain, but the action is undercut by unusual foregrounding: the music—that is to say, its performer, Sam—is positioned in the foreground, close to the camera. We learn something from the couple's entrance, of course, but the narrative is concerned with Sam's reaction. The comparison of sound and image also brings to attention cases of what Chion calls negative sounds (the image calls for them, but they are absent) and negative images (sound calls for them, but they are absent). The most common example of negative sound is found in the footfalls that are routinely missing in the classical cinema, an omission that is surprisingly common even today. Similarly, machine noises—especially automobiles—tend to be minimized. Not absent, they are mixed lower than would be expected from real-world aural experience. Noises of background human activity are also frequently minimized or absent, a good example being the train scene from *North by Northwest* to be discussed in the next section: obvious movement and speech are rendered wholly silent. Negative images, on the other hand, are difficult to ignore: the compulsion to seek the source of a sound is strong. The negative image is the basis of offscreen sound and, of course, a cliché in horror films.

Chion offers a very detailed analysis of the opening of Ingmar Bergman's *Persona* (1968), to which the reader is referred (Chion 1994, 198–205). For sake of a brief example of this kind of analysis in relation to image, consider again the first dance from *The Dark Corner,* discussed in chapter 1. The sequence starts at 21:22 and runs through 21:58. At first we hear only a dance band playing at a high sound level; they begin in midphrase with a scale flourish in the piano; shortly thereafter a relaxed lyrical melody enters in the clarinet; the music is a rumba. Ten seconds later, a man's voice enters at the same high level, and the music drops in volume almost immediately. In a middle-register voice with clear articulation, the man continues to speak through 21:55 at a consistent volume and in a consistent tone of voice. There are several pauses, the most notable being near the end, after which a note of tension suddenly enters his voice with the affirmation " . . . and belongs to me." A woman's voice in its middle register says only "sweetheart," and after another two or three seconds a phone rings loudly. The conversation might even have been direct recorded: the microphone is close by (above them), and we hear not the reverberant silence of a sound studio but other noises of an uncertain character, perhaps the swish of clothes as they and others nearby dance. Those sounds disappear briefly after the woman speaks, but we still hear the music, which drops abruptly in sound level with the cut a second or less before the telephone rings. Overall, then, music is the only element in the sound track initially, but after that it shares the sound track with the voice. Though the latter predominates, voice, music, and effects are kept very distinct. The extra resonance in the voice due to the close miking is noticeable. The voices drop out, music continues (backgrounded but not quiet), and the phone interrupts with a surprisingly high, tinkling ring. I might also note that the music continues after the ring: that is, the common strategy of taking music out under a foregrounded effects sound is not followed here.[4]

For such a short passage, it is difficult to say much of interest about audiovisual phrasing that is not already accounted for in the details described above. The abruptness of the opening is mitigated by a sound advance: that is, we hear the introduction to the song during the final moments of the previous scene, and what we might call an accent of surprise, created by the suddenly louder sound level with the cut to the orchestra, is promptly mitigated by the entrance of the melody. After that entrance, the temporal articulations might well have been determined by the phrases of the music—but that does not occur; instead, a second chorus, with saxophones carrying the melody, simply starts up under the conversation. Needless to say, the entrance of the man's voice is a strong moment of articulation equal to the earlier entrance of the music. But the passage ends in a curious way: the closing accent (in the voice) is not his but hers (the interjected "sweetheart"). This comment receives negative emphasis by the "silence" that follows (no voice, only music), but it is then linked by proximity to the accent of the phone ringing. Overall, then, the passage features a smooth, mostly continuous pairing of voice and music until the two interruptions (disruptive accents by voice and phone) at the end. The one element present continuously throughout, however, is music.

On to the fourth stage (comparison): music enters with the cut to the band, and the sound, loud as it is, is appropriate to the tight framing (see again figure 1.1a). Music and sound diverge slightly with the pan, as the increasing distance from the band ought to be—but is not—matched by a drop in volume for the music. One might also note that the pan is relatively slow and thus is consistent with the relaxed character of the music: the camera does not seem to be in any hurry to get across the room and reveal the lead couple. The pan, however, does accomplish this much: it takes attention firmly away from the band's performance and repositions the music as diegetic background sound. The band, which is quite large, the *mise-en-scène,* which is elegant, and the dancers are all giving us the same narrative information: this is a party of peers at the home of a wealthy person. Medium close shots (from waist level moving to shoulder level) clearly coordinate with the tight miking of the man's voice.

The oddities are the final accents. When the woman answers, she is turning away from the camera. The effect is to undermine the accent (her first speech) but also to attribute that undermining to him (the turn does seem abrupt, overly forceful). The combination of sync point and unusual action opens up a narrative gap. ("Why did she speak that way? Does she not share the feelings that the man has just expressed? Why did he seem to turn her roughly?")[5] The music, in the meantime, has become neutral, perhaps at this moment even anempathetic, its pleasant amiability out of sync with the dialogue, as it is with the final accent: the phone ringing in another room, perhaps a library or den, and answered by the butler. This last is, of course, a cliché: we expect something significant to happen next, and probably not something good.

Thus, the three sound track elements, all present and yet always distinct from one another, are marshaled in service of the depiction of an elegant household where not everyone is happy (we hear it at the last moment in the insistence in his voice and in the absence of personal affection—or is it conviction?—in hers).

Chion takes the term "dominant" from Roman Jakobson, for whom it is "the element that in any text or tradition subordinates all others" (Lapsley and Westlake 1988, 142). The same can be applied to the later stages of this analysis. Robert Lapsley and Michael Westlake note that Stephen Heath describes the dominant as "a form of narrative causality reliant on temporal and spatial systems. . . . In classical cinema, space becomes subordinated to the requirements of narration, which entails that the spectator is always placed in the optimum viewing position in each shot" (142). Thus, Chion can be said to set up a vehicle for close viewing/hearing, but the end of the process always comes back around to narrative, or, as an astute early observer of film and its musics, Virgil Thomson, put it, "the aim and problem of the narrative film is nothing more or less than effective narration" (1981, 152).

Visual and Aural Codes:
The Big Sleep (1946), Second Car Scene

The brief scene to be discussed here occurs not far from the end of *The Big Sleep*. Phillip Marlowe and Vivian Greenwood, the characters played by Humphrey Bogart and Lauren Bacall, have escaped from one dangerous encounter and are heading toward another. They talk over their situation (though he, in fact, does the majority of the talking), and they admit, for the first time, genuine romantic feelings. The scene consists of twelve shots and lasts one minute and forty seconds.[6] Dissolves (overlapping shots) at beginning and end create a clearly defined frame for the scene, whose design is determined by the grouping of two-shots of Vivian and Marlowe, within which two sets of alternating close-ups are positioned (stills selected from each shot appear in figure 2.1).

Figure 2.1. *The Big Sleep* (1946), screen stills from each of the twelve shots in the second car scene. (After Raymond Bellour, "Obvious and the Code," in *The Analysis of Film*. Reused by permission of Indiana University Press.)

Raymond Bellour analyzes the scene in detail. His goal is essentially to describe the workings of several visual and aural codes that underlie and enable what he asserts is "the simplest narrative fact imaginable—two characters talking in a car" (2000, 72). Indeed, there is little to decipher here. Any narrative requires, first of all, a space, a story world, a diegesis. In this case, the diegesis has an internal and an external component: the inside of the automobile where Bogart and Bacall sit and the vague night world we see flying by outside and through which the automobile is moving (shot 1). Granted, this scene does probe the limits of the audio-viewer's generosity with respect to the diegetic representation, given the obvious car body on a rocker and the process shot that creates the exterior. A viewer in the period, however, would understand this convention very well and was unlikely to have taken it as negating diegetic representation as the scene follows a standard progression from exterior (in the manner of an establishing shot) to interior, moving gradually closer until the close-ups in shots 3–6, after which the pattern from shots 2–6 repeats in 7–12.

Itemize. Since Bellour is concerned with speech and image but not effects and music, I have added details about the latter to his itemization of the elements: see columns 6 and 7 in table 2.1. Music is continuous. "Talking" (speech) is more or less continuous, with occasional brief pauses, but it begins several seconds after the scene starts and stops several seconds before the end. Sound effects are limited to one screech of tires as the car swerves for an unknown reason (this occurs during shot 7). Both speech and the tire-screech effect are diegetic—they obviously originate from and resonate in the story world. The music is closely synchronized but nondiegetic.

Characterize. Voices are somewhat dry, with relatively little resonance, and as such are appropriate to the environment (interior of a car). With one exception, there is little emotion in either character's speech. They speak in a tone and at a moderate pace that seem to match the acoustic space. The exception, ironically, is not either character's declaration of love (shots 6 and 10) but Marlowe's extended and increasingly excited challenge to Vivian, which takes up most of shot 7 and climaxes with the sudden swerve and sharp tire-noise effect. The registral distribution of music and voice tracks is clear and tends to keep the different elements in separate layers. At the bottom (lowest) is the continuous car noise in the lower strings. Just above that are the two voices, Bogart's being barely lower than Bacall's, which is unexpectedly deep (she had trained to lower her voice for *To Have and Have Not*). Theme statements and the tire-noise effect are spread across the register of the voices and a higher pitch register.

Music provides another complete set of codes that might have been integrated very readily into Bellour's description. In the simplest sense, we can characterize the music as adding its own temporal imprimatur to the scene, first through its continuous presence and second through its consistent figuration in the accompaniment. The scene is a conversation carried out "on the way," in the midst of a movement of machine and time as expressed visually by the car and the passing nighttime landscape, respectively. Associative themes are embedded in the cue in a manner closely synchronized with dialogue. Under the Music column in table 2.1, "Movement," "Love," and "Carmen" are labels applied to these themes in the studio cue sheet. These are also indicated in the music summary of figure 2.2. Although I refer to them as themes, they are of very different character: "Love" is a proper melody, "Carmen" is a two-note motive, and "Movement" is an automobile-sound "gag" (as the composer, Max Steiner, called such musical imitations of sound effects). "Movement" has already been heard more than once in this automobile-heavy film. The simple but often menacing motive "Carmen" was also heard early on, when Vivian's wayward younger sister was introduced in scene 1.

Table 2.1. Table of codes operating in the "car scene" from *The Big Sleep*

#	Framing/ characters	Angle	Time	Speech	Music	Effects	Elements of narration
1	MS → M2S	↗	+ (6)	—	"Movement"		[Exterior of car]
2	2S	←	+ (5)	MV			[2–12: interior of car]
3	CU, M	↗	− (6)	M	Brass buzz / "Movement"	Low car noise throughout	
4	CU, V	←	− (4)	MV			
5	CU, M	↗	− (7)	M			
6	CU, V	←	− (5)	MV	"Love"		V: "I guess I am in love with you."
7	2S	↗	++ (43)	MV	4": cont. 12": "Movement" / brass buzz 8": "Love" 14": "Movement" 5": "Carmen"	Tire screech with the swerve; low car noise	Marlowe's movement as he takes a corner
8	CU, V	←	− (3)	M	"Movement" / "Carmen"		
9	CU, M	↗	− (4)	M	"Movement"		
10	2S	↗	+ (11)	VM	Cont. / "Love"	Low car noise	M: "I guess I am in love with you"
11	CU, V	←	− (2)	—			
12	2S	↗	+ (5)	—	"Love"		Vivian puts her hand on Marlowe's arm

*Note: After Raymond Bellour, "The Obvious and the Code" (2000). Some editing and correction were done in columns 2, 4, and 5, and I added columns 6–8. In column 4, the symbols +, -, and ++ are Bellour's indications of relative length; in parentheses I have added durations in seconds. Note that these do not always agree with Bellour's symbols. Based on a figure in Raymond Bellour, *The Analysis of Film*. Reused by permission of Indiana University Press.*

MS = medium shot
M2S = medium two-shot
2S = two-shot
CU = close-up
M = Marlowe
V = Vivian

↗ = camera at 45° angle from characters
← = camera straight on
(#) = shot duration in seconds
+ = slightly longer than average shot length
++ = much longer than average
− = shorter than average

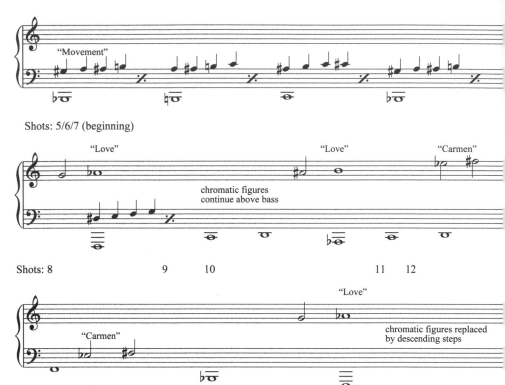

Figure 2.2. *The Big Sleep,* second car scene, music summary. "Movement," "Love," and "Carmen" are themes or motives. (Based on sketches in the Max Steiner Collection, Brigham Young University.)

Here it is folded into the brass figures. "Love" was first heard on the sound track when Vivian and Marlowe kissed in a parallel car scene, and it was quite vivid in the scene preceding this one when Vivian helped Marlowe escape from a gangster's house. Here it appears twice, once for Vivian's declaration, again for Marlowe's.

The functional registers of the music are kept distinct in the layers of accompaniment and melody. The accompaniment imitates (indeed, generates) the sound of the car engine purring along at highway speed and maintains tension through punctuating brass chords, while the melody introduces a variety of linear and chordal fragments. The remarkable result of Steiner's embedding the automobile effect in the underscoring—something one might disparage as hypermimetic—is that of an overlapping of the diegetic/nondiegetic. Yet the overall character or function of the underscore in this context is nevertheless rather unremarkable.

Analyze sync points. For all its punctuations in the underscore and its concentration on dialogue, the sound track in this excerpt really has only three sync points: the two appearances of "Love," which are very distinctive timbrally and expressively and which rise out of the continuity of the underscore; and the screeching tire. The latter—this isolated sound—might seem to be an enigma (*punctum?*), but in fact it serves a useful articulating role as an end-accent for Marlowe's animated speech during shot 7. At one level, it is a subtle reminder of the dangers they still face (and that Marlowe is rehearsing at the time), but at another level, it serves as a physical jolt to Marlowe's self-possession, after which only a few additional moments are required before he can acknowledge his feelings for Vivian.

Compare sound and image. The deep conventions of narrative would tell us that the nondiegetic is not strange: the film narrator's register is always assumed, or at least is always available as potential to be realized. What Steiner's musical cue provides, in effect, is a musical voice-over, a layer of ongoing allusional commentary that cannot refrain from naming the characters or redundantly describing the action: "See, the car is moving"; "Yes, the two of them do seem to have feelings for each other (remember when they kissed earlier?)"; "He mentioned Carmen and the family's troubles"; and "Yes, the two of them have now acknowledged that they are forming a romantic couple." "Now, on to the next scene" (= lap dissolve as music continues).

Visually, an interior/exterior opposition correlates with a warm/cold opposition in this scene: the "interior," a (relatively) warm, womblike car, is set against the "exterior," a cool, misty night (images of the passing countryside are prominent in the background). This "warmth" is part of the coding system that predicts the mutual admissions of love, and it is further subdivided into quiet/active and settled/dangerous oppositions, expressing narrative codes to which Bellour does not make reference: Vivian is comfortable, resting her head against the seatback, and physically quiet: she moves her eyes, only rarely her head, during their conversation. (Only in the last shot does she move her hand in a slow gesture to rest it on his shoulder.) Marlowe, on the other hand, is jittery, frequently turning his head and swaying much more obviously than she to the movement of the car. (The flickering background accentuates this, since we can see movement outside the windows behind him during his close-ups but never during hers.)

Interpretation (1): implicit meanings (with a critique of Bellour). Bellour's goal is to draw attention to what he calls the "elementary but subtle operations" that underlie—one might say guarantee—the simplicity or "obviousness" of this scene (2000, 72). Given the variety in the materials, Bellour initially claims that the large number of shots for a scene that consists of nothing but two persons talking in a car suggests a level of discontinuity, but then he demonstrates that the effect is mitigated by "a profound tendency toward repetition" (75). He isolates the functioning of six cinematic codes that accomplish this task (refer again to table 2.1). The first and fourth of these are gathered in column 2: framing and the presence or absence of characters in the frame. The remaining codes are given separate columns: camera angle (that is, head on or tilted at 45°), time (duration of the shot), and speech (the person who is talking). I have deleted one code—static or moving shot—because all the values are the same (moving) after the beginning.

Symmetry of design is Bellour's main analytical conclusion: this short scene is an exemplar of the apparently effortless, technically skilled mode of classical Hollywood practice. The points to be emphasized particularly are the patterned alternation of two-shots (that is, Viviane and Marlowe together) and close-ups, the two-shots at beginning and end whose framing function is reinforced by camera angle and the absence of speech, and the symmetrical but not numerically rigid positioning of the extended shot 7 (note that shots 1–6 take thirty-three seconds, shot 7 lasts forty-three seconds, and shots 8–12 take twenty-five seconds). It is, in fact, the subtle variation within the repetitions that drives the design. For example, Bellour highlights differences between the series of close-ups before and after the central two-shot (which, as noted above, is unusually long for this context and so forms a natural axis): in the first series, or shots 3–6, Marlowe is shown first, while in the second (shots 8–9), Vivian leads; in the first series, both talk at some point (not always onscreen), while in the second series, only Marlowe talks (Vivian talks during the two-shot in shot 10); and so on. Bellour claims these differences generate or reinforce the direction of the narrative, as attention shifts from discussion of their dangerous situation to expression of their love for each other. Temporal discontinuities, then, provoke assessment of design and may lead to interpretive conclusions, as in this case where the excessive duration of shot 7 leads Bellour to take this shot as an axis about which groupings of shots can be organized.

In Bellour's analysis, as I extend it, music is a code. Claudia Gorbman isolates three codes as essential to the interaction of image and music: the pure musical code (where attention is to performance), the cultural musical code (generally accepted meanings—topics, for example), and the cinematic musical code (the system of music-narrative associations developed within an individual film) (Gorbman 1987, 12–13).[7] These three codes do inadvertently reinforce the idea of music performance as separate and therefore seem to support the Romantic idea of music as autonomous or even transcendent. Music in film and concert share the cultural and cinematic musical codes (essentially generic expectations and internal design elements, respectively), but only diegetic music in film can approach the state of pure performance without undermining image/sound relations. Thus, Gorbman can actually say that "music, indeed, is constantly engaged in an existential and aesthetic struggle with narrative representation" (13)—certainly an opening for any critic who wants to argue for music's special character! But, citing filmed performances, Gorbman emphasizes their atypicality and reasserts the priority of narrative (and with it the visual): "Although film music undeniably possesses its own internal logic, it always bears a relationship to the film in which it appears" (14).

Using Gorbman's three types, we note first that the pure code is absent from this scene: we would have to construct it arbitrarily by listening closely to Steiner's music, blocking out other sound track elements. Peter Larsen attempts this by "reading the score," treating Steiner's entire cue as a "cohesive 72-bar composition" (2005, 113–18), but in order to do this, he is obliged to add mimetic "walking music" and clear cadential close on a B♭ major triad that belong to the following scene. Such transitional overlapping is very common, but a cadential close, as in this case, is definitely not.

Unlike the pure code, the cultural and cinematic codes will be at work in virtually any music in film. The question is not their presence but the degree to which they are active. The extreme case of minimal activity would occur with the most deliberately fashioned neutral music, the sort of aural "wallpaper" that Igor Stravinsky accused all film music of being (Neumeyer and Buhler 2008, 131). As here, Steiner frequently approaches the opposite extreme, as he weaves a dense web of constantly shifting topical and thematic references in musical cues that are pushed forward in the sound mix, following Warner Bros. house style. The reunion scene in *Casablanca* is a particularly striking example, but the technique is also at work in this second car scene in *The Big Sleep*: the entire cue consists of two topics (the car noise "gag" and the brass stingers [chordal accents or sforzandos]) and several thematic citations with links to dialogue. "Movement" (the car "gag" itself) counts as a theme because it has been used several times earlier in the film (hence, it has become a motif). Its recurrence here invites the audioviewer to make connections to those previous instances and in so doing helps to reinforce the idea of the film as a coherent narrative.

At the level of the scene, the music attempts to capture both aspects of the scene's basic interior/exterior, warm/cold opposition. The warmth of the "Love" theme stands out sharply against the background ostinato figure and motivic fragments that seem to threaten, as it were, from outside. But Steiner's treatment is not so simplistic as this characterization might make it seem. The "elementary but subtle operations" that Bellour ascribes to the director, Howard Hawks, apply quite as well to Steiner's score. First of all, though Vivian admits her love in shot 6, the "Love" theme has already entered with shot 5, a close-up of Marlowe. Later, to a brief comment of hers, he finally admits his love in a duplicating pattern: he repeats her language, and the "Love" theme enters a shot earlier than his statement (that is, in 10 rather than 11). This time, however, the emphasis turns toward Vivian and toward the couple: shots 10 and 12 are each two-shots, and shot 11 is a close-up of Vivian (this is one of the inversions Bellour mentions). Thus, what we might call the "image/music system" helps to effect a clean articulation by finishing a pattern and emphasizing it through the restatement of the "Love" theme. The close-up of Marlowe earlier is balanced by a close-up of Vivian, the pattern of close-up(s) followed by a two-shot (shots 5–7) is repeated in shots 11–12, where there is no dialogue. At that point, the larger narrative situation (expressed in most of the scene's dialogue) is suppressed in favor of the emotional resonance of the new couple (the "Love" theme overlaps slightly into the following scene as well).[8]

It is hard to resist the conclusion that Steiner was at least as good an analyst of the scene as Bellour.[9] Music brings to this scene the perfection of Steiner's underscoring art, which he had been developing for a dozen years by the time he came to work on this film. And, as we have just seen, a straightforward analysis easily falls in line with Bellour's reading. At the beginning, Steiner ties music tightly to the movement of the car and the landscape outside its windows. The car "gag" adds greater regularity but in doing so ties itself very closely to the landscape: the fog rolling over the car, then the exterior, seen flying by through the car window. When speech intrudes, however, everything changes: the music-effects combination recedes to its proper role as *mise-en-scène*, all the more so because speech moves quickly, too, taking control of the "tempo space" or pacing that the other elements had established earlier. Thereafter, music rises only in fragments when prompted to set off some brief stinger figures or the "Love" theme: music names what is important for us to "see" or "hear" in the characters.

Interpretation (2): symptomatic meanings—the ideology of the voice. Despite its omnipresence and all its richness of detail, Steiner's music really does nothing that might effect a displacement of the voice's authority. Analogously, elements of the *mise-en-scène* never interfere with the focus on Bacall's or Bogart's face. Except for the two statements of "Love" and the clear invocation of a *misterioso* topic, the music does little more than the exterior that passes outside the windows in making itself a point of attention. We can double-check the status and function of the sound track elements by asking the question, "What if there were no music in this scene?" The answer is that very little would change. We would receive the same information from dialogue, we would see the same obvious motion of the car down the highway (reinforced by Marlowe's comment "if we can get there in time"), the same (small but definite) physical manifestations of their attraction to each other. On the other hand, the lack of background sound would undermine the image. We would expect some level of noise from a moving vehicle, noise that should be heard even inside it. Furthermore, that expectation has been fulfilled and reinforced any number of times already in this film. Even the parallel car scene provides a negative confirmation. In that instance, we see the interior of the car, but since they have stopped by the side of the road, we hear no noise. Of course, a silent background would also contradict the principle of the integrated or multiplane sound track. Steiner's car "gag" was a substitute for the effects track that would have been necessary otherwise.

Bellour refers to "the simplest narrative fact imaginable—two characters talking in a car" (2000, 72)—but for our purpose, of course, we want to be able to fit sound and music into that very typicality. Should there be music? Yes and no. Consider the following points: (1) Max Steiner has established an expectation for a great deal of music through earlier sections of the film (including an earlier and obviously parallel scene in a car); (2) the sound is so intimate and the meanings in the dialogue so clear that music is redundant, except, ironically, for its role as effects; (3) there is, nevertheless, a very well established convention for music in love scenes, subdued though this one is; (4) for the genre (basically, *film noir* or the detective film), one expects less music relative to other genres (with the exception of romantic comedy and the filmed stage play) and more often for action than as dialogue underscore; and (5) by the mid-1940s, a trend was in place to reduce the amount of underscoring in feature films generally, and thus there could

Table 2.2. The "five binaries" with descriptions

Terms/oppositions	Description
(principle: balance of narrative levels)	
1. Clarity	1. Priority to efficiency in presentation of narrative
2. Fidelity	2. Priority to accurate reproduction of the acoustic environment of the physical world depicted in the narrative
(method: mix and balance of sound track elements)	
1. Foreground	1. Sound that is forward in the mix, or a sound track that draws attention compared with the image
2. Background	2. Sound that is low in the mix, or a sound track that draws little attention
(space: sound in relation to space/levels of narration)	
1. Diegetic	1. Sound belonging to (anchored in) the physical world depicted in the narrative
2. Nondiegetic	2. Sound belonging to the level of narration or the narrator
(time: temporal and logical coordination of sound and image)	
1. Synchronization	1. Close, realistic coordination of sound and image
2. Counterpoint	2. Nonrealistic treatment of sound/image simultaneity
(agency: emotional coordination of sound and image)	
1. Empathy	1. Close, sympathetic coordination of sound and image
2. Anempathy	2. Ironic or distanced treatment of sound in relation to the image

have been external pressure to reduce the number of minutes including under-score. On balance, one would have to say that the first three of these points over-rule the last two.

The Five Binaries: Film Music's Functions

Chion's audiovisual analysis routine helps to insure close attention to the sound track. Additionally, Gorbman's three codes for music in film are a useful way of gathering the material of basic modes of understanding, whether or not one's orientation is to a language-based (or, more generally, discursively semi-otic) model. Nevertheless, it will be more efficient for our purpose here to think in terms of a set of functions that are common to all the codes, functions that can be understood to underlie the material of those codes. Gorbman herself de-velops a list of seven rules for classical Hollywood underscoring that amount to a set of narrative functions, and in the intervening years since the publication of *Unheard Melodies* it has been shown that the rules work remarkably well as basic categories for film music of almost any kind, whether or not classical, from Hollywood or limited to the underscore.

Figure 2.3. *The Dark Corner,* conversation in the High-Hat Club; includes all the expected, or unmarked, characteristics of the classical sound track. Screen still.

The underlying structure for audiovisual analysis consists of a small set of functional oppositions, or what I call here the "five binaries": see table 2.2 for terms and descriptions. The table is set up to follow a model of asymmetrical oppositions, where the more general or common term is unmarked, the narrower, more specific or limited term is marked. The first term in each of the five binaries is unmarked, the second term in each is marked. The table thus also identifies a set of correlations that applies to all five binary pairs.[10] There is one discrepancy—between the first pair and the others—that should be noted, however. The first term, clarity, set against its opposing term, fidelity, is the aesthetic priority for the sound track that guarantees the functional priority of the other four. The pair is included here even though it represents an overriding principle because the tension between clarity and acoustic fidelity can sometimes have expressive effects. (The opposition not included here and even more fundamental is presence/absence: whether, in any particular instance, a sound element is in the sound track.)[11]

The remaining terms are correlated in terms of Altman's "for-me-ness"—as if the onscreen characters are in a conversation with you, the viewer, for whom all the elements of the film are ordered for the sake of ease in following the narrative. Pairs 2–5 each begin with a term or condition one would intuitively associate with a normal conversation between two people: one expects to be in the same physical space (diegesis), speaking directly to or listening attentively to the other person (foregrounding), hearing the other person's words as he or she speaks them (synchronized), and being engaged in the conversation (empathic). The image in figure 2.3 suggests how a film typically meets all these requirements easily.[12]

One can readily confirm or test the presumed state of narrative clarity by invoking a cluster of the opposing terms: backgrounded, unsynchronized, nondiegetic, and anempathetic sound is the murmur of an unseen crowd (as if of ghosts), or a subdued neutral underscore, or perhaps a threatening murmur of nonspecific ambient sound.

North by Northwest, *Dining Car Scene*

A brief case study will draw attention to each of the pairs. In discussing music's unique freedom to cross the diegetic/nondiegetic divide, Gorbman cites two "familiar" cases: background "music that suddenly ceases as a character leans over and turns off a radio; or, conversely, as in a scene in, what seems like piped-in music in a train's dining car becomes more and more clearly nondiegetic" (1987, 3).[13] Gorbman draws this last example from Royal S. Brown, who cites it as an instance where music passes from diegetic to nondiegetic without obvious justification in design or narrative. His description: "A kind of bland music accompanies the opening dialogue . . . [and] the audience presumes that this is . . . Muzak [actually, a foxtrot by André Previn written a year earlier for a different film, *Designing Woman* (see figure 2.4a)]. As the conversation amorously heats up, however, the 'Love Theme' composed by Bernard Herrmann for the nondiegetic music track takes over without missing a beat [figure 2.4b]." There is a problem with this, however, because neither theme is foregrounded. Brown is particularly bothered that Herrmann's theme is not distinguished from Previn's: "One could argue that the low volume level of the Muzak offers a clue that it is intended diegetically, save that the love theme comes across at pretty much the same level." Nevertheless, this discrepancy between (presumed) significance of the theme and its low status in the mix gives Brown a convenient opening for interpretation. He is able to construct two possible readings. First, and more plausibly, "the innocuous quality of the initial music offers something of a nondiegetic comment on the lukewarm state of [Cary] Grant and [Eva Marie] Saint's relationship at the onset of the conversation, whereas the more impassioned Herrmann strains carry us into the budding sexual relationship" (1994, 69). Second, "the passage from the Muzak to the 'Love Theme' in this scene . . . fortifies subliminal audience perceptions that [Roger Thornhill] and [Eve Kendall] have passed from an ordinary to an extraordinary level of existence"—that is, from the "real" world of the diegetic to the "unreal" world of myth and emotion that nondiegetic music enables (69–70). This latter reading is rather weak on two counts: (1) the innuendo-laden banter between Grant and Saint never suggests that anything more than casual sex is in the offing; and (2), as we learn later, Eve has an ulterior mo-

Figure 2.4, a–b. (a) *North by Northwest* (1959), "Muzak"—actually music composed by André Previn for the film *Designing Woman* (1957), "Fashion show" theme; (b) Bernard Herrmann, music for *North by Northwest*, "Interlude," beginning. Transcriptions from the sound track.

tive for her actions: she is playing to character as the mistress of the film's villain (played by James Mason) in order to prevent Thornhill from discovering that she is, in fact, a government spy participating in an elaborate deception.

The relatively stable level of the Muzak and "Love" theme is a subtle design element—in other words, I am not at all sure one needs to go to the interpretive lengths that Brown does. Position in the mix—which usually means relative loudness (especially for monoaural sound)—is essential to an audio-viewer's reading. Brown does not mention the very low-level but constant sound of the train running over the tracks, the fact that the dining room is full of guests but no one can be heard speaking (other than the host and a waiter early on), or the very close miking for the couple, which, for most of the scene, effectively positions the audio-viewer at the camera, as if situated in adjacent chairs at the compact dining table (a somewhat overbearing for-me-ness in this instance; see figure 2.5a–b). The couple's intimate dialogue is all too plainly paramount: clarity, not realism, is being served here. Oddly, then, although loudness levels are important, they are measured against physically plausible sound only within a (generous) range and in accordance with the hierarchy of sound track elements.

In this case, it is possible to respect point of location (where the sound comes from) and sound scale (relative loudness with respect to apparent distance from the camera). Generally speaking, in the classical cinema either or, more often, both are sacrificed in order to guarantee clarity of speech. The dining car scene, nevertheless, has to be considered an exaggerated instance of sound assisting narrative clarity—exaggerated because the nearly complete suppression of other voices has an unnatural quality about it, as if the dining car is a tableau rather than a realistic scene of activity, the other passengers props rather than people.

Figure 2.5, a–b. *North by Northwest,* train scene, Roger Thornhill (Cary Grant) and Eve Kendall (Eva Marie Saint) when Herrmann's "Interlude" begins. Screen stills.

In this sense, Brown is correct in speaking of the "unreal," but here that applies to a radical division of empathy (for the couple) and anempathy (for all the others), though I should emphasize that this applies to speech and effects, not to music. On the other hand, Gorbman's characterization of the music as turning "more and more clearly nondiegetic" is problematic. The hallmark of the scene's two musics is, as Brown notes, how much alike they are and how nearly the same is their presentation. It is true that the music is "cued," since it enters just after Eve invites Roger to her room, but Herrmann's melody rises into consciousness almost entirely because of the cutting timbre of the oboe (see again figure 2.4b). Di-

Table 2.3. *North by Northwest*, dining car scene, analyzed in terms of the "five binaries"

Five binaries	Summary
Clarity/fidelity	Clarity of dialogue is paramount. With the exception of some ambient train sounds that are properly positioned in the physical space (and are so realistic that they sound live recorded), fidelity is sacrificed. The acoustical realism in location and sound scale are accidental by-products of camera position.
Foreground/ background	In this context, the foreground/background divide is exaggerated in both image and sound tracks. This is especially obvious in the sharply different treatment of the couple at their table and the rest of the guests and staff in the dining car. Within the sound track, sound levels of voices and music are also exaggerated.
Diegetic/nondiegetic	The diegetic/nondiegetic distinction is of little significance because of the music's low volume.
Synchronization/ counterpoint	Synchronization is very close in the dialogue; temporal counterpoint is exceedingly rare in classical Hollywood films. One instance of dubbing that Hitchcock fans like to cite (changing an overly suggestive word to something more innocuous) is invisible to the normal viewer. The music is not closely synchronized (mickey-mousing), nor are there any clear sync points (even the entrance of Hermann's theme is barely noticeable).
Empathy/anempathy	Music approaches the anempathetic only tentatively in the form of a neutral "Muzak" sound. Previn's soft-colored, sophisticated fox-trot is stylistically (that is, topically) appropriate, but it adds little beyond its presence. Its neutral quality is also reinforced retrospectively when Herrmann's slightly more emotionally charged cue enters.

egetic plausibility is thus left (almost) undisturbed, while Herrmann is able to get in a first iteration of what will become a significant associative theme (it dominates the extended bedroom scene that follows). Whether by Herrmann's choice or, more likely, by decision of the sound editor, the theme's low position in the mix here avoids the melodramatic overstatement that was commonplace in the 1930s and 1940s and would have rendered the music schmaltzy. Like "screwy," "schmaltzy" was very nearly a technical term in the classical studio era. Max Steiner, for example, used it frequently in his notes to orchestrators, along with joking variants such as "schmalzando" or "molto schmalzione."[14] Herrmann mocked this style of "Love" theme, with its soaring violins cliché, in both *The Trouble with Harry* (1955) and *Vertigo* (1958). By comparison, the treatment in *North by Northwest* is considerably more subdued. See table 2.3 for a summary of the analysis in terms of the treatment of each of the five binaries.

Casablanca: *The Band Plays, the Singer Sings, People Talk*

Martin Marks (2000, 173) notes that, as famous as "As Time Goes By" may be, we do not hear it in *Casablanca* until more than half an hour of viewing time has passed. Before that, in addition to underscoring for the opening credits, prologue, and first action scene, music consists of a dozen performances during the first evening at Rick's Café Américain. Of those dozen, I have chosen two as representative of different treatments of diegetic music.

The first of these is a featured performance, Sam (Dooley Wilson) singing "Knock on Wood," which was written specifically for this film and which the producer, Hal Wallis, hoped might become a hit (it did not, but Rudy Vallee's reissued recording of "As Time Goes By" from 1934 did). The performance is highlighted but is barely a minute long (one chorus) and is broken up visually as the camera registers two significant events: Rick hides stolen exit visas in Sam's piano, and Ferrari (Sydney Greenstreet), Rick's competitor as owner of the Blue Parrot café, enters (his first appearance in the film), sits down, and nods to Rick. The basic mode of this number, nevertheless, is Gorbman's pure musical code, and in accordance with that, attention to physical space and to foregrounding are the highest priorities for the sound track.

The frame of the performance begins and ends offscreen with audience applause. We first hear it offscreen from the casino room while Rick and Ugarte (Peter Lorre) are finishing their conversation about Ugarte's theft of the letters of transit and murder of the letters' couriers. Cut to a posed shot of the entire band, Dooley Wilson and his piano in lower center, with audience behind (at which point we might realize that the applause was unsynchronized: no one is clapping). The band quickly finishes their intro, a spotlight appears on Sam, and he sings. The applause is of particular significance because it signals activity in another area of the café, and it contributes to tying together the two principal spaces of the café as one larger physical space. Earlier activity at the door to the casino room had already managed this, but this moment calls particular attention to it. Speech (not lyrics) and effects are not absent but are restricted to the audience members' responses to Sam's calls ("Who's unlucky?" etc.).[15] See table 2.4 for a summary of the scene in terms of the five binaries.

The dozen performances in the film appear at all levels of the diegetic, from highlighted songs such as "Knock on Wood" to neutral backgrounded instrumental pieces played entirely offscreen. In another circumstance, the diegetic status of these last might be uncertain, but in *Casablanca* the confirmation of the physical space is so strong that there is no question even for these. It is true that the performances, all recorded separately, are not positioned well when the instrumental music is offscreen (that is to say, we can't be sure quite where the band is when we can't see them, especially if the volume level is relatively low), but that level of acoustical fidelity is largely irrelevant.

The second performance to be discussed here is considerably more complex than "Knock on Wood." Sam plays "Speak to Me of Love" (Parlez-moi d'amour) when Ilsa and Laszlo enter the café. This happens about ten minutes of viewing

Table 2.4. *Casablanca* (1943), "Knock on Wood," analyzed in terms of the "five binaries"

Five binaries	Summary
Clarity/fidelity Foreground/background	As a featured performance in this film, this is primarily spectacle, and therefore clarity is served through visual focus on the performers and audience, and music and its associated effects are strongly foregrounded. Cutaways are used to distinguish between narrative and performance.
Diegetic/nondiegetic	Performance is framed by offscreen applause, which also serves to link different physical spaces in the café.
Synchronization/counterpoint	The applause at the beginning is unsynchronized, but it is in the nature of a blooper (the crowd is not clapping) and not significant. The performance was prerecorded, but screen actions closely match in any case.
Empathy/anempathy	Address to the audience and the call/response patterns are highly empathetic. Because of references to luck and optimism, even the cutaways are empathetic rather than neutral, since Rick and Ferrari are two important social figures who represent luck (the means to escape Casablanca) and optimism (or at least the distracting pleasantness of a night's entertainment).

time later and just before Ilsa asks for Sam to come to her table, thus initiating the reunion scene, one of the film's most famous sequences and one to which we will give particular attention in chapter 4. Instrumental music plays continuously for several minutes, switching almost imperceptibly to another song, "Love for Sale," along the way. "Speak to Me of Love," as Marks notes, "emphasizes the moment with a poignant change of mood (it follows a breezy rendition of 'Heaven Can Wait') and brings to mind thoughts of Paris and romance in preparation for the flashback scenes to come" (2000, 174). Strictly speaking, the viewer has no inkling of all this yet, but Sam certainly does. He continues to play but turns his head and wears an alarmed look on his face as Ilsa and Laszlo pass by him—even the musical performance is affected, as we hear a clumsy moment of rubato. "Speak to Me of Love" is best interpreted at this point in the film as a reference to the entrance of a beautiful woman into the café (a point emphasized shortly afterward through a greeting by the lecherous Captain Renault (Claude Rains), the local chief of police).

Music comes in with the cut to the café entrance. The couple are just walking through the door, and when Laszlo speaks, it is in a gap of the introduction to the song. The volume level rises awkwardly as they approach and pass the piano, with Sam in medium close-up and the couple behind him. At this point the volume level is quite high, and one might suppose that unusual attention to acoustical fidelity is the cause, the narrative point being to draw attention to the fact that Sam recognizes Ilsa. As they continue walking and the camera cuts away to them, however, the volume level does not drop, and, although this does make it easier to cut back to Sam again, the music adds unusual intensity to what is (merely) the couple walking. With the cut back, Sam shakes his head, and we suspect that the volume level (like the earlier rubato) is more an emotional marker of his feelings than anything to do with fidelity. (This is, incidentally, also the first time we have seen him in close-up since the "Knock on Wood" number.) With the next cut we see the couple in long shot reflected in the bar mirror. The music continues but drops in volume to a level where dialogue is clear once they are seated and begin talking to one another. Still, we know exactly where the piano is (thanks to their transit), and the sound level is plausible for the distance.

All this time—that is, up to the point they sit and begin talking—we have heard the crowd noises we would expect of a busy evening. At first these noises seem direct recorded. We do hear the maître d' shuffling menus at his station, and the level of Paul Henreid's voice is barely above the level of the room noise. Once they move through the room, the crowd noise lessens unnaturally and becomes less specific, more muted, as if at the fringe of a unidirectional microphone. We do not hear footfalls. Ilsa and Laszlo's entrance, in other words, is not out of the ordinary for a lead or significant supporting couple, except for the music. (Ilsa does cast a glance at Sam as she passes, but the look is nothing more than one might expect of anyone noticing the entertainer. A definite jolt of recognition on her part only comes later, after they have walked on farther into the room.) Initially, the crowd noise might be synchronized, but even then it doesn't matter. The scene might well have been designed with more prominent music throughout and little if any ambient sound.

Two things happen because of the specific way the sound track is formed: (1) what might otherwise have been an unremarkable entrance of an elegant couple is disrupted—marked—by a certain amount of sonic chaos; and (2) music participates in this chaos not to mark the arrival of Ilsa but to mark Sam's reaction. If we consider this in terms of the correlations of the binaries, the pairs foreground/background and empathetic/anempathetic are momentarily thrown off center—by which I mean imbued with an expressive ambiguity reminiscent of the "fantastical gap"—while at the same time the diegetic/nondiegetic and synchronized/nonsynchronized are intensified. Image depth is split into three parts, with the middleground of the walking couple added to Sam's foreground and the patrons' background. As an attempt to compensate, the sound in the foreground is exaggerated, more resonant, closer, but the result is an uncertainty in the empathic dimension of the sound: the camera tells us to follow the couple, but sound cues direct us to follow Sam instead. The discrepancy is not easily resolved, even once Sam is offscreen and the couple is seated. On the other hand, the spatial depth of the opening and the camera's careful following of the couple as they walk and talk, along with the persistence of the music offscreen, tie sound and space together with unusual tightness.

Spotting Beethoven in *Prénom Carmen* (1983)

Making choices about where music should be added—commonly referred to as "spotting"—is one of the most basic of all tasks in the creation of a feature film, presence or absence being even more basic than the five binaries, as I noted earlier. It can be productive for analytical or critical purposes to ask what happens when one adds music to a scene that has none to begin with. A few measures from the first movement of Beethoven's String Quartet in A Minor, op. 132— will be inserted into a film sequence with the expectation that the familiar work, with its familiar affect and devices, will be transformed into something different but will at the same time—by the phenomenon of "added value"—effect a reinterpretation of the image track. Ironically, as we shall see, our few seconds of Beethoven fit too well, contradicting the director's priorities, which overall are to place music and image next to one another, as it were, emphasizing filmic stratification.

This particular exercise is by no means so arbitrary as it might sound, since the film is Jean-Luc Godard's *Prénom Carmen* (First Name: Carmen), which, at its most readily comprehensible narrative level, is about an ensemble rehearsing for a performance of late Beethoven string quartets. As they practice, the second violinist seems distracted (Claire, played by Myriem Roussel). Music consists entirely of quotations from those quartets.[16] The film unfolds in a parallel narrative construction whose other story, in rough outline at least, is the same as Bizet's famous opera. A bizarre tale of Carmen the bank robber and Joseph the policeman is set side by side with the quartet's rehearsal, which is filmed throughout in medium and close-up shots, sometimes with tightly framed close-ups of Claire. Only at the end do the two narratives meet, when the robbers attempt (and fail at) a kidnapping in a luxury hotel where the quartet is performing.

After the mid-1960s, Godard planned both sound and music in considerable detail before production (that is, shooting sessions) began (Musy 2000, 33). In this film, especially, "the music has a certain control over the images" (Bachmann 1998, 133). For example, Godard claimed that the idea of opening the film with a bank robbery staged as a military-style assault occurred to him "after I heard a certain part of the 10th Quartet [op. 74]."[17] As to the disparity between the title story and the musical score, he insisted that "I didn't choose Beethoven, it's Beethoven, in a way, who chose me. I followed the call" (130). He makes the symbolic importance of the quartets very clear: "What I wanted was to have what I would call 'fundamental' music. I wanted music which had marked the history of music itself, both its practice and theory, and the Beethoven Quartets represent this" (130).

As Miriam Sheer (2001, 183) has noted, movements from five quartets are quoted, roughly in order of opus number and movement. Although Sheer does say that opus number and movement order are strictly maintained, Davison (2004, 95n26) states that the "overall chronology" is correct but that the third and fourth movements of op. 132 are intermixed, and internally in several other movements the chronology is not maintained. Sheer found each quartet to be associated with a single narrative sequence: op. 59, no. 3, with what she calls the "exposition" (which takes place in a mental hospital, where we meet "Uncle Jean" [Godard himself] and Carmen [Maruschka Detmers], who visits him); op. 74 with the bank robbery; op. 131 with the cross-country escape of Carmen and Joseph; op. 132 with their love scenes in Uncle Jean's beach house; and op. 135 with the painful dissolution of their relationship (in a Paris luxury hotel, as the gang plans the kidnapping).

The first movement of op. 132 is not quoted in the film (we hear only the third), but the strictness of Godard's design allows us to make a very plausible placement.[18] The time frame is extremely limited: one minute and twenty-five seconds from DVD timing 28:42 (when the last quote from op. 131, seventh movement, goes out) to 30:07 (when the first quote from op. 132, third movement, enters). Here is a breakdown of this sequence: (a) a police constable in his car at a gas station along the highway; he opens the door to get out; (b) cut to the couple in the large but empty beach house:

28:42	Joseph in interior hallway taking off a boot; with the cut Carmen enters, opening the door and accidentally pushing him out of the way
28:47	Carmen hits the door roughly
28:51	Carmen walks offscreen
28:55	Carmen walks onscreen, then off again (at 28:57), then on (at 28:59)
29:01	Carmen pushes Joseph's leg aside and walks offscreen
29:03	Joseph: "Sorry," then Carmen: "No, I'm sorry" (offscreen)
29:05	Carmen onscreen; they talk
29:20	Carmen goes offscreen; Joseph, boot not quite off yet, hops to next room
29:23	cut to new room; Carmen laughs offscreen (29:24) then enters; pan with her as she goes across the room to the window
29:31	Joseph throws boot, bangs doors
29:37	Joseph: "Sorry" offscreen
29:40	Joseph goes to opposite wall (which is in the dark)
29:44	Carmen to the door of a third room, strongly backlit from outdoors; she returns
29:49	Joseph to the door of the third room; we see him in a mirror
29:54	Joseph/Carmen in a rapid series of grabs and repulsions
29:59	cut to the gas station; the police detective runs out and gets in the car, and the policemen drive off quickly
30:08	cut to Carmen in extreme long shot walking on the beach

In this brief sequence, which acts as a prologue to the much longer group of scenes that follows, sound works as outlined in figure 2.6.

Godard edits the sound track in an unconventional manner but with (for him) unusual consistency and a relative simplicity that keeps the sound track generally quite understandable. The Beethoven quotes vary greatly in length, but most are short fragments of two to three seconds. Music rarely plays in an obvious

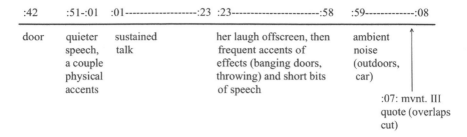

:42	:51-:01	:01------------------:23	:23-----------------------:58	:59-------------:08
door	quieter speech, a couple physical accents	sustained talk	her laugh offscreen, then frequent accents of effects (banging doors, throwing) and short bits of speech	ambient noise (outdoors, car)

:07: mvnt. III
quote (overlaps
cut)

Figure 2.6. Sound in a brief sequence (28:42–30:08) from Godard,
Prénom Carmen (1983).

way against the screen action, and thus we are free to look for a passage (or passages) in the first movement that can parallel the barely pent-up sexual energy that both Carmen and Joseph increasingly struggle with. The tension is apparent immediately in Carmen, in her rough movements and nervous pacing; at this point Joseph seems quite calm. When they move to the next room, the situation reverses: she has relaxed herself with a laugh at her uncle (who has left a tape recorder in the refrigerator), but Joseph begins pacing and banging window shutters. This second stage in their vigorous prelude to foreplay is the best moment for music. I have chosen bars 182–88 from the first movement of op. 132, the end of the first recapitulation. This is a passage that features abrupt dynamic contrasts and sharp rhythmic shifts from bar to bar—changes that mirror the impulsive movements of the characters (figure 2.7). At the end, the "correct" C major chord is missing, the sonority that would properly be the end of the movement if there were only one recapitulation and we were following all the conventions of sonata form (except monotonality).

The urgency in the music lies in accelerated motion toward a conventional conclusion. The question of key is long over and done with—and in that sense the music works well, because from the moment of their escape from the bank, Carmen and Joseph are plainly headed toward a sexual encounter. They are not quite ready, apparently, as Carmen says "Scram!" then "Grab me!" but Joseph walks off, and the cut back from a brief intervening scene of policemen finds Carmen walking alone on the beach. When the couple do move toward intercourse, it is the third movement from op. 132 that Godard employs as background (we hear both the chorale and its trio), a disconcerting but in its way also very traditional mingling of the sacred and the profane, spiritual and carnal.[19]

This short fragment of music, analogous to Godard's choices elsewhere, is not only concretely tied to the screen but tied so tightly that it resembles the very close synchronization, or "mickey-mousing," common in classical Hollywood sound film. Joseph's speech ("sorry") from offscreen during the sharp articulations of m. 182 contrasts with his silent physical action (walking across the screen) in m. 183; mm. 183–84 reverse this pattern as the two walk quickly past each other (action matched nicely now to the rhythmic propulsion of the dot-

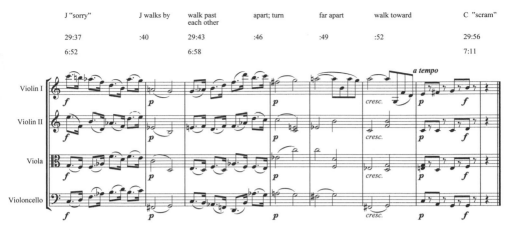

Figure 2.7. Beethoven, String Quartet in A Minor, op. 132, I, mm. 182–89, beat 1, with spotting annotations for *Prénom Carmen*. Timings for the music were taken from a recording by Quatuor Vegh, V 4406 Auvidis Valois (1986).

ted-note figures). They then stop and turn just as the music does, with its *piano* half-note chords. They are farthest apart as the dominant chord/harmony is expanded (that is, the dominant resists resolution, just as they are resisting their own physical desire) in m. 185, but they walk toward each other, just as the dominant is pulled to the tonic chord that begins m. 187. At that moment, four isolated chords provide parallels in accent to the quick sequence of physical actions, which we hear more than see, as they take place in the short, darkened section of the wall (darkened by backlighting of open doorways on either side).

It is tempting to make an argument based on a parallel between Godard's idiosyncratic treatment of film and Beethoven's similar treatment of musical conventions in his late period, but Godard himself contradicted that interpretation in the interview quoted above: he saw Beethoven as representing the continuity of tradition, "music which had marked the history of music itself," not its disintegration. Sheer argues that the late quartets are part of a complex and intricate web of associations that have formal, narrative, and autobiographical qualities: "Godard . . . uses this music in a way that continually infiltrates the narrative and visual scene" (2001, 182). By contrast, Davison emphasizes the narratively disruptive effects of the music—and of the quartet that plays it. She argues that "the purpose of the [musicians] is to embody a locus of confusion: [this quartet] lacks narrative motivation; and, it undermines the role(s) of music as defined by classical Hollywood scoring and exposes such scoring practices as 'conventional' rather than established by 'natural law'" (2004, 83).

My own view is closer to Davison's than to Sheer's. Although there is much that is of value in the many connections that Sheer makes, I would argue that the formalisms introduced by such connections are not the main point: that is, the webs of association may be interesting devices, but they are present in order to enable and intensify the kind of disruption that Davison describes. I do believe, however, that the true or primary diegesis is unequivocally the series of rehearsals (along with the brief meetings between Claire and Joseph). Given the conventional view of Godard's depictions of women (which are considered complex at best, misogynistic at worst), it may perhaps be difficult to conceive of *Prénom Carmen* as a sympathetic story about a somewhat downtrodden second violinist's construction of an imaginary parallel narrative to the Beethoven quartets as the group rehearses them. In this view, Carmen would represent the "other" Claire; Joseph would remain Joseph. Carmen's bid for sexual power (which includes her rejection of Joseph) would then mirror Claire's (private) bid for equality and acceptance among her male peers in the quartet.

A clue to the centrality of these pairings is in Godard himself: as the crazy uncle, he helps Carmen create a film; as the (actual) filmmaker, he makes Claire's story for her. The uncle's film is a ruse by the gang to facilitate and cover their kidnapping of Claire's father. The uncle's presence in the final scenes also points to the appropriate narrative register when the quartet performs in the hotel. Here, their role is completely different from the rehearsals; now they are not in the "real world" but in Claire's imagination, as Carmen is. Godard's treatment of the Beethoven quartet quotations is consistent with stream of consciousness for Claire's split attention between rehearsal realities and her construction of the Carmen narrative. (Claire's status as a professional musician, by the way, can also be said to account for the story itself—it is reasonable that a person of her background and experience might have thought of the Bizet opera as a starting point for her own imagined narrative.)

How all this can be reconciled with Davison's argument about this group of four musicians as a disruptive agent is not difficult to see: the natural dimensions of narrative are simply inverted. Davison's "central narrative" is really a dream, and the quartet ironically deconstructs everything in sight, from that dream to the group's own narrative, from the music they play to the idea of realist narrative film itself (in the Hollywood tradition).

With all this in place, we can look back on those few seconds of op. 132, first movement, and consider how the fragment may be said to function within the narrative I have just outlined. The quote seems to exemplify a sense of strong but contained emotion, and its timing fits neatly with the action of the scene. In its co-opting of the cadence (and equally so in the failure of that cadence to consummate), we hear the same teleology of desire that Susan McClary (2000, 18) finds embedded in traditional tonality, now constructed—or reconstructed—in a musician's imagination in performance. The one weakness of this fragment is that it serves too well the functions of nondiegetic music in the classical tradition; that is to say, it reinforces the "invisible style" of continuity editing and therefore threatens to narrate (as if in voice-over) and thus reveal Claire's central role by putting her own desire too directly into sound.[20]

Throughout much of *Prénom Carmen*, music competes with or even drowns out the voice, but it is as if we are hearing the music the way Claire is, in the aural "extreme close-up" of a player within the quartet. Easily understood, then, as a highly specialized mode of hearing, the quartet passages and fragments serve essentially as conveying a point-of-view sound. Although I have demonstrated that our twenty seconds of the first movement can fit the details of the scene surprisingly well, by that very fact they are out of line with the more artistic and flexible counterpointing of image and sound that Godard employs everywhere else in the film. Apart from the highly specialized case of dramatic silences, the concert composer never has to confront the issue of presence or absence. For filmmakers, it is among the most important questions, and the most basic.

Rebecca (1940), Establishing Sequence and First Scenes

Alfred Hitchcock's first American film was very successful with audiences and quickly became a classic of what would eventually coalesce as the genre of women's gothic (Neumeyer and Platte 2012, 46).[21] The opening seven minutes of Rebecca are divided into five segments that cover a variety of scene types and music functions. To my purpose here, they are ideally suited to explore categories of the voice in relation to diegetic and narrative spaces and a cluster of related terms and their correlations: these are, in addition to diegetic/nondiegetic, onscreen/offscreen, embodied/bodiless, vocal/mute. In order to prepare for the analytic and interpretive discussion of these film scenes, my first considerations will be theoretical; specifically, I will address the oppositions onscreen/offscreen and diegetic/nondiegetic.

Because of the fundamental relationship between sound and physical space, it is perhaps not surprising that, in film, the diegetic/nondiegetic pair is complex in its effects. Still, we can plausibly reduce the basic states or categories involved to four by combining narrative levels (as represented in diegetic/nondiegetic) with framing (the camera's presentation). The schematic in figure 2.8 can help us understand these effects. Physical space is represented by framing as onscreen/offscreen (on the vertical axis) and narrative space by the diegetic/nondiegetic pair (on the horizontal axis). Illogical as this may seem—onscreen/offscreen are attributes of the diegesis, after all, not separate and equal filmic elements—it is nevertheless the state of the cinema. The diegesis is never unqualified: narrative is always foregrounded by the presence of the camera in the form of framing. Thus, the opposition between what the camera shows us (onscreen) and what it does not (offscreen) is a fundamental property that we understand as separate from the diegetic. The latter has its own opposition based on the body between exterior (real) and interior (psychological)—see the shaded quadrants in figure 2.8. Another related opposition is world and mind, which can be read as "diegetic world" and "mind of the narrator" or can be extrapolated to the opposition between presence and transcendence.

The "default" case (or unmarked pairing) among the four options in figure 2.8 is the one that directly serves the idea of a plausible diegesis or story world. Clearly, that requirement is satisfied by onscreen and diegetic (lower left quadrant), the province of a character's speech or of a sound made by a visible source. In other words, synchronized sound, however much it might be a construct, ap-

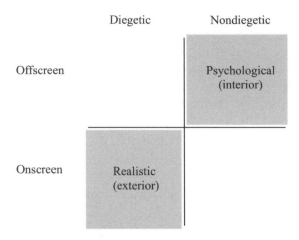

Figure 2.8. Relations of the diegetic/nondiegetic and onscreen/offscreen pairs.

pears to us as a natural state of sound. At the same time, synchronized sound can only present the exterior of the characters. The realistic (at the lower left) is necessarily opposed to the upper right quadrant: it is "antipsychological." Whatever we learn of a character's psychology must be inferred from dialogue, body language, vocal intonation, and so forth, but that psychology remains as opaque to us as any person we might encounter in our world. In this sense our perspective remains objective and external: we have no privileged access to a character's interior. As a simple illustration, consider again figure 1.1c along with the close-up in figure 2.9. Only in the final seconds of this scene from *The Dark Corner* do we get a sense of Clifton Webb's and Cathy Downs's characters as anything other than an elegant couple dancing. The change comes in the tense firmness of his "belong to me" and her minimally affectionate "sweetheart" (in the image, he has just finished, and she is just opening her mouth to speak). Here the band music's inability to tell us anything more is the surest sign of its neutral status. (Incidentally, here is also an example of sound's power to cover over weaknesses in continuity: if you will compare figures 1.1c and 2.9, it will be clear that Webb and Downs are noticeably closer to one another in the latter—both voice and music continue over and "hide" the jump.)

By the time we see the couple, the band is offscreen but still diegetic. Positioned in the upper left quadrant in figure 2.8, this mode is most often of a neutral or subdued character, as if part of the sonic background, which typically includes low-level ambient noise or environmental sound. The lingering sense of offscreen sounds and agents that are not entirely explained and therefore not in our control, however, is the basis for a peculiarly negative power. We saw this notion played out in a very small way in the beach house scene from *Prénom Carmen*. Recall that Carmen initiates their early and quite physical foreplay: Joseph attempts to take off a boot, but Carmen abruptly pushes him aside, nearly knocking

Figure 2.9. *The Dark Corner,* Hardy and Mari Cathcart during the dance scene. Screen still.

him down, and then walks offscreen. Joseph says "Sorry," but then Carmen, still offscreen, responds "No, I'm sorry." Though the inflections in their two voices are not markedly different, Carmen retains the upper hand by the fact of her distance (emphasized by the offscreen position): she might say she is sorry, but she is also physically and therefore perhaps emotionally distanced (we don't know; being offscreen maintains the mystery). Carmen returns, they talk, and then she goes offscreen again. We hear her laugh, she returns and walks across the room to the window. Here, the offscreen laugh signals that she has something to tell us. She is in control of the narrative, and, with Joseph, we wait for her to reveal the odd fact that Uncle Jean has left his tape recorder in the fridge. Not that this turns out to be all that illuminating, except as to his eccentricity, but it will help to confirm our impressions of the significance of the tape recorder as a motif (and also an icon of the sound track).

The offscreen nondiegetic (upper right quadrant of figure 2.8) makes possible the development of a subjective perspective. In the case of the onscreen diegetic, we are restricted to inference. Similarly, with the offscreen nondiegetic, we lose the specificity of anchored sound. In compensation, as it were, we gain access to a character's psychological state. Here music is particularly powerful. Even if nondiegetic music cannot in fact express directly what a character feels, we can

Tools for Analysis and Interpretation 79

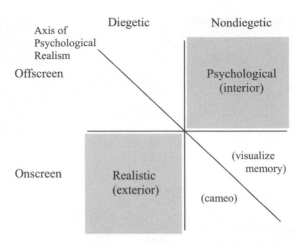

Figure 2.10. Relations of the diegetic/nondiegetic and onscreen/offscreen pairs: the four quadrants divided along an axis of psychological realism.

nevertheless understand the music as a representation of that character's psychological reality. We sense what has affected the character at this level, and the music can alert us to exterior bodily gestures and words that might correspond to that state. Even small changes in underscoring can generate relatively large changes in our understanding.

As the site for underscoring—but also for the most common type of voice-over narration—the offscreen nondiegetic is obviously an important relation between sound and image.[22] Onscreen diegetic sound and offscreen nondiegetic sound, taken as an opposed pair, define an axis of "psychological realism" (see figure 2.10). Most dramatic narrative film presupposes this axis as a normal state, which is one reason it seems so unproblematic to an audio-viewer. The normative state of this axis is also the primary reason that digressions from it can be so powerful: they can be used to channel desire, either ours, as a part of the narrative process, or a given character's, as a representation of that character's desire. Alternating between these options creates a particular kind of fluctuation along the axis of psychological realism.

In figure 2.10, the axis of psychological realism bifurcates both the offscreen diegetic and onscreen diegetic quadrants. If the offscreen diegetic has particular power (a possibility that I shall explore at some length below), the onscreen non-diegetic seems to have very little, to judge by its rare uses in mainstream cinema. Onscreen nondiegetic sound understood as exterior is usually treated in a "picture-in-picture" manner, more occasionally as an insert. When understood as exterior, it is usually represented as a brief narrative intrusion or comment—the cameo in a corner of the screen being typical. Onscreen nondiegetic sound understood as interior is easily tied to a character's thoughts, feelings, or memories

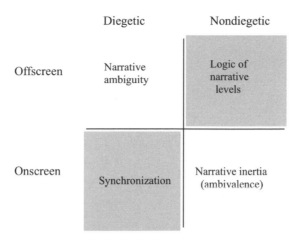

	Diegetic	Nondiegetic
Offscreen	Narrative ambiguity	Logic of narrative levels
Onscreen	Synchronization	Narrative inertia (ambivalence)

Figure 2.11. Relations of the diegetic/nondiegetic and onscreen/offscreen pairs: the four quadrants conceived in terms of narrative functions.

as a direct visualization of them: it is indicated in the diagram by the shortened label "visualize memory."

Figure 2.11 summarizes the relationships of the quadrants: lower left and upper right balance the straightforwardly diegetic with the level of narration or narrative voice, where upper left and lower right balance ambiguity with ambivalence. Given these balances, we can also conceive the relationships among the quadrants in terms of a Greimassian square of oppositions (see figure 2.12). To follow the form of these squares, the quadrants have been rearranged: since the onscreen diegetic is the typical situation of the sound film, it is placed at the beginning as the first and unmarked term. Its contrary (the term balanced against it in figure 2.11) is at its right: the offscreen nondiegetic. Its contradiction (negation) is here construed to be the onscreen nondiegetic, which undermines synchronization by visualizing both diegetic and nondiegetic space simultaneously. Similarly, the offscreen diegetic undermines the distinction of narrative levels that is the particular province of the offscreen nondiegetic at the same time that it wrestles the realism of synchronization by expanding diegetic space, threatening the camera's authority, so to speak, by contradicting the unity implied in framing.

Returning to figure 2.10, the bifurcation of the upper left and lower right quadrants does suggest particular problems for exterior and interior positions of the offscreen diegetic. Exterior offscreen diegetic sound is unproblematic: this is the place of ambient sound or of neutral background music, such as the band in *The Dark Corner* or Sam in *Casablanca* once they have gone offscreen. The interior offscreen diegetic, on the other hand, is highly problematic, as it requires either that a person's psychological state be somehow manifested without being shown

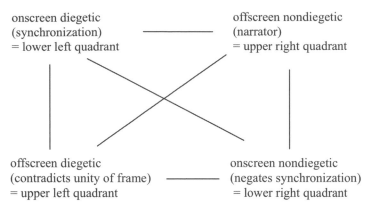

onscreen diegetic
(synchronization)
= lower left quadrant

offscreen nondiegetic
(narrator)
= upper right quadrant

offscreen diegetic
(contradicts unity of frame)
= upper left quadrant

onscreen nondiegetic
(negates synchronization)
= lower right quadrant

Figure 2.12. Relations of the diegetic/nondiegetic and onscreen/offscreen pairs: the relations of the four quadrants understood in terms of a Greimassian square.

or that an offscreen character or a physical sound evoke an emotional reaction that is foregrounded. But how is this separated from the sound itself? Even in the simplest case, a person hearing a familiar melody playing offscreen, the diegetic status of that melody would have to be firmly established to keep the music from collapsing back into the nondiegetic. Offscreen diegetic sound, in other words, is fraught with ambiguity when considered in relation to onscreen characters, and it will come as no surprise to the reader that this attribute is exploited frequently in the sound film.

In its more genial manifestations, offscreen diegetic sound is often played for comedy. A clever instance that ties directly into expectations of musical form occurs in *Sons of the Pioneers* (1942), the fifth of eight Roy Rogers releases in 1942. The series' usual comic characters, Gabby Hayes and Pat Brady (the bassist for the Sons of the Pioneers), mistakenly believe that Roy has died, and they ride down an open road singing a sad slow waltz, "He's Gone, He's Gone up the Trail." When they reach the end of the second chorus, they pause and hear Roy yodeling. Initially, they are not surprised, assuming these are vivid memories of the vocal tags Roy put on many performances at this point in the design. Soon, however, they begin looking around. A cutaway to Roy on the hillside above lets the audience in on the gag, but when Roy emerges on horseback from the trees, the two men turn and ride off quickly, having been thoroughly frightened. Note the irony: the audience understands that Roy has been "deacousmatized"—his power as a ghost dissipates—but Pat and Gabby do not.[23]

At its most benign, offscreen diegetic sound may be the voice of a known person or music anchored in a familiar source (for example, a piano we have already seen in the next room or one that is mentioned by an onscreen character). At the opposite extreme, offscreen diegetic sound may derive from a transcendent being (angel, devil, and so on) or from the impossible voice of someone dead. These are instances of what Michel Chion (1994, 129–31; 1999, 140–51) labels the acousmêtre, or acoustical being, who holds a unique power. His six categories for the acousmêtre are the voice of a master behind a veil, a case of mistaken identity, someone speaking without identifying his or her location, a dead person, a prerecorded voice, or a "Machine-Being" such as a computer (1999, 36). The acoustical being establishes an axis of deviance at a tangent to that of psychological realism, and it is the ability to maintain this alternate axis that defines its power. The acousmêtre exists in the diegetic space but is placed consistently offscreen and, thus, being heard but not seen, is defined wholly in terms of diegetic sound. The figure of the acousmêtre is distinct from the voice-over narrator, since the voice of the acoustical being is taken to occur in the same time frame as the diegesis (therefore is "offscreen, but present"), whereas narration is necessarily after the fact, even when the voice of the narrator is also that of a character in the diegesis. Due to our understanding of the axis of psychological deviance as abnormal, the acoustical being is also typically malevolent. The principle of psychological realism endows the diegesis with a force that pulls toward embodiment, but the power of the acoustical being is measured by its power to block that force. The blockage maintains the axis of deviance yet at the same time produces a "leakage" that dissolves the integrity of offscreen diegetic space. The distinction between offscreen diegetic and offscreen nondiegetic threatens to wear away, a change that exposes the careful management of offscreen space, working to convince us to accept the diegetic as real.

Though the acoustical being is not a frequent character in sound film, its complex inhabiting of offscreen space suggests reasons why synchronization, despite its presumed redundancy with the image, is such an important facet of sound film. Synchronization is an act of closure. At levels beyond the immediate, such closure usually is almost imperceptible, an aspect of the play of sync points (sound accents) in low-level audiovisual phrasing (that is, the groupings created in the sound track by sync points). Sometimes the deferral of a sync point can be used to structure a sequence, in which case, its systematic deployment seems to operate metaphorically as a sign of a character's unrealized desire, as in the scene from *The Dark Corner* where Webb's sudden tightening of the voice and Downs's somewhat overloud response are sync points, end accents for the scene, as it were. The acoustical being turns such deferral into the very definition of character, stretching deferral to the breaking point where synchronization—as deacousmatization—represents the loss of being, that is, death: the monster is shown; the monster dies.[24] The malevolent acousmêtre is an especially striking narrative treatment of sound, but it is by no means the only option for an offscreen diegetic character. For example, one famous acousmêtre, the Wizard of Oz, may appear pompous and even threatening but turns out to be pathetically incompetent in the end. In his case, the deacousmatization is the revelation of that impotence.

Nondiegetic music, too, appropriates the power to speak from a transcendent realm beyond the image, nowhere more so than when music represents the structuring presence of an absence: the force of the dead on the living. Chion notes that "ever since the telephone and gramophone made it possible to isolate voices from bodies, the voice naturally has reminded us of the voice of the dead. . . . In the cinema, the voice of the acousmêtre is frequently the voice of one who is dead" (1999, 46). In films such as *Rebecca* (1940) and *Laura* (1944), the title characters are first of all musical entities, that is, the music "names" these dead persons with associative themes and does so in the clearest possible way by stating the theme against the main title. Rebecca, however, is never seen onscreen, even in flashback, but Laura eventually does appear, alive after all, from which point her theme becomes firmly associated with her status as an object of love. Through music we sense the extent to which these characters determine the action in the diegesis even when the image can detect only their fragmentary traces. The constant presence of the kitschy, haunting theme in *Laura* betrays something obsessive about the diegetic world, shifting as it does from a reasonable concentration on the cause of her supposed death to the competing romantic interests of the detective, Mark McPherson (Dana Andrews), and Laura's mentor, Waldo Lydecker (Clifton Webb).[25] Rebecca's case is little different. The fact that Maxim de Winter (Laurence Olivier) refuses to speak about her only succeeds in piquing his second wife's interest, and her quest for information quickly turns into a fearful fixation, which Franz Waxman's extensive underscore abets through repetition of Rebecca's theme in a distorted, ghostly orchestration.

When nondiegetic music is combined with a voice-over narrator, however, the situation is somewhat different. Being somehow situated in the same "space," the music can readily be understood as assisting, augmenting, or even substituting for the narrator. Music adopts the voice of the narrator, as in *Sunset Boulevard* (1950), where William Holden's character, Joe Gillis, talks just before his dead body is seen in a swimming pool. He keeps tight control of the exposition throughout the film, even speaking after the long flashback returns to the point of discovery of his body—he goes on nearly to the last moment of the famous ending, Gloria Swanson's descent of the staircase. Speaking almost continuously until fourteen minutes into the film and entering with additional, often extended voice-overs more than a dozen times thereafter, Joe tells his story, and the music conforms to it. Though admittedly an extreme case in its controlling narration, *Sunset Boulevard* is so effective in harnessing musical commentary to the narrator's status that one is left to wonder if that may be nondiegetic music's proper function.

In figure 2.13, I have positioned voice types in relation to narrative space by rewriting the terms of figure 2.10: the "onscreen diegetic" of figure 2.10 becomes "character speaks onscreen" in the upper left quadrant of figure 2.13, and so on. The default case in the synchronized film is Chion's anacousmêtre, literally the "being that doesn't lack an embodied voice." In terms of its physical match, the anacousmêtre is of course opposed to the acousmêtre, the voice without a body, but in terms of its screen presence, the anacousmêtre is opposed to the offscreen character who speaks or to the voice-over narrator, who is presumed to have a body somewhere in the diegesis or perhaps in the nondiegetic narrative space. The acousmêtre negates the offscreen diegetic voice by existing nowhere as a

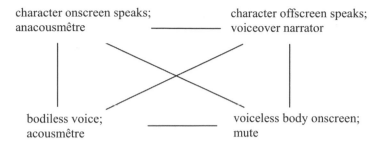

character onscreen speaks;   character offscreen speaks;
anacousmêtre   voiceover narrator

bodiless voice;   voiceless body onscreen;
acousmêtre   mute

Figure 2.13. Figure 2.12 redrawn with categories of the voice.

body (see the lower left of figure 2.13), while its opposite, the mute body, negates the anacousmêtre by existing without a voice (lower right).

Although Chion is quite correct to put special emphasis on the acousmêtre, none of the four basic combinations of body, voice, and space identified in figure 2.13 is unknown to the classical cinema. We need look no farther than the opening of *Casablanca* for examples. In a commonly used design, a prologue substitutes for the transition from the main-title credits to the film's first scene. A voice-over narrator (in at 1:14) speaks over a slow montage of maps and refugees. The voice is that of a solemn newsreel announcer. Not the film's narrator, not its author, and not a character, he is not a bodiless voice either. From his knowledge and his speech to us, we presume that he exists somewhere in our physical world and is reporting events to us. Music accompanies him discreetly and in a similarly solemn mood and tempo. In the opening scene, the roundup of suspected Free France sympizers (2:25–4:00), the first diegetic speech is anacousmatic, that of a Vichy officer calling out over the police radio about the deaths of two German couriers. Music stops, gets out of the officer's way. In the action-spectacle that follows, an aggressive music dominates, and very few individuals speak, especially not—with one exception—the poor suspects being herded into trucks and then, at the end of the scene, into police headquarters. In this, we can see a fundamental difference between the acousmêtre and the mute: the former is assumed to have power, the latter is not. The one Resistance fighter who does speak is unconvincing and promptly loses his power as well, indeed becoming the extreme kind of voiceless body, as he is shot dead by the policemen. Only one category is missing: *Casablanca* has no acousmêtres. The unseen powers that pull on its characters are of a different, more abstract kind: painful memories and noble causes. We will consider their effects in the chapters of part 2.

Strictly speaking, the title character of *Rebecca* is not an acousmêtre, as we never hear her speak, but her character is richly established by every other filmic means, including the speech of others who constantly refer to her, often nearly citing her words. Rebecca, in other words, is so palpable a presence that part of her power is that she might speak and thus be "revealed" as a true acousmêtre. Multiple moments in the film suggest this, but the climax is clearly the confession scene, when Alfred Hitchcock's camera follows the invisible Rebecca around the room: we "see" but do not hear her (we hear only her husband's account of their final confrontation). As we shall discover, Rebecca is only fully deacousmatized and her power dissipated by the final madness of her surrogate, Mrs. Danvers, in the fire that kills her while also destroying the couple's mansion.

Rebecca was the first wife of Maxim de Winter. For the second wife, the story begins when this wealthy but moody man, age forty-two, gives his attention to her. She is the twenty-one-year-old paid traveling companion of a much older, and difficult, wealthy woman. The mystery only deepens when he proposes to "I" (the only name we will know her by), the couple marry, and they leave Monte Carlo for Maxim's fabled mansion in Cornwall: Manderley. Not surprisingly, "I" (Joan Fontaine) feels hampered by her inexperience and insecurity, even though Maxim makes it clear that he values her qualities, in considerable part because they are utterly different from those of his first wife, who died a year earlier. "I" is actively opposed by Mrs. Danvers (Judith Anderson), the matron of the house and fierce defender of Rebecca's memory. After Rebecca's body is found inside her sunken sailboat and it is established that another person had mistakenly been buried as her, suspicion falls on Maxim. Eventually we learn that Rebecca had terminal cancer and (in the novel) goaded Maxim into shooting her or (in the film) attempted to goad him but actually died after falling and hitting her head.

The deacousmatization of Rebecca takes place in stages over the course of the film. Her status as an acousmêtre must be established first, of course. We learn almost nothing about her early on, but the fact that Maxim is reluctant to talk about her is enough to establish the mystery. Only after the return to Manderley, however, does Rebecca become a proper ghostly presence: Mrs. Danvers has kept the house as it was, now a kind of mausoleum, and she resists any attempts at change. Through Mrs. Danvers's malevolence (greatly exaggerated by Hitchcock in comparison with the novel, incidentally), Rebecca also becomes a threat. When her body is discovered and Maxim must endure an inquest, the threat only increases. (We never see the body, so that the sense of a "power beyond death" is maintained more easily.) The turning point is in Maxim's confession to "I," when he tells her the story of Rebecca's adulterous behavior and the events of the night when she died. After this, armed with knowledge and the confirmation of Maxim's love for her, "I" gains confidence, and the power of the ghost begins to recede. "I" protects Maxim, guides him past the inquest, and accompanies him to the office of a London physician, where they are told of Rebecca's fatal illness.

The novel is written as a memoir, and its first-person voice would have been a liability in filming. There is no hint of that voice anywhere in the film after the prologue, this despite the producer's publicly stated intention to remain faithful to the book. Nevertheless, the film does succeed surprisingly well in realizing David O. Selznick's goal. Its only serious weakness is that it cuts short—and so minimizes the impact of—three long conversations, the first of them a lovers' quarrel between Maxim and "I," the second an extortion attempt by a drunken cousin of Mrs. Danvers, and the third a confrontation in Rebecca's room between Mrs. Danvers and "I." Two major changes were forced on Selznick by the censor: Rebecca's manner of death and Mrs. Danvers's own death in the fire she sets that destroys Manderley.[26]

Selznick started his career with MGM, was called in to improve the mediocre A-film products of the youngest of the major studios, RKO, in 1932, but then in 1935 started an independent studio to concentrate on prestige productions.[27] He had worked with Max Steiner at RKO, and the two now collaborated on reviving and extending for sound film the high-quality performance traditions of the major urban picture palaces of the 1920s (see Neumeyer and Platte 2012, 124). It was not Steiner, however, who wrote ninety minutes of symphonic underscore for *Rebecca*: he was too busy finishing up Selznick's biggest project, *Gone with the Wind* (1939). Instead, Franz Waxman did the work. A young composer who worked for MGM and had recently managed the creation of a complex, partly compiled score for Selznick's *Young at Heart* (1938), Waxman earned his second Academy Award nomination for *Rebecca*. Its success also was a major factor in his eventual move to Warner Bros. in 1943.[28]

The first eight minutes of *Rebecca* divide cleanly into five segments: studio logo, main-title sequence, prologue, opening scene, and hotel lobby scene. Music is continuous throughout. After a fanfare (written by Alfred Newman) that offers a "succinct evocation of grandeur" (Neumeyer and Platte 2012, 96), the main-title cue alternates between suspense and lush melody, an appropriate juxtaposition of topics for this film centering on a glamorous but mysterious woman, an acousmatic femme fatale. Waxman's design of the musical materials is compact and effective. The sections of suspenseful figuration are based on C♯, in the first instance as V of F♯, the key in which we first hear the "Rebecca" theme (see figure 2.14a), in the second instance as a bass note that undermines the A major tonality of the second statement of the theme and leads back toward F♯, which is now V of B minor (figure 2.14a, from 0:60 to 1:24). The key of B minor—it can be called "the key of Manderley"—remains primary from this point through the opening moments of the hotel lobby scene, as we hear two statements of the "Manderley" theme over this key at the end of the main-title sequence and then immediately hear it again in the opening of the prologue (figure 2.14b), when "I" names the house and we see its ruined main gate.

The formal frame of the main-title sequence, along with the reiteration of "Manderley" at the beginning of the prologue, establishes a prominent pair of associative themes and at the same time sets them in opposition to one another by mode (major or minor), expression (rich, full, loud or spare, reduced instrumenvtation, quiet), and mood (expansive and confident or melancholy and tentative). Throughout the prologue, "Manderley" and its qualities prevail, as the music shifts its manner into the accompanimental mode of synchronized dialogue underscoring. The oddly static yet shifting dream state is maintained by staying close to B minor and to "Manderley" but at the same time inflecting them, first through changing a single note that brightens a second-inversion B minor chord to G major for the word "spirit" (at 2:14), then by restating "Manderley"

(a)

0:13
throughout: images of Manderley
park with fog music enters just
before image

0:32
throughout: images of Manderley
park with fog music enters just before
image

0:60

Major + minor triads in A major,
plus G major triad

Rebecca theme

Rebecca

F♯add6   (appog.   F♯7   E7   Aadd6
           chord)

1:21

1:24

1:40
to black

Manderley

$\frac{A_{add6}}{C\sharp}$ C♯ø4/3   F♯   (7,♮9 in
                                                    figuration)   b ⸺

(b)

1:40   2:14   2:36 2:52   3:00   3:27
images: moon; gate; walk; Manderley ruins
throughout: voiceover

Manderley on b   on c   on b♭

          "spirit"   "light" "cloud"   "dreams"

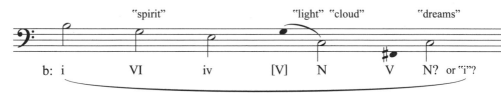

b: i   VI   iv   [V]   N   V   N? or "i"?

deleted:

                                                    V   i

Above and facing. Figure 2.14, a–d. *Rebecca* (1940), (a) music in the main title sequence,
sketch; (b) music in the prologue, bass sketch; (c) music in the opening scene, sketch;
(d) transition from opening scene to hotel lobby scene, sketch. (Based on sketch and
other materials in the Franz Waxman Collection, Syracuse University, and Harry
Ransom Humanities Research Center, University of Texas at Austin.)

(c)

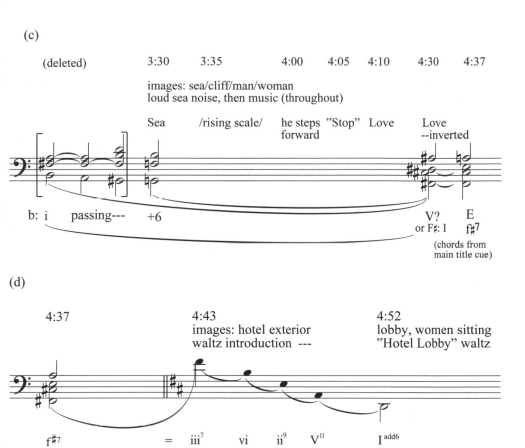

(deleted) 3:30 3:35 4:00 4:05 4:10 4:30 4:37

images: sea/cliff/man/woman
loud sea noise, then music (throughout)

Sea /rising scale/ he steps "Stop" Love Love
                     forward   --inverted

b: i passing--- +6

V? E
or F#: I f#7

(chords from
main title cue)

(d)

4:37 4:43 4:52
images: hotel exterior lobby, women sitting
waltz introduction --- "Hotel Lobby" waltz

f#7 = iii⁷ vi ii:9 V¹¹ I add6

on upper and lower leading tones of B minor (C minor at 2:36 and B♭ minor after 3:00). Similarly, C minor momentarily brightens to C major at 2:52 for "light," then darkens again for "cloud." The Neapolitan chord (of B minor) generated this way reappears at the end, but it is uncertain whether we are to hear it as such or rather as a displaced tonic chord in B minor, an uncertainty that is an apt reflection of the instability of "dreams" (see the end of figure 2.14b). Although the effect is striking, Waxman's original intention was actually to follow through on a cadence in B minor, but the chords shown at the lower right of figure 2.14b were deleted in later editing, as were the beginning moments of the opening scene cue (see figure 2.14c).

In the prologue, the voice-over narration is foregrounded. Music occupies the peculiar position of dialogue underscoring that is not pushed down low in the mix—not so much backgrounded, or even "middlegrounded" as it is "at the narrator's side," commenting, elaborating, and filling in coloristically. If one were obliged to construct a physical space, it would be not the film's diegesis (which is still obscure enough at this point) but the space of the narrator, where we would

Above and facing. Figure 2.15, a–j. *Rebecca,* opening scene. (a)–(c) Maxim on the cliff; (d) Maxim hears a voice and turns; (e) the source of the voice; (f)–(g) "I" approaches, and they talk; (h)–(j) Maxim looks after her, turns to look again at the sea, turns back. Screen stills.

find "I" standing in front of an orchestra, as if in performance of a monodrama. Such a picture must be suppressed, however, as the orchestra must stay in the nondiegetic realm, whereas "I" occupies the in-between position of a nondiegetic voice-over narrator but is always also capable of appearing in the diegesis (as indeed she does during the opening scene in the form of her younger self). Waxman's music follows the narrator with great sympathy: there is no trace of anempathetic distance. Things will change, however, in the two subsequent scenes.

The shift from dream to waking reality—from nighttime dream to daylight world—is abrupt and effective. The voice-over narration of the prologue drops out with the fade to black, and loud effects noise unexpectedly introduces into the sound track a strong sense of tension. This rises along with the slowly ascending pitches of the scale emerging out of a "Sea" theme and the camera's framing, which moves up the cliffside (without changing pace), finally reaching a human figure in silhouette (a man wearing a suit and hat) (see figure 2.15a). Then follows a relatively sharp disjuncture: a cut to a close-up of the man's face followed by two brief shots from behind, the first being a slightly dizzy high-angle shot from above the man's head, with the bottom of the cliff visible but out of focus in the background (figure 2.15b), the second a close-up of feet and shins, with one foot slowly edging forward. All these are Hitchcockian visual idiosyncrasies. The man halts at a woman's cry ("No!") offscreen, he turns (as she calls out "Stop!"), the two approach one another, they appear in a two-shot and speak briefly (figure 2.15, c–g). We learn from the music what we do not yet see in the image track: a "Love" theme, which will become one of the film's most prominent recurrent musical fragments, particularly in the latter half.[29]

In this scene, a great deal of narrative information is offered in a very short time and almost without dialogue. The contrast with the prologue could hardly be greater—and would have struck the film's early viewers even more, as this brief but dramatic scene is not in the novel, where Maxim and "I" first meet during what becomes the hotel lobby scene in the film (in the novel, it is the hotel lounge, to be precise).[30] In the prologue, speech was continuous throughout. Here it is intermittent, tentative (with the obvious exception of "No! Stop!"). The scene is one of action, opening with the spectacle of Maxim's thwarted suicide attempt and finishing with a bumbling, embarrassed conversation where the words mean little. "I" rushes off, and Maxim is left to stand looking after her, bemused (figure 2.15, h–j).

The unsynchronized sound effect of crashing waves at the beginning is a strong sync point, by far the strongest effects sound in the film and, indeed, one of the strongest sync points of any kind. Music is present under the noise but is nearly inaudible. Quickly, however, tension rises along with a turning figure, the "Sea" theme, and a steady scalar pattern—mostly whole tone but with some chromatic steps mixed in—that moves over what has to be called an augmented sixth chord in this context (figure 2.14c at 3:30). In a triumph of clarity over fidelity, as the tension rises, the wave noise, implausibly, disappears.

Waxman's music notes show that he planned to end with Maxim staring over the cliff edge (or very possibly with the movement of his foot forward) (Neumeyer and Platte 2012, 98, 149).[31] But when Selznick requested that music continue through the rest of the scene, Waxman obligingly added a thinly scored extension that includes the first statement of the "Love" theme for solo clarinet. The added music does have some distancing effects. The tentative conversation hardly deserves the overwrought shapes and saccharine sound of "Love." But Waxman sneaks the music in: we hear it first quietly on a medium shot of "I" before she approaches Maxim, and it speaks to her interiority while he barks harsh questions at her from offscreen. The music gradually grows during the course of the two-shot (figure 2.15, e–f) as Maxim grows calmer and his voice more sympathetic. We certainly learn something from the details of the melody. The first interval (D5–F4) is the inversion of the distinctive framing interval of "Rebecca" (C♯4–A♯4), and the remainder is the chromatic turn that we have just heard in "Sea." Finally, though, one might complain that we learn something intimate far too early. Maxim in particular suffers: his appearance as a confident man of affairs in subsequent scenes is rendered less plausible.

If the contrast between the quiet entrance of "Love" and Maxim's offscreen demands suggests anempathy, Waxman's treatment of the final seconds of the scene makes it abundantly clear that he could appreciate and express irony. The inverted sixth of "Love" was not a coincidence. As Maxim, alone, stares offscreen (figure 2.15, h–j), we hear "Love" again, now in a more diatonic form but inverted. The initial leap is now E♯5 up to A♯5, and the melody is made to sit atop the two chords that harmonized the "Rebecca" theme on its first appearance: F♯$^{\text{add6}}$ and F♯ minor^7 (compare figure 2.14a at 0:32 and 2.14d at 4:30). Thus, if "Love" overpromises in its plaintive romantic figures, its inversion follows up by quickly undermining that promise, distancing the viewer from Maxim's hope that an innocent love will be possible without complications from his past: Maxim looks toward "I" but also turns to stare at the sea one more time.

With the hotel lobby scene, the film "proper" begins, starting with traditional establishing shots of Monte Carlo at night and then the exterior of the hotel, followed by a cut inside to the lobby, where we see two women sitting on a chaise. Music had already entered with the exterior shot, the introduction to an elegant waltz. Just after the cut inside, the waltz itself begins. In such circumstances, one might well hear waltzes from a hotel orchestra, and indeed an orchestra is mentioned in Daphne du Maurier's novel near the end of the couple's conversation during lunch (this follows the hotel lobby scene in the film): "The restaurant was filled now with people who chatted and laughed to an orchestral background and a clatter of plates" (1938, 27). In this scene, however, diegesis is uncertain: the volume level is too loud, and the sound is acoustically too present. Nevertheless, its reference to place clearly supports our impressions from the image track: an expensive traditional hotel in which it soon becomes clear that although Maxim de Winter and the wealthy Mrs. Van Hopper fit in, "I" does not. Mrs. Van Hopper is condescending, Maxim is rude, and "I" is flustered and embarrassed. Through the course of this, the waltz goes on in a neutral fashion, indifferent to the nuances of conversation or mood, although it is not impossible to read this indifference as confirming the social powerlessness of "I."

The hotel lobby scene and its waltz end the film's first part. Waxman's waltz does connect to three others by Josef Lanner and Johann Strauss, Jr., for the ensuing luncheon scene, but the music's B minor–based tonal design is abandoned. The five strains from three waltzes are arranged in the key sequence B♭–B♭–E♭–E♭–D. The transition to the final waltz is made in an abrupt four-bar introduction typical of Viennese waltzes: E♭–E half-diminished^7–A^7. A strong close in D brings the music back to its starting place as the terrace scene starts up in that key with a theme and orchestration that are reminiscent of the prologue.[32]

Where, then, might Rebecca—who hovers over everything but is absent—fit in the terms and relations we charted in figure 2.13? We will need to add to the lower left term the phrase "voiceless body, offscreen," which, granted, might sound as counterintuitive as "onscreen nondiegetic" did earlier (recall figure 2.12). To fill things out completely, we should also add "bodiless voice, onscreen" to the lower right-hand term of figure 2.14 (see figure 2.16, which places the characters under the appropriate terms).[33] The "bodiless voice, onscreen," at least, is straightforward: the acousmêtre suits it when its voice is situated as if onscreen, when we can hear—and physically place—a body but cannot see it. In *The Invisible Man* (1933), Claude Rains fits this in most instances, as the camera is constantly trying to match his voice and presumed position onscreen. Rebecca very nearly

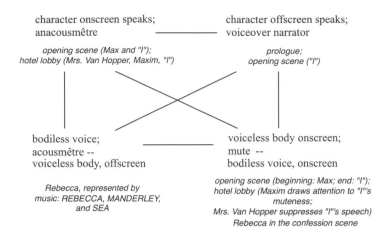

Figure 2.16. Figure 2.13 with annotations for voices in the opening sections of *Rebecca*.

becomes the same during the confession scene, which includes the famous (but not necessarily praised) stylized moment referred to earlier, in which the camera follows Rebecca about. At any moment, that onscreen unseen body could be expected to speak, perhaps even to appear. In retrospect, it is also not hard to hear Rebecca's voice in Maxim's head during the opening scene, urging him to jump, rather like Mrs. Danvers's actual voice later on, when, acting as a surrogate for Rebecca, she does urge "I" to leap from the window of Rebecca's bedroom.

Moving clockwise through figure 2.16, note that there is no lack of the fully synchronized voice but that it shows up late, after the prologue, and even then the few awkward words between Maxim and "I" barely count as normal conversation. The two types of the offscreen voice are neatly represented by the prologue (voice-over) and opening scene, as the first diegetic voice is also "I"—offscreen, shouting. The voiceless body is rendered in a symmetrical pattern in the opening scene: Maxim, mute, at the beginning and "I," mute, rushing offscreen at the end. In the adjustments noted above, the other instance of this term is the bodiless voice, onscreen: it is represented abundantly by Rebecca in the confession scene. Finally, the almost-acousmêtre of Rebecca's near-constant presence in the speech of others, in the *mise-en-scène* (monogrammed napkins, china figures, her room, the seaside cottage she used for assignations, Manderley itself), is represented early on in the music as well. The trio of themes "Rebecca," "Manderley," and "Sea" are the exclusive thematic material of the beginning through the first appearance of "Love" in the final moments of the opening scene. Recall also that even there "Love" was not only derived from "Rebecca" plus "Sea" but promptly undercut by its "Rebecca"-like mirror.

The voiceless body, offscreen, is the generalized figure or threat of the ghost. Chion links the ghost and the acousmêtre:

Burial is marked by rituals and signs such as the gravestone, the cross, and the epitaph, which say to the departed, "You must stay here," so that he won't haunt the living as a soul in torment. In some traditions, ghosts are those who are unburied or improperly buried. Precisely the same applies to the acousmêtre, when we speak of a yet-unseen voice, one that can neither enter the image to attach itself to a visible body, nor occupy the removed position of the image presenter. The voice is condemned to wander the surface. (1999, 140)

Rebecca may be gothic melodrama, but (in the film version at least) it ends as romance, when Maxim and "I" finally banish ("properly bury") the ghost in all its forms. The threat of Rebecca's body and the inquest is removed when the doctor reveals the cancer diagnosis; Mrs. Danvers, the surrogate, dies in the fire; and Manderley, which Rebecca had effectively stolen from Maxim, burns to the ground.[34]

Rebecca was an agent without a body, a presence without a voice. Manderley is her funeral pyre, and music goes with her: the final seconds of the sound track are overwhelmed by an unburdened "Love."

Conclusion

The five binaries are the functional categories by which sound, image, and narrative in a film are elaborated. In early film theory, questions of clarity and fidelity, synchronization and "counterpoint," were the centers of attention. The practices of the classical cinema, however, suggest that diegetic/nondiegetic, with its accompanying pairs onscreen/offscreen, as we explored them in the previous section, is particularly rich in possibilities for analysis and interpretation. A sense of physical space creates the diegesis, agency motivates it, onscreen/offscreen interprets it visually, and the diegetic/nondiegetic distinction interprets it aurally. What the agent is to the image track the agent's voice is to the sound track. If the sound track has an irreducible principle, that is it.

Part II

Music in the Mix: *Casablanca*

3   Acoustic Stylization: The Film's Sound World

David Neumeyer and James Buhler

Casablanca is unquestionably one of the best-known films from America's studio era. To be sure, it is not an example of the system at its mechanical, factory-production best (scriptwriting and shooting schedule were notably chaotic), but the film does show what Hollywood professionals could do under pressure. In terms of narrative presentation, it is not a particularly efficient film (by Warner Bros. standards, at least), yet it is all the more interesting because its various elements evince remarkable creativity and skill. It is also a film rich in music. The three chapters of part 2, taken together, constitute an extended reading of *Casablanca*'s sound track and its music.

In chapter 1, I argued for the sound track as a whole, with its internal dialectic, as the object for study. This idea receives its most elaborate treatment in the present chapter, where James Buhler and I extrapolate to a conception of the film's sound track as analogous to a musical composition. Sound tracks, like image tracks, are "composed," not merely recorded. Here we consider the sound track of *Casablanca* as a whole in order to demonstrate how the "composers" of the sound track manage the complex interaction of elements in the sound track under the concept of vococentrism. In chapter 4, attention turns to the narrative functions of music and pitch design in the famous reunion scene, where Humphrey Bogart's Rick and Ingrid Bergman's Ilsa first encounter one another in Casablanca. Chapter 5 widens the scope, placing our reading of the reunion scene in its filmic contexts through similar readings of two closely parallel scenes, both of them confrontations between Rick and Ilsa (after hours on the first night in the café, and after hours on the second night in Rick's living quarters upstairs). The underscore cue for the first confrontation is in fact the original version that its composer, Max Steiner, adapted and developed for both the reunion scene and the second confrontation. Finally, we circle back to the concept of acoustic stylization—sound track as "composed"—with an examination of the atypically complex sound track in the film's airport finale. The reunion scene and confrontation scenes, along with the finale, collectively chart the course of Rick's harrowing journey from utopias—built, crushed, remembered—through disillusionment and cynicism to ultimate affirmation.

Introduction:
Image Track/Sound Track Stylization

The power of the image track derives not from some mystical aesthetic unity but, as I argued in part 1, from the way editing productively structures the tensions among its various components—*mise-en-scène,* lighting, framing, blocking, and so forth. Evaluating the effectiveness of music with respect to the narrative context requires moving analysis beyond the purely musical to a view that conceives the two tracks, image and sound, as in a dialectical tension, each track structured in turn by its own internal dialectic. A central claim of part 1 was that this internal dialectic also serves to confirm the internal hierarchy of the sound track as the starting point for analysis and interpretation. Such an interpretive framework requires evaluating the particular contribution of music to the *mise-en-bande.* That emphasis on understanding music in a film's sound design allows interpretation to probe the rich tensions, complexities, and contradictions that music helps articulate.[1]

If music is a structuring of sound in time, as many twentieth-century aestheticians have claimed, then conceptually the *mise-en-bande,* with its complex interplay of music, dialogue, ambient sound, effects, silences, and so forth, can be understood as a kind of musical "composition." Aural analysis then includes both technical musical analysis and Pierre Schaeffer's "concentrated hearing" (*écoute réduite,* translated as "reduced listening" in Chion 1994, 29), which involves close scrutiny of the qualities and characteristics of individual sounds (Nattiez 1990, 95).[2] Analysis also requires a specifically musical sensibility that can be brought to bear on the sound track as a whole, its relation to the image, and its contribution not just to the narrative but to the act of narration itself. Interpreting a film in this way is perhaps the most "musical" way of reading it, more so than treating the score as a relatively independent component of the film, an analytical strategy that takes as its object music *for* film rather than music *in* film. If this preference for music *in* film seems to violate the principle of the vococentric cinema, one of whose goals is to divert us from the analytical and interpretive routines of music studies, in fact it simply transfers those routines to the sound track as a whole.

Vococentrism remains the hierarchical principle that dialogue serves in order to anchor the sound track, just as the human figure, especially the face, serves to anchor the image. This is a descriptive principle, not a prescriptive one. We recognize that other configurations of cinema are possible (as in silent film) but presume that vococentrism has a certain basis in human perception and cognition, and we take for granted that it is the dominant cinematic practice. Because dialogue is above all a figure of sense and meaning,[3] it operates primarily at the level of denotation; denotation here is used in Stuart Hall's (1999, 512) sense of the term as that which has a relatively fixed, consensual, and determinate meaning.

Denotation is neither an absolute nor a universal meaning, however, but merely what is foregrounded, obvious, most demonstrative, and insistent—similar to Barthes's (1977b, 52) level of information, which is oriented toward communication. Denotation might be understood as the baseline of meaning that must be extracted from the film for its point to be intelligible, for it to make sense, assuming that the film's point requires making such sense.

The very ubiquity and centrality of dialogue, however, make it a poor medium for structural articulation or for the expressive effects of coloring tone, of establishing mood, setting, or inarticulate feeling. Structural articulation and expressive effects are both important considerations for effective narrative. Novelists confront this challenge in the literary text and can marshal the resources of language (which consist in more than just dialogue). Although it deploys language, sound film can only with difficulty make use of the more intricate linguistic devices for structural articulation and expressive effect, because the priority of the vococentric means that the film's language takes form primarily as dialogue. Film, however, has many other nonlinguistic devices at its disposal. These are generally stylistic figures that perform structural and expressive functions and that are not, strictly speaking, necessary to the denotative sense of the film. In terms of meaning, figures operate primarily at the level of associative (Hall 1999, 512) or symbolic meaning (Barthes 1977b, 52–53), that is, connotation rather than denotation. To put it another way, the meaning these figures supply is implicit rather than explicit. As such, that meaning is less determinate and therefore possible to overlook without the film ceasing to be intelligible. Connotation may alter denotation a great deal or not much at all—in the former case by subverting, ironizing, or destabilizing denotation; in the latter case by confirming, reinforcing, or clarifying it. (We might want to disavow the implicit meaning of connotation on either end: because it makes denotation too obvious or because the transformation of meaning seems too fraught, given the denotation.)

Structural articulation affects meaning by ordering the representation. It establishes priority, hierarchy, and points of comparison and contrast. Although the principle of vococentrism states that the position of the voice determines the composition of the sound track, this means only that the placement is always of central concern, never a contingent factor. It does not imply that the voice is always centered any more than the face is always centered and in medium close-up in the image track. Vococentrism in this sense claims only that we recognize in an immediate way when the voice has moved off-center and interpret the configuration accordingly as an expressive effect or as an excessive stylistic flourish.

Finally, the notion of an excessive stylistic flourish brings us beyond denotation and connotation to a third level, one that is positioned at the edge of meaning. Barthes calls it "obtuse" (1977b, 54) and understands it as a "signifier without a signified" (61), the classic definition of nonsense. Often we recognize its presence in a certain "touching stupidity" (66n1). He sees its function as primarily one of blunting the obviousness of the first and second levels, adding a tangible excess of semiotic imprecision, which endows "a rich perceptual field" (Thompson 1986, 136). The result is to unsettle the denotation—as the supporting network of connotation modifies it—by opening it to what Barthes calls *signifiance,* the indeterminate field of meaning defined by the totality of signification, the "infinity of language" (Barthes 1977b, 55). In this way obtuse meaning unhinges the obvious, forcing the latter to struggle to rearticulate itself and thereby earn its ultimate significance. For Kristin Thompson (1986, 134–35), the resulting tension between the obtuse and the obvious, or what she calls the excessive and unifying elements, is the very basis of aesthetic form. She defines excess as any filmic device that exceeds motivation (134), as "those elements [that] escape unifying impulses" (141). Classical cinema usually domesticates (without eliminating) excess by using it to dramatize its struggle with the obvious, so that the impression of clarity is strengthened (as a lesson or moral) while meaning is divided, to rewarding multiple interpretive strategies (Maltby 1996).

Our analysis of *Casablanca* seeks to demonstrate the working of these nonlinguistic devices on the sound track, in both their structural and expressive functions, and to track the obtuse play of nonsignifying, audible stylistic flourishes. In that respect, we pay attention to almost every element of the sound track except the actual words in order to consider how those words—their denotations, their obvious meanings—are set off, inflected, structured, and called into question. We also examine those elements in their connection to the image track and larger narrative concerns. In short, our object is to reconstruct how the principle of vococentrism is realized and sustained throughout the film and how filmmakers turn the principle of vococentrism to thematic advantage.

Methodologically, we presume the category of voice itself to be divided in two ways: first, the speaking voice and the singing voice are distinguished, as in chapter 1; second, those voices are themselves divided into sense and "grain," adopting Barthes's well-known term, if not quite his meaning (1977a, 181). For our purposes, grain consists in every material aspect of the voice that is not reducible to the production of meaning, the voice on the sound track that cannot be reduced to script (Chion 1999, 1). Grain is the opposing principle to vococentrism, the noisy oppositional ground vococentrism requires to establish the centrality of its order. Under grain we will include categories such as accent, intonation, and timbre to the extent that they either serve as barriers to meaning or signify in a capacity beyond words. Grain can also be deployed to create structural articulations as the characteristic sounds of individual voices interweave with one another as sound rather than meaning to become structurally significant on the aural plane of the sound track. In such cases, voices can recur like musical themes, and the changing mode of expression (anger, melancholy, gruffness, and so on) and form of address (public, private, formal, informal) resemble variants of musical themes and characteristic mood music. Voices, in other words, can function as narrative motifs. The singing voice—the actual vocal object around which Barthes developed his term—also has a grain that cannot be reduced to its musicality. In Barthes's terms, it would be better understood as the distinctive way a particular voice assimilates the material particles of language into its musical tone, the way it transforms the resistance of language to musicalization into an aesthetic value. Understood thus, we might reappraise the grain of the speaking voice analogously as the distinctive way a particular voice assimilates the body into language, or as the way it transforms into a value the resistance of bodily sound to being a bearer of denotative meaning. But transforming nonvalue (mere noise, contingent sound) into a value immediately raises the question: A value of what? Here we find the obtuse meaning of the voice, its excessive quality.

Music in the Sound Track

Casablanca certainly offers some purchase for a reading based on music as semiautonomous, as music *for* film. Consider, for example, the obsession with "As Time Goes By."[4] Once it enters the film with Ilsa's muted singing in the prelude to the reunion scene, the song's various transformations and incessant presence underscore and give insight into Rick's shifting psychological state. The music in fact treats Rick rather like a hysteric, his interior opened up and scored in the fashion of women in melodrama.[5] In some respects, *Casablanca* even resembles a talking cure film without the psychoanalysis, where Rick manages to confront the traumatic bad object, dissolve the repression he had constructed around it, and tell a new story about the relationship. "As Time Goes By" becomes a signifier of this bad object—Caryl Flinn (1992, 108) calls it a "souvenir" of what Rick remembers as a perfect relationship with Ilsa in Paris. As the signifier of the bad object, this souvenir at first takes negative form: a taboo on the song and cynicism toward a world that can only offer the semblance of true relationship. The song in fact never appears whole in the film—usually we hear only the A-phrase of the thirty-two-bar AABA chorus (the verse does not appear at all)—but it only disappears from the sound track in the last moments, when Rick comes to terms with his loss of Ilsa and allows that relationship to be past. In this respect, the displacement of "As Time Goes By" through an apotheosis of "La Marseillaise" signifies that Rick is no longer in thrall to his desperate attempt to relive what is no longer, what can no longer be. Far from being an unreflective exercise in nostalgia, *Casablanca* becomes through Max Steiner's underscore the story of mastering and overcoming the debilitating effects of trauma.

The approach to analyzing the music of the film represented by this brief interpretive sketch can clearly yield genuine insight into the work music does in film and the relation of music to narrative, but it entails an abstraction from music as it exists in the film, where it shares space on the sound track with dialogue and sound effects. Abstracting film music from the sound track places it where nineteenth-century idealist philosophy tells us it belongs: in a realm apart. For those who want to locate the art of film music in the underscore, the concept of nondiegetic or "background" music serves a covert ideological purpose: it separates music from what the narrative represents, places the music beyond the diegetic world. It is a question of whether the music belongs to the narrative representation (diegetic) or is outside it (nondiegetic), that is, a question of narrative level. Music as representation of emotion does not (normally) belong to the level of the diegesis. We do not (normally) believe that the character hears the same background music we do but only that the music represents the emotion the character feels or the emotion that we are supposed to feel about the action depicted in the world. Music, thus, is granted special powers. Its absence from the diegetic world seems to promise access to a transcendent, utopian space—existing nowhere but in the mind—where the emptiness of the diegetic world is filled, indeed overflows, with meaning.[6]

Moreover, a reading concerned with music alone must remain relatively silent about important factors of music *in* the sound track. For instance, the music that underscores the portentous voice-over in the prologue grants the image the dignity and pathos of a world-historical event. Similarly, Rick's Café Américain is enlivened by the careful regulation of the sympathetic noise of the patrons, who listen to this music in order to forget, if only for a moment, their woes. The play between foreground and background music in the café, again controlled in large part from the mixing board, likewise encourages our attention to flit from a popular music apparently indifferent to the plight of the patrons to the desperate deals being made at the tables.

Two moments in *Casablanca* gain particular narrative importance from the mixing of music into the sound track. The first is the lead-in to the famous flashback. As Rick sits in the darkened, empty café after seeing Ilsa for the first time since Paris, the sound is dead, indeed painfully silent, a signifier of Rick's emptiness. We hear only the most narratively pertinent effects, sounds that mark Rick's descent into nihilism: the sound of alcohol being poured, the clink of a glass. Sam speaks. Rick answers Sam's suggestions with progressively more force. Rick is reduced to wild, if pure negation in response: "no . . . no . . . no." Like a modern-day Orpheus, Sam attempts to counter the despair the way he does generally for patrons in the bar: with music. Rick responds with a more measured but still essentially nihilistic reflection. He breaks off. He refuses Sam's attempt to console him. He takes control of the sound track, commanding Sam to stop improvising something of his own and instead play "it" for him (figure 3.1a). "As Time Goes By" quickly fills the sound track, displacing all dialogue and sound effects. As the orchestra enters, first in support of the piano but quickly engulfing the entire sound track, Rick is reduced to a last inarticulate, grunted sigh as he loses the world in his thoughts. The image dissolves from him to the Arc de Triomphe just as "As Time Goes By" dissolves into the trumpeted head motive of "La Marseillaise" (figure 3.1b, c). The progression here, from spare diegetic sound to almost bombastic nondiegetic music, marks a passage from the real to the ideal in the same way the audio dissolve in a film musical does, but for quite a different purpose (Altman 1987, 62–74). But far from the musical's ideal, which establishes the presence of a charmed world, an anticipation of what is not yet but might still be, Rick's reverie is sentimental, taking hold of an irrevocable but also unrecoverable past.[7] If "As Time Goes By" marks the presence of an absence, namely Ilsa, the explosion of "La Marseillaise" bursts Rick's emotional dam, proclaiming the absence of a presence, Rick's actual idealism, which has been blocked by the trauma of Paris and shows itself only in inversion, as a deep cynicism. We will return to this point—the importance of this contrast—below.

Figure 3.1, a–c. *Casablanca*, Rick and Sam after hours. (a) Rick tells Sam to play "it" (that is, "As Time Goes By"); (b) Rick staring ahead as Sam plays; (c) dissolve to Paris flashback—we hear "La Marseillaise." Screen stills.

The musical battle between "Die Wacht am Rhein" and "La Marseillaise" is the second place where the sound track mix lends special pertinence to filmic meaning. German officers stand around a piano singing. Victor Laszlo, a prominent leader of the resistance in Europe and husband of Ilsa, decides to challenge the Germans on the ground most sacred to German culture, that of music.[8] He asks the musicians to play "La Marseillaise." A bit apprehensive, the musicians look to Rick, who signals his approval with a brief, silent nod. As "Die Wacht am Rhein" withers under the instrumental (and mixing board) onslaught, the music swells into a mighty chorus. (The producer, Hal Wallis, was behind this. In his music notes, he writes: "On the [Marseillaise], when it is played in the café, don't do it as though it was played by this small orchestra. Do it with a full scoring orchestra and get some body into it" [Harmetz 2002, 260].) The musical allegory is hardly subtle, but it can be given depth by recognizing that Rick for the first time takes sides, albeit tacitly, without sonic reinforcement. Thus, if "La Marseillaise" had at the start of the flashback served to displace "As Time Goes By" as a figure of loss—a negative trace of his idealism—its diegetic presence now begins to reclaim that idealism and ground him in a community. As Paul Allen Anderson puts it, "Musical performances undertaken in the name of collective or shared remembrance extend an ambitious performative promise: they will not merely reference some 'elusive entity' through the ritual of commemoration; they will bring it into being. Thus the live performance of the 'Marseillaise' in *Casablanca* transforms the cafe's multinational crowd into something at once new and old, a newly unified collective that can give form to an originary and indestructible entity through song" (2006, 484).

The musical battle suggests that this collective, even if it is a ragtag chorus, when supported by sufficient instrumental resources can trump even the most rigorous musical discipline. This effect is emphasized through the mix by bringing various voices forward, most prominently with a close-up on Yvonne, who before the "battle" had been chastised for flirting with the German officers but who is now presented teary eyed and proudly defiant. Along with the visual close-up, the mix focuses on her voice, allowing the passion of her singing to be heard clearly. The subjectivization of the mix, the elevation of her voice in the communal chorus, marks the significance of conversion, of Yvonne's return to the community, and so also prefigures Rick's full conversion, his return to the fight. Peter Franklin (2011, 121–22) claims that this musical contest is undermined, is made "effete" to some degree, by the fact that both anthems are offered in the same key. He believes that the music, though "a rather impressive contrapuntal and harmonic *union*" (122; emphasis in original), thus misses a chance for a "manly," dissonant "Ivesean" collision.[9] Such a critique requires accepting a Modernist framing of the issue in terms of gender that is at odds with the general argument of Franklin's book. One could very well make the contrary point: the very stakes of this musical battle reflected the current moment and situation in the Casablanca of the film. This was not so much a battle about abstract ideals but a battle over a specific piece of common ground (the café). How much more powerful to refuse the Germans even the consolation of retaining the right to their own tonic key.

Diegetic/Nondiegetic Levels and Acoustic Stylization

Our reading of the first scene above—the lead-in to the flashback—would lose much of its richness without the supporting recognition of how music is slowly removed from the diegetic world and taken someplace else. It is the gap opening up between what we see and what we hear in this sequence that seems to motivate the narrative shift to the idealized fantasy of the flashback. This device, Altman's audio dissolve, is much less common in dramatic films than in musicals and perhaps the more striking because of that; it is also one of the most clearly foregrounded instances of Robynn Stilwell's (2007) "fantastical gap." Here, the progression of music from the diegetic to the nondiegetic world underscores that the flashback is a vision of another world.

At the end of the flashback sequence, an abrupt visual transition is marked by a similarly abrupt audio transition from an extremely passionate orchestral variation of "As Time Goes By," through the sound effects of the train pulling away from the station, and back to the lonely piano—in other words, movement from a rich, nondiegetic music back to a rather plain diegetic music. The latter cannot maintain itself, however: it is broken off by Rick's collapse, as he drops his head on the table, a metaphor, perhaps, for the total collapse of the rich fantasy world of the flashback and also the empty, cynical world of the Café Américain. It is at this moment of collapse and utter despair that both Ilsa and the nondiegetic music return. Her presence is announced by the same distinctive, accented chord that marked the recognition at the first meeting, this time made more piquant by raising the F♮ to F♯ (see figure 3.2). At the same time, in the opening of this later scene, "As Time Goes By" is conspicuously absent. Earlier, it had flowed directly out of and moved on top of the stinger chord, but now we hear instead a slow-moving chromatic descent in octaves. The absence marks a distance that now appears absolute and unbridgeable. Rick seethes with anger. Ilsa tries to calm him, which, despite Rick's sarcasm, does succeed in evoking the tune. She attempts to retell the story of her absence from the train, beginning with the account of her relationship with Laszlo. The music turns to Laszlo's theme, but before she can complete the story, Rick lashes out, and the music likewise veers abruptly away. Eventually it returns to the same musical mark of absence, the descending chromatic line, heard after another stinger chord when he asks the fatal question: "Who was it that you left me for?" His anger in effect transforms the taboo into harsh negation, a vicious attempt to purge that memory, which ironically requires absenting Ilsa herself from that memory and therefore leaving him with only the song, the presence of an absence.

The play between diegetic and nondiegetic music draws interpretive attention to the narrative pertinence of the music, but we must also be able to account for an even more basic distinction: the play between presence and absence of music. Whether controlled by composer, director, or sound editor, the placement of nondiegetic music, or "spotting," is a fundamental task with important consequences for a film scene. Music in *Casablanca* is extremely well placed, and the spotting makes broad connections between structure and theme. For instance, it is surely

Andante

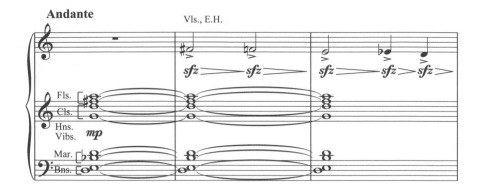

Slowly

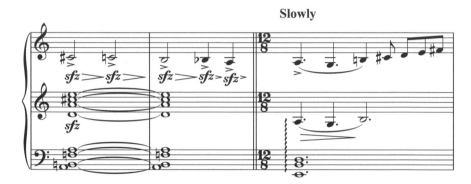

Figure 3.2. *Casablanca,* music for Ilsa's late-night return to Rick's Café Américain, mm. 1–6. (Based on sketches in the Max Steiner Collection, Brigham Young University, and materials in the Warner Bros. Collection, University of Southern California.)

significant that no nondiegetic music appears with scenes of the café until Rick sees Ilsa.[10] Another example is the "sober" encounter between Rick and Ilsa in the market after their angry meeting the night before. This scene is most poignant because of its sound. The sequence is wholly bereft of music, as if in rejecting Ilsa's attempt to narrate her story and so also the presence of "As Time Goes By" in the underscore Rick has drained the world of music. Rick and Ilsa's dialogue is set in counterpoint to the chatter of the vendor. For her, the value of friendship with this new Rick plummets as quickly as the price of the linen.

The relevant categories for this film's use of music, then, are these: presence/absence and, within the former, diegetic/nondiegetic. This simple schematic, however, suggests that the categories are not only discrete but fixed hierarchically. For purposes of interpretive practice, it will be more fruitful to consider them as functionally equal, as different modes of acoustic stylization, or means of rendering the filmic world of sound. Absence or silence, which at its extreme would be a silent sound track (such as at the nadir point in the café before the flashback), is a pared-down sound world. Nondiegetic music, on the other hand, belongs to a displaced sound world (its extreme would be a wholly nondiegetic music, such as the music over the titles or the apotheosis of "La Marseillaise" at the end). Diegetic sound, then, can be understood as an effaced stylization, where rendered sound is taken—and mistaken—for real. What we have is a cluster rather than a binary: silence, nondiegetic (presence), and diegetic (presence).

The point here is not to use stylization as a continuum along which the binary of diegetic and nondiegetic is displayed—they remain distinct levels when viewed in terms of narration—but rather to accommodate the use of music to vococentrism. If music is understood as a stylized mode of representing the sound world, then sound is placed on a par with visual means of cinematic signification. In fact, music has often been theorized along the lines of such stylization— as a signifier of excess used to fill in what would otherwise be absent.[11] Nondiegetic music represents, as it were, something otherwise masked by the screening of reality: how the world feels, say, rather than how it appears. And it is the stylization that indicates the expressive effect. In this sense, music is not unlike stylized lighting and sets (as we noted in chapter 1 in connection with background and neutral scoring).

The theoretical treatment of stylization of the sound track has been quite different from that of the image track. In the case of nondiegetic music, for instance, the audience is construed as hearing music the characters do not; that is, unlike the visual realm, we presume that the appearance of the acoustical realm is naturally stratified.[12] A good deal of music is taken to be screened from the characters, to exist for us and our world, but not for the characters and theirs. This theoretical screening serves, paradoxically, as a means of naturalizing the presence of music in the film. Music is extracted from the diegesis, made nondiegetic so that its signification can become external, supplemental to the representation. By excluding background music from the world screened, diegetic sound, particularly synchronized sound, can then be made to anchor a film's representation of the reality, even when—or especially when—the visual field is highly stylized. As was discussed in chapter 2, a clear distinction between the representational registers of diegetic and nondiegetic sound (including music) helps a film project a world of psychological realism constructed on a split between an external world of character action and an internal world of character feeling. Sequences such as the flashback momentarily suspend the distinction for a particular effect (in *Casablanca* to represent the descent into an overly idealized past). This distinction is only routinely ignored in films that are not particularly committed to a world of psychological realism, such as musicals. Even in those cases, the lack of distinction is typically associated with a suspension of mundane reality so that an ideal world, enchanted by music, can emerge by contrast.[13]

If, instead of understanding sound along this vector of psychological realism, we conceptualize it in terms of stylization, much diegetic music in dramatic films appears as an acoustical backdrop not all that much different from nondiegetic music. Of course, the distinction between ambient music and sound, on the one hand, and nondiegetic music, on the other, is frequently less than clear. Both the "Arabian" music in the prologue and the similar music at the Blue Parrot café

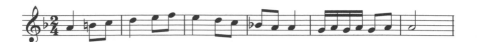

Figure 3.3. *Casablanca,* music for the Blue Parrot, opening (from *Charge of the Light Brigade* [1936]). Transcription from the sound track.

later in the film, for instance, hover nebulously between diegetic and nondiegetic sound. Martin Marks (2000) interprets both as diegetic sound because it seems that this music could emanate from that space (the "Blue Parrot" music also is not included in Steiner's score).[14] Yet running against this reading in both cases is the lack of musicians to anchor this sound. Though musicians are briefly present in the background of the Blue Parrot, for instance, the music is not really handled as diegetic sound. It does not accord with the musicians we see as Rick enters the Blue Parrot and again later as he passes Laszlo on his way out, and it does not change levels significantly as the characters move through the space—the levels are adjusted, like background music, only to make room for dialogue. In fact, it is treated rather like nondiegetic mood music, much as nondiegetic music over an establishing shot is often used to evoke the sonic ambience of the place—in other words, still another instance of the "fantastical gap." The ambiguity in the case of the "Arabian" music emerges because the music appears somewhat less stylized, its tone somewhat less distant, than typical establishment music (see figure 3.3). The music does not appear, as it were, to gaze upon the world screened from outside; it does not sound at a level of abstraction from the diegesis.[15]

In cases such as the "Arabian" music, the function of the ambiguity seems primarily to establish not just a sense of place but its fundamental musicality. Not securely anchored to any particular sounding body, the entire place seems suffused with music, with just this music, a style topic composed to evoke unambiguously the music of the other, which is why we can identify it as "Arabian" in the first place. If the clarity of this style topic projects an easily decoded sign of the primitive that, despite—indeed because of—its apparent presence in the diegesis, holds the other fixed in a colonizing gaze, the ambiguity of its status is perhaps even more problematic. Even when purportedly authentic indigenous music is used, it would suffer a similar fate in being marked as "other" insofar as it is used to point to what stands outside the norms of modern social conventions. The logic of the colonizing sign appears whenever it emphasizes what is exotic in the music rather than what is human. The unruliness of the music—the indeterminate nature of its stylization; the way it floats between diegetic and nondiegetic; the relative crudeness of its use of tonality, particularly its resistance to "proper" tonal (or even modal) progression—underscores the apparent "dangers" of a place that does not follow established conventions. In that sense, the uncanniness of this sort of music draws on a power similar to the acousmêtre. If, unlike the acousmêtre, this music is not exactly allied with the irrational and fantastic, it is nevertheless employed as the representation of what is not yet rational, an apparently "primitive" culture unmarked by the articulations characteristic of an advanced (that is, technologically dependent) society.[16]

Ambiguity reinforces at a narratological level the marked exoticism more audible in the style topic itself. In this sense, interpreting sound in terms of its mode of stylization places emphasis on the *work* of the sound track, on the play between categories. Rather than stopping at a formal description of the status of the music, say, giving priority to the stylization that music brings to the sound track reveals decisions, both implicit and explicit, made about how music, how the sound track as a whole, will participate in the construction of filmic meaning. Because they are typically motivated in terms of realism, narrative pertinence, and aesthetic terms such as mood and ambience, decisions about sound contain an ideological content buried deep in the political unconscious. Interpreting sound in terms of its stylization and drawing attention to an excess over and above its expressive function is one way to bring that unconscious closer to the surface.

Purposeful ambiguity between diegetic and nondiegetic sound is not restricted to marking exotic locales. For instance, the flashback as a whole operates in a highly ambivalent sonic fantasy zone that continually erodes the distinction between diegetic and nondiegetic sound. A brief scene of dancing uses an arrangement of the song "Perfidia"; clearly scored for dance band and synchronized to some extent with the dancing, it seems like diegetic music. Yet because it is seamlessly integrated with the orchestral score that surrounds it, because it underscores the general mood, because the synchronization of dancing and music is less than perfect, and because visual dissolves occur over it, "Perfidia" also seems to function somewhat like nondiegetic music. (In fact, as with the "Blue Parrot" music, a recorded track was reused from *Now, Voyager,* released earlier in 1942: according to an agreement reached between the studios and the musicians' union in 1939, all reuses, such as this one, were to be newly recorded. The musicians' strike in 1942, however, nullified that requirement for the time being.)

Similarly, the flashback portrays the German assault and capture of Paris with images of war machines loosely synchronized to harsh, grinding music that is hard to distinguish from sound effects, the announcement of the impending German occupation through a loudspeaker, and the muffled sounds of artillery—all are handled in such a way that each threatens to dissolve the fantasy world of the flashback. Narratively, each serves to underscore an interruption, a cutting off, that plays into the whole castration anxiety around which the flashback is structured. The images of the advancing German troops appropriate music to "sweeten"—or rather "demonize"—the sound, especially the mechanical instruments of war—trucks, tanks, and planes; the loudspeaker projects the voice of an absent power whose catastrophic presence is imminent; the distant artillery set in counterpoint to a variant of "As Time Goes By" suggests that the music cannot much longer hold the world from encroaching on the romance.

Even in a case where music would almost inevitably be interpreted as nondiegetic, such as the final sequence of the flashback where Rick waits at the train

Figure 3.4. *Casablanca,* music at the moment that Rick reads the note from Ilsa. (Based on sketches in the Max Steiner Collection, Brigham Young University, and documents in the Warner Bros. Collection, University of Southern California.)

station, it might still be taken instead as stylized sound. Sam brings Rick the fateful letter from Ilsa. The words begin to smear as Rick reads it, as if the letter itself were weeping with Rick's sorrow. At the same moment, music cries out with the pain of a passionate climax, a slow waltz variant of "As Time Goes By" (see figure 3.4). Although this music would clearly be nondiegetic in standard narrative analysis, it might also be taken instead as a highly stylized sound effect: the sound of a breaking heart, not literally the searing sound Rick hears inside his head at that moment but a sonic metaphor for the world, both visible and audible, weeping in sympathy with him. Just as the letter runs with tears, so too the sound track is drenched by the sound of pathos-laden rain clouds sent by heaven. A train whistle wails, signifying the encroachment of harsh reality as the letter falls from Rick's hand, and he stumbles to the train. The train, which had promised escape and a life together, now signifies only emptiness: the music dissolves into the mechanical sound of the train's departure.

The Sound World of *Casablanca*

For its era and genre, the sound track of *Casablanca* is surprisingly lively. Once the prologue's voice-over narration gives way to dialogue, the sound track is rarely without diegetic sound for more than a few seconds at a time. Much of this time is given over to dialogue, punctuated by diegetic music performances in the film's first third and accompanied thereafter by fluid dialogue underscoring. The film's almost unbroken chain of short, dialogue-centered scenes provides a norm against which the occasional audiovisual accents introduced by music and effects stand out as points of contrast. Framed in these terms, large-scale design in *Casablanca* might be understood as a direct temporal sequence where plot and story (mostly) coincide, over which is laid a complex set of large-scale articulations (with the exception of the prologue and the flashback to Paris, the film follows a fairly strict chronological succession of three days and nights, with priority emphatically tipped to the latter).

Although lively, *Casablanca* is absolutely typical of classical Hollywood practice in using sound effects to mark bodies with immediate narrative pertinence. Sound gives guns, whistles, sirens, propellers, bottles, glasses, and so forth special emphasis in a scene. Indeed, the customary absence of other sounds allows the recurrence of these few effects to structure the sound track in a striking way. Just as a love theme might recur to mark further development of the narrative

Table 3.1. Transformations of the alarm-answer syntagm

	Alarm	Answer
Prologue	Police whistle	Gunshot
Ugarte's arrest	Gunshots	~~Arrest~~
Closing the café	Strasser's warning	Renault's whistle
Flashback	Loudspeaker (French)	Orchestral noise
	Loudspeaker (German)	Cannons
(Last kiss)	Cannon blast	Glass tipping
(Train)	Train whistle	Piston
Second confrontation	~~Gun~~	~~Watchtower~~
Finale	~~Whistle~~	Gun
	Phone call	
	↓	
	Buzzer	
	↓	
	Horn	
	↓	
	~~Phone~~	Gunshot
	Bottle ←——————→ Bottle	

Note: Struck-through words indicate absent elements in an alarm-answer pair as the result of inversion. The two-way arrow marks the double displacement of Renault's act in discarding the bottle of Vichy water.

thread of romance, so too these sound motifs might recur to draw similar narrative associations.

For instance, whistles and gunshots are two sounds fraught with special significance in *Casablanca*. These sounds are originally paired in the segment of the opening prologue involving "rounding up the usual suspects": the police whistle shrieks, the resistance fighter is shot. Chion emphasizes the importance of the "only three noticeable sound effects— . . . whistle, . . . gunshot, and [plane]"— early in the film. He understands these as sync points, sounds that "function like three points organizing everything else. The lush symphonic music prepares the police whistle, builds up to the gunshot (and stops momentarily to make the gun audible), and finally blends into the decreasing noise of the airplane, to give way to a dialogue scene with no music, at the city's airport." In this context the music is "a continuous ambient texture," while the sound effect is "the narrative event: the whistle is blown on a suspect, a man is gunned down, and an airplane lands in Casablanca" (2009, 76, 77).

Whistle and gunshot are thus formed as two sides of a menace: the one sounds the alarm, the other responds to the call and delivers. This is the first instantiation of a minimal syntagmatic unit (alarm-answer) that recurs at numerous points in the film (see table 3.1). Though this sequence sets up a definite linkage between whistle and gunshot, the pairing never again appears quite so baldly—or, rather, each recurrence entails a transformation of that initial coupling. Thus, the reports of Ugarte's gun as he tries to escape the police invert the original pair in sequence and meaning. The gunshots surprise because the alarm has not been sounded. The gunshots, however, are also impotent. The gun reports, the bullets perhaps even hit him, some of the policemen chase him, but none of it matters; Ugarte does not escape. The gunshots thus become an inversion of the original state. They stand in for, indeed become, the otherwise absent alarm, summoning the police, whose arrest of Ugarte in turn fills the gunshot role in the original syntagm.

When Renault closes the café at the insistence of Major Strasser, the German officer sent to capture Laszlo, the relationship is flipped again. Where Ugarte's gun had substituted for the absent whistle, here the whistle substitutes for the absent gun. Strasser warns vocally rather than through effect, and Renault's whistle delivers on that threat, announcing the closing of the café. When Ilsa pulls a gun on Rick, the transformation is again one of inversion, this time accompanied by pure absence: no gunshot, no whistle, though the menace is present in the form of the gun but also in the watchtower we see outside the window.

Likewise, the last meeting with Rick, Renault, Ilsa, and Laszlo in the closed café begins a long transformation that works by absenting and then restoring effects. Renault's knock on the door announces his presence but does not yet threaten. Arresting Laszlo, he clutches his whistle as if he is about to call in his men. Rick pulls his gun, keeping Renault's whistle silent. Whistle and gun retain their threat, but they do not yet sound. At this point the process begins to reverse. Renault calls Strasser, warning him of the plot, which leads to increasingly emphatic alarms: the buzzer to call his car, the car horn as he rushes to the airport. Like Renault earlier, Strasser picks up the phone to sound the alarm. But the alarm does not sound. Instead, Strasser and Rick exchange gunshots, and Strasser falls; the sudden presence of that sound eliminates both the menace and the alarm. An inverted coda of sorts starts from this point. The shots call the policemen to the scene, but Strasser's death has released Renault from his burden: he is free to decide his course. Rather than delivering (that is, arresting Rick), he releases him. As the policemen remove Strasser's body, Renault throws the bottle of Vichy water away. The ringing sound of the bottle hitting the trashcan and the musical stinger that accompanies it in this interpretation become a final, emphatic displacement of the whistle that never sounded, but it is also the sound of Renault's delivery. Displaced alarm, it also serves as answer, as present resolution of Renault's conflict.

The transformations of the flashback are even more complicated than those of the ending. There are two pairs of paired transformations. The first is centered around the loudspeaker and sounds of the German army. The loudspeaker, without underscoring, brings bad news of the collapse of the French front, which is followed by images of German troops advancing, underscored, as noted above, by violently dissonant music hardly distinguishable from the mechanical sound of trucks, tanks, and planes that also fills the sound track. Here, the loudspeaker takes the place of the alarm and the sound accompanying the German troops, the answer. Yet in both cases, the threat remains at a distance: the voice speaks French, and the troops are still far from Paris. In the second, the threat is imminent. The loudspeaker, also without underscoring, again sounds the alarm, but this time in German, and the answer is rendered more literally like gunshot in the muffled sound of the cannons. Taken as a pair, these two sets of transformations also follow the same organization on a higher level: the first warns of an impending threat, the second stands on the cusp of the fall of Paris.

The final two transformations in the flashback occur at the end. First, a single cannon blast is heard just before Ilsa and Rick kiss "for the last time." This is followed immediately by the champagne glass being knocked over, an action emphasized by a sharp stinger. Here the cannon blast warns of the separation, and the glass delivers, since this is Rick's last glimpse of Ilsa until she turns up in Casablanca. (It is worth noting that a second tipped glass occurs immediately after the end of the flashback, bringing Sam's playing of "As Time Goes By" to an end and seemingly conjuring up the late-night return of Ilsa to the café.) Second, on the platform, we hear the whistle of the conductor and then of the train as it pulls away from the station, with the pistons firing as the engine wheels turn sounding very much like the cannon fire heard earlier. Here, the whistle warns of the departure, and the sound of the train delivers. As above, these two transformations are also organized as a pair on a higher level: the "last kiss" warns of separation, while the train ensures the final parting that places Rick in the throes of despair. Then, too, these larger pairs are also organized as a pair: the loudspeaker/German pair warns, the "last kiss" / train pair ends the romance as the music that had accompanied most of the flashback dissolves into the disenchanting sound effect of the departing train.

The structure of the sound track on which these transformations track, produce, and reproduce narrative movement is ensured by what is held invariant, namely, the sounds themselves. For instance, to return to the gunshots again, the one in the prologue that kills the resistance fighter is answered by Rick's at the end that kills Strasser. (The structural parallel would have been even more pronounced had Rick simply killed Strasser, as in the original screenplay, rather than shooting him as Strasser turns his pistol and fires on Rick, as the Hays Code required.) Between these two gunshots are the ineffective ones fired by Ugarte as he tries to evade capture and the sounds of the cannons in the flashback.

More important, however, is the sound of an airplane, which is likewise heard four times: (1) in the prologue, when the plane, even though German, as it turns out, is represented as embodying the refugees' desire to escape; (2) late in the first evening, as Rick and Renault talk outside the café ("the plane to Lisbon"), when Ilsa and Laszlo are first mentioned; (3) during the flashback, when planes of the Luftwaffe are shown as part of the German advance; and (4) at the end, when the propeller sound, as if on cue, marks the end of Ilsa and Rick's final conversation. (Here, in a parallel with the train station, that train and this plane present two antithetical takes on parting. The difference is underscored by the sound track, which isolates the train sound, presenting it only once, whereas the plane sound returns at important narrative junctures.) Thus, with the dramatic certainty of tonal cadences, these effects accents—alarms/shots and plane noise—remind us of beginnings while also bringing action to a close. Each begins in the prologue and returns at the end with distinct moments of medial punctuation in the film—the broadest sweep of audiovisual phrasing in the film.

Large-scale accents not accounted for by effects are cleanly managed by music. The most important of these are the half-music, half-effects stinger chord, discussed above, that registers the traumatic shock of recognition, and Sam's foregrounded diegetic performances near the beginning, which find their counterpart on the second evening in the battle of anthems. The partitioning of music is even starker than the three days of the plot design. The film's most striking single sound moment—the audio dissolve that shifts Sam's coerced performance of "As Time Goes By" into the nondiegetic dialogue underscoring—is the small-scale instantiation of an audio dissolve that covers the entire film and uses this famous moment as its fulcrum. With allowance for the battle of anthems and the nondiegetic music of the main-title sequence and prologue, the first twenty-seven minutes have only diegetic music, the remaining seventy-four only nondiegetic music. Only "As Time Goes By" and the national anthems pass the barrier.[17]

Finally, then, the complex design of the sound track in *Casablanca* combines a massive, middleground audio dissolve in the music (as just described) with a constant background of dialogue and the large, structuring articulators of sound effects. A large-scale progression, a teleology, a *grande ligne* (after Boulanger) or *Urlinie* (after Schenker), if you will, overlaps the gunshots (a resistance fighter dies, but later the villain, Strasser, dies), the whistles (warning when sounded but eventually falling silent), the airplane sounds (the forlorn hope of refugees with the flight that brings the Nazis to Casablanca turns later to an active decision to resist, as Ilsa and Laszlo escape and Rick and Renault leave), and the effects-like stingers (shock recognition turning first to Rick's determined anger but finally to Ilsa's determination and his sense of danger).

Conclusion

In this account, we have mostly detached the film from its history in order to examine its textual effects, whatever the intention might have been during production. In other words, we have essentially isolated the film and its sound track as a textual (discursive) system. At first glance, such patterning might seem remarkable, incredible, even fantastic, suiting the commonly held but "romantic notion that this film was almost magically put together, as if it practically dictated its own shape through a kind of organic growth" (Telotte 1993, 62)—an idea encouraged by one of the film's principal screenwriters, Howard Koch (Harmetz 2002, 13).[18] No doubt at least some of what we note was accidental, but it is more likely, given the efficiencies of studio production by the early 1940s, that the strong parallelisms in this film—especially the parallel scenes, which Steiner, with his sharp eye and ear, then enhanced—arose in large part as the work of a production staff of experienced professionals who were trying to wrest order from chaos, to make *any* sense they could of a material they couldn't hope to control through subtlety and careful planning, given the pressure of meeting a tight production schedule with a constantly changing script.[19] As J. P. Telotte says, in his praise of Aljean Harmetz's account of the production, the case of *Casablanca* demonstrates "how the studio system in its most productive period worked, and how, almost in spite of the sort of assembly-line principle that guided much of its operations, it could consistently produce meaningful and enduring works" (1993, 62). In chapter 4, we will see that, even when speaking of the details of a single two-minute scene, the same can be said to be true.

4   Music and Utopia: A Reading of the Reunion Scene

David Neumeyer and James Buhler

Production for *Casablanca* finished on 3 August 1942, and the film editor finished his postproduction tasks by the end of the month. Max Steiner had already been assigned in July to write the underscore. He complained about using "As Time Goes By" sometime in August, but the film was still ready for its New York premiere on Thanksgiving Day.[1]

On 2 September the film's producer, Hal Wallis, wrote a detailed set of cutting notes about music placements to the music department's director, Leo Forbstein. Among his comments was the following for the scene that leads to the reunion meeting of Rick and Ilsa:

> Start the piano as Ilsa and Laszlo come in the door. You can stop the piano playing at the table with Ilsa when Renault brings Strasser over to the table. Then don't start the music again until Sam introduces the guitar player. When Ilsa calls Sam over to play, let that go on just as it is until the scene is interrupted by Renault coming back, saying: "Oh, you have already met Rick." Now, at that point, when Rick and Ilsa exchange glances, on the first of their close-ups, start an orchestration using "As Time Goes By." And *score* the scene. Let Steiner do this. And carry this until right through the Exterior until the lights go out. (quoted in Behlmer 1985, 216; emphasis in original)[2]

And that is exactly what happens.

The Reunion Scene

The reading in this chapter consists of a very detailed description of action, image, and sound in the reunion scene, with particular attention to the stinger chord that signals the fraught nature of Rick and Ilsa's reunion. "Stinger" is a venerable industry term for a sudden chordal accent. Often a single chord but sometimes two or three and perhaps including a brief melodic figure, the "stinger" might be best described as a kind of "sforzando gesture." To link this particular chord to the narrative situation, we will call it the "gaze sonority." Our discussion will include specific attention to the mechanics of the music's design, the habits of Steiner's underscoring practice, and the treatment of diegetic and nondiegetic space.

The reunion scene begins near the end of the first evening at Rick's Café Américain, an evening that spans nearly thirty minutes of film duration and is apparently chronologically continuous. This first act of the film nevertheless feels both compact and heterogeneous as performances and conversations alternate and we are introduced to a variety of characters. All of this activity is interrupted at one point by a gunfight and arrest (see table 4.1 for a summary of the events and music).[3]

The arrival of Ilsa and Laszlo at the café (just after 25:00) takes place shortly after the dramatic arrest of Ugarte. Martin Marks notes that the couple's entrance coincides with Sam "playing a favorite sentimental waltz of the thirties, 'Parlez-moi d'amour,' . . . a poignant change of mood (it follows a breezy rendition of 'Heaven Can Wait') and [one that] brings to mind thoughts of Paris and romance in preparation for the flashback scenes to come" (2000, 174). Only when Laszlo leaves the table to find his contact in the Resistance (at about 31:00) does Ilsa ask to speak with the "piano player," and Sam dutifully appears, pushing instrument and bench ahead of him. After their famous exchange over "As Time Goes By," Sam begins singing, and Rick emerges from the casino room. Once the gaze sonority sounds, the underscore runs continuously through Ilsa and Laszlo's departure and a final pan up to a darkened café sign—a nice symmetry, as we had last seen this sign, brightly lit, much earlier, as the evening started. Then, it was a sound advance, but here, it is an almost gratuitous moment of doom, lingering on a shot of Renault smoking, his thoughtful, almost scowling look timed to a prominent shift from a D♭ major to a D♭ minor triad. If the first appearance of the café sign promised a pleasant evening of entertainment, Renault's stare (he is watching the taxi that has just departed with Ilsa and Laszlo) reminds us that trouble is still ahead in the coming day.

The high point of the reunion scene in fact occurs near its beginning, a climax that has been prepared in stages, beginning with Ilsa and Laszlo's entrance into the café. The conversations that follow are little different from those we have already heard from everyone else: comments on their European past, refugee status, paying for exit visas. Even Ilsa's asking for the piano player is hardly out of character, since performances by Sam or the band have been a constant throughout the evening. Nor is the close miking that foregrounds Sam unusual— it matches the image, after all, though it would perhaps be more typical of the style to favor Ilsa, since she is the more central character (see figure 4.1 for the three microphone positions during the reunion scene). Only when Ilsa contradicts Sam with "You used to be a much better liar" does the mood shift. There is clearly a mystery behind this interaction, and it involves not only this beautiful woman and the piano player but also Rick (Sam's all-too-obvious reason for lying is to protect Rick). The link somehow is the song she insists that Sam play and sing, a point amply confirmed by the very long close-up of Ilsa as he complies and

Table 4.1. *Casablanca,* summary of the first evening in Rick's Café Américain, 6:25–36:00

THAT EVENING AT RICK'S—RICK AND UGARTE
EXTERIOR: RICK'S CAFÉ—NIGHT

	6:29: music in with shot of sign outside café		
1	[Song 1] "It Had to Be You" (Gus Kahn, Isham Jones)	Background/visual vocal: Dooley Wilson	F

INTERIOR: RICK'S CAFÉ—MAIN ROOM—NIGHT

2	Connects to [song 2] "Shine" (Lew Brown, Ford Dabney, Cecil Mack)	Visual vocal: Dooley Wilson; then instrumental offscreen	E♭
	8:20: music fades awkwardly just after cut to casino room		

INTERIOR: RICK'S CAFÉ—GAMBLING ROOM—NIGHT

	9:12: music in with opening of casino door		
3	[Song 3] "Crazy Rhythm" (Joseph Meyers, Roger Wolfe Kahn, Irving Caesar)	Offscreen instrumental	E♭
	10:00: music goes out with closing of casino door		

BACK IN THE CAFÉ: RICK, YVONNE, SACHA—RICK TALKS TO RENAULT OUTSIDE
INTERIOR: RICK'S CAFÉ—MAIN ROOM—NIGHT

	12:42: music in as a sound advance just before cut to main room		
4	[Song 4] "Knock on Wood" (M. K. Jerome, Jack Scholl)	Visual vocal: Dooley Wilson	F
5	Connects to [song 5] "The Very Thought of You" (Ray Noble)	Visual instrumental, background instrumental	A♭

EXTERIOR: RICK'S CAFÉ—NIGHT

	17:10: music out		
	17:20: music in with cut inside		

INTERIOR: RICK'S CAFÉ—MAIN ROOM—NIGHT

6	[Song 6] "Baby Face" (Benning Davis, Harry Alest)	Visual instrumental, background instrumental	C

INTERIOR: RICK'S CAFÉ—OFFICE—NIGHT

	18:16: music goes out with office door closing		

STRASSER ARRIVES—UGARTE IS ARRESTED—STRASSER INTERVIEWS RICK
INTERIOR: RICK'S CAFÉ—MAIN ROOM—NIGHT

	20:32: music in as office door is opened; effect is of a sound advance		
7	[Song 7] "I'm Just Wild about Harry" (Noble Sissle, Eubie Blake)	Background instrumental, visual instrumental	F

INTERIOR: RICK'S CAFÉ—GAMBLING ROOM—NIGHT

22:18: music out under gunshots

INTERIOR: RICK'S CAFÉ—MAIN ROOM—NIGHT

22:45: music in when Rick tells Sam to start playing again

| 8 | [Song 8] "Heaven Can Wait" (Eddie DeLange, Jimmy Van Heusen) | Visual instrumental, background instrumental | E♭ |

23:55: music goes out as band finishes number

ILSA AND LASZLO ARRIVE

25:18: music in with the cut: the couple walks into the café

| 9 | [Song 9] "Speak to Me of Love" ("Parlez moi d'amour" by Jean Lenoir) | Visual instrumental, background instrumental | G |
| 10 | Connects to [song 10] "Love for Sale" (Cole Porter) | Background instrumental | E♭ |

27:55: music out as Strasser comes to their table

28:52: applause offscreen; music in with cut to singer 28:59

| 11 | [Song 11] "Tango delle Rose" (F. Schreier, A. Bottro, and Carol Raven) | Visual vocal, background vocal: Corinna Mae | e/E |

30:48: music out with end of song

31:34: music in when Ilsa asks Sam to play

| 12 | [Song 12] "Avalon" (Al Jolson, Vincent Rose, and B. G. De Sylva) | Visual instrumental | G |

32:04: music out when Sam turns to speak to her

32:30: music in when Ilsa hums/sings

| 13 | [Song 13] "As Time Goes By" (Herman Hupfeld) | Visual vocal (Ingrid Bergman, Dooley Wilson) | D♭ |
| Reel 4,7 | Connects to underscore (sketches = 2 34+, 33:32–36:06 = 2:35 | Cue begins in d, ends firmly in D♭/d♭ | d/D♭ |

EXTERIOR: RICK'S CAFÉ—NIGHT

36:06: music out with end of scene

Source: Information from Marks (2000); studio cue sheet; published scripts; and Max Steiner's sketches (Max Steiner Collection, Brigham Young University). Timings from DVD.

Column 1: Scene label from script; song number

Column 2: Song titles, entrance/exit and events at those moments

Column 3: Status of the performance: "visual" = onscreen; "background" = offscreen

Column 4: Key: uppercase = major; lowercase = minor

performs, almost entirely offscreen, the first half of the chorus from "As Time Goes By." The sound track subtly emphasizes this difference (albeit by coincidence more than design, undoubtedly). Before he sings, Sam's voice is direct recorded (not dubbed), and so is the piano playing (one can easily recognize that the position of the piano is offscreen by its subdued resonance: it sounds exactly like a piano being played behind another piano).[4] But when Sam starts singing, the sound changes. The performance was prerecorded with proper studio miking and then filmed to playback. The sound, dubbed in, amplifies the sense of detachment and bemusement in Ilsa's face during the long close-up. It was probably to ease this transition from direct recording on the set to studio recording that prompted the slightly closer miking of Sam throughout the sequence, but it produces a nice expressive effect in that it seems to attribute the intimacy and proximity of the sound increasingly to Ilsa's own aural perspective.

Indeed, Ilsa's gaze increasingly turns inward as she listens, which transforms Sam's performance and Ilsa's hearing into an instance of what narratologists call internal focalization (Bal 2009; Verstraten 2009). We see Ilsa hearing, and we see the intensity of her reaction, even if the exact contours of this feeling remain uncertain. Seeing her listen and recognizing the intimacy of the sound encourage us to intensify our own listening, to plumb this music for the emotions that she is apparently finding in it. As Peter Franklin writes of this shot, Ilsa "hears and sees the internal re-run of a moving complex of past experiences and emotions of whose nature we are as yet unaware" (2011, 118). The effect of all this is that the long-held shot of Ilsa's inward gaze seems set up as preparation for an eyeline match. We await the cut that will show what she sees and that will turn the implicit internal focalization of this hearing into an explicit internal focalization of her whole perspective. Rick's flashback in the café later on will follow precisely this procedure, giving us the explicit stylized signs in both image and sound that allow us to confirm the crossing to the explicit internal focalization of the flashback itself. In the case of Ilsa and Sam, the shot (presumably of some memory) that would complete the eyeline match to her interior gaze never comes. Instead, it is the exterior motivation for that memory, the body of Rick himself, in the present, that fills the direction of her gaze. Her recollection of Paris, we eventually learn, requires "As Time Goes By."

The song provides not only diegetic music for the reunion scene but also, as we shall explain below, the overall design of the underscore. In its published, sheet-music form, "As Time Goes By" follows the familiar verse-chorus design of the popular music of the time. A four-bar introduction is followed by a twelve-bar verse that uses diatonic cycle-of-fifths figures circling about the dominant. There is no melodic or motivic connection to the chorus that follows, whose design is the typical thirty-two-bar AABA. The first A closes with an imperfect authentic cadence on the tonic (by far the cadence heard most often in the film), the second A has a perfect authentic cadence, and the bridge turns toward the subdominant before eventually settling on the dominant to lead into the reprise of A, whose closing cadence changes the ending to a rising $\hat{3}$–$\hat{5}$–$\hat{5}$–$\hat{8}$ for the final iteration of the title words. The bridge and reprise appear only once in the film, during the

Figure 4.1, a–c.
Casablanca,
microphone positions
during the reunion
scene: (a) foreground,
over Sam and the
piano; (b) background,
behind the arch;
(c) over the table.
Screen stills.

Table 4.2. *Casablanca*, uses of "As Time Goes By"

Reel/no./title	Medley position	Music in (DVD timing)	Action	Song source (chorus)
REEL 4				
14. ATGB		32:29	Ilsa sings	Bars 1–2
15. "		32:37	Sam plays	Bars 1–2
16. "		32:45	Sam sings	Bars 1–16
17. "		33:31; 33:37	Cue 4,7 (reunion)	Bars 1–8, then 1–3 (waltz version), intervening passage, then 1–8
REEL 5				
19. Medley	a. ATGB	38:16	Rick tells Sam to play it	Bars 1–12
	f. ATGB	40:15	Rick and Ilsa talk ("penny for your thoughts")	Bars 1–3, brief intervening passage, then bar 3?, bar 4
20. Medley	a. ATGB	41:13	Kiss	Bars 1–2
	d. ATGB	42:15	Sam sings in La belle Aurore	Bars 17–32 with altered melodic line in 17–21 and ^5 rather than ^8 in bar 32. Combined with item 16 above, this makes a complete "consecutive" performance of the chorus
21. Medley	a. ATGB	43:13	They talk in La belle Aurore	Bars 1–3 (development)
	e. ATGB		Kiss, with sound of German guns in the distance	Bars 1–5 (waltz)
	h. ATGB	47:15	Letter	Bars 1–8 with substantial development, some it the waltz version
	i. ATGB	47:51	Sam is singing as flashback ends	Bars 1–2, beat 1 (cut off)
REEL 6				
22. Medley	b. ATGB	48:45	In "first confrontation scene"	Bars 1–8 (waltz)
	g. ATGB	50:46	End of "first confrontation scene" (as Ilsa leaves)	Bars 1–2

REEL 7				
26. ATGB		1:07:50	Second evening at Rick's Café; Rick tells Sam to play	Bars 1–5
REEL 8				
30. Medley	a. ATGB	1:16:15	Laszlo and Ilsa talk; he reports on Rick's refusal to sell the exit visas	Bars 1–2
31. Medley	a. ATGB	1:17:08	Laszlo and Ilsa talk; he asks her about Paris	Bars 1–3
REEL 9				
32. Medley	d. ATGB	1:18:40	As Ilsa leaves the hotel	Bars 1–2
33. Medley	c. ATGB	1:21:30	Second confrontation scene; gun	Bars 1–3
	e. ATGB	1:22:29	She breaks down	Bars 1–8 (waltz)
34. Medley	a. ATGB	1:24:55	End of scene: Ilsa says she won't leave Rick	Bars 1–8
	d. ATGB	1:26:38	As Rick tells Carl to take Ilsa home	Bars 1–3
REEL 10				
37. ATGB		1:28:45	After Laszlo is arrested	Bars 1–3
38. Medley	b. ATGB	1:32:07	Closed sign on café door	Bars 1–3
39. Medley	b. ATGB	1:33:12	As Laszlo and Ilsa arrive	Bars 1–8
40. Medley	a. ATGB	1:34:14	Rick with gun	Bars 1–3
REEL 11				
41. Medley	a. ATGB	1:36:15	Rick says "Mr. and Mrs. Victor Laszlo"	Bars 1–8 (expanded); 1–8 (waltz)
	e. ATGB	1:39:09	As Laszlo and Ilsa turn away to walk to plane	Bars 1–3
	h. ATGB	1:40:40	Above "Deutschland" quote	Bar 5

Notes: Titles from studio cue sheet (corrected), with entry point (DVD timing), action, and material used from the song.

"Medley" is used in the studio cue sheet to refer to a continuous cue with inserted quotations.

ATGB = "As Time Goes By"

Column 1: Numbers are cue numbers from studio cue sheet; titles are also from the cue sheet.

Column 2: The lowercase letter indicates position in the series of themes cited in that medley.

flashback.[5] The verse is not used at all (see table 4.2 for a list of all the appearances of "As Time Goes By").

The reunion scene is typical of Steiner's dialogue underscoring practice in its complexity, its close alliance with screen action, and its fluid treatment of devices, gestures, and melodic quotation. To summarize the musical elements that were described in much greater detail in our first reading (from chapter 3): in little more than two and a half minutes, the music cycles through the following in a shape that roughly suggests the structure of the chorus from "As Time Goes By":[6]

Scene, part 1: as if A (stating the theme phrase) (0:05–0:51)[7]
1. Gaze sonority (to 0:05½) as introduction.
2. Main theme phrase of "As Time Goes By" played over the gaze sonority, which is held until a three-chord cadence at 0:30–0:36. (The final chord is held to 0:42¾, its bass note eight seconds beyond that.)

Scene, part 2: as if A' (repeating the theme phrase) (0:51–1:21)
3. Fragments of "As Time Goes By" (0:51–1:21), first with a harmonically unstable waltz accompaniment (0:51–1:00), then a new stinger chord (at 1:00), against which we hear "Deutschland über alles" in a minor key.

Scene, part 3: as if B (the bridge should bring in something different) (1:21–before 1:45)
4. Neutral, nonthematic music used as an "unhurried hurry" to accompany movement of characters onscreen (1:21–1:45). ("Hurry" was a term applied in nineteenth-century theatrical contexts—and carried over into the silent cinema—for music that signaled or accompanied action and movement.)

Scene, part 4: as if A" (reprise of the theme phrase) (1:45–the end)
5. Fragments of "As Time Goes By" in three different guises (1:45–2:34⅔), first with slow-moving mid- or lower-range chords (at 1:45) derived from the earlier three-chord cadence, then, after 2:03, an even slower-moving derivative that is rhythmically flattened out (that is, all chords are now of the same duration, except the last, which is sustained), and from 2:19 to the end, another rhythmically flat, three-chord series, now as a wedge. (The bass moves downward stepwise, but the upper voices, which are still quoting "As Time Goes By," ascend, also stepwise.)

In our reading below, the overlay of the chorus design is seen as reflecting the subterranean structuring effect of the diegetic world brought about by discursive pressure from the nondiegetic space, which seems to reflect the tension between the utopian ideal embodied by a complete performance of the song and the barriers to that realization as the music instead follows the conversational drift. The inability of the music in the scene to maintain a consistent tonal level and coherent thematic organization in this sense is a by-product of the fluctuating status of the relationship between Ilsa and Rick and the peculiar conversational situation they find themselves confronting, in which they are forced to speak in a kind of veiled code.

The tonal design of the cue is also divided based on two performances, not one. When Steiner became involved in postproduction, the interaction between Ilsa and Sam had already been filmed and recorded. It had also been tightened up somewhat. Among the many image and sound editing notes written by the producer, Hal Wallis, are these: "Lose the long shot of the waiter bringing the bottle and glasses. Cut to Bergman right on her line, 'Ask the piano player to come over.' . . . Take out that long look of Bergman looking around before she says, 'Where is Rick?'" (Harmetz 2002, 261). The editing worked out in such a way that we get an awkward "preview" of Bergman's long close-up: there was apparently no other footage to drop in at that moment. It is probably coincidental that the first of the "old songs" Sam plays is in G major, but he plays and sings "As Time Goes By" in D♭, a tritone away—which we might take as a symbol of his discomposure.[8] Whether or not that's the case, Steiner does not take advantage of it in the subsequent underscore. Instead, he builds the cue from a much more salient opposition: Ilsa's wordless singing in F, Sam's singing in D♭. It is this opposition—a kind of abstract double tonic—that hovers over the cue and marks the poles of the scene's emotional movement.

The Reunion Scene: Agents, Motivation, Narrative, Music

The meeting of Sam and Ilsa is the introductory segment of the reunion scene. Sam then sings "As Time Goes By" for Ilsa, and Rick emerges from the casino room, pausing briefly to survey the café's main room. Something seems to disturb him, and he quickly moves forward and out of the frame. The next shot picks up Rick as he rushes toward Sam. Rick's image fills up the frame faster than the camera can dolly back, and the sound of his footfalls also rises in volume as he approaches the microphone (which, recall, is placed over the piano). Just as he seems ready to burst out of the frame again, he stops at the piano, and Sam also ceases playing. Crossly, Rick rebukes the musician: "Sam, I thought I told you never to play . . ." trailing off before stating the name of the song or even supplying a pronoun that would make the thought into a grammatical utterance. What seems to be a slightly mistimed acting cue—Rick's line trails off before Sam makes the gesture toward Ilsa that would have naturally interrupted Rick's line— has the expressive effect here of emphasizing the missing song title, as though the song is so traumatic that the very thought of it fractures his thinking. Sam gestures toward Ilsa, and Rick's eyes follow. The next shot is motivated by an eyeline match, a close-up of Ilsa, tears welling in her eyes and looking up to meet Rick's gaze—from the same camera position, however, that we had seen her previously listening to Sam (see figure 4.2a). The effect is a little uncanny, as though he was simply stepping into a position that had been prepared for him all along—the completion of the internal focalization discussed above. As we will see, the music in the reunion scene does something similar to the extent that we attribute it to

Figure 4.2, a–b. Interlocking gazes: matched close-ups of Rick and Ilsa. Note the asymmetry of the eyeline axis if we presume that Rick and Ilsa are looking at each other. Ilsa is presented more or less along Rick's axis of vision, but the image of Rick is much farther removed from Ilsa's axis. Screen stills.

Figure 4.3. *Casablanca,* music for the reunion scene (cue 4,7), two-stave reduction, part 1; "As Time Goes By," bars 1–8. Timings are from Max Steiner's sketches. Music reproduced by permission of Alfred Publishing Co., Inc. *Casablanca* by Max Steiner. © 1942 (Renewed) WB MUSIC CORP. All Rights Reserved. For Europe: Warner/ Chappell North America Ltd, London W8 5DA; reproduced by permission of Faber Music Ltd; all rights reserved.

Rick, which implies that he has somehow overheard Ilsa and Sam's musical exchange.[9]

With the close-up of Ilsa cued from the eyeline match, the nondiegetic orchestra erupts with the famous stinger chord, our gaze sonority (see figure 4.3, m. 1). As with Sam's performance, direct recording is displaced by recorded cue. The gaze sonority, held for an astounding thirty seconds, first alone and then with the opening tune of "As Time Goes By" unfolding in F major over the ambiguous harmony, quivers with the dissonant shock of recognition as their gazes lock. The music for a moment seems to put this exchange of looks into temporal parentheses, where the passing of time slows almost to a halt. Although synchronized with the close-up of Ilsa and thus plausibly expressing the feeling of this vision (ostensibly Rick's shock), the chord extends beyond the close-up to the reverse shot of Rick, motivated from Ilsa's point of view but not quite a match to her axis of vision (see figure 4.2b).

With the reverse shot, the music nevertheless loses secure anchorage in Rick much the way the sonority appears through its duration to float free of any definite tonal function (the question of its tonal function will be considered below). Oblivious to its tonal impulses, the chord is more a sonority than a functional harmonic entity, less dissonance in need of a resolution than a yearning that stops even musical time. For a moment it is as though the diegetic world has been canceled, and in this interval outside of time another space is opened up, cre-

Music and Utopia 129

ated, enveloping Rick and Ilsa in their own sonic shell every bit as much as the exchange of close-ups uses framing to exclude the world from their images. Outside the unfolding of musical time, the chord nevertheless seethes with a desire that it seemingly cannot discharge: it remains a charged sonority, defying the gravitational pull of tonal function. The sonority becomes, in other words, the audible symbol of the connection, or force of attraction, between them. The status of this audible gaze is even more ambiguous than the cinematic one, seeming to spring from the very interlocking of gazes rather than from any particular point of view.

The remainder of the scene is reaction—a long, slow denouement. The most significant narrative movement involves Renault's attempts to sort out the mystery. If we assume that the overriding key of the reunion scene cue ought to have been D♭, the key in which Sam sings the tune, then Rick's shock of recognition is well reflected by the abrupt shift of the gaze sonority up a half step. When the chord sounds, F in the double-tonic complex is amplified by the D minor grounding of the harmony (the notes of the chord are also scale degrees $\hat{6}$ up through $\hat{4}$ of an F major scale). As we note below, the structure of the chord in F suggests C^{13} with a missing root and a diatonic eleventh substituted for the more typical ♯11. This omission of the root, however, is crucial to its ambiguity, as it deprives the sonority of any possibility of clear functionality. Through parts 1 and 2 of the scene, the double-tonic complex, then, is represented by F major and D minor, the latter of which both substitutes for D♭ major as a psychic displacement and associates itself more easily with F major, the key Ilsa had used to introduce the song. It is only over the course of the scene that the arousal gradually subsides, the significant moment being Rick's deflation after Ilsa and Laszlo leave, when Rick slumps down into a chair while the music misses its proper D minor[7] chord by a whole step, allowing D♭ to reassert itself for the conclusion of the cue.[10]

Sam witnesses the encounter between Ilsa and Rick, of course, but his presence is marginalized. The tight shot / reverse shot close-ups of Rick and Ilsa exclude him, along with much of the rest of the diegetic world (note the blurred backgrounds behind both), just as the nondiegetic score similarly displaces the diegetic music (and sound) associated with Sam and the café. When Sam tries to extricate himself and the piano from the scene as unobtrusively as he can, he interposes himself briefly between Rick and Ilsa (see figure 4.4). This intrusion of the diegetic world into the nondiegetic space is also marked by the mingling of direct and studio-recorded sound tracks at this moment. We hear sounds of the piano or bench as Sam gathers them to leave (remember that the microphone is immediately overhead [figure 4.1a]) and also an emphatic marking in the underscore. Steiner "catches" the momentary disruption of the gaze: as Sam crosses between Rick and Ilsa, the music becomes motivically active, engendering a statement of "As Time Goes By" in F over the ambiguous gaze sonority. Steiner thus subtly draws attention to Sam as a highly problematic figure, one who plays the structural role of a catalyst indispensable to moving the action (and music) forward, but one who, when all is said and done, remains a marginal figure in the plot. As we shall see below, however, he is the central figure in the establishment of the "personal utopia" that envelops Rick and Ilsa in this scene. It is his singing,

Figure 4.4. *Casablanca,* reunion scene. Sam is caught between Rick and Ilsa. Screen still.

and not the gaze sonority, that signifies this utopia; the gaze sonority is in fact the singing's semiotic inversion, its dystopian double.

On Sam's departure, the melody moves forward, following the contour of "As Time Goes By" even after the arrival of Renault and Laszlo. (Their arrival is the third set of male footfalls, to parallel the earlier ones of Sam and then Rick. Each time, the footfalls announce the presence of new characters, as well as an important turn in the action.) With Renault's introduction of Ilsa to Rick, the note that concludes the third statement of the motive is lengthened (bars 4–5 of figure 4.3). Musical unfolding once again briefly stops, leaving nothing sounding but the gaze sonority. Thus far, Ilsa and Rick have not taken their eyes off each other, despite the arrival of the two men, but with the formal introduction of Laszlo, the diegetic world fully intrudes, and the gaze sonority associated with it slowly dissipates. Ilsa breaks the gaze first, since she needs to acknowledge and introduce Laszlo, and Rick soon follows. The breakdown of their intimate nondiegetic space is made concrete in the score: the tonally ambiguous gaze sonority is first reorganized into a tonally intelligible ii^7 over tonic pedal (bar 6 in figure 4.3).

After this, and coinciding with talk among the men, functional harmony takes over, leading to a half cadence on A, a definite affirmation of the bass note in the gaze sonority as the tonic of D minor. Even here, though, there is a complication: a first-inversion triad on A♭ in bar 7. This chord is the first hint of an active tension between D minor and D♭ major; the $A♭^6$ here substitutes for an expected diatonic A minor^6 (see again figure 4.3). This substitution has all the hallmarks of keyboard improvisation, of composing at the piano, which was known to be Steiner's standard mode of working.[11] In this passage, the ancient chaconne-bass descent steps down diatonically from D to A in the bass, but instead of a conventional chord above C, he writes a chromatic chord.[12] This A♭ triad is much less some deeply complex functional substitute and much more a "similar" chord that surprises but also lies well under the fingers and is easily shifted to—perhaps why David Lewin, in his *Generalized Musical Intervals and Transformations,* gave the transformation involved the label SLIDE (1987, 178). The alteration also happens to fit nicely a small nuance in the dialogue, as Rick surprises Renault by saying he will join the group for a drink.

From this first instantiation of the abstract double-tonic complex F/D♭ flows the design of the materials in the rest of the cue. Steiner builds on it, producing an opposition between Rick and Ilsa's special musical space of D minor / F major and the flat keys. As we shall see, the latter eventually dissolve that space: at the tonal design level, the strong cadence to D♭ major at the end of the cue, which is also a major structural division of the film, is readily understood as a displacement of the key of D major, just as the A minor^6 chord was displaced by A♭^{6} near the beginning.

Up to the point the A major triad is reached at the end of the chaconne-bass descent, the tonal design hovered between D minor and F major, between the underlying implications of the harmony and the transposition level of "As Time Goes By." At this point the music pauses until Ilsa speaks again: "I wasn't sure you were the same." With these words—a direct reference to their past acquaintance—the second section begins a new statement of "As Time Goes By," now compressed into slow waltz time and accompanying Rick and Ilsa's talking with one another. This slow-waltz-time version of "As Time Goes By" has considerable significance later on, as Steiner uses restatements of it to mark strong moments of crisis in Rick and Ilsa's relationship: just before they separate in Paris (she already knows that her husband is alive and that she will abandon Rick—see no. 21e in table 4.2); then as Rick reads her letter before boarding the train (21h); at one point in the first confrontation scene (22); when she breaks down after threatening Rick with a gun (33e); and in the film's final minutes, when Rick reveals that Laszlo, not Rick himself, will accompany her on the plane to Lisbon (41a).

As Rick mentions the club La belle Aurore, the motive overshoots its mark: instead of the original C (figure 4.3, bar 3), the melody reaches D♭ on the downbeat of the final $\frac{3}{4}$ bar before 1:00 (see figure 4.5). Up to this moment, the connection between Rick and Ilsa—the gaze sonority and the "As Time Goes By" melody—anchored the music, giving it a kind of tonal coherence. Although ambiguous, the earlier music in the cue always seems sure of itself, its ambiguity calculated to seal a special nondiegetic space off from the rest of the diegetic world. Here, on the contrary, the music begins to wander and disintegrate; with it, the non-diegetic space that it had sustained begins to dissolve as well. The recollection of the last day in Paris—"Not an easy day to forget," Rick growls—imperils this nondiegetic space as the scene begins to mirror those earlier events. Ilsa cannot speak forthrightly, cannot tell her story to Rick, because others are present. As

Figure 4.5. *Casablanca*, music for the reunion scene, two-stave reduction, part 2; "As Time Goes By," bars 1–4 or 9–12? Timings are from Max Steiner's sketches. Music reproduced by permission of Alfred Publishing Co., Inc. *Casablanca* by Max Steiner. © 1942 (Renewed) WB MUSIC CORP. All Rights Reserved. For Europe: Warner/Chappell North America Ltd, London W8 5DA; reproduced by permission of Faber Music Ltd; all rights reserved.

in Paris, she must decide between the utopian nondiegetic space she shares with Rick and the realities of the diegetic world—between past and present—between "As Time Goes By" and more commonplace sounds. She again chooses, as she did before and as she must now, to live in the diegetic world, a decision Rick comprehends no more now than he did in Paris. The music explodes in an enigmatic diminished seventh chord on E♯ over an F♯ pedal at 1:00, enigmatic not because its tonal function is unclear (it is obviously vii°7 of the bass's F♯) but because the F♯ as a functional chord (much less a potential tonic) appears out of nowhere. Instead, this diminished seventh is another absolute sonority, a distorted mirror of the original stinger chord. Both operate extratonally, outside tonal progression, as enigmatic symbols, ciphers for what must remain unsaid. But whereas the gaze sonority creates a nondiegetic space, the harsh mirror chord sounds like a gaping wound—it breaches the illusion of that space, calls it into question.

A fragment of genuine counterpoint, highly dissonant and polytonal, prolongs the chord, reflecting a loss of connection, a deep divide, between Rick and Ilsa. Ilsa abandons the nondiegetic space for the diegetic, as her reference to the Germans marching into Paris summons up "Deutschland" (in G♯ minor), the first motivic intrusion into the nondiegetic space demarcated by "As Time Goes By" and the gaze sonority. Rick, on the contrary, struggles to hold on: the "As Time Goes By" motive, restored to its proper melodic level of F (= E♯ in relation to the bass note F♯) and rhythmically elongated to emphasize this pitch, is especially poignant, recalling the nondiegetic space as something already lost and not

Figure 4.6. *Casablanca,* music for the reunion scene, two-stave reduction, part 3. Timings are from Max Steiner's sketches. Music reproduced by permission of Alfred Publishing Co., Inc. *Casablanca* by Max Steiner. © 1942 (Renewed) WB MUSIC CORP. All Rights Reserved. For Europe: Warner/Chappell North America Ltd, London W8 5DA; reproduced by permission of Faber Music Ltd; all rights reserved.

to be recovered—at least not here. The prolongation of the mirror chord dams up tonal impulses, which are allowed to dissipate rather than being released, as they had been through the half cadence earlier in the scene. This time the music goes nowhere; it remains as cryptic as Ilsa's line "I put that dress away. When the Germans march out, I'll wear it again." (This passage, with its polytonal counterpoint between "Deutschland" and "As Time Goes By," appears again in the film, not, as one might expect, in the flashback, with its scenes of Paris, but at the airport, when Rick shoots Strasser and after Ilsa has left with Laszlo. That it reappears after Ilsa has departed adds credence to the idea that we should understand this music as being from Rick's point of view.)

Laszlo interrupts: "Ilsa, I don't wish to be the one to say it, but it's late." The next section of the underscore begins on his last three words, another abrupt change to a distinctly less committed, even motivically indifferent "neutral" music that vaguely follows the kinetic activity of the scene: the characters standing up and moving. Explicit reference to "As Time Goes By" disappears, although the initial five-note motive, echoed six seconds (two bars) later, does hint at the central motive (see figure 4.6). The music no longer directly sustains a nondiegetic space but remains in the sound track for continuity—the music cannot stop, because it has more work to do at the end of the scene—and perhaps to demonstrate that the shock continues to reverberate. Though no longer audible on the musical surface, "As Time Goes By" exerts a subterranean influence, as Rick and Ilsa continue to attract each other. A prolongation of an A♭–F complex from 1:21 to 1:35 moves to

Stinger chord/gaze   incomplete gaze sonority
sonority transposed
at T$_{-6}$

Figure 4.7. Derivation of the held chord at the
end of figure 4.3 from the stinger chord that starts
cue 4,7.

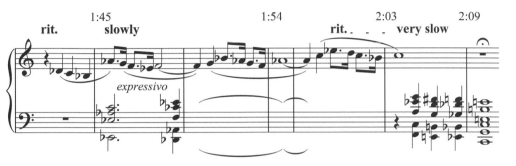

Figure 4.8. *Casablanca,* music for the reunion scene, two-stave reduction, part 4; "As Time Goes By," bars 1–4. Timings are from Max Steiner's sketches. Music reproduced by permission of Alfred Publishing Co., Inc. *Casablanca* by Max Steiner. © 1942 (Renewed) WB MUSIC CORP. All Rights Reserved. For Europe: Warner/Chappell North America Ltd, London W8 5DA; reproduced by permission of Faber Music Ltd; all rights reserved.

a transposed incomplete analogue of the gaze sonority at about 1:40 (final chord in figure 4.6; for the derivation, see figure 4.7). The structural bass likewise moves from A♭ at the beginning of the passage to B♭, which is precisely the motion of the structural bass in the bridge of "As Time Goes By" when the main key is that of the published song, E♭. At 1:45 (see figure 4.8), "As Time Goes By" does in fact return, and now it is in E♭. The nondiegetic space of the tune may have temporarily receded, but the underlying pattern of harmony suggests that the space itself still exists—or, perhaps, that Rick and Ilsa recognize there is unfinished business from their past to which they will soon need to attend.

When the incomplete gaze sonority (B♭–F♭–A♭–E♭) sounds, Rick again looks intently at Ilsa, reopening the nondiegetic space on the musical surface, but the space has lost some of the mysterious immediacy it had at the beginning of the scene. Transposed a tritone from E to B♭, the sonority here lacks not just the lower pedal and two pitches (D♭ and C♭) from the aggregate but, more immediately,

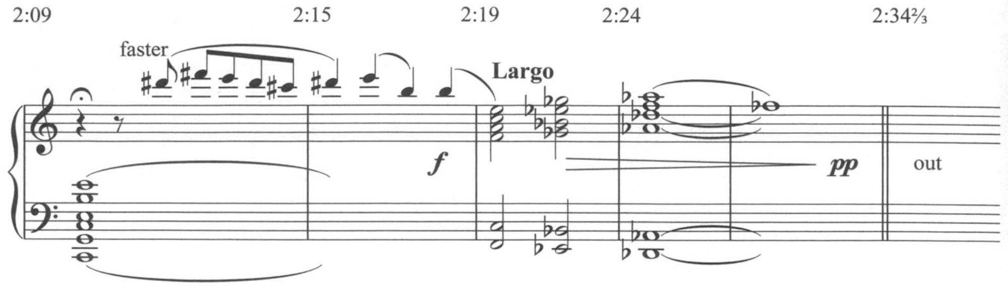

Figure 4.9. *Casablanca,* music for the reunion scene, two-stave reduction, part 5; "As Time Goes By," bars 5–8. Timings are from Max Steiner's sketches. Music reproduced by permission of Alfred Publishing Co., Inc. *Casablanca* by Max Steiner. © 1942 (Renewed) WB MUSIC CORP. All Rights Reserved. For Europe: Warner/Chappell North America Ltd, London W8 5DA; reproduced by permission of Faber Music Ltd; all rights reserved.

the orchestration and spacing that do so much to produce the distinctive aura of the gaze sonority. What remains, however, is hardly insignificant: a pair of fifths, separated by a minor seventh, with the lower one diminished. Recall that in the original sonority, as separated in two staves in Steiner's sketch, the lower part is a half-diminished seventh chord, the upper part a minor triad plus a perfect fifth below. Rick, for the moment, confronts the nondiegetic space alone, and the music perhaps reflects this through use of an incomplete sonority. But as Ilsa returns his gaze, the Db–C–Bb extended anacrusis to the "As Time Goes By" motive (*ritardando* before 1:45—see the beginning of figure 4.9) slyly completes a pitch-class collection (Ab–Bb–C–Db–Eb–Fb) that matches the contents of the gaze sonority in later scenes, where the equivalent of Cb is changed to C♮ (more on this below). The tone of the melody is detached, recalling the opening, but distantly, the intimate oboe having been replaced by the orchestral violins. The utopian nondiegetic space still exists, but Rick and Ilsa, looking at one another, are also gazing on that space from outside, as something irrevocable. Hence, the nostalgic tone, the feeling of lost plenitude captured by the fragmenting of the melody—the motives no longer flow into one another. Instead, the joints between the motives expand, isolating the individual motives, which dot the nondiegetic space as monuments to a past. That the space still belongs to Rick and Ilsa is apparent from the fact that the motivic entrances coincide with their dialogue: first motive at 1:45—Rick: "Any time"; second motive a bar later—Ilsa: "There's still nobody in the world who can play 'As Time Goes By' like Sam"; third motive the bar before 2:03—Rick: "Good night."

After the third statement of the motive, Ilsa and Laszlo exit. Even nostalgia is no longer sufficient to support the nondiegetic space; it collapses, and as Rick slumps down in his chair, a series of parallel minor ninth chords, dripping with portamento, mimics his descent (see the end of figure 4.8) to the rhythm of the words "as time goes by." A clearly audible swish (sliding shoes) provides a higher-register counterpoint as he shifts position to put his hands on the table.

The chords overlap the cut outside to Ilsa and Laszlo. After the E♭ minor^9 chord, the underscore lands on a C major^{maj7} chord (end of figure 4.8; also beginning of figure 4.9), yanking the music out of E♭. We hear a final set of footfalls as the two have a short exchange: Laszlo: "A very puzzling fellow, this Rick. What sort is he?" Ilsa: "Oh, I really can't say, though I saw him quite often in Paris." Ilsa's evasive response is undercut by a final statement of "As Time Goes By": the second phrase with its cadence. Now in E major but sounding over the prolonged C major^{maj7} chord, the motive sounds out of tune, ethereal, almost unreal. Its tonality and scoring isolate it from the preceding E♭, even though it is the formal completion of the song's A section. The joint has expanded too far and burst, the E major fragment being the last, displaced remnant of the nondiegetic space.

This last fragment, however, is unyielding; it resists further reduction. In an even more emphatic version of the cadence that closed part 1, the bass descends F–E♭–D♭, pulling the harmony decisively toward a close on D♭ (announced by an equally decisive car door shutting—this happens between the E♭ and D♭ chords), albeit not in a traditional functional progression such as IV–V–I but in a Hindemithian three-chord modal cadence, complete with parallel fifths reinforcing the chord roots in the bass.[13] The melody, however, remains stubbornly in E: D♭ has been imposed on recalcitrant material. On the one hand, a return to D♭, the key of Sam's earlier interrupted performance, closes a wound—itself symbolic of the interrupted relationship—that had been left open in the diegetic world. On the other hand, D♭ intrudes from the diegetic world, and its presence in the nondiegetic space threatens a musical closure that might put an end to "As Time Goes By," to this musical nondiegetic space, forever. The melody does not yield to D♭. Even after the cadence in D♭ seemingly appropriates the melody, interpreting the melodic G♯ enharmonically as A♭, E affects the physics of the space like a gravitational force: F falls to F♭. But the world is unyielding, too: the note change happens as we see a thoughtful Renault and are reminded of the true weight of the larger diegetic world in which the characters find themselves. Secure in his power, Renault's puff of cigarette smoke coincides with the F♭ in a gesture more worthy of an unscrupulous cynic. Steiner adds a subtle bit of color that brings attention to this final note despite the relatively low dynamic. The two vibraphones, which had been playing chords during the cadence, now strike an octave E4–E5.

In summary, then, the tonal levels and the joints between the motives appear as though they have been put under extensive pressure. The melody wanders from strong definition of F major in the first half to E♭ in the second but at the last moment is pushed upward to E major. The harmony, by contrast, takes us from D minor to E♭ major and finally D♭ major. Relative keys, D minor and F major, are paired at the beginning, but this connection comes unglued at the mention of Paris and the invading Germans. Spurred by the analogue gaze sonority, melody and accompaniment move together in E♭ major in part 3, but this, too, is undone by the sinking extended chords at 2:03, after which the melody shifts up a half step, and the accompaniment continues downward. The A♭, enharmonically G♯, is both $\hat{5}$ of D♭ and $\hat{3}$ of E, and of course D♭ can be understood as enharmonically VI of E major. The F–F♭ movement in the final chord, however, restores—

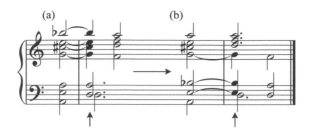

Figure 4.10, a–b. "Proper" position and resolution of the 4,7 stinger chord according to traditional voice leading in D minor: (a) the model with A^flat9; (b) with the 4,7 chord.

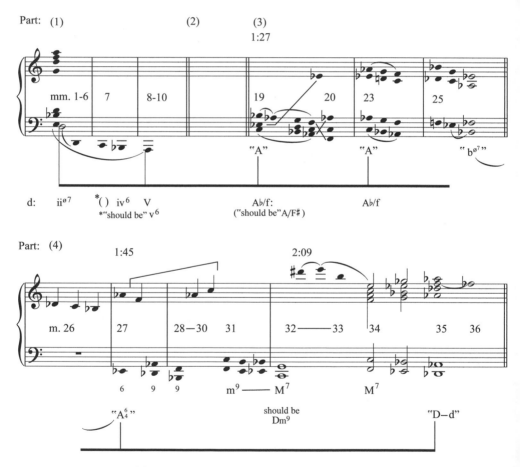

Figure 4.11. *Casablanca*, reduction of cue 4,7 and bass-line reading as if in D minor/major.

Figure 4.12. The "correct" ending of cue 4,7 in D major/minor.

Figure 4.13. The "correct" ending of cue 4,7 in E♭ major/minor.

for an isolated but exposed few seconds—the relationship of relative keys from the beginning, now a half step lower: C♯ minor (enharmonically D♭ minor) and E major.[14]

Taking into account all of the materials of the cue and the keys of the song performances before and after, it appears that there were in fact several possibilities for an appropriate ending. The first is a monotonal option: D minor of the opening becomes D major (then minor) of the ending. The second is the "deflation" option that Steiner employs: D minor of the opening becomes D♭ major of the ending, as the "proper" D major drops by a half step. Third is another progressive tonal option in which D minor of the opening becomes E♭ major in the ending. The final statement of "As Time Goes By" is thus followed through in its proper key and also looks forward to the next scene, where Sam plays "As Time Goes By" in E♭ major. Finally, any of these might be complicated—or undermined—by replacing D minor at the opening with the key pair D minor / F major. Of these options, of course, the most traditional conception of tonal organization and voice leading would give priority to the bass in the opening, and on those terms we can say that the cue "should have been" in D throughout. Proper voice leading shows how the gaze sonority could easily derive from suspensions in a V^{flat9}–i progression in D minor. Figure 4.10a shows the traditional progression with correct voice leading. Figure 4.10b gives the altered version that produces the voicing of the gaze sonority (at the arrow). Note that the only concession we were obliged to make in figure 4.10b was to move the ninth out of its "textbook" position at the top of the chord.

The voice-leading graph in figure 4.11 shows a comparison of the D minor/major and the "deflation" models. If D♭ displaces the proper D, then the whole is an elaborate process of alteration, in which the "wrong notes" are the majority of actual pitches, and a "background" bass identifies the significant corrected pitches in D minor/major. The graph shows a shorthand version of the cue with only what we regard as the critical moments—not necessarily those that are important expressively or narratively, but those that are essential to overall pitch design. The two staves show actual notes in the cue, and the beam underneath is aligned with and corrects certain chords according to a monotonal reading in D minor/major. One complication with this "correction scheme" is that, if we follow strict transposition from the ending back, the D minor^9 would have to be C♯ minor^7, as shown in figure 4.12. Thus, what we marked as "should be D minor^9" in figure 4.11—the next half-step transposition down in the series of minor ninth chords—would actually be a second level of deflation: in the series of minor ninth chords, the bass should be D2, but correctly transposed for D major it should be C♯2, and yet it is actually C2. The D minor^9 *would* have worked if the transposition had been conceived in terms of E♭—an entirely plausible choice, of course (see figure 4.13). Given the D minor^9 as properly the next chord in the chromatic sequence, one can easily imagine Steiner had the E♭ ending in mind as his goal but changed direction as he approached the cadence. Either E♭ or D♭ would fit the theme of lowering toward the flat keys, but the D♭ ending is certainly more emphatic, as it adds additional aural weight to Rick's dejection, to the evening's end with a car door closing and driving off, and to hints of a fateful tomorrow as reflected in Renault's face.

The Reunion Scene and Vococentrism

The reunion scene as a whole traces the opening of a utopian space and its tentative closing off. In this respect, too, the D♭ ending is dramatically effective, tonally rounding off the key of Sam's interrupted performance. The gaze sonority enters as an interruption and seems to offer an alternative to the tonal pull of diegetic reality, which nevertheless proves too powerful. It must be remembered, however, that this image of utopia is damaged by and founded in the very diegetic reality that it ostensibly opposes—Rick and Ilsa's presence in Vichy-era French Morocco. That is to say, the condition for that utopia is our understanding of an opposition between the city of Casablanca in the film's present and the Paris now lost, dislocated temporally and physically from the present. It takes twenty-four seconds before Rick and Ilsa greet each other, with quick "hellos," but a few seconds before that Renault—for most of the film the very symbol of Vichy and the one character who professes to have no interest in music—has already reasserted the diegetic world by walking into the frame and saying "Well, you were asking about Rick earlier, and here he is." A comparison of the figures of Sam and Renault on this account is instructive. Sam sings, the world of the diegetic present seems to dissolve with the sound of his voice, and he does everything in his power to disappear even when his singing is interrupted so as not to impose on the vision. Renault, by contrast, not only intrudes but insists on the reality of the diegetic present. One could argue that the utopia is really established not when the gaze sonority first sounds but with the reassertion of diegetic reality and the refusal of the music throughout the scene to recede and disappear. Renault clearly articulates the implausibility of this utopia, even as the music affirms it in the face of diegetic impossibility. The role of the gaze sonority, then, is to alert us to the emotional intensity of the connection between Rick and Ilsa, something that can only come out of the past, and it testifies to the continued influence of that past on the present. In that respect, Paris is precisely *not* a nostalgic image. The past it symbolizes does remain traumatic for Rick, and so its appearance is musically dysphoric. Nevertheless, that appearance—the memory trace in the music—leaves an opening: the present, the diegetic reality, could be otherwise.

Though we may seem to have wandered far away, what this all suggests, in fact, is the importance of attending to the principle of vococentrism. The voice remains central, the voice ("you were asking") firmly grounded in the diegesis ("and here he is"). The opening of the reunion scene also has a direct parallel in the first confrontation scene, where three versions of the gaze sonority are coupled with a chromatic descent. These last for fully twenty-seven seconds before Ilsa finally speaks, only to dissipate their effects with a very direct assertion of the voice's prerogative: "Rick, I have to talk to you." The principle of vococentrism helps us be alert for such overdetermining effects, as well as resistances to them.

If the moment the utopia is formed can be shifted from the gaze sonority to Renault's speech against it, it can even more appropriately be moved earlier. "As Time Goes By" is introduced into the film not by the underscore but by the voice: Ilsa requests that Sam play the song, and then, when he claims not to remember it, she uses wordless singing to prompt him. Ilsa therefore introduces both the title of the song and its tune. When Sam responds literally to her request by playing the piano, she quickly rejects it and insists on *him* singing. It is only then, when Sam sings, that the song finally achieves its proper form.[15] If, as Chion claims, attention by habit goes to the voice and its source, then the singing voice is, as noted in chapter 1, the best cinematic instantiation of music: texted music centered in the body of a character-agent. A subtle aural sign of the change from speech to song during the reunion scene occurs in the secondary musical materials. When Sam shifts from playing to singing, the manner in which he accompanies the melody changes rather markedly. The piano, which had subtly entwined melody and accompaniment, now turns into pure accompaniment in support of the tune carried by his voice. The resulting stratification of the music into voice and accompaniment is the epitome of vococentrism, reproducing the hierarchical divisions of sound film into foreground voice and background sound (whether music or effects). This allows Sam's voice to assume the character of fantasy object, to disappear, with the status of a transparent signifier, into the past world of the "old songs." The moment releases the utopian energies that will propel the remainder of the narrative and motivate much of the subsequent music.

When Rick appears, as though conjured by Sam's voice and answering the call of Ilsa's desire, the past world comes back to Rick in a rush, albeit in dysphoric form. The music of part 1 (gaze sonority, "As Time Goes By," all above the chaconne bass) seals their mutual recognition of their shared memories. At that point, the underscore is no longer really needed from the standpoint of the narrative. Ilsa's attempt to speak casually about Paris and the actions of getting up from the table and leaving the café are clear and sufficient in themselves. So is the larger filmic articulation: narratively, in the visual figures it is quite obvious that the long evening sequence is ending. Even the final reference to Paris, Sam, and "As Time Goes By" is rendered effectively by nuances in Bogart's and Bergman's voices. Strictly speaking, music is superfluous in the sense that much of the scene at the table could survive its absence.[16] From the standpoint of vococentrism, however, the issue is not so much music's necessity, since music that is not diegetic is rarely necessary. Vococentrism does not prescribe or proscribe the background but only insists that we proceed from the centrality of the voice and interpret what happens on the sound track accordingly. A change in the music would alter the configuration of the voice, its placement in the field of meaning.

One question remains to be asked: How are the status and placement of the voice affected by the choice of music? However appropriate the music might seem for a scene, we should nevertheless not delude ourselves into believing it to be more than one possible alternative. We are meaning-making creatures, and given any conjunction of music and narrative in film, it would be very unlikely that we could not construct a persuasive interpretation of that conjunction. Vococentrism does not intervene in this hermeneutic impulse but simply insists that any conjunction be considered from the standpoint of how it affects the placement of the voice in the field of meaning.

Methodologically, this question can be framed as a simple commutation test: How do the words resonate in the presence or absence of the music (or with different music)? If there were no underscore at all, we would still have the invocation of a shared past through the nostalgic song. Its echoes would just have been fainter. Such a scene, however, limited to the characters' bodies and their dialogue, would be reticent, restricted. Without underscore here (even more café music in the background would have done something), the emotional outburst precipitating the flashback would have seemed like an explosion, something out of the blue. As we shall see below, the cultural model under which classical Hollywood worked could not permit the male lead to do this first or alone. The music's underscoring may seem simply redundant, apparently contributing nothing that is not already there (Germans enter Paris, cue distorted "Deutschland über alles" in G♯ minor, etc.). Nevertheless, its excessive presence may still add something: a sonic richness or stylistic flourish that resists being reduced to meaning or diegetic reality. In the case of the reunion scene, what would be lost in the absence of music is not just the tenuous status of the memory of Paris that fluctuates with the conversation but also the fascinating, if not quite symmetrical, hold that it exerts on both Ilsa and Rick across the scene. Furthermore, if we take Sam's performance of "As Time Goes By" as introducing the utopian figure, then the fact that the scene ends in *his* key of D♭ suggests a prolongation of this figure, the way the figure reverberates through the scene, the past offering a palpable counterpoint to the conversation and the diegetic reality in which it occurs.

Singing, Performance, and the Figure of Sam

If we bracket off the levels of narrative space, the two poles of the classical sound track are the speaking voice and instrumental performance: the one is devoid of music, and the other is devoid of speech. Singing, as the combination of voice and music, is in a middle place, yet it poses more problems of categorization than that would suggest. Since it is often foregrounded (especially if sung by one of the film's leads), a song is presented as a performance, frequently interrupting narrative flow. Performance in that respect poses a challenge to the primacy of narrative representation; and, as noted in chapter 1, the spectacle of the singer's body always threatens to eclipse the musical sound of the voice. Performance therefore resembles in many respects the image of woman in Mulvey's (1975, 11) influential analysis, where she notes that the image of woman likewise serves as the spectacle that claims the spectator's gaze at the price of arresting narrative flow. On the other hand, songs are texted and are therefore allied to the discursive specificity and control of the speaking voice.

In line with studio priorities, which were also a means of managing the potential disruptive textual effects of singing, there are no uninterrupted song performances in *Casablanca,* despite their initial foregrounding. In some ways, the first of the performances has the strongest potential to be complete. With the cut to nighttime and the exterior of Rick's Café Américain, an extended sound advance has Sam singing "It Had to Be You." The music continues (and the sound clarifies) with the cut inside and a slow pan across the club's patrons, the camera finally settling on Sam himself as he finishes a chorus, then follows up immediately with a new song, "Shine." But the camera jumps away, and the music's volume drops under a series of short conversations, finally fading entirely as the head waiter, Carl, enters the casino room.

Sam's performance of "Knock on Wood" a few minutes later provides a sustained vocal performance for an entire brief song (it runs about a minute and a quarter), but here again the narrative intrudes extensively on the image track once the premise of the performance has been set up. Rick strolls into the middle of the performance, stopping at the piano purportedly to glance over some music but in actuality to hide the letters of transit in the piano. Later during the performance, Rick's competitor, Ferrari, enters the café, is seated at a table, and then exchanges glances with Rick across the room. For none of these actions, however, do we hear any associated sound effects, and the extensive cutting throughout the second half of the song does not lead to significant changes in the sound levels, as is the case in many of the nonhighlighted performances (and even some of the highlighted ones). The nature of the performance, with its extensive audience participation, may partially explain the relatively integral treatment of the song on the sound track. The scripting of the audience into the chorus has the effect of eliminating the background chatter that otherwise pervades the café, even the above-mentioned "It Had to Be You," where the gradual emergence of the song out of the crowd noise and the foregrounding of Sam's performance combine to form a figure of efficient sound track exposition that immediately characterizes the space of the café. As Martin Marks notes, the lyrics of "Knock on Wood" are also suggestive rather than decorative: "The jaunty music enables [the club's patrons] to make light of their troubles, but the song's superstitious lyrics also anticipate impending turns of fortune's wheel: Ugarte's arrest, Ilsa's arrival" (2000, 173). If "Knock on Wood" offers a complete musical performance on the sound track, the important narrative action of hiding the letters of transit, the song's thematic connection to the larger plot as noted by Marks, and the anticipation of the power of musical performance to organize collective action all seem to reflect the speech pole of the axis.

The other complete performance is also the one that has perhaps the least autonomy as "pure" music of any of the performances in the film—"La Marseillaise," in the battle of the anthems. Although its integrity as a musical performance—the fact that it drowns out "Wacht am Rhein" and continues triumphantly to its goal—defines its very meaning and significance in the sequence, this meaning resides not in the beauty, purity, and expressivity of the performance qua performance, which gives precisely the feeling of being ragtag, but rather in its power to organize collective action into mass force without eradicating individual difference.

The early performances of "It Had to Be You" / "Shine" and "Knock on Wood" do offer considerable exposure for Sam as part of the diegesis, but one late change in the screenwriting personnel made a remarkable difference for shaping his role into a dramatic one as well. On the first day of shooting (25 May 1942), Hal Wallis hired one last screenwriter. Casey Robinson was expected to do some fine tuning during the first two weeks of shooting, but in fact he worked for three and a half weeks. Ironically, since he was compensated at $3,000 a week, in addition to salary, Robinson ended up being the highest paid of all the film's writers (Osborne 1997, 190).[17] His special skill, the reason he drew the highest regular salary among the writers at the studio, was making emendations that would solve problems with the censors; he had recently done this for two very difficult scripts— *Dark Victory* (1939) and *Kings Row* (1942) (Harmetz 2002, 174). Here, Robinson's task was "to work on the love angle between Rick and Ilsa [that] Wallis and others thought needed improving," and an important part of his strategy was to make more of "As Time Goes By" as an emblem of Rick and Ilsa's relationship (Osborne 1997, 190).[18]

Sam was already an important character in the film before Robinson joined the film—the Paris scenes in La belle Aurore were the ones filmed on the first day—but with the upgrading of the song's presence elsewhere, Sam's role was significantly enhanced (Osborne 1997, 190; Harmetz 2002, 176).[19] The scene between Sam and Ilsa, in particular, is important, as it is the first time we see Sam speaking in a personal way rather than as a professional performer and Rick's employee. This seems to have been Robinson's doing. In notes (dated 20 May and likely the reason he was subsequently brought on), he says, "Play the stuff at the piano where she asks Sam to play some of the old songs, and then insists on 'As Time Goes By.' Play up very strongly Sam's trying to avoid playing this. I'm sure this material will tell the audience that there is something of great significance to this music, and something of romantic significance" (quoted in Harmetz 2002, 176).

Robinson's idea seems to have been to make Sam into a sign of the romance between Rick and Ilsa, where the displacement of Rick by Sam's voice establishes a powerful attraction between Rick and Ilsa at the same time it succeeds in skirting a number of problematic issues that representing the relationship in any detail would pose within the Production Code. According to the final version of the script, Ilsa was married to Laszlo at the time of the relationship in Paris, although she believed he was dead. Just as she and Rick were about to leave Paris, Ilsa learned that Laszlo was in fact alive, belatedly making her relationship with Rick adulterous. This somewhat convoluted scenario was the compromise Joseph Breen, in charge of enforcing the Production Code, required to allow the production to go forward (Miller 1992, 120). Because the relationship was adulterous, even though inadvertently so, the Production Code also required that it be handled discreetly, with little attention to the romance and as much deniability as possible (Maltby 1996). Robinson's notion of turning Sam into a sign of the romance that could displace Rick was his solution to the problem. Indeed, Robinson thought so much of the effect of this displacement that he argued that Rick should not be a part of this scene at all but that he and Ilsa should meet first after hours (Harmetz 2002, 180), a recommendation that was not, of course, followed.

The scene between Ilsa and Sam in the Café Américain was clearly meant as a parallel to the one in La belle Aurore in Paris (which will occur in the flashback several minutes later). Sam's role is significant in both. We have already discussed the scene between Ilsa and Sam above and will have more to say about it in a moment, but we should pause briefly to consider the La belle Aurore sequence. This sequence begins much like "It Had to Be You," which served to establish the location of the Café Américain. A shot of sunshine falling on the Paris café's floor with the shadow of the window sign clearly legible is accompanied by the offscreen sound of Sam singing the bridge of "As Time Goes By." As with "It Had to Be You," Sam's voice is initially treated with reverb and a lowered level to give the impression of distance. When the camera tilts up as though to look for the source of the sound, Sam is in the background, with Ilsa listening intently at the piano (figure 4.14a). Rick is in the foreground at the bar getting champagne. Near the end of the bridge, just after Sam sings "and man must have his mate," Rick brings the bottle and glasses to the piano, his footsteps clearly audible as he passes through the somewhat deserted café with the camera dollying after him and the sound gaining in proximity, both growing louder and mixed with more direct sound. Rick arrives at the piano just as Sam comes out of the bridge and

Figure 4.14, a–b. *Casablanca,* La belle Aurore: (a) Ilsa listens to Sam; (b) Ilsa appears disconcerted. Screen stills.

begins the return of the main phrase. As Rick pours the drinks and Sam sings "a case of do or die," Ilsa breaks her focus on Sam and looks at Rick. For no reason yet evident in the film, this seems to disconcert her (figure 4.14b), and she will continue to appear anxious and evasive, mostly avoiding looking at Rick, until the cut outside to the loudspeakers.

The sequence is therefore divided by the song structure, Rick's position (the change of which is signaled on the sound track by footsteps that intrude on the music), and Ilsa's look, which first falls intently on Sam and then seems to avoid Rick. The La belle Aurore sequence therefore anticipates or reflects the reunion scene, depending on whether we give priority to chronological or plot order. In each case, Ilsa's fantasy of the romance evidently requires the presence of Sam's voice but the absence of Rick's body: Ilsa's fantasy (and the desire on which it is founded) involves the *idea* of Rick; the desire is—like all desire—always already a semiotic construct involving an originary displacement. Rick's presence disrupts Ilsa's fantasy. Rick's body, literalized in both cases with footsteps, intrudes on the music of romance, in the case of the reunion leading to its interruption and transposition to the score. By embodying the Parisian romance in Sam's voice, Robinson succeeded in deflecting attention from the physical relationship and transformed it into one of pure desire (we might almost take the pun here seriously, Sam's voice signifying pure desire as chaste desire). In the process, Sam becomes a more important character and his role one of the most serious for an African American actor in mainstream movies of the 1940s.

Casablanca as *Film noir*: A Critique

Given the discussion above, we will have to disagree with one aspect of Peter Franklin's reading of *Casablanca,* which interprets the film as following the conventions of *film noir.* Franklin assumes a homology between the conventional structure of *film noir* and Carolyn Abbate's analysis of the plot stereotype of the "undone woman" in nineteenth-century opera. Based on this, Franklin posits that Ilsa "plays a dual 'musical' role, as both allegorical representative of Music—with all its ancient danger to masculine rationality and control—and its experiential victim (as we surmise from the play of recollected emotion that 'As Time Goes By' arouses in her" (2011, 122). Although *Casablanca* does bear many attributes of *film noir,* Franklin's larger interpretive point is weakened by the fact that the homology with operatic undoing requires him both to bind Ilsa to music and to interpret the connection to music as the source of her "undoing." This general framework works to some extent for *film noir,* where the *femme fatale* is often a singer, the films typically do not use much other music, and her initial allure for the hero is staged to a large extent on the ground of musical performance, which can therefore assume the status of existential threat to the hero's initial rational commitments. In particular, music serves as the antirational pole opposed to the rational pole of efficient communicative exchange that otherwise seems to guide the interactions in the world.

As Franklin acknowledges, *Casablanca* does not really fit the model, because Ilsa relates to music primarily through Sam, which means that the "dark link between the powerful female voice and Music (as *femme fatale*) is broken, or at least further complicated" (2011, 118). That is, unlike a *femme fatale*, Ilsa does not represent Music in its antirational form. As we have seen, if anyone fills this role, it is Sam, who provides the music for much of the first part of the film. In fact, the irrationality, the danger, here lies in the café itself, in the subdued but fearful lives and conversations of the refugees, and, one should add, implicitly also in Rick himself, who controls the music in order to neutralize its traumatic effects on him.

Although Rick may see Ilsa as *femme fatale* (she destroyed their relationship and ruined his life) and may recognize the musical danger, Ilsa herself has other things on her mind. Moreover, Ilsa's relationship to the music is actually the more traditionally masculine one compared to Rick's. In the scene where she coaxes Sam to play "As Time Goes By," as analyzed above, Ilsa listens, perhaps rides an emotional wave that the song seems to engender for her, but we are not privy to her thoughts. We remain on the outside and may in fact wonder what she is thinking and feeling. But Sam's performance is not music of interiority as Hollywood of the period understood it, even if the long close-up (recall figure 4.14a) adds pressure to interpret the face and an expectation for a matching shot to her inward gaze. Ilsa, however, was sensible enough to demand to hear Sam sing, a precaution that Rick neglects to take in the parallel scene leading to the flashback. Vococentrism means that diegetic status of the singing voice is more secure and less likely to dissolve into the ambiguities of the fantastic gap than is instrumental music (or music represented as recorded). Diegetic performance, however, always poses the threat of shifting attention from the narrative to the song and from the sound of the voice to the spectacle of the singer: it is this threat the performing *femme fatale* frequently exploits in *film noir*. The asynchronous treatment in the reunion scene—Sam's voice, Ilsa's face—and the interrupted performance neatly sidestep those issues. Sam's voice, by which we mean not just his voice but his singing voice, can therefore serve as a signifier, implicitly of the time in Paris, as in Franklin's interpretation (through Sam's singing voice Ilsa sees Rick in Paris)—though perhaps Ilsa is just moved by the sound of Sam's voice. We can't be sure. Sam's absent body nevertheless holds the image in place, allowing Ilsa's thoughts to remain her own, veiled. The film answers the long close-up not with the picture of interiority we might expect and probably desire but with an external shot, most emphatically not from Ilsa's point of view, of the presumed object of her thought, that is, Rick. The point-of-view shot we have been expecting comes only when Rick sees Ilsa and we hear the gaze sonority.

At this moment, we have already penetrated Rick's interiority in a way we have not Ilsa's. If the cut back to Rick in close-up (recall figure 4.14b) seems to grant some access to Ilsa's interiority, it is only on the condition that Rick has already prepared the ground; their space, not hers. Throughout the conversation that ensues, few shots suggest Ilsa's direct point of view, though the axis of representation is certainly between Rick's view and hers. The shots of Rick and most of the rest of the table are generally over her shoulder or from behind Ilsa, but close-ups of Ilsa are all motivated from Rick's point of view and without the intervening shoulder. This analysis of Ilsa's presence in the shots of Rick differs from Ray (1985, 93), who reads it as a mark of her "true allegiance." Since she also appears in the shots of Renault and Laszlo, the better interpretation would be to say that it figures her as a "linking object," as Ray admits is the case in the parting shots. As linking object her loyalties are in a sense divided. Nevertheless, it is also important that shots from Ilsa's axis are presented externally with her body in the frame, whereas those from Rick's are presented internally, with no intervening body.

Although such gender-specific allocation of shots is typical of classical Hollywood cinema, which favors tighter close-ups of women with indistinct backgrounds that destroy placement in space compared with wider shots of men in deep focus that establish definite spatial coordinates (Mulvey 1975, 12–13), this scene problematizes its allocation. If the close-up generally serves to stake a claim of possession, suggesting ownership by the bearer of the look (Doane 1991, 48), this scene concerns precisely a lack of possession, even the feeling of dispossession, when framed in these terms. Aside from one medium shot of Laszlo during introductions, shots from Rick's side of the axis are focused exclusively on Ilsa (or on the pair of Ilsa and Laszlo during the parting). The only shot plausibly from Ilsa's side of the table in which some part of her is not visible is a medium close-up of Laszlo. The placement of the camera for this shot of Laszlo is difficult to read in terms of the axis of representation, as it seems to be positioned somewhere between Rick and Ilsa, a camera setup we do not see elsewhere in the scene, except perhaps in the medium shot of Laszlo during the introductions. The conversation would initially attribute it to Rick's side of the axis, but the succeeding shot of Rick is over Ilsa's shoulder, suggesting a comparison with Laszlo as seen from Ilsa's side of the axis (and mirroring the comparison in the conversation between Rick's work and Laszlo's).

Attending to the depth of field of the close-ups, we find it most pronounced in Laszlo's, even though the background is not particularly inviting for depth-of-field photography. The close-ups of Rick and Ilsa, by contrast, are quite similar, with blurred rather than indistinct backgrounds. Rick's close-ups nevertheless give a stronger sense of space because the room is open behind him. The shots from behind Ilsa, including those of Rick, all have extremely pronounced depth of field. As is customary, Ilsa's close-ups are also generally tighter than Rick's and held longer. Finally, the shots from Ilsa's end of the axis divide the table: Rick, on the one hand; Renault, Laszlo, and Ilsa, on the other. The full table is given only at the beginning and end of the sequence. Such analytical editing of space is absolutely typical of the style, as is the division of the space into groups that underscore thematic oppositions (here, the isolation of Rick with Ilsa's body as the fulcrum on which the opposition pivots).

Although the reunion scene is therefore fully consistent with the representational system of classical Hollywood, the overall effect of the scene works not to establish Rick's mastery but to undermine it. Rick may be granted the bearer of

Figure 4.15, a–b. *Casablanca*, reunion scene, Laszlo and Rick introduced and compared. Screen stills.

the look in the close-ups of Ilsa, but he sees only lack, what he does not have. Indeed, his representation in general lies closer to Ilsa's; Laszlo, even though he does not bear the look, is nevertheless coded in the more secure masculine position: the matched shots of Laszlo and Rick during introductions (see figure 4.15a–b) position Laszlo in a much greater depth of field, and twice during the conversation Rick must defer to Laszlo's superiority of accomplishment ("One hears a great deal about Rick in Casablanca"; "This is a very interesting café"). Moreover, Rick is "burdened"—to use Heather Laing's quite appropriate term (2007, 10)—by the presence of music throughout the scene. The emotional identification of the music may occasionally pass to Ilsa as well, but as the analysis of the scene above suggests, music hardly seems her burden here, with the possible exception of the mention of Paris, where the musical explosion of dissonant counterpoint registers a dangerous turn in the conversation. This musical outburst illustrates that Ilsa's burden, in fact, is the conversation itself, which she must conduct on two levels that match the division of the editing between Rick, on the one hand, and Renault and Laszlo, on the other.

Vococentrism allocates to the underscore primarily the supplementary function of connotation, to inflect a scene to mean something different from what it otherwise would. Its burden, in a general sense, is that its supplementation implies an insufficiency in denotation: "To music is always delegated the task of pinpointing, isolating the moments of greatest significance, telling us where to look despite the fact that the look is inevitably lacking" (Doane 1987, 97). Although Doane frames music's supplementation in terms of vision—whereas in actuality dialogue is probably more important to sound film's construction of rationality than is anything in the image—the basic point holds: music burdens the characters it underscores because its use suggests that the character cannot or will not adequately express himself (or more commonly herself) in words or action. The burden of supplementation thereby moves from the representational plane to that of the character, and the scoring of character is typically gendered. As Laing notes, "The sense of interiority usually associated with the female character derives from association with a musical theme that can be varied or developed according to changes in her feelings" with the result that we come to "believe we understand the woman's thoughts and emotions to an intimate degree" (2007, 141). In the classical model, this device is reserved for female characters: "In the emotional representation of men, . . . this particular configuration is usually avoided" (141). Because music remains connotation, its indefinite play of tones suggests not so much emotional depth as a subjective interior buffeted by unmastered emotion, which is why Laing suggests it is typically not found in Hollywood's musical representations of men. This is, however, what happens to Rick.

Let us briefly compare Ilsa's listening to Sam to the parallel scene leading to Rick's flashback, analyzed more fully below. For Franklin, who does not deny the effect of music on Rick, the fact that Rick succumbs to the music on account of his desire for Ilsa is sufficient to indict her, to turn her into the figure of Music that must be expunged for Rick to reclaim his masculinity. But it is not Ilsa who is "reduced to woman's-picture femininity" (Franklin 2011, 123) in the music leading to the flashback but Rick, who is initially scored very much like a woman in a melodrama. Laing notes that such reversals of subjective scoring are occasionally found in films treating male trauma and troubled male adolescents (although the music is usually more dissonant than is typical for scoring a woman) and also suggests that films working with *noir* thematics frequently transpose the musical threat to the nondiegetic scoring: "The transfer of the music from the diegetic to the nondiegetic level in this context seems almost an antidote to the conscious or unconscious appropriation of the man's music undertaken by the female listener. As the *noir* hero is pursued by the musically signified female influence, he risks increasing weakness and compromise. Only by resisting this latter-day siren song can he emerge intact in his masculinity, in the way of Rick . . . in *Casablanca*" (2007, 146). Like Franklin, Laing here attributes the music to Ilsa; through intense listening, evidently, Ilsa claims Sam's music (or is it Rick's?) as her own but then transmutes it into its signified as song passes to score.

This concentration of attention on Rick and Ilsa distracts from the fact that the power of music, the power of its performance in the sense of an operatic character, belongs to Sam, not Rick or Ilsa, who hold only the power to command (and in Rick's case extract profit from) performance. For nothing of Ilsa's musicality survives in the film unless it is her rather nondescript wordless singing or the intensity of her listening (and she does not show herself to be an especially adept listener otherwise). What does survive musically, besides the strains of "La Marseillaise" that accompany Rick and Renault's stroll into mythical mists at the end, is the score's obsessive use of "As Time Goes By," as well as all the performances in the café that dominate the first act. Ultimately, the *sound* of the café would seem to represent Music in the sense that Franklin (2011, 119–22) uses that word, an idea that is certainly compatible with his own discussion of the band and Sam's popular music numbers as undermining Modernist aesthetic hierarchies. Put another way, even when trauma forms a hard, cynical shell that provides no musical window to subjective interiority, the café is at least one place where music is still possible, even if, up to the point of Ilsa's arrival, it operates under the condition of a musical taboo and labors under the requirement of profit.

For Rick and Ilsa, it is Paris and the past that Sam embodies and can still signify through his singing and playing, but we know from the outset that Paris is not Ilsa's unique possession: it belongs to Rick and Ilsa together. Sam, as the material signifier, is in the middle, for one brief moment quite literally. He is instrumental to cementing the tie between "As Time Goes By" and Paris: it is first mentioned in a conversation between Ilsa and Sam; and its history is fleshed out after a conversation between Rick and Sam, who also appears singing the song in Paris in the ensuing flashback. Sam even reappears on the second night to play (not sing) the song again at Rick's command at a time when all the bonds seem to have been broken and prospects for reconciliation seem bleak. Rick and Ilsa's encounter over "As Time Goes By" is a classic moment, to be sure (she does "own" the song to the degree that she names it first and commands its performance), but we realize retrospectively that Sam must be its "proper" owner, certainly its keeper; in any event, only he can reproduce it and conjure Paris out of nothing more than the sound of music. Ilsa must cajole him to perform it, to pull it out of his pocket and show it, as it were, and his first response is to offer an imperfect version (instrumental), after which she must resort to a peremptory command ("Sing it, Sam"). The effect is definitely not "to hypnotize him into performing it" (Franklin 2011, 118) but to play to his identity as a performer, to his desire to satisfy his audience, which overrides his obligation to respect the will of his boss. Although for Rick, "clearly this music is threatening" (118), Ilsa herself resists being drawn into Rick's anger and recrimination, and "As Time Goes By" does seem to function for Ilsa from the outset more like the souvenir that Caryl Flinn (1992) calls it (and as Rick perhaps comes to understand it in the end). In that sense, the song is never Ilsa's music when scored from her perspective but always theirs—and up to the second confrontation scene it is always past. In any event, her primary goal is not to reclaim Paris; her memory of it is wistful and nostalgic, not traumatic. In the first confrontation scene, she spends her time trying to explain the situation to Rick; she only succeeds much later, during the second confrontation. Almost all the time between she spends trying to secure the letters of transit that will give Laszlo and her the right to leave. Only at her breakdown does she lose this as her central concern, surrendering to the notion of love in the present (if she does surrender to that notion), a character conversion that is far from convincing. We will return to this point below.

Ilsa's relation to "As Time Goes By" is therefore complicated. Sam is required for its initial production; Paris belongs to the couple; the score burdens Rick, not Ilsa, with the song. To associate the song primarily with Ilsa in order to read the gender dynamics of the film is really to interpret those dynamics through the distorting lens of Rick's trauma: Ilsa loses (is lost) because Rick wins, secures his masculinity by expunging the feminine object of desire so he can rejoin the beautiful fraternity of fighting men. But in that event she has lost before the film has even begun, the moment she is reduced to her signifying function within a traumatic vision that the film itself pathologizes and disavows. This interpretive tack exhibits a myopia that resembles Rick's inability to read the signs of Ilsa's withdrawal in his flashback. Ilsa indeed seems more the victim of Franklin's interpretive plotting than of *Casablanca*'s actual plot, and his interpretation must remain silent on the fate of Sam, whose symbolic sacrifice in the film is at least as large as Ilsa's, and more hidden.[20] Although perhaps overstuffed with the theme of sacrifice, noble and otherwise, *Casablanca* is in the end neither melodrama nor *film noir*. Who is undone in the film? Everyone—since sacrifice is required of all—and no one, if our benchmark be opera's usual, deadly method of undoing, unless it be the villain (Strasser), the thief (Ugarte), the German couriers, or the anonymous Resistance fighter shot in the street during the roundup of the usual suspects in the opening establishment sequence.

Umberto Eco and *Casablanca* as Comedy

The best one can do along the lines of undoing would be to accept Umberto Eco's (1985, 9–10) claim that the film's happy ending disguises the fact that everyone in the film winds up unhappy. For Eco, this incoherence is symptomatic of the virtuosic bricolage technique used to assemble the film, which he seemingly cannot help admiring even as he seeks to contain by marking it as an essential property of the cult film rather than the artistic film. Or perhaps he recognizes in the film's untamed sublimity a quality that is always lost when it is domesticated under the banner of art but that he hopes can be preserved by classifying the film as cult. Whatever the case, the distinction between art and cult that Eco deploys and the implicit hierarchy that it presumes belong to the discourse of late high Modernism. The opposition Eco constructs does not, however, follow the usual gendered lines that Franklin traces in the discourse of Modernism—the wild and the sublime are not properties of the feminine in that discourse, even when they are given the name "nature" and placed in opposition to the speech of men (11). Indeed, Eco substitutes for the gendered opposition precisely the contrast of classic hero and renegade hero outlined in *Casablanca:* Laszlo and Rick: "Quite subliminally, a hint of Platonic Love is established. Rick admires Victor, Victor is ambiguously attracted by the personality of Rick, and it seems that at a certain point each of the two plays out a duel of self-sacrifice to please the other. In any case, as in Rousseau's *Confessions,* the woman is an intermediary between the two men. She herself does not bear any positive value (except, obviously, Beauty): the whole story is a virile affair, a dance of seduction between Male Heroes" (10).[21] If this little allegory of platonic love between art and cult film is accepted, the usual gendered opposition of Modernism is sidestepped only by engendering an intermediary without positive value. And what is this intermediary?

We should not forget that what Eco terms "the magic key" (the letters of transit) is hidden in the piano: "Casablanca is like a musical piece with an extraordinarily long overture where every theme is [initially] exhibited according to a monodic line. Only later the symphonic work takes place" (1985, 7). Despite this prominent musical metaphor, which organizes the second half of the essay and which implicitly recognizes the large musical articulation of the film (the passage from popular song to symphonic scoring), Eco is remarkably silent about the film's actual use of music. Sam, for instance, warrants only two passing references in Eco's text (8, 9), one of which is included primarily because Woody Allen made a film based on a commonly misremembered quotation, and "As Time Goes By," despite its ubiquity, appears only obliquely in that same quotation. Beyond that, the opposition between the exotic and "La Marseillaise" in the main title sequence is noted, as is the melodramatic demonization of the Germans' arrival with a distorted version of "Deutschland über alles," the later battle of the anthems, and a very obscure reference to "Knock on Wood" (7–9). That is it.

Music, then, evidently stands in the place of Ilsa: beautiful, but without positive value for the film. We are apparently not so far from Franklin's interpretation. Gender may not be the undoing of Ilsa or music, but any romance based on gender is seemingly beside the point in Eco's interpretation, which unites the divergent worldviews of men so they can remake the world according to a universal patriarchal ideal. Robinson's scriptwriter strategy of turning the music into a sign of romance seems to open it to the field of an uncontrolled semiosis, but it passes well beyond its intended mark, displacing not only Rick and Sam but Ilsa as well before landing on Laszlo and closing the circle by returning to Rick. The slide along the signifying chain has the effect of being a solvent of difference, as first race and then gender disappear as contingent matter into the transparent sign of general signification. The issues of race and gender, however, are complicated, even more so when they are approached from the standpoint of semiotics. Race and gender are marked categories whose difference is inscribed in the very materiality of the sign. This makes them somewhat recalcitrant signs, ones whose materiality refuses to fade into contingency, which allows them to reverse—or rather reveal—the workings of the semiotic process. If we return to the beginning of the chain, Ilsa's ostensible substitution of Sam's voice for Rick's body, we can examine how race functions in the displacement. On the one hand, the black body serves as a barrier that forces signification. The Production Code bars miscegenation, so under that system Sam cannot serve as the object of romance for Ilsa. The Production Code therefore insists that we read Sam as a signifier rather than a signified: if Sam's music means that romance is in the air, then its object must lie elsewhere. Sam's race seemingly makes his body a safe displacement for Rick's. On the other hand, the very censorship that forces this signification also destabilizes it: Does Ilsa love Rick, or does she think about Rick to justify the intense pleasure of listening to Sam's singing? Is her romance in fact with Sam's voice? In the two moments in the film where Ilsa is shown listening to Sam, Rick's bodily presence disturbs Ilsa's reverie. Both instances suggest that Rick's body is not in fact the principal object of desire, that the signified of romance again lies elsewhere.

The apparent conclusion, that pure desire has no object proper to it, has a Lacanian ring to it. Even if one is unconvinced by the Lacanian union of psychoanalysis and semiotics, it should not be a surprise that music might appear both absolutely indispensable to the film and yet completely superfluous. How else can the opposition between Rick and Laszlo come to seem self-sufficient? How else can the romance of these two positions come to define the world of possibility? It falls to the intermediary of female gender to perform the role of supplement and the intermediary of a racialized body to play the music for "the dance of seduction between Male Heroes." Eco's brief analytical sketch tells us that Sam's act in the Café Américain, the music for this dance between art and cult, is the distant echo of a tinny piano played in the downstairs parlor of a New Orleans brothel.[22] Art and cult are supported at base by—and are impossible without—an entertainment sphere where the energies of sexualized and racialized difference (and no doubt innumerable other differences as well) are gathered, exploited, and released into a psychosexual economy that produces and reproduces the conditions of general culture.

It is not the configuration but the repression of difference that is at issue: that the patriarchal culture of privileged men is sustained in virtue of a system of exclusions that it can neither acknowledge nor do without. Romance is the sign of impossible union in the film, and its displacements across the signifying chain are the mechanism of repression; Rick's trauma is its symptom. The taboo is the secret stitching it together. Sam is the keeper of this secret, and Ilsa holds the key. Only when thought together does the symptom appear; only when thought together do race and gender reveal themselves to be something more than intermediaries without positive value: together, they too might change the world. After the flashback the film keeps them apart.

Conclusion

Rick's trauma is a symptom, and the gaze sonority is its sound. *Casablanca* on one side of that chord's first sounding is different from the film on the other side. Returning to that moment—and the beginning of its underscore—in chapter 5 we work simultaneously inward and outward: inward to an analysis of the musical structure of the gaze sonority itself, outward to its connections in the rest of the film. Surely fitting the role of music as stylized sound, as we discussed it in chapter 3, the gaze sonority also acts in the role of harmony as motif, for it recurs twice prominently in parallel dramatic situations (that is, emotional encounters between Rick and Ilsa). Even in its pitch design it can be related to a number of other punctuating chords, beginning as early as the film's prologue, and often in ways that are narratively substantive.

5   The Reunion Scene's Contexts

David Neumeyer and James Buhler

The Gaze Sonority and Other Stinger Chords

The gaze sonority appears in the film for the first time during the reunion scene, but Max Steiner had already composed the cue for Rick and Ilsa's after-hours confrontation, where the chord also appears, and in an equally striking way: cue 4,7, the underscore music for the reunion scene, bears an instruction from Steiner to his most trusted orchestrator, Hugo Friedhofer, to "orchestrate like Reel 5 Part 4 Bar 1."[1] Writing cues out of order was hardly unusual for Steiner or, for that matter, almost anyone else in the studio music departments: like filming in order of story chronology or of script order (that is, plot chronology), composing the underscore from beginning to end was the exception, not the rule. For reference, table 5.1 lists the reuses that Steiner marks in his sketches for *Casablanca*.[2] Not surprisingly, the majority of them are internal reuses late in the film: cue 4,7 is the important exception. The note at its beginning is the only forward reference in Steiner's sketches. It reveals that he saw the first confrontation scene as a crucial dramatic moment and therefore as a good starting point from which he could develop the basic materials for his underscore.[3]

In this chapter, we will use "Reel 4, Part 7," "cue 4,7," or simply "4,7" interchangeably for the underscore in the reunion scene. Similarly, either "Reel 5, Part 4" or "5,4" refers to the confrontation that immediately follows the flashback, and "Reel 9, Part 2" or "9,2" refers to the second confrontation closer to the end of the film as Ilsa makes one last attempt to convince Rick to give her the exit visas that she and Laszlo need to leave for Lisbon.

A comparison of the full scores for the stinger chords that open cues 4,7 and 5,4 shows that Friedhofer did follow Steiner's instructions but by no means slavishly (see figure 5.1). The winds are identical in their voicings, but the changes in the other instruments clearly suggest that the opening of Reel 4, Part 7, was meant to be softer in timbre, more "swimmy," as Steiner writes in other contexts. In the prologue, for example, where he marks the final chord of what he calls the "refugee march" as "sort of misterious—swimmy" (the spelling is very possibly due to a trope on "mist" and "mysterious" rather than evidence of the composer's

Table 5.1. *Casablanca*, Max Steiner's Sketches, Annotations for Reuses, with Comments

Cue	Source	Measure	Comment
Main title	*Gold Is Where You Find It* (1938)	2	Steiner's trademark music for Warner Bros. studio logo (see Marks 2000, 164).
Reel 4, Part 7	"orchestrate like Reel 5 Part 4 Bar 1"	1	Begins the reunion scene.
Reel 5, Part 2	"Perkins: We might be able to use Now Voyager Reel 5 Part I"	15	"Perfidia"—Rick and Ilsa are dancing. "Perkins" is Hal Perkins, who was responsible for all the nonsymphonic arrangements.
Reel 5, Part 2	*Confessions of a Nazi Spy* (1939)	8	For the first war montage during the flashback. From a similar scene in Reel 9 of the earlier film.
Reel 5, Part 3	*The Life of Emile Zola* (1937)	10	In the train station, the 25″ of music before the Letter insert. From music for a scene in Reel 3 following the defeat of France at Sedan during the Franco-Prussian War.
Reel 9, Part 2	Reel 5, Part 4	5	The first 25″ of the Second Confrontation scene.
Reel 9, Part 2	Reel 5, Part 4	8	Second Confrontation scene: source is the climax (1:05–1:36) of the First Confrontation scene, transposed up a step.
Reel 9, Part 2	Reel 5, Part 3	15	After Ilsa breaks down midway through the Second Confrontation scene: intense waltz version of "As Time Goes By" (Steiner marks the final bars "ecstatic")—from flashback, waltz version leading up to the final kiss, transposed a step down.
Reel 10, Part 4	Reel 8, Part 4A	7	Laszlo's theme, music leading up to Rick with the pistol. Source is the scene following Rick's refusal to give Laszlo the exit visas.
Reel 10, Part 4	Reel 9, Part 3	5	Follows immediately on the preceding—accelerando version of "As Time Goes By" phrase. Source is the second-night after-hours scene, when Rick tells Carl to take Ilsa home.
Reel 11, Part 1	Reel 5, Part 3	8	At the airport, after the opening quotation of "As Time Goes By." Source is the first part of the flashback waltz version that leads to the kiss, beginning when Ilsa touches Rick's chin.
Reel 11, Part 1	Reel 9, Part 3	7	Follows from preceding, rhythmically altered and embellished "As Time Goes By," A. Source is the last part of the Second Confrontation scene, after the cut-away to the tower.
Reel 11, Part 1	Reel 5, Part 3	10	First page reproduced in Marks (2000, 169). At dialogue "But I've got a job to do." Source is again the flashback, waltz version leading up to the final kiss, transposed a step down.
Reel 11, Part 1	Reel 8, Part 4A	7	Laszlo theme, after the brief cut to Strasser in the air on the way to the airport. Source is the scene before Ilsa confronts Rick: Laszlo and Ilsa talking at night, starting when he says "I love you very much."

Source: Based on sketches in the Max Steiner Collection, Brigham Young University.

4,7 - chord

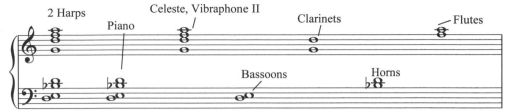

Figure 5.1. *Casablanca,* two stinger chords, orchestration details. (From materials in the Warner Bros. Collection, University of Southern California.)

shaky command of English spelling). Note also that the one major triad lurking in the pitches of the 4,7 chord, B♭ major, is entirely suppressed in the orchestration. Perhaps the most significant change from Reel 5, Part 4, however, is the missing Vibraphone I: in the reunion scene it is saved for the immediately ensuing quote from "As Time Goes By," coloring the clear tones of the oboe to shift the tune just a little off-center timbrally.

As figure 5.1 shows, the two chords are also not precisely the same in pitch design: Martin Marks (2000, 168) reproduces the entire first page of the sketch for Reel 4, Part 7, but ironically the reproduction is so clean that it suppresses a smudge in the original sketch: the sharp accidental on F has been erased. There is a similar erasure on F in bar 2 of the tune. An F♯ in the latter case would have been a mistake if Steiner intended to follow the melody exactly, but his original intention seems to have been to intensify the opening as a complex and prolonged G minor sonority (that is, at the tritone from D♭, the key in which Dooley Wilson was just singing). Still, it is hard to imagine that this version survived past bar 3, when the motive moves upward through the F major scale and the alteration of F♯ to F♮ turns G minor into the supertonic in F major.

Another possible way to look at this opening is in terms of the melody itself. It is clearly in F major, and interpreting the gaze sonority strictly in F means we can hear it—very easily in fact—as a C^{13} chord. The F♯ in the 5,4 chord, then, would make sense, since it forms the conventional raised eleventh, according to jazz theory and swing-era practice (see figure 5.2 at left, where the presumed bass C2 is added; likewise for the 4,7 chord at right). That C is missing and F♯ is lowered

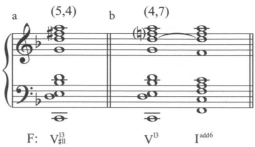

Figure 5.2, a–b. *Casablanca,* (a) the "5,4" chord and (b) the "4,7" chord, understood as V¹³ chords in F major.

obviously increases the expressive power of the gaze sonority at the same time it obscures its functionality. All this, again, would have occurred to Steiner by the time he was composing bar 3, and the end result is the overwhelming of F major implications by D minor in part 1 of the reunion scene, as discussed in chapter 4. The relationship of sustained chord to melody moving within is the same in both cases: in figure 5.3a, the initial and prominent notes of the two motivic segment are F♯4 and D4; in figure 5.3b, the initial tetrachord of "As Time Goes By" is B♭4–A4–G4–F4.

In addition to borrowing, then altering, the opening stinger chord of cue 5,4 for the gaze sonority of the reunion scene, Steiner might have taken the idea of chromatic deflation (recall that D minor ends as D♭ major/minor in the reunion scene) from the opening passage in cue 5,4. The chords shown in figure 5.4 accompany the determined and slow chromatic descent, the expanded moment after Ilsa reappears. At bar 6, the tension comes down a bit, and the harsh upper notes relax as well: F♯ becomes not C♯ but G♮ in the potential third chord, which matches the underlying E minor seventh chord in bar 6.[4]

Although the film's action scenes contain their full share of stingers, all of them are easily heard as conventional devices of underscoring: expressive, dramatic, but also attention grabbing. The gaze sonority, on the other hand, acquires a considerably greater depth of significance. We will refer to its version with the F♮ as the 4,7 chord, the one with the F♯ as the 5,4 chord. All told, they appear four times: (1) with F♮, at Rick and Ilsa's reunion (33:34; Reel 4, Part 7); (2) with F♯, at Ilsa's late-night return (48:10; Reel 5, Part 4); (3) with F♯, the second night as Rick enters his apartment over the café and sees Ilsa (1:19:37; Reel 10, Part 2); and (4) with F♯, very near the end of the film, almost inaudible as the plane's engines start up (1:38:44; Reel 11, Part 2).[5] (Note: In this tally, we have not counted the internal repetitions of the chord within the cues named.)

Steiner was quite fond of dissonant stinger chords, and many of those in *Casablanca* are quite traditional, consisting of a diminished seventh chord (as for Renault's emphatic discarding of the Vichy water) or of a triad or seventh chord above a conflicting bass note. Two examples among many are the moment in the

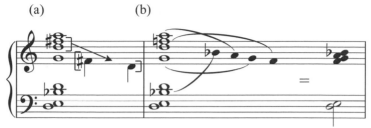

Figure 5.3. *Casablanca,* (a) the "5,4" chord with the interval frame of TROUBLE; (b) the gaze sonority and the first motive in "As Time Goes By."

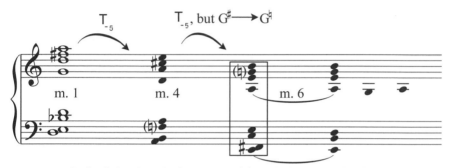

Figure 5.4. The "5,4" chord (with F♯) transposed directly down a perfect fourth in bar 4, then its transposition another fourth down, with one alteration: G♯ becomes G♮ (in the box), and finally the actual music in bar 6.

reunion scene when the Germans' marching into Paris is mentioned—E♯°⁷ over an F♯ bass—and, in the consolation scene, a D°⁷ chord over an E♭ bass (Marks 2000, 169). Occasionally, less traditional chords are employed for harsher dramatic moments, as when the Resistance fighter is shot trying to escape from the police in the opening scene: an F+ᵐᵃʲ⁷ chord is heard at that moment, immediately followed by a sustained B♭ minorᵐᵃʲ⁷ chord. And in the final minutes of the film, multiple stinger chords of all types are heard, including an A minor ⁶₄ chord when Renault arrests Laszlo but turns to see Rick holding a gun (1:34:35); an A♯ half-diminished⁷ chord on the subsequent cut to Major Strasser on the phone; E half-diminished ⁶₅ after he calls for his car; D°⁷ chord over a bass E♭ on the cut to the airport (1:36:15); F minor with a split fifth on the cut to Strasser in his car (1:37:48); plus the gaze sonority, the "Vichy" chord, and a string of dissonant, sharply articulated chords for the final confrontation between Strasser and Rick.

The first time we hear a stinger chord, remarkably, is less than four seconds into the film. Steiner's trademark studio-logo music, as Marks aptly describes it, starts "firmly in C major, [but] lands as firmly on a B major chord after a measure and a half, or [less than] five seconds later" (2000, 164) (see figure 5.5). Innocent though it all sounds, "such a sequence of harmonies can be manipulated to

Figure 5.5. *Casablanca,* basic chord progression in the opening seconds of the film.

lead to any key one wishes, and in this case the goal turns out to be F minor." The movement is certainly abrupt, and the resounding dissonance (at the asterisk) certainly creates the surprise effect of a stinger chord, even though it is only marginally louder than its predecessors. The accompaniment for the "Africa" theme that will follow in another ten seconds starts up underneath, and the held chord is there "long enough to define it as a dissonance needing resolution," which it finds in an open fifth, F and C, which in turn Steiner fills in with the minor third, the first held note of the "Africa" theme.

The motivation for such an aggressive opening is unclear, all the more so as the energy and volume suggest that the film to follow will be an action drama, which *Casablanca* patently is not. The prominent stinger chord that ends the main-title cue (at 1:05), on the other hand, is deliberately and clearly connected to the drama. This chord—unquestionably a stinger in its effect yet with an oddly muffled orchestration—sets the final pitch of "La Marseillaise" and earned this marginal annotation from Steiner: "Hugo. An ominous note intrudes on 'La Belle France.'"[6] Figure 5.6a reproduces the chord in the voicing of Steiner's sketches along with the ostinato chord underlying the "refugee march" that comes immediately after. This ostinato chord simultaneously represents a transposition of what we will call the "Marseillaise" chord down a half step—note especially that the dissonant A♮ shifts down to G♯—while effecting a resolution to a D minor triad. That is, the bass and primary dissonance of the "Marseillaise" chord move down by half step in the ostinato chord, whereas the rest of the chord formation—a minor triad (A♯ minor versus D minor)—is built a fifth above the root in the first case but on the root in the second. If we apply the transposition to the "Marseillaise" chord itself, the result is as in figure 5.6b. In order to facilitate comparison of the pitch materials, the "Marseillaise" chord and the 5,4 chord have, respectively, been converted to scale form in figure 5.6c. It takes only deleting the note G5 (crossed through) to see that the two chords are inversions of one another: in pitch classes, <8,9,0,2,4> inverted about the axis E♭ or A becomes <2,4,6,9,10>. The individual changes are mapped onto the original chord voicings in figure 5.6d: thus, A remains the same, while D and E switch places, C becomes F♯, and G♯ becomes B♭.

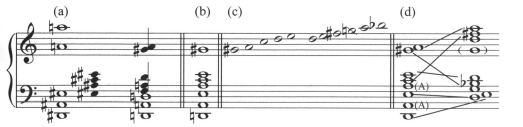

Figure 5.6, a–d. *Casablanca*, the axial pitch relationships of the main-title "Marseillaise" chord and the "5,4" chord: (a) the "Marseillaise" chord and the "resolution" used under the ensuing "refugee march"; (b) transposition of the "Marseillaise" chord down a half step; (c) the version in (b) and the "5,4" chord arranged in scalar form; (d) the axial relationships of the two chords (about D/E, or Eb).

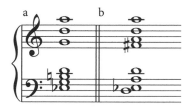

Figure 5.7, a–b. *Casablanca*, inversion around F/F♯: (a) the "Marseillaise" chord in the voicing of figure 5.6b; (b) the refugee chord from figure 5.6a.

The symbolism of the connection is obvious: the generalized events and dangers represented in the main-title cue and prologue are drawn down to the very personal in the first confrontation scene. The 5,4 chord is so distinctive in its structure that it is plausible Steiner might have built inverted forms literally and then adjusted them. In figure 5.7a, the "Marseillaise" chord, transposed down a half step, as in figure 5.6b, easily generates a structure close to the later stinger chords by inversion about F/F♯. These not only are significant pitches but as an axis of inversion also have the advantage that they hold constant the fifth D–A. In this case, that fifth is moved from bottom to top, replaced at the bottom by a stack of thirds above Eb. Inversion of the refugee chord (see figure 5.7b) generates the D major chord in the upper parts while introducing a second in the bass.

A caveat: although we suspect this reading based on symbolic inversion is correct, still, without confirmation, it is impossible to say for certain. The reason for hesitation is that Steiner does not exploit inversion in an obvious way in any other of the several dozen scores—all of them characteristic of his practice—that we have examined in detail over the years. And, although he routinely uses chords

Part 1

Part 2

Part 3: see Figure 5.11a
Part 4

Figure 5.8. The tetrachordal motives of "As Time Goes By" in the four parts of the reunion scene.

Part 3: see Figure 5.11a

mm. 11-18

(lacks G♭)

(lacks E♭)

Figure 5.9. The tetrachordal motives in part 2, with "Deutschland" (below) and the aggregate (at the right).

that are dissonant with their bass notes (or a held upper-voice pitch) and does make use of out-of-phase layering, he rarely uses clearly defined, functionally explicit extended tertian chords. The *Casablanca* chord may well have been his first inspiration for the film's underscore, and its implications may have shaped the music in unusual ways.

The Tetrachords of "As Time Goes By"

The urge to construct and manipulate a small set of distinctive stinger chords may well have had its source in the melodic structure of "As Time Goes

Figure 5.10a. The tetrachordal motives in Part 3 (variants of those in the bridge of "As Time Goes By" [see figure 5.10b]).

Figure 5.10b. The tetrachordal motives in the bridge of "As Time Goes By."

By." Every phrase (including the bridge) repeats and transposes (or otherwise alters) a single motive and ends with a slower-moving cadential tag. The principal phrase uses tetrachords (see figure 5.8). As we noted in the list in chapter 4, part 1 has the original, diatonic version of the theme; part 2 pushes motive B a half step higher (motive F) before correcting itself, but the fourth iteration (G) is cut off; and part 4 moves the melody down a step to E♭, maintaining the first three motives (H, J, K ≅ A, B, C) but pushing the last one (L) up a half step.

The half-step distortions are enough to make it clear that Steiner was aware of the song's repeated motives (how could he not be?), but that he also understood and was willing to manipulate them as tetrachordal shapes is clear from the developments of parts 2 and 3. In part 2, there is in fact a fourth iteration of the tetrachord, as the first to fourth scale degrees of the minor-key version of "Deutschland über alles" (see figure 5.9). This tetrachord is identical to motive F except for octave: thus, the expressive distortion in one case becomes attached to a key center in the other. The aggregate of the four iterations in part 2 is interesting in its own right: ten pitch classes, excluding only G♭ and E♭, the latter being the tonic of the key in which "As Time Goes By" will appear in part 5.

A more complex but equally telling instance occurs in part 3. The "walking music" may use melodic shapes that are different from the principal phrases, but

Figure 5.11. *Casablanca,* reunion scene key scheme, with tetrachords.

there are four of these shapes, and all can be understood as distorted transpositions of the first, which has the same interval order as motive B and the same pitches as that motive's analogue in the E♭ major statement of part 4 (that is, motive J) (see figure 5.10a). We have marked the second iteration "T4"—it is recognizable as a transposition up a major third, but the uppermost note has been pushed a whole step higher, from D to E. The third iteration moves the initial motive up an octave, and the final one, which is barely recognizable, goes up another perfect fourth, to the position of the "goal key," E♭. The design is the same as the bridge in "As Time Goes By" (see figure 5.10b). The tetrachords in the bass clef are obviously not the same. What Steiner has done with his "walking music" is to map the tetrachordal motives of the principal phrase onto the phrase design of the bridge.

Finally, the combination of the tetrachords with the key scheme for the reunion scene allows a particularly clear view of a reiterated process in parts 1 and 2 and in part 4 (see figure 5.11). The initial D♭ is the key in which Sam sings and to which the cue ultimately returns. Motive G is the diatonic correction of motive F's distortion, but it is at that moment that the underlying key goes askew, with the F♯ pedal tone in the bass and "Deutschland" in G♯ minor in the midregister. Once E♭ major is reached in part 4, the process is repeated. This time the key remains stable under the distortion (motive L), but immediately afterward the key changes in order to accommodate the melody, which concludes the phrase in its new position on E. The end result is the same: the melody has forced the harmony to move in a different direction.

The Flashback and First Confrontation Scene

Once the reunion scene ends, there is an obvious temporal gap, a jump to the darkened bar after hours, with Rick sitting and Sam playing the piano some fifteen feet away. Once the long flashback (a sequence as famous as the reunion scene) has finished, time runs continuously again as Ilsa reappears and the couple argue. Music goes out with the scene—a dissolve transitioning to the next day—and is effectively gone for ten minutes,[7] until we again see the café sign, and the second evening's activities commence (notably among them, conversations in Rick's apartment, the "battle of anthems," and the closing of the café by Renault).

Figure 5.12. *Casablanca,* Rick, Ilsa, and Sam in La belle Aurore. Screen still.

The flashback to Paris, then, intervenes between the reunion scene and the first confrontation. Structured as a long, slow-moving montage, the flashback fills in a substantial amount of information, principally about Rick and Ilsa's romance but also about Sam's role and, finally, about the mystery of Rick's disgruntled, cynical pose as the owner of a café in Casablanca. The after-hours scenes, however, begin before the flashback, with the conversation between Rick and Sam in the darkened café. Following directly from the reunion scene, Rick's emotional deflation at the end of the reunion scene has now become a drunken stupor, and where Sam had pleaded with Ilsa to stay away from Rick, now he urges Rick to go away, to get out of town. Sam is obliged to replay his earlier performance of "As Time Goes By"—though he plays rather than sings—and he triggers the flashback by doing so. Brief citations of the song appear in the first part of the flashback, but the central moment is the short scene in La belle Aurore, analyzed above, which finds Sam at the piano again. The core moment of the Paris utopia is here (see figure 5.12). Sam is no longer playing when Ilsa resists Rick's suggestion to marry, and at the end of the flashback a tortured orchestral rendering of "As Time Goes By" is wholly internal to Rick as he reads the parting letter from Ilsa. Only he can "hear" what the song means, and it is up to Sam to act in the diegetic world as he pushes Rick onto the train. On the return to the café and current time, Sam has no more music; instead, he resets the overturned glass and straightens a chair. Ilsa at that moment appears in the doorway to the sound of the 5,4 chord. After

Table 5.2. *Casablanca*, reunion and first confrontation scenes, invariant structure and additions

Invariant structure	Additions
Ilsa or Rick alone (no music)	
Sam enters	
Dialogue	
	Request for Sam to play (reunion scene only)
Sam plays	
Request for ATGB	
Refusal	
Second request	
Sam plays ATGB	
	Third request (reunion scene only)
	Sam sings ATGB (reunion scene only)
Close-up	
	Flashback (after-hours scene only)
Interruption of Sam playing by Rick	
Chord with Ilsa	
Sam exits	
Music under dialogue	

close-ups of Rick and Ilsa, Sam is simply gone. The reemergence of Paris for both Rick and Ilsa in the reunion scene became Rick's feverish reimagining of it in the flashback, but now, with Sam absent, it turns dystopic in Rick's persistently harsh accusations, which Ilsa is given no real opportunity to counter.

The flashback and the first confrontation with Ilsa, taken together, can be seen as a radically expanded version of the reunion scene itself: the song is played and the shock is replayed, now drunkenly ("Of all the gin joints . . ."); the utopia is rebuilt or reimagined; and "Paris" is crushed by Ilsa's abandonment of Rick. Table 5.2 traces the parallels in detail. Like the conversation scene after the gaze sonority, this confrontation scene can be divided into four parts aligned with the underscore cue. The first part (at 48:10) begins with the 5,4 chord, the analogue to the gaze sonority (see again figure 4.1). The slow-moving, sharply articulated chromatic octaves (the first appearance of what we will call the "Trouble" motive) that wind their way through the middle registers of the 5,4 chord statements are the mirror of "As Time Goes By" in the reunion scene: the earlier scene's diatonic melody floating upward over a soft, if slightly ambiguous, diatonic chord has become in the later scene a determined chromatic line moving downward and generating a string of dissonant conflicts with the sustained chords as a result.[8] As in the reunion scene, however, it is Ilsa who dispels the tension foregrounded in the music: she speaks, saying that they need to talk. Rick reluctantly agrees, and

Figure 5.13, a–c. (a) *Casablanca,* confrontation between Lisa and Rick, motive referred to by Steiner (my transcription); (b) parallel motive in *Tosca,* first option ("Qual'occhio al mondo," opening); (c1–c2) parallel motive in *Tosca,* second option: (c1) the clarinet before "O dolce mani"; (c2) Tosca leaps to her death. (From a figure of the author's in *Wagner and Cinema,* edited by Jeongwon Joe and Sander Gilman [2009]. Reused by permission of Indiana University Press.)

in part 2 (at 49:25) Ilsa begins her explanation. Her speech is bifurcated: the first half is an attempt to calm Rick down, a plea to his sympathy, and the second half is about Laszlo and her attraction to him as an idealist and activist.

The first of the two motives is labeled "Tosca" because Steiner has added a marginal note in his sketch: "A poor man's Tosca" (see also figure 5.13a).[9] He is apparently referring to a melodic resemblance either to the opening of Cavaradossi's act 1 aria "Qual'occhio al mondo" (figure 5.13b) or to the clarinet motive that precedes his "O dolce mani" in act 3 and figures prominently throughout that act, most spectacularly at the end, the moment of Tosca's leap to her death (see figure 5.13c1–c2). Whether Steiner deliberately introduced this motive in order to make a subtle reference to the plot parallel (Rick could save Laszlo, as Scarpia could save Cavaradossi) or simply noticed the resemblance after the fact is unknown. Because Steiner did not write the score in the chronological order of the film, however, it is possible that he decided on the motivic citation while writing music for the final confrontation, a scene that might easily be misconstrued to suggest that Rick would ask for sexual favors in return for the exit visas, as Scarpia did of Tosca in return for Cavaradossi's release (the issue is actually more complicated, as we shall see below). Still, even then, the introduction of the motive does not align with any strongly parallel dramatic moment (such as revealing the gun, the analogue to the knife with which Tosca kills Scarpia). The motive, instead, first appears when Ilsa makes another allusion to their time together in Paris ("Richard, we loved each other once").

The association of "Tosca" with sexual tension between Rick and Ilsa seems more plausible in part 3 (at 50:06), when Rick reacts dismissively, becoming more and more bitter, until his final words prompt Ilsa to leave ("Or are you the kind that doesn't tell?"). In part 4 (at 50:40), utterly deflated, Rick lets his head fall to the table within a last reminiscence of "As Time Goes By," generating another mirror reversal in relation to the reunion scene: in the latter, the song is first stated in F, then near the end in E♭, but here it is the opposite: the statement in E♭ is paired with the later one in F.[10] The scene ends with a quick fade to black at 51:00, followed by a fade-in to Strasser and Renault consulting in the latter's office.

Thus, cue 5,4 is clearly a compositional source for much of the material in cue 4,7, but in terms of formal or sectional design this applies only in the opening. The gaze sonority accompanies an associative theme ("Trouble"), then gives way to a neutral action music, then to "As Time Goes By" (in E♭ in both cues). Looking at the two scenes in a different way—from the standpoint of the song statements—we can see the first confrontation scene as an expanded reversal of the reunion scene: speech in the middle with quotations of "As Time Goes By" at (or near) the end, with the keys switched as noted above. Rick has reached his nadir in the moments after Ilsa leaves, but ironically the song, its last quotation like the first being in F, leaves him where he started at the moment he saw Ilsa in his café earlier that evening.

Both "Trouble" and "Tosca" appear here for the first time, and one could certainly argue that their significant expressive roles later in the film, roles that succeed in part because of the associations established within this scene, would justify their presence here. At the same time, and by analogy to the reunion scene, music might well have dropped out, perhaps as early as bar 6, or, to preserve the connection to the immediately preceding flashback through the citation of "As Time Goes By," perhaps by bar 16, then returning somewhere between bars 31–35 or in bar 39 for the sake of the final song quotation. The emotional intensity of the scene is carried with great effectiveness by the voices on their own; the music offers some associative links and some dramatic intensification. The starkness of conversation without music here would also have been convincing. The principle of vococentrism recognizes that little on the sound track except the voice is strictly necessary and that alternative configurations of the sound track therefore always exist. Vococentrism does not require that the voice always be centered on the sound track but that the analysis always take account of the place of the voice, that it place the voice in the field of meaning. The centrality of the voice concerns its placement in analysis and interpretation rather than on the sound track. The analytical consequences that should be drawn from this are that we need to describe and evaluate how the rest of the sound track positions the voice.

The Second Confrontation Scene

When Ilsa returns to the Café Américain after hours on the second night, she has hidden in Rick's apartment and confronts him with great emotion, demanding that he surrender the letters of transit that will save her husband's life. She eventually pulls a pistol on him and all but calls him a cad and a scoundrel. This scene is considerably longer and more diffuse than either the reunion or first confrontation scene, but most of the music is repeated from the latter or from the flashback. This scene was another of Casey Robinson's suggestions, his goal being to make subsequent action, including the finale, more plausible (Osborne 1997, 190). It is effective in the larger narrative context (the intensity of Ilsa's emotion and commitment in the early minutes eventually get through to Rick, who then develops his plan to get Ilsa and Laszlo out of Morocco), and it is certainly acted well. Nevertheless, this second private interaction between Rick and Ilsa also reveals the film's most ill-fitting seams. It not only includes some embarrassing dialogue (including the notorious clinker "You have to think for both of us . . . for all of us") but also uses the crisis to reverse the positions of Ilsa and Rick in terms of initiative and their romantic relationship.

We share the opinion of virtually all the film's commentators that this is the film's weakest plot element. Up to this point, Rick has been the one burdened with music. He has been traumatized by the relationship, and the underscore music has generally reflected this fact. Ilsa has also been a fairly active character, with the primary goal of obtaining exit visas and a secondary one of explaining herself to Rick. As mentioned, she comes to the apartment not for romance but in the hopes of convincing Rick to surrender the letters of transit. Rick's actions so far, by contrast, have been mostly reactive or emotionally overwrought. From the moment Ilsa arrives in the café to the point she draws the gun on Rick, the film treats him somewhat like the emotionally vulnerable woman in the stereotypical Hollywood relationship and Ilsa somewhat more like the rational and detached man.

The reversal of their characters to the default Hollywood positions occurs in extremely short order, and the bulk of the task is accomplished in a prominent ellipsis that leaves motivations unspecified. It relies on a tacit convention of gender roles to explain the shift and the intimation of a sexual encounter to justify concealing it. Their kiss is followed by a dissolve to a watchtower outside, then a second dissolve to Rick standing near the window, and finally a two-shot with Rick standing and Ilsa sitting on a couch. Rick's standing near the window, his somewhat hurried "and then" (as if the dissolve covered an extended explanation from Ilsa), and the two-shot showing her sitting on the couch and him standing are all an attempt to cover over the awkwardness by suggesting that they have been in conversation all this time. The implication was certainly not lost on the censor, but he insisted only that no bed be visible and that a dissolve be used rather than a fade (which would have suggested a greater passage of time) (Harmetz 2002, 163–64).[11] In any event, the titillating question of what happened during the ellipsis is ultimately a red herring that distracts the viewer from the radical character realignment that emerges from it, even more so because the conventional morality implied by the ellipsis requires that Ilsa and Rick remain chaste—that they not yield to "socially unsanctioned desires"—if the love she subsequently professes is in fact true and transformative of character, especially toward the conventional norm (Maltby 1996, 441). Yet if nothing censorable in fact happened during the interval, there was no reason to conceal the moment's transformational event other than the fact that it proved impossible to represent convincingly within the constraints of the story the sudden conventional realignment of gender representation under the power of love. This is the wide gap in the plot that the cutaway to the tower attempts to hide.

Steiner does what he can to help: the passionate waltz version of "As Time Goes By" ends with the kiss, but its final chord is $E\flat^{\flat 9}$, an oddly tenuous sonority that is sustained by the strings and given an enigmatic splash of color by the arpeggiating harp; it is held through the dissolve to the tower and the subsequent shot of Rick at the open window, up to his "and then."[12] The decision to hold the chord throughout and beyond the dissolve is an effective way to minimize the sense of any significant amount of time passing. One has to wonder what else Steiner could possibly have done except leave music out altogether so that the scene would have a neutral, prosaic feel. That would not have been a solution either, since the emotional level of the scene needs to be high in order to make Rick's change of attitude and subsequent actions convincing. Ironically, the scene might well have succeeded without music if we were only concerned with Ilsa: unlike the first confrontation scene, she commands the conversation throughout, and the emotional level of her performance is the highest it is anywhere in the film. Rick, on the other hand, is passive, mostly watching: we see little in his eyes or his body until he is truly disconcerted by Ilsa's breakdown (in a nice nod to Bogart's earlier typecasting as a tough guy or gangster, he seems genuinely surprised when she doesn't shoot him).

Steiner wrote two underscoring cues: Reel 9, Part 2 runs up to the dissolve; Reel 9, Part 3 enters after the ensuing conversation and runs through Rick's telling Carl to take Ilsa home. In the first of the scene's five segments (at 1:19:37), Rick enters his apartment over the café and realizes Ilsa is there. The 5,4 chord sounds as he turns on the light and looks across the room. It continues on a quick pan over to her. This differs from both the reunion scene and the first confrontation scene in that the chord accompanies a shot of Rick instead of Ilsa, but it duplicates the situation of the reunion scene in being associated with Rick seeing Ilsa. In the first confrontation scene, by contrast, Rick is looking down at the table when Ilsa comes through the door, and he lifts his head noticeably after the sounding of the chord.

TROUBLE

Figure 5.14. *Casablanca,* part 3 of the second confrontation scene, underscore (reduction). (Based on sketches in the Max Steiner Collection, Brigham Young University, and materials in the Warner Bros. Collection, University of Southern California.)

The opening measures of the music are a direct citation of the beginning of cue 5,4, followed by a development of same: "Trouble" thus lasts nearly a minute, up to a long-held note. The second section begins (at 1:20:34) as Rick walks away toward the window. She follows, speaking more intensely of Paris, and "Tosca" intervenes in a complicated set of transpositions of its earlier forms. After Rick walks back into the room and Ilsa calls him a coward (section 3, at 1:21:05), "Trouble" returns (see figure 5.14) and continues till he lights a cigarette, turns, and sees Ilsa with the gun (section 4 at 1:21:35). At this point, "As Time Goes By" makes its first appearance in the scene in a distorted version of the reunion scene opening that is quickly displaced by a minor-key version of the "Laszlo" theme (when Rick mentions him and the "cause"). When she breaks down (section 5 at 1:22:10), "Trouble" sounds again, but before long it melts into a charged form of the waltz version of "As Time Goes By" as Ilsa refers to the "last day in Paris." In the orchestration of that moment, the music is being replayed from the flashback, just after the German loudspeaker sounds and she asks "Is it cannon fire . . ." As we noted above, its closing Eb^{flat9} chord is held through the dissolve (1:23:04), nearly up to the two-shot at 1:23:15. Music is out until Ilsa says, "I can't fight it anymore" (at 1:25:05), and cue 9,3 starts with a serene statement of "As Time Goes By." A sudden burst of *agitato* intervenes at 1:25:37 as Laszlo and Carl run toward the café, and the *misterioso* affect continues in a series of figures until a final, striking statement of "As Time Goes By" in woodwind octaves, augmented by celesta and vibraphone, all over an Eb minor $\frac{6}{4}$ chord in the bass register and held until the scene ends at 1:27:05.

The design overall, then, is much like that of the first confrontation scene: a series of citations and variations of a small set of themes: "Trouble," "Tosca," and "As Time Goes By." In all this, the version of the gaze sonority from the reunion

missing

Figure 5.15. *Casablanca*, gaze sonority transformations in opening of cue 9,2.

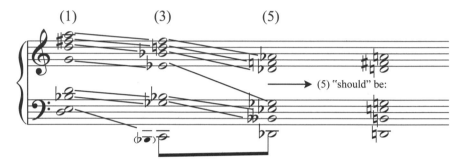

(1)   (3)   (5)

(5) "should" be:

Figure 5.16. *Casablanca,* cue 9,2: chords that begin parts 1, 3, and 5 show the "deflation" device again.

scene never appears, but the 5,4 chord and several variants do, repeatedly. As we noted in the summary of the scene above, the opening is a literal restatement of the opening of the first confrontation scene, but the T-5 transposition has now become T-6 (see the second chord in figure 5.15). The third chord in the figure exploits the deflation device even more, going to T-9, but it adds to that a distortion—an irregular transposition—that brings the third chord back to 5,4 in a registrally compacted version. As the "Trouble" motive moves down from F♯5 to C♯5, however, the chord changes into an identifiable A^{flat9} over a pedal D, that is to say, the functional chord in D minor to which we traced the gaze sonority earlier (figure 4.10). That functional connection, which had significant consequences in the reunion scene, is much more tenuous here: the effect is of a dominant of the dominant, as the music continues in G minor.

On a larger scale, the three appearances of the 5,4 chord to begin sections—in the opening and sections 3 and 5—work out the deflation device as well. The chord that opens part 3 is a T-4 transposition, but, like the second chord in figure 5.15, it lacks the bass note and thus clearly sounds like an extended form of a half-diminished chord (see figure 5.16). And, also like the opening of the scene (see again figure 5.15), the third chord in the series is a distorted transposition: the four upper voices and G♭3 move down at T-9, but B♭3 is only at T-7, and the bass actually moves up to D♭ (the note that B♭ would have taken in a completely parallel transposition). The end result is a nearly exact repositioning of the 5,4 chord at T-12 (in parentheses) but deflated at an additional half step.

The Finale: Max Steiner, Reluctant Hero

In the previous section, we have conjured up and dwelt on the image of the composer, pen in hand, thinking about notes: chords, themes, instrumental colors. Managing his creative task like any composer, regardless of medium or genre, Steiner manipulates notes, sometimes abstractly—as we saw in the variants of the 5,4 chord and the motivic tetrachord—and sometimes formally, thematically, in terms of development of material. At the same time, recall that this composer is sitting at a desk (or in Steiner's case, more likely at the piano) on which lies a detailed cue sheet prepared by a studio music editor. Chords, themes, and instruments are marshaled according to their narrative functions and effects.

We know that Steiner was reluctant to use "As Time Goes By": he had just written a theme song for *Now, Voyager* that was published as "It Can't Be Wrong" (with lyrics by Kim Gannon), and he saw in *Casablanca* an even better chance to produce a hit. Having accepted the situation as it was, however, Steiner made the most of it, helping to create a soundscape that, for its time, is remarkably subtle, complex, and varied. The underscore is present for much of the film's first six minutes, including the establishing sequence and prologue. During the next twenty-seven minutes, we hear more than eleven minutes of diegetic music from the band or Dooley Wilson but no underscore. Once the gaze sonority sounds, the underscore predominates: of the remaining seventy minutes, about thirty-eight have underscore; diegetic music adds another six. Left to his own devices and habits, Steiner might well have written another ten minutes of music here and there, perhaps even more.

Although it seems to have been a matter of temperament in part, this tendency on Steiner's part toward "wall-to-wall" underscoring came out of the early 1930s, from his collaborations with David O. Selznick at RKO. As noted in connection with *Rebecca* in chapter 2, Selznick had a decidedly conservative but at the same time remarkably aggressive attitude toward sound and music: he was a strong proponent of the idea of film as art, but he looked back to the picture palaces of the 1920s, where orchestral music had predominated, as his model for high-class film production and presentation. After some early, not entirely successful experiments, notably including *Bird of Paradise* and *Symphony of Six Million* (both 1932), the exotic-fantasy extravaganza *King Kong* (1933) was a spectacular success. After 1935, when the original dramatic score was recognized as an Academy Award category, it was assumed that prestige films would have a substantial underscore. As Michel Chion complains, "The mid-thirties witnessed a

Table 5.3. *Casablanca*, table of sound track elements in the final fifteen minutes

Time	Action	Speech	Music (all underscore)	Effects
1:27:00	Rick in café downstairs talks to Laszlo, who was injured	Continuous (Rick, Laszlo; predominantly Laszlo)	Out	Conversation direct recorded: we hear buzzer, footfalls at the end
1:28:30	Police break into the café; at 1:29:04 dissolve to Rick and Renault at Renault's office talking	Policeman speaks; after dissolve continuous (Rick, Renault; predominantly Rick)	In; out 1:28:40; in 1:28:48 with "As Time Goes By" quickly, but then it slows down, overlaps slightly with dissolve	
1:31:28	Dissolve to Blue Parrot: café view, then conversation in office	Continuous (Rick and Ferrari; balanced)	Blue Parrot music in background; louder than in earlier scenes?	Direct-recorded conversation between Rick and Ferrari: tea cups; flyswatter
1:32:12	Nighttime car approach to café; Renault enters, they talk; others arrive; Renault arrests, is interrupted by Rick; Renault calls "airport" (actually, Strasser)	Rick and Renault: equal, hurried; short conversations mostly in pairs after that; ends with Rick and Renault	Music in; out 1:32:43. In 1:33:09 just after car is heard outside; out 1:34:00 with letters/Renault; in 1:34:18 Renault turns, gun; 1:35:00 phone call; music out 1:35:30, after dissolve to airport	Renault knocks on door; with cut inside you can tell the mike is near the front door—Rick's footsteps get louder as he approaches and opens it; occasional sounds from Renault later
1:35:25	Dissolve to airport; dispatch officer on phone; 1:35:45 car arrives; Rick and Renault talk	Mike above while Rick and Ilsa talk, almost unnaturally foregrounded	Music in 1:36:17 after Rick names Laszlo and Ilsa for visas (agitato "As Time Goes By")—underscore is lower below dialogue than typical (they're also speaking quickly)—ends with "here's looking" and "As Time Goes By" comes forward more—end of A' phrase with clear tonic	Car sound is heard while it wraps around the hangar; persistent rain sounds; phone noise when hung up, and footsteps; car comes under a mike near entrance (loud engine noise till turned off)

Time	Shot	Speech	Music	Sound effects
1:37:49	Cut to Strasser in car; back to airport; now Rick and Laszlo	Rick and Laszlo talk	Effects chord, with car horn; chord holds over into cut back to airport, well into it. Music back in under conversation at 1:38:20	Car horn; footsteps as Laszlo approaches from outside
1:38:42	Cut to airplane; then back to Rick, Laszlo, and Ilsa	Laszlo and Ilsa talk—only a few short sentences, then Rick, too	Music under the airplane, then emerges	(Loud; like an insert) then back to conversation (engine is softer, as if at correct physical distance)
1:39:30	Cut back to Rick and Renault, they talk	Rick and Renault, foregrounded	Music continues under	Engine noise much subdued
1:39:55	To plane, and Strasser arrives	Renault and Strasser talk; Rick and Strasser	Low-level music under effects	Louder briefly with shot of plane; then car noise as Strasser arrives; repeated as plane leaves
1:40:29	Shot; car arrives; plane; car gone by 1:41:08		Music continues—pops out with Vichy stinger	Pattern of speech, music, plane continues—car arrives. Some low-level noise of policemen carrying Strasser away; car leaves. "Vichy" water opening is foregrounded
1:41:29	Plane takes off [after "Vichy"]	No speech		Loud noise (music effect, too) of plane taking off
1:41:46	Last conversation	Rick and Renault talk	Music rises gradually as they talk, then takes over	Rain sounds barely audible at beginning
1:42:35	End			

tidal wave of films sporting obtrusive musical accompaniments. Sandwiched between equally prolix doses of dialogue and music, noises then became unobtrusive and timid, tending much more toward stylized and coded sound effects than a really fleshed-out rendering of life" (1994, 146). In 1936, when Steiner moved from RKO to Warner Bros., he found studio executives who were supportive not only of large amounts of dramatic music but also of foregrounding that music in the sound track.

The climax of this trend in Hollywood prestige films came at the end of the decade in prestige films covering a variety of genres: *The Adventures of Robin Hood* (1938), *The Wizard of Oz, Dark Victory, Gone with the Wind, Wuthering Heights* (all 1939), and *Rebecca* (1940). Also by this time the construct of the "constant-level sound track," and with it a fully formed classical aesthetic, had been achieved (Altman 1992, 56): volume was the unifying constant, and the balance (amount and prominence of each) of the sound track elements was negotiated within that frame. Patterns and teleologies of design in the individual sound track elements were of course still possible, even as these designs were being negotiated in the context of a unifying, multiplane sound system (Altman 2000, 339, 357–58). The constraints under which Steiner worked on *Casablanca,* in other words, were more than simply a matter of working around all the source music. To be sure, that practical problem for him did work to the film's advantage, as its sound track, in terms of its music, is more varied (and, we would argue, more interesting) than almost any other Hollywood film of its time.

It is the film's final minutes, however, that demonstrate what was possible in those early years of the classical, multiplane sound system: they are among the most intricate and aesthetically interesting in the studio-era Hollywood film repertoire. One can get a sense of those qualities by looking at table 5.3, a table of the action along with descriptions of sound track elements for the last fifteen minutes of the film (which encompasses all the action after the second confrontation scene). A quick glance will confirm the amount of activity in all three of the sound track elements. Before the dissolve to the airport (at 1:35:25), effects are generally subdued—with the important exception of Renault knocking on the door of the café—but rain, car sounds, and other noises become more prominent and, crucially, persistent. There is some irony here, of course, in that the distinctly live sound quality comes in significant part from the open space of the hangar and the nighttime "exterior" (actually all of it was built inside a studio, a point that would have been obvious to any viewer at the time). The film's final five minutes complete the trajectory: effects leap to the front with the cut to the airplane and the loud noise of its engines starting up (at 1:38:42). From that point on, until the plane takes off, the three sound track elements do an intricate dance, as speech is sometimes foregrounded, music is unusually low (ceding its place to effects) but then suddenly emerges (as in the "Vichy" stinger), and airplane noise moves in and out, forward and back.

The Vichy stinger—which serves to punctuate one of the score's more distorted renditions of "La Marseillaise"—and the airplane sound that follows the chord mark the formal end of the film's action and the beginning of a brief epilogue, which consists in Rick and Renault walking into the fog accompanied by the strains of a hymn-like rendition of the French national anthem as they discuss joining a "free French garrison." Music here reasserts itself as the principal accompaniment to the voice, and, as Nicholas Reyland (2012, 64) points out, drawing on Robert Hatten's (1991, 76–82) concept of "expressive genre," solidifies the ideological point of the film by shifting the orchestration of "La Marseillaise" so that its national anthem topic is inflected with the religious, moral tone of the style topic of Laszlo's theme, which is used more generally to represent the idealism of the just cause. "La Marseillaise" is transfigured, the juxtaposition of two renditions at the end of the film (the distorted form associated with Vichy, the ethereal form with the Resistance cause) plays out in small form the large form of its symbolic transformation across the film from opening credits to closing end card: "The anthem began its life in the score denoting location (French-occupied Morocco), but ends up symbolizing notions of liberty more attuned to its revolutionary origins. Its meaning pivots midway through the film in the duel of the anthems sequence, in which the action is directed, in turn, by the thematically and ideological pivotal Laszlo," the representative of the film's "moral center" (Reyland 2012, 66, 63).[13]

Equally important to the ideological project of the film is the shift on the sound track from emphasizing diegetic effects in the finale, especially the plane but the gunshot too, to the nondiegetic score in the coda. This play between effects and score as accompaniment to the voice is thematic. The insistence of the sound effects throughout the finale asserts the immediate demands of the diegesis. Music often seems an afterthought. In any event, the music is overwhelmed by the sound effects again and again. Whatever the music attempts to assert as an emotional, idealized, or affective setting of the words and actions is quickly overtaken by events and pushed aside by sound effects that announce the next segment of action. In the parting scene, sound effects are in fact minimal, and Rick's story of Ilsa's visit to his apartment is accompanied by Laszlo's theme as though to sanctify the words (whatever Renault or we might make of them). Nevertheless, the scene is concluded by the loud intrusion of the airplane engine starting up, which obliterates every other sound and so immediately answers the idealized, even fairy-tale speech with an all-encompassing diegetic demand. Sound effects here pull the words and their referents toward grounding in the immediate diegesis; music pushes them out to imagine the world otherwise. The diegetic present is overbearing, oppressively closing in toward a singular point of determinate conclusion (the syntax of tragedy), but the music stubbornly persists through most of the sequence as the mark of hope, as the sign that the world cannot be reduced to its diegetic appearance. The plane, however, crosses this opposition as both the most intrusive and insistent sound effect and the very vehicle of salvation and escape.[14]

It is important that we do not yield to the temptation to attribute to the music alone what is in fact the effect of the sound track and music's place in it. The ideological project of the film is much less persuasive without Steiner's music, to be sure, but it receives its purchase—delivers its "closing vision of ideologically charged grace" (Reyland 2012, 67)—through its placement on the sound track. The music itself is hardly up to the task (and any music that was up to the task on its own would be unlikely to manage the task as part of a film score). This is one of the principal lessons to be drawn from vococentrism.

And so we end where we began: with the "musical" construction of the sound track, the *mise-en-bande,* in the context of which Max Steiner's preference for close synchronization plays itself out as a virtuosic interweaving of underscore with dialogue and prominent effects based on a fine-tuned understanding of the sound editor's work.

Part III

Topics and Tropes:
Two Preludes by Bach

Introduction to Part 3

When, by about 1910, narrative films began to dominate cinema exhibition, the change affected the screening and therefore the production of movies. At that point, the role of music as performed live in the theater shifted from a semi-independent focus on performances of concert and salon works to a more integrated role in supporting the film's narrative (Buhler and Neumeyer 2014, 18–21).[1] After 1927, in the sound film, music was irrevocably (that is, physically) integrated into a complex (vococentric) sound track, a sound track that was in turn conceived in a give-and-take with the varying demands of the visual image.

With respect to the musical repertoires involved, one line of aesthetic debate and creative opportunity ran along the high art / low art—or concert/popular—divide, while another ran along the existing music / newly composed music axis. Although the emphases varied at certain points in the historical trajectory (the cinema counts its historical articulations—its "periods"—by the decade), the overall treatment of music was heterogeneous. As is so often the case, that heterogeneity can be difficult to uncover and recover in a later generation. For example, Tchaikovsky, Gounod, and Auber would have been highbrow in 1920, certainly when played by a professional ensemble (quality of performance was a distinguishing trait in cultural status). This is a particularly important consideration as late as *The Jazz Singer* (1927), which makes extensive use of the Russian composer's *Romeo and Juliet,* but more to signal high production values than to apply the lush romanticism or sexualized emotion usually ascribed to it.[2] Tchaikovsky remained highbrow even later, at least under the right conditions, as for example in *The Great Lie* (1941), where the First Piano Concerto figures prominently in a tale about a concert pianist. By 1950, however, with the general turn toward more dissonance in concert music, Tchaikovsky sank to a decidedly middlebrow level, as represented by pops concerts and the early stereo LPs of Mantovani, 101 Strings, and the like.

As another example, the expressionism of the Schoenberg school was initially typed for horror, rather than for the strong sense of psychological interiority that Schoenberg himself would undoubtedly have favored. Nevertheless, he seemed to encourage that outcome, as in the three cues he wrote for a German publisher's silent-film library in 1928, which he titled "Danger," "Fear," and "Catastrophe."[3] The last of these is the most extreme category—akin to the intersection of "Climax" and "Grim" (*Höhepunkt; Düster*)—in Hans Erdmann and Giuseppe Becce's exhaustive catalog of musical topics for silent-film performance, the *Allge-*

meines Handbuch der Film-Musik (1927). The direct connection to Hollywood, however, was made by Hans Salter, a student of Alban Berg who became Universal's in-house expert on music for horror films. In the 1950s, as Tchaikovsky's music succumbed to an evaluation as middlebrow, dissonant expressionist styles were more generally accepted and so seemed amenable to a broader range of expressive uses. However, as exemplified by Leonard Rosenman's underscore for *Freud* (1952) and Jerry Goldsmith's for *The Planet of the Apes* (1960), that expressive range appears to have been limited for the most part to psychological and futurist realms. In recent decades, especially, historical European styles have been exploited for their "classical" traits, but historical high-art styles of other cultures have occasionally been treated in a similar fashion. The opening of Kurosawa's *Rashomon* (1950), for example, uses Fumio Hayasaka's evocation of medieval Japanese court music the way a European composer might use a quotation from Mozart. And we may speculate how the opening of *Holy Smoke* (discussed in chapter 1) would differ if its establishing sequence had been accompanied by sitar and tabla rather than by a song by Neil Diamond. Obviously, the gradual passage into and through the fantastical gap that Stilwell observes would evaporate. Instead, the distance implied by unsynchronized, nondiegetic music—as found, typically, in the music for the opening credit sequence—would be maintained. Instead of zeroing in on a person (it doesn't take the audio-viewer long to catch on to the parallelism between "Holly Holy" and Kate Winslet's character), the music would offer a vaguer notion of the exotic by referring to India.

The exotic is an example of a musical style topic, an intermediate category in Robert Hatten's typology, where (1) *gesture* is concrete, immediate, an aural translation of embodied movement into figure, textural type, or theme; (2) *topic* refers to culturally settled clusters of gestures, "patches of music that trigger clear associations with [the still larger levels of] styles, genres, and expressive meanings"; and (3) *tropes* are creative combinations of topics, or "the interpretive synthesis of, for example, otherwise contradictory topics that are juxtaposed in a single functional location or rhetorical moment" (Hatten 2004, 2–3).[4] The sense of clarity or recognizability as an essential element is also apparent in Gerald Prince's definition of the synonymous "topos": "any of a stable disposition of motifs that frequently appears in (literary) texts" (1987, 88). Byron Almén, similarly, posits that "as a locus for a network of correlations, *topic is expressively static*. By contrast, as a manifestation of the playing-out of a fundamental opposition, *narrative is expressively dynamic*" (2008, 75; emphasis in original).[5]

Hatten's understanding of the word "trope" is narrower and more specific than its use in literary studies, where it is generally synonymous with "figure of speech" (McLaughlin 1990, 81).[6] The distinction between topic and trope, as maintained here, is close to one made in traditional rhetoric between stock devices (or schemata) and those figures of speech that change the meanings of words (Baldick 1990, 226, 230). From this we can derive the sense of topics as stable (even though they are, of course, contingent on a historical scale) and tropes as shifting, creative, or altering.

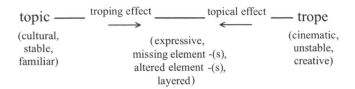

Figure 6.0a: Topic and trope: a continuum model.

Pragmatically, for the sake of interpretation of specific musical cues in a film context, I believe it is most effective to treat topic and trope in the form of a continuum (see figure 6.0a). One might think of this as oscillating between Claudia Gorbman's cultural musical code (relatively stable, generally understood) and cinematic musical codes (developed or reconceived in the context of an individual film, therefore both unstable and creative). A troping effect is laid on a topic when it is treated in an expressive rather than neutral fashion, an effect that is cumulative. Thus, a single altered element (such as guitar rather than piano, added reverb, slower or faster than expected tempo, or a distinctive articulation such as *non legato*) may or may not significantly alter the topic, but more than one ("-(s)" in figure 6.0a) almost certainly will. An analogous topical effect is laid on a trope by repetition, as in the establishment of motifs (whether visual, verbal, or aural).

We could, of course, argue that troping is inevitable because figures of speech are inevitable; indeed, the meaning of "troping" is all too easily expanded to become synonymous with "creative writing." With respect to film, troping can be said to be inevitable because of Michel Chion's principle of added value: the music *must* change the image (and vice versa). Although differences in tempo and instrumentation will certainly play a role, I will follow Chion here in that I understand the greater potential for a strongly expressive troping as occurring not within the music cue itself but between the image and the sound. I invoke the continuum, however, in order to emphasize the idea that, for purposes of interpretation, such expressive juxtapositions are best understood and evaluated as a matter of degree. From a methodological viewpoint, the utility of this construct is what the several readings in chapters 6 and 7 are designed to demonstrate.[7]

Two simple examples will suffice to get the idea across in a preliminary way. As another substitution exercise, suppose that we removed Eddie Heywood's band from the dance scene in *The Dark Corner* discussed in chapter 1 and replaced it with an early twentieth-century hotel orchestra of the kind Waxman invoked for the hotel lobby scene in *Rebecca* (recall chapter 2). The latter, with its moderate-tempo waltzes and lush but largely desexualized tangos, would certainly signal elegance appropriate to Hardy Cathcart's home and to the occasion of the party. In 1946, however, such hotel orchestras were rapidly disappearing along with their style of music, as the war years had accelerated the cultural institutionalization of the swing band. Thus, contemporary music of a jazz-based dance band was far more appropriate to the *mise-en-scène*. The hotel orchestra, in other words, would have had a stronger troping effect than could be claimed for the contemporary dance band.

Historical concert works also are not immune to topical transformation through repeated use over a period of time. J. S. Bach's Toccata and Fugue in D Minor, BWV 565, is certainly historical, but its repeated use in films—beginning with film performance well before the sound era—led to its cliché status. This piece, as deployed in horror films of the 1930s, apparently beginning with *Dr. Jekyll and Mr. Hyde* (1931), or, even more, as a joke about early horror films, as in *Sunset Boulevard* (1950), became a style topic through cinematic practice, an instance, in other words, of Gorbman's cinematic musical code "hardening" into the cultural musical code.[8]

Here we are once again at Christian Metz's lament—cited in chapter 1—about a film being easy to understand, and also at Robert Scholes's closely related characterization of the cinema as needing to work at conceptualization. In the first instance, musical topics in film are rarely difficult to understand. As James Buhler puts it, "A musical topic can be defined as a conventional musical sign with an unusually clear signification. . . . As scholars of film music have long noted, scores have deployed musical topics to gain clarity in signification" (2014b, 208).[9] The topical repertoire is relatively limited, and the audio-viewer generally does not need to know titles or other specific information to follow the essentials of how a particular instantiation of a topic relates to the narrative. This lack of requirement for specificity has less to do with narrative clarity than with the effects of Carolyn Abbate's notion of stickiness: music's ambiguities tend to disappear in the immediate audiovisual experience. The driver is Chion's synchresis (1994, 63; 2009, 214): if music and sound are presented to us as an entity, which means "at the same time," then we will work to find ways to combine them, to read them as a unit. Thus, paradoxically perhaps, if troping is inevitable because of the principle of added value, it tends to be suppressed in the experience of film because of synchresis. Only if distance is created—most easily managed by textural or tempo alterations—can the kind of parallelism arise that Royal Brown describes: "Excerpts of classical music compositions that replace [an] original film score no longer function purely as backing for key emotional situations but rather exist as a kind of parallel emotional/aesthetic universe" (1994, 239). Musical topics, then, tend to be easily assimilated, and the cognitive process of synchresis takes care of the rest.

Beyond the immediate image/sound connection, Scholes's point comes into play as one seeks to interpret the moment in context, which in most instances means narrative context. The audio-viewer "reads" musical topics first, quickly and intuitively, and then seeks a functional explanation in relation to narrative. Song performances offer a clear example, since they typically appeal to a single topic and are easy to understand in and of themselves as spectacle or in terms of Gorbman's "pure" musical code. Especially when instrumental, they do not have to signal anything more, but in many instances they do, especially when they are vocal and highlighted, as is the case with "Am I Blue?," one of the three scenes from *To Have and Have Not* analyzed in chapter 1. The song itself tropes in obvious ways on a popular ballad style and the blues—although it contains rather more of the former than the latter. Motivation for the performance is not obscure. We were already introduced to Cricket as the hotel band leader, and here he is simply doing his job. Slim, who needs money to get home, has been taken on as a singer. The only question we might want to ask is why the performance is so short (barely over a minute) if it is meant to be highlighted, which is certainly the impression we get from the cleanly ordered and leisurely progression from one band member to the next, ending with Slim. Such abbreviated performances, however, were typical of Warner Bros.' house style in the 1940s.

The topics and their troping match the situation: the ballad style is one of a small number we would expect of a hotel or bar performer in 1944, but the blues adds a transgressive element that makes us wonder about Slim (or at least the persona she is presenting through the performance). The specific element of spectacle—the focus on Slim singing—introduces ambiguities that appeal to narrative and are largely answered by the image editing. We see Slim at first with Thompson, a luckless tourist who failed to catch any fish and is now planning to skip out without paying his boat fees (he dies in a police raid a few minutes later), but after she starts singing, several cuts back and forth make it clear that she intends to pursue Harry as a more likely sucker. The combination of this with the previous scene, the first of several memorable verbal jousts between Slim and Harry, has her emerge as a kind of tough-girl siren, but certainly not a *femme fatale* in the manner of *film noir*. One of the few weak points in the script, however, is a lack of clear motivation for her largely abandoning this pose later in the film.

I will not attempt to offer a catalog of style topics here: as Raymond Monelle succinctly puts it, "Comprehensive lists of topics are probably of little use and are not the way to do topic theory. . . . Topical analysis works best when we proceed ad hoc, allowing musical texts to suggest new topics as they arise" (2006, ix–x). Following that advice but for a medium different from the one Monelle was concerned with, I will use just a pair of familiar historical compositions that are used topically in films—the C Major Prelude from *The Well-Tempered Clavier,* Book I, and its close cousin, the Prelude from the G Major Cello Suite—and will employ close reading to investigate what happens to them in different filmic settings.[10]

The two preludes can be gathered under a single musical topic—the kinetic perpetual-motion étude—but they differ from, say, Chopin's C Major Étude in that the tempo is relatively slow (or should be in a proper performance) and there is less obvious attention to a virtuosic surface. The repeated arpeggio patterns, especially in a slower tempo, can invoke for a modern listener qualities of the pastoral, extending to nostalgia or potentially even to minimalist trance. The C Major Prelude, specifically, varies markedly in its signification according to tempo. The simplicity of the figuration and lack of a strongly profiled melody lend the work considerable expressive flexibility. Figure 6.0b maps out the main possibilities in the form of another continuum. I associate the C Major Prelude with études, not with the extreme options (shown at the far left of figure 6.0b), represented by the concert étude and the *perpetuum mobile* toccata, with their

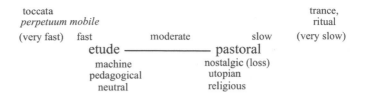

Figure 6.0b: Johann Sebastian Bach, *The Well-Tempered Clavier,*
Book I, Prelude in C Major: topical categories in relation to
pedagogical étude and pastoral.

virtuoso displays, but with the pedagogical or preparatory exercise, in accordance with early nineteenth-century understandings of *The Well-Tempered Clavier.* (See the opening section of chapter 6 for more on this.) In both its "fast" and "very fast" manifestations, the étude represents emotional qualities of speed and control, perhaps also (or alternatively) stress and agitation. The pastoral topic, by contrast, emerges unmistakably when the Prelude is played at a *moderato* to *andante* pace, where it is also capable of taking on the qualities of the religious pastoral—unequivocally, as we shall see, in Gounod's "Ave Maria," an effect created by the combination of the long held notes Gounod introduces and the rippling water effect of a quiet but moving accompaniment. At a still slower tempo, minimalist traits of bliss, transcendence, or trance take over. Whether invoking the religious pastoral or a more extreme minimalist trance, the Prelude may suggest a utopian or transcendent realm.

The tempo of the G Major Prelude varies far less than the C Major Prelude in recorded performances, but both pieces maintain the eighteenth-century prelude's connection to the toccata heritage: both in fact take advantage of it in their dramatic climaxes and in their long pedal points near the end. The oscillation between étude and pastoral, however, provides a remarkable range of opportunities for treatment in specific filmic situations, even with minimal changes in the musical materials or their presentation. As we will see, despite their limited means, the two preludes can indeed fit situations ranging all the way from a merely kinetic background to the evocation of metaphysical or transcendent states. On the other hand, these musical cues will usually require diegetic circumstances (a performer) to achieve any clear sense of interiority or character subjectivity.

Chapter 6 begins with an introduction on the history of the C Major Prelude and a second introduction on archetypal treatments of the two preludes in underscore and in diegetic performance. The latter is then explored in a variety of mostly recent films (post-1980). Chapter 7 takes up the former by offering close readings of four film scenes in which the C Major Prelude is used as underscore. The analyses combine details of the music (as score and as recorded sound), of the montage (that is, continuity editing), and of staging within the shot (following Bordwell 2005).

I should emphasize that I will not claim the film scenes discussed here are all aesthetically perfect examples of film art or of the use of music in film art, even less that the prelude cues have special prominence or significance—only that they are all adequate to their task. Naturally, of course, I will spend most of my time with the ones that best reward close description and interpretation. Comments on several others may be found in the notes.[11]

I should note that the overwhelming attention to early sound film repertoire in parts 1 and 2 will be mitigated in part 3 in that all but one of the films discussed are much more recent. As one might expect of these repertoires, the examples chosen are, by and large, more complex constructions of sound, image, and the sound track elements, even if the basic structure of the classical paradigm still prevails (Thompson 1999, x). Nevertheless, throughout these chapters the points made in part 1 will continue to support, and be supported by, the analyses: the notion of the vococentric cinema and the three principles, these being a distinction between music *for* and music *in* film; an understanding of the sound track as constructed, with clarity as its objective; and the assertion that any music in a film is film music.

6   Performers Onscreen

Prelude to the Prelude

The C Major Prelude in the Eighteenth Century

Opening a chapter on the paradoxical notion of a text-centered contingency, Robert Scholes asks a rhetorical question, "Why won't the text stand still so that one could indeed be true to it or false to it and know which is which?" (1985, 149). This image of an unstable text is particularly well suited to reception studies. Bach's C Major Prelude has a specific, definite textual history (as a written score), but it did not "stand still," in Bach's own hands or in anyone else's. It is by no means unique in *The Well-Tempered Clavier* in that there are preliminary versions that were expanded and polished for inclusion in the published volume, and it is well known that Bach continually returned to his own (and occasionally others') work as sources for new compositions. David Schulenberg refers this practice of "composition by variation" to a broader tradition of composition and pedagogy that embraces not only figural and ground-bass variations but also improvisations on figured basses and reworkings of existing pieces. The training that "Bach apparently received as a child from his brother Johann Christoph must have included not only figured bass realization but also score notation." In his own teaching, Bach used the same method, avoiding altogether the abstractions of species counterpoint: "In this approach to composition, melodic material was understood as . . . a variation of simple three- or four-part counterpoint that could be represented by figured bass (as it was in [Friedrich Erhardt] Niedt's treatise [of 1706])." The fundamental conception of composition linked it inextricably to improvisation, then, and both were understood to be "in essence nothing more than a very elaborate variety of figured bass realization" (1995, 24).[1]

A suite in C major by Johann Adam Reincken, a composer whose work Bach knew well, provides a good example of how figured bass variation, improvisation, and composition were related. The work is a variation-suite (Schulenberg 1992, 8): in effect, the courante, sarabande, and gigue are all figural variations of the allemande (see figure 6.1). The allemande also happens to trace the octave line and parallel tenths of Bach's C Major Prelude (see the schematic version of the opening of the allemande in figure 6.2, top system). The allemande lacks the chromatic touches of Bach's C Major Prelude, but bars 1–3 and a variant that follows in bars 4–6 include the suspension-based sequential dissonances. The final detail in this

Figure 6.1. Johann Adam Reincken, Suite No. 2 in C Major, incipits of Allemande, Courante, and Sarabande, showing the latter two as figural variations of the first. (From Johann Adam Reincken, *Sämtliche Werke für Klavier/Cembalo,* edited by Klaus Beckmann [1982]; reprinted by permission of Breitkopf & Härtel KG.)

speculative connection is in the second system of figure 6.2: the opening bar of the sarabande gives us exactly Bach's first chord and its voicing, plus very nearly its figure.

Thus, it is hardly surprising that the first two versions of the C Major Prelude are in a pedagogical collection, the *Clavier-Büchlein vor Wilhelm Friedemann Bach,* the earliest version under erasure below the second. The three versions are given in figure 6.3, without the sixteenth-note figuration and with corresponding bars aligned vertically: the earliest version (at the top) is twenty-four bars long, the *Clavier-Büchlein* version is twenty-seven, and the final version is thirty-five bars.[2]

Finally, in his extended exposition of the method of variation writing to which Schulenberg refers above, Friedrich Erhardt Niedt (whose treatise was known to Bach) takes a single figured bass and creates from it no fewer than eleven dances (two complete suites), plus doubles for the courantes and a prelude that consists of a toccata and a chaconne, each of which is based on the progression. The opening bars of the model are shown in figure 6.4a. In most instances, Niedt sets a

Figure 6.2. Johann Adam Reincken, Suite No. 2 in C Major, incipits of Allemande and Sarabande in schematic form, aligned with *The Well-Tempered Clavier*, Book I, Prelude in C Major opening.

basic melody of $\hat{1}$–$\hat{2}$–$\hat{2}$–$\hat{3}$ against the first four bass notes, but at the "tutti" (return of the chaconne after a trio) he writes what appears in figure 6.4b. It is hard to imagine that Bach's contemporaries—in northern Germany, at least—would miss the C Major Prelude's reference to this moment.

Now, why Bach should have chosen five voices is not at all clear (for more on the implications for analysis of this five-part texture, see chapter 7). We might say that he ignored simpler three- or four-part textures because more complex textures were common in arpeggio preludes.[3] That assumption, however, gets us no farther than a reference to a genre that sets *The Well-Tempered Clavier* firmly (at least in its opening gesture) in a tradition of German keyboard practice, a notion that seems to be confirmed by the old-fashioned ricercar-like fugue that follows (but in four voices, not five, as in the other ricercar fugue from Book I, the B♭ minor). That he is referring to a tradition of "preluding" is obvious, though it is unusual to begin the prelude in an upper register. Examining the repertoires of both German and French composers, I found no other instance of a prelude beginning so high. Indeed, most begin with a bass note in the third octave, and a significant number start in the second octave. For a notable example of the latter option, the first of the remarkable eight *préludes* François Couperin composed for his *L'art de toucher le clavecin* begins with five voices, but stretching from C2

Figure 6.3. Johann Sebastian Bach, *The Well-Tempered Clavier*, Book I, Prelude in C Major, three versions (two preliminary versions and final version) aligned. In the final version, m. 22a (in parentheses) is a later eighteenth-century addition known as the "Schwenke measure."

Figure 6.4, a–b. Friedrich Erhardt Niedt, *The Musical Guide:* (a) opening bars of the thorough-bass model; (b) Chaconne, beginning of reprise.

to E4, a dark, resonant sound reminiscent of the well-known rondeau "Les barricades mystérieuses."

If a reference to historical styles in the C Major Prelude is doubtful (five-part textures in sixteenth-century vocal music? the five-part string orchestra of Lully?), the progression that follows is clear: the slow-motion cascade from top to bottom of the keyboard range (on any of the instruments of his day, roughly C2 to C6) elaborates a descending form of the *rule of the octave* (harmonization of a descending scale; Wason 2002, 103) that is made more difficult by the five-part texture and tight voice-leading constraints of several 2–3 bass suspensions.[4] Bach achieves a kind of dramatic clarity along with a demonstration of craft in this prelude that amounts to an announcement of the seriousness of the entire project of *The Well-Tempered Clavier.* Thus, the C Major Prelude is prelude to the entire cycle, not only to the first fugue.

The C Major Prelude in the Early Nineteenth Century

Robert Wason has argued that two Chopin études are "clear cases of Chopin troping on traditional structural archetypes" derived from preludes in *The Well-Tempered Clavier* (2002, 109).[5] The first of these, the C Major Étude, op. 10, no. 1, stands at the head of the two collections of études, just as Bach's C Major Prelude stands at the head of the two volumes of *The Well-Tempered Clavier,* a work Chopin knew intimately. Wason recounts observations of earlier writers about similarities between the basic voice leading of the opening sections ($\hat{4}$ as neighbor note to $\hat{3}$ over I–V–I), then notes a "consistency of pattern" in the Chopin étude such that "the arpeggios are completely consistent registrally, so that the voice leading comes through." He extends the earlier literature by noting structural parallels in later sections of the C Major Étude in the form of particular cycle-of-fifths patterns in the middle section, which elaborate an "octave descent . . . accompanied by tenths in the bass, just as it was in Bach" (109–11).

Putting both the C Major Étude and the C Major Prelude in a slightly larger context of early nineteenth-century pianism, specifically keyboard performance methods and collections of graded and "finishing" études, we note first that *The Well-Tempered Clavier* was considered to be one of the most important historical documents for keyboard pedagogy. This use was encouraged by a phrase in Bach's own title: "For the use and improvement of musical youth eager to learn" (translated in Ledbetter 2002, 2). Indeed, Ledbetter says that "the 48 is the apex of Bach's clavier teaching programme. . . . [H]e puts the educational intention first, before the 'rare entertainment of those already skilled in this discipline'" (126). Composers and piano teachers—notably Chopin but also Beethoven, Mendelssohn, Schumann, Liszt, and others (Eigeldinger 1986, 135n136)—regarded *The Well-Tempered Clavier* as important to the development of piano technique, especially legato playing. The collection, in other words, was used in much the same way as the methods and étude collections that began appearing in great numbers in the first decades of the nineteenth century, beginning with Johann Baptist Cramer's *Études* (1802) and including among their best-known products Clementi's *Preludes and Exercises* and *Gradus ad Parnassum*.[6] A student of Chopin in the 1830s, one Madame Dubois, recalled that she studied pieces from both Clementi volumes under Chopin, along with "Bach's forty-eight Preludes and Fugues." That Chopin thought of *The Well-Tempered Clavier* in terms of pedagogical and musical values is clear from his advice to Madame Dubois on their last meeting (a year before his death): "Practice Bach constantly—this will be your best means to make progress" (quoted in Eigeldinger 1986, 61).

Simon Finlow, who works hard to distance Chopin from the perceived inadequacies of his contemporaries, points particularly to the preludes of *The Well-Tempered Clavier* and their representation of "the more general features of [Bach's] keyboard writing" (1992, 69) as having an influence on Chopin. Another student, Jane Stirling, "returning to the piano after the death of her teacher, wrote: 'I started with some Bach Preludes, as he always advised'" (quoted in Eigeldinger 1986, 136n137).[7] Finlow adds that Chopin's appropriation of Bach "establish[es] . . . an essentially contrapuntal tension between the linear, horizontal aspects of the piano figures and the underlying harmonic ground-work" (1992, 69), and it is this tension that helps to raise Chopin's étude writing above that of most of his contemporaries in terms of aesthetic value. Nevertheless, Finlow finds that Chopin's C Major Étude completely reverses the priorities of Bach's C Major Prelude: in the latter "the linear elements unfold through a figuration of secondary importance whereas in [the former] . . . it is the figuration ([that is,] the technical element) that is realized through the harmonic structure" (71). To be sure, arpeggio playing is a specific, well-defined problem in piano playing, and, given the incipient Bach cult and the iconic status that *The Well-Tempered Clavier* quickly attained for both pianists and composers, it would not be surprising to find Bach's C Major and C Minor Preludes figuring in such pedagogy, not just

Figure 6.5. Robert Schumann, *Impromptus,* op. 5, introduction and theme, first half.

in the later stages of training ("His own Etudes op. 10 and 25 he entrusted only to the most advanced students" [Carl Mikuli quoted in Eigeldinger 1986, 60]) but also at lower levels.

Janet Ritterman (1992, 28–29) observes that Ignaz Moscheles and Franz Liszt were influential in introducing *The Well-Tempered Clavier* into the concert repertoire in Paris. Both gave series of recitals in 1837 that included a wide range of music—Moscheles is noted as having including preludes and fugues from *The Well-Tempered Clavier.* It is worth noting the irony that the rising status of *The Well-Tempered Clavier* as repertoire coincided with the historical moment when the practice of "preluding" so plainly represented in its first number gradually went into decline: "As respect for the role of the pianist as interpreter increased, improvisation became regarded as one of the less necessary skills for the pianist to demonstrate in concerts." In particular, this change affected improvised variations or fantasias, but also "the custom of 'preluding'—that is, of performing a brief passage, generally of scales, arpeggios and chords, in order to introduce the mood of the piece to follow and to establish its key. Although students were still encouraged to develop the skill, its application in public concert situations seems to have been gradually discouraged" (26).[8]

Clara Schumann's introduction of *The Well-Tempered Clavier* into her recitals may have had a motivation beyond the promotion of Bach as the greatest historical icon of German music (following the argument of Johann Nikolaus Forkel). Rather, one source may have been personal, in her early experiences with Robert. Even before finishing a relatively brief period studying composition under Heinrich Dorn, Robert studied closely Friedrich Wilhelm Marpurg's fugue treatise (which is based on Bach), and when his formal study ended in April 1832 Schumann spent a period of time intensively studying the music of Mozart and Bach, in particular *The Well-Tempered Clavier,* which Schumann

Figure 6.6. Schumann, *Impromptus,* op. 5, variation 3.

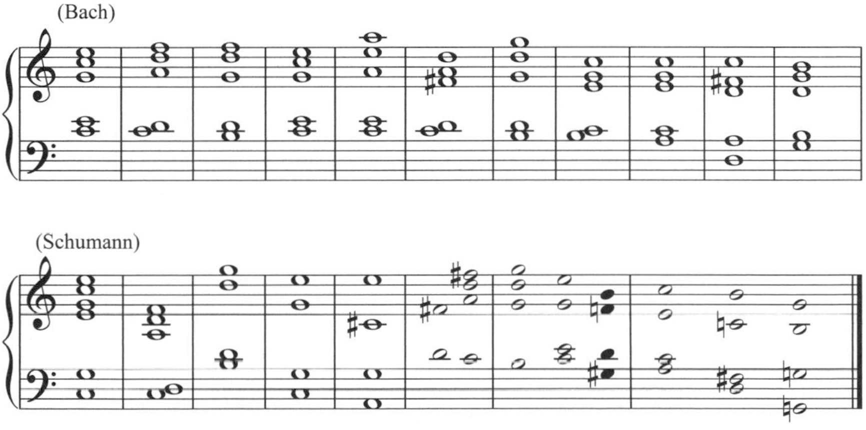

Figure 6.7. Schumann, *Impromptus,* op. 5, variation 3, first section, voice leading aligned with the opening of Bach's C Major Prelude.

later labeled the "Work above all Works" (Bischoff 1997, 450).[9] Only a month later, he and Clara played through a half dozen Bach fugues together, and by his own account Schumann went home in a mood of euphoria to improvise portions of what became the *Impromptus on a Theme by Clara Wieck,* op. 5 (Köhler 1981, 27). He even claimed to have derived the opening bass formula directly from this experience of sight-reading (Daverio 1997, 108). In their personal and creative interactions at the time, Clara (only thirteen years old) and Robert used the typically Romantic image of the shadow or spiritual double, the *Doppelgänger.* The theme of the *Impromptus,* which are actually a set of (increasingly) free variations, is shot through with this symbolism. See figure 6.5, where the melody is from a *romanze* by Clara, the harmony is by Robert (thus the two are each other's "shadows"), and the bass begins with the formula "CF.GC," whose symmetry Robert emphasizes with that internal period.[10] The theme ends with the identical formula. To these we might add a nod to the tradition of ground-bass pieces, as the entire bass line of the theme appears first, unaccompanied (not shown in the figure). Thus the introduction is history unaccompanied, as it were, while the theme sets above this "history" a modern and expressive melody: so, history as the shadow of the present.

It seems reasonable also to extend this idea to variation 3, the only one in which Schumann significantly alters the bass progression, with the result that the first half tracks the C Major Prelude surprisingly closely: see figures 6.6 (score) and 6.7 (comparison). The only problem with this story is that variation 3 was not written in 1832. It may have been the impending Bach centenary year or just nostalgic personal memories of the role of Bach's music in Schumann's warm and playful early relationship with Clara (Daverio calls op. 5 the "first in a long and impressive series of 'Clara' pieces" [1997, 109]), but Schumann returned to his op. 5 in the late 1840s, revised it, and published the new version in 1850.[11] The new variation pushes the functional pattern in CF.GC back from actual pitches to the (slight) abstraction of chord roots, enabling an homage to the C Major Prelude in a similar abstraction of its chords and voice leading that stands among and behind the shifting chordal elaborations.

Another factor we need to consider in connection with nineteenth-century understandings of the C Major Prelude is the so-called Schwenke measure. In 1783, as the story goes, a sixteen-year-old student named Christian Friedrich Gottlieb Schwenke copied out the C Major Prelude and, for reasons that remain unknown, added a bar between mm. 22 and 23 (Ledbetter 2002, 146): refer again to figure 6.3, where the addition appears in parentheses and is labeled m. 22a. Thanks to its inclusion in early nineteenth-century editions of *The Well-Tempered Clavier* (notably, Carl Czerny's, first published by Peters in 1837), this bar was assumed to be authentic throughout much of the century. One can readily understand the motivation of Schwenke (or perhaps of some other, unknown person who made a change that Schwenke copied).[12] The insertion comes at a spot that is doubly problematic: not only is the bass progression F♯–A♭ peculiar, but the five-part part writing is compromised for the only time in the prelude: there are five pitches, but only four can be chord tones. The added bar fixes the problem in the bass but not the part-writing problem. Heinrich Schenker specifically repudiated this version by noting that stem directions in Bach's holograph lead F♯ (stems up) and A♭ (stems down) directly to the dominant G in bar 24.[13] Schenker's curmudgeonly gesture was unnecessary, however, as Hans Bischoff had established the authentic version of the C Major Prelude several decades earlier using the holograph and a number of other authentic, early manuscripts. Still, editions with the Schwenke measure retained currency for many years, into the twentieth century.

The derogation of the Schwenke measure is a telling element in J. A. Fuller-Maitland's critical appreciation of the C Major Prelude. By Fuller-Maitland's time, half a century after Chopin's death, *The Well-Tempered Clavier* had become something altogether different from a link to historical traditions of keyboard training and composition. Of the C Minor Prelude, for example, Fuller-Maitland writes briefly and abruptly: "To some superficial critics it has seemed 'like an exercise'" ([1925] 1970, 13). He does not identify the critics, but he does make it clear that *The Well-Tempered Clavier* is no longer a part of everyday music making or pedagogy. Instead, it has been transformed into a work of heroic perfection, even more than that, into something ascetic and holy: "There are shrines that can only be approached after the worshipper has performed some lustral rite, and the need for such purification meets us at the threshold of the great temple we are now to enter." The enemy of the true believer in this case is none other than Charles Gounod, who undermined the ability to reach "the real meaning of the Preludes and Fugues" and therefore any hope of "the spiritual blessings they can convey" by producing "a certain dreadful piece of sentimentality which was for many years fashionable even among people who ought to have known better" (12). Gounod's *Méditation* (universally known in its vocal setting as "Ave Maria") is a "sugary tune placed on the top of the first Prelude" and cannot possibly satisfy contemporary listeners, who "will feel that they prefer the prelude without Schwenke's extra bar, which, as we might expect, is required for Gounod's *eau sucrée*" (13). The severe, the serious, and the perfect go together in Fuller-Maitland's view: "The whole point of the Prelude in C is its negation of a defined melody; it is in one aspect a transformation of the arpeggio prelude in common use, which generally means nothing whatever, into a creation of perfect loveliness, the ethereal beauty of which is due in great measure to the subtle suggestions of its harmonies. Like many other flawless works of art, it seems as though it had sprung forth spontaneously, as though it could not ever have gone through any process of development" (12).

Thus, Fuller-Maitland's views on both musical spirituality and its mechanics are very much akin to Schenker's. For both, the goal is to create a yawning and unbridgeable gulf between genius and hack (for Fuller-Maitland, the severe and monkish genius versus the sentimental and worldly hack), between genius and "foreground composer," between grand, inspired architecture and the inconsequential chaining of short ideas. The typical Schenkerian language for levels that reflect these biases—"surface" versus "deeper" (or "higher")—is a jumble of metaphors in Fuller-Maitland: exterior and interior of a temple (in the first quote above), "common" (everyday) and "perfect," "common" (vulgar) and "ethereal." There is even a hint of an immaculate conception myth in "sprung forth spontaneously" versus constructed or made by a "process of development" (strangely enough, the C Major Prelude is implicated directly in this myth in Jean-Luc Godard's *Je vous salue, Marie*—see the discussion in chapter 7).

Presumably, Fuller-Maitland would not be pleased to be reminded of the early versions of the C Major Prelude nor to be told of Bach's use of copying (and alteration) as a teaching tool. At the very least, we sense that Fuller-Maitland's "flawless work of art" is somehow not the same once we recognize that Bach was drawing on everyday clichés of figured-bass performance, was probably making an overt homage to Niedt's textbook, and may even have lifted a bar from Reincken's sarabande. Nor is it the same once we admit that the aesthetic distance from the quite adequate *Clavier-Büchlein* version to the one in *The Well-Tempered Clavier* is really rather small. Did Bach himself think the latter version was better, rather than merely of different utility, needing as it did to be a bit longer in order to open a large public document, no longer just an exercise in a private collection of teaching pieces? It can safely be assumed that Bach, like any serious professional, was interested in creating the best possible forms of his compositions, but it is by no means obvious (and the evidence of the student copying exercises suggests that it is very unlikely) that he thought he was performing a "lustral rite . . . at the threshold of the great temple" in opening *The Well-Tempered Clavier*. Or, to return one more time to the fluid interplay of elements of musical training in Bach's time:

> The student went to a master and learnt everything from him: tuning and maintaining the instruments, notation and copying, technique, improvisation, and composition. . . . Even making a little musical sentence out of a finger exercise is an act of composition. In addition, the boundary between improvisation and composition was very imprecise: one of the objectives of writing fugues was to improve one's technique of improvising them. One often has the impression with pieces in the 48 that the early stages . . . were improvised but that later, more intricate and less playable developments were worked out at the desk. (Ledbetter 2002, 138)

The C Major Prelude in the Twentieth Century

As Gounod's "Ave Maria" and Fuller-Maitland's criticism of it suggest, by the later nineteenth and early twentieth centuries little if anything was left of the historical associations of the C Major Prelude with toccata, preluding, pedagogical exercise, or concert étude. In the cinema, specifically, Bach's music found little place. There are no listings at all in Erno Rapée's collection *Motion Picture Moods* (1924) or his *Encyclopedia of Music for Pictures* (1925), for example. In the European catalog of Hans Erdmann and Giuseppe Becce, there is only one item (to be discussed later in this chapter). Among the more than three thousand musical excerpts they list, early eighteenth-century music in general is very weakly represented, mostly through operatic excerpts by Handel (eleven) and Rameau (fourteen). It should be remembered, however, that Becce and Erdmann's *Handbuch* was concerned with orchestral presentation and, strictly speaking, is only representative of film exhibition with higher production values in the context of European practices. At the opposite extreme of the exhibition spectrum, however, the pedagogical history of the C Major Prelude might very well have allowed it to survive in the United States in neighborhood or even rural theaters where a lone pianist did his or her best while armed with a limited repertoire acquired for the most part from piano lessons. Almost certainly, however, the C Major Prelude in its accompanimental role for Gounod's "Ave Maria" was much more likely to be heard in local theaters. All this, unfortunately, is impossible to document. On the other hand, we can say with confidence that, in the early decades of the sound film era, the C Major Prelude on its own appears to be virtually nonexistent. Indeed, except for some scattered cantata quotes, the music of Bach is represented almost entirely by Gounod's "Ave Maria" and the horror-movie chestnut Toccata and Fugue in D Minor.[14]

By the middle of the twentieth century, if the music of Bach had a place, it was very specific: intellectual high culture in the fugues and equally high religious values in the cantatas. Modernist attitudes and a much broadened range of musical textures and instrumentation in underscoring eventually brought Bach and *The Well-Tempered Clavier* back into the cinema as well, an early instance being the Eb minor fugue from Book I in Ingmar Bergman's *Wild Strawberries* (1958). The C Major Prelude does make a spectacular appearance in Jacques Demy's *Lola* (1961) but thereafter appears only sporadically—if in a few instances memorably—in subsequent decades. In recent films, one is far more likely to hear what I earlier called the C Major Prelude's topical twin, the Prelude from the Cello Suite in G Major, as well as the preludes and dances from the other cello suites, all this in line with an increasing tendency to use music for string instruments, from solo violin to quartets to strings-heavy orchestral scores, in both source and underscore contexts.

My exploration of the topical use of these preludes begins with two strongly contrasting examples, the first featured in the nondiegetic underscore, the second appearing in a diegetic performance. Both are stable or neutral topical importations. The unflagging étude-like manner of many recorded performances of the C Major Prelude minimizes expressive qualities of the music and can lead to its use as neutral underscore or as narratively indifferent end-credits music, one instance of which is found in *Allegro* (2005). A pairing of performance and the kinetic in the diegetic realm follows in arguably the most remarkable instance in the film repertoire: the G Major Prelude as played by a group of young cellists while riding on an urban transit train, a scene from Pere Portabella's *Die Stille vor Bach* (*The Silence before Bach*; 2007). In *Allegro,* blending or synchronization is dominant, whereas the scene from *Stille* foregrounds the juxtaposition of image (the train) and sound (the music) while disconcertingly suggesting the train noise as a kind of mediator.

Next I introduce a series of examples that emphasize degrees of troping. All involve scenes with performers, both professional and amateur, that seem to emphasize the étude, especially the pedagogical étude or exercise, but that also signal the pastoral. In *Ma saison préférée* (*My Favorite Season*; 1993), failed attempts at performance accompany and illustrate a young woman's disappointed hopes. Another brief turn to the G Major Prelude—a short scene from *The Pianist* (2001)—mingles the erotic with a moment of poignant loss for a professional musician. Similarly varying treatments can be found in *The Chronicle of Anna Magdalena Bach* (1968; a young Wilhelm Friedemann plays from his *Clavier-Büchlein*); *Entrapment* (1999; a mingling of amateur performance, the erotic, and high art as wealth); and *Following Sean* (2005; age and nostalgia as loss). Finally, in *Bagdad Café* (1986), a performance of the C Major Prelude that emerges from a young man's practicing is set in the form of a short parallel narrative accentuating disjunctions in the sound track that undermine competing effects of eroticism (treated comically) and a transcendence tied to high-art nostalgia.[15]

Introduction: Two Preludes, Two Treatments of the Perpetual-Motion Étude

Among other things, the two chapters of part 3 might be regarded as a "corrective" to my radicalized notion of the sound cinema as vococentric. David Bordwell, after all, does say in connection with his study of cinematic staging that "the filmmaker who wishes to tell a story is obliged to pursue pictorial strategies. He or she narrates visually, and in this project the deployment of figures in space is critical" (2005, 238). Earlier in the same volume, he comments at some length on the importance of nonverbal gestures and movements as conveying narrative information (37–38). On the other hand, he says that "despite critics' complaint that [contemporary] movies are packed with chases, explosions, and gun battles, the standard scene remains a conversation" (22), as was the case in the classical studio cinema. He identifies two basic types as used by film practitioners: "stand-and-deliver" and "walk-and-talk," both of which are self-explanatory (22, also 29). What I will do here, then, is not so much provide a "corrective" as an "addition" to—or, better, a "filling out" of—the vococentric model by looking more systematically at the details of music/sound and image relations. The strategy is to begin from the characteristic habits of audio-viewers, who "concentrate on the faces, the words, and the gestures, testing each one for its relevance to the ongoing story action" (8). Although narrative remains the highest priority, there is more to the experience: "The faces (and the bodies), the words (and the reactions to the words), and the gestures (and the interplay of gestures) are all working together. At every instant, in most storytelling cinema, cinematic staging delivers the dramatic field to our attention, sculpting it for informative, expressive, and sometimes simply pictorial effect" (8). The way in which sound and music participate in or influence this process is the point of interest here.

We do need to distinguish between staging (arrangement of figures) and movement, between movement of agents and movement of the camera, and between the individual shot and an edited sequence of shots. The first example below, a conversation in a car (from *Allegro*), uses a typical mixture (Bordwell 2005, 22) of editing and staging; its "stand [strictly speaking, "sit"]-and-deliver" mode is complicated by a voice-over. The second example, the train scene from *The Silence before Bach,* is a long take with sitting figures and a slowly meandering camera. Except for brief framing shots at beginning and end, the scene is a single long take. There is no speech.

The C Major Prelude as Neutral Underscore in Allegro *(2005)*

Allegro is a musician's film that offers us biography for barely more than the first third of its runtime, during which we learn (partly by means of animated drawings) that Danish pianist Zetterström was an introverted, socially awkward, but talented child who grew up to be a successful concert artist, abruptly left his home, and as abruptly reappeared ten years later. Sometime earlier he met and fell in love with a neighbor, Andrea, a woman whose need for an emotionally responsive love was as great as Zetterström's inability to offer it. After her pregnancy is aborted, he withdraws further, and she drowns herself in a canal.

The remainder of the film, starting with Zetterström's return to Copenhagen, is about his gradually uncovering his suppressed memories, which are represented in surreal fashion by a closed-off area of the city everyone calls "the Zone." He enters and returns to this district several times, in the process making his concert agents increasingly nervous, till he finds Andrea at the moment of falling into the canal and jumps in after her, to no avail. The geographical area of the Zone then collapses back into reality, and the voice-over narrator tells us that Zetterström plays the best concert of his career.

The film does make clear that Zetterström comes to terms with Andrea's death (which was really two deaths, her own and their child's) and receives a gift of emotional depth that he can finally express in performance. Apart from its morally repugnant premise (high art justifies someone *else's* sacrifice?), *Allegro* is a well-made film that holds the viewer's interest. Not a small part of that is due to the music, all of it Bach after an opening nod to Liszt. The sources are mostly the keyboard concertos and *The Well-Tempered Clavier,* and they include the C Major Prelude. The second movement of the Concerto in F Minor, BWV 1056, is the most prominent, however, being both motif (by virtue of several repetitions) and symbol (of the emotion that Zetterström cannot feel on his own).

The C Major Prelude, by contrast, plays a small and, in my view, negligible role in comparison with the F Minor Adagio. Zetterström is shown talking on the phone in his hotel room (the city is apparently New York). After he confirms that he is indeed returning to Denmark, the music enters, the briefest of sound advances before a cut (at 25:00) to the interior of a car going from the airport into Copenhagen. Zetterström and his agent are passengers in a limousine; as it moves through the night, they talk. The music functions in the manner of a montage cue, the simple fact of its continuity tying together a layering of voice-over narration, cutaways motivated by that narrator, and the conversation. Music goes out about 26:20, fading out rather than ending. The tempo is relatively fast—quarter note = 76—and the sound level is moderate, in the background below the narrator's and the characters' voices. As neutral underscoring, the cue would serve its purpose without any need for synchronization, but there is in fact fairly close coordination. The A minor[6] chord (C Major Prelude, m. 5) is first heard on an insert (a letter that will provide Zetterström access to the Zone), and the first arrival on I (m. 19) is reached at the end of their conversation, so that the ensuing dissonances match a surreal moment when the glove compartment opens to reveal Andrea sitting on a stool in the dark.[16]

The stylistic markers of Baroque music or of high-art music are not relevant, as so much other music accomplishes that task in a more prominent manner. The C Major Prelude does work well as neutral underscore, especially under the conditions here: the performance is not strongly profiled, but its tempo and precise

Table 6.1. Parallel design in Johann Sebastian Bach, *The Well-Tempered Clavier*, Book 1, C Major Prelude, and Cello Suite no. 1 in G Major, Prelude

C Major Prelude		G Major Prelude
Part 1: mm. 1–4	Neighbor-note figure	1: mm. 1–4
Part 2a: mm. 5–11	Descending bass to V	2a: mm. 5–10
Part 2b: mm. 12–19	Same, transposed to I	2b: mm. 11–19
Part 3: mm. 20–24	Cadence approach	3: mm. 20–24
Part 4a: mm. 24–31	Dominant pedal point	4a: mm. 25–41
Part 4b: mm. 32–35	Tonic pedal point	4b: m. 42

articulation suggest a professional performance; the music is also not placed high in the mix.[17] When Nicholas Cook introduces his description of Heinrich Schenker's analysis of the C Major Prelude, he offers a pragmatic summary of an initial encounter with the piece: it "has no marked dynamics, no rhythmic change, no thematic, textural or timbral variation. By a process of elimination, then, we can say that its structure as a piece of music must be principally harmonic" (1987, 28). Nevertheless, within those narrow parameters, the C Major Prelude does offer the possibility of close sychronization and some level of dramatic or emotional emphasis by means of its several distinct sections. By far the most often heard in film sound tracks is the neighbor-note figure of the opening four measures; I will call these part 1 (see again figure 6.3). The subsequent section (mm. 5–11) begins with the A minor⁶ chord, which initiates a sequence that combines registral accent in the right hand with suspension dissonances in the bass; this is part 2a. As *Allegro* shows, this passage—like the very similar mm. 12–19 (part 2b)—can be used to emphasize a dramatic moment (in this case, the letter insert), but part 3 (mm. 20–24, or the approach to the cadential V) is more intense (used here for the revealing of Andrea, symbolic of the uncovering of Zetterström's suppressed memories). Part 4a (mm. 24–31) is the prolonged dominant pedal point, whose steady chromatic progress in the melody up to G4 is well suited for climactic moments, leading quickly to the final section's denouement, the tonic pedal of part 4b (mm. 32–35).

The G Major Prelude as Performance in Die Stille vor Bach *(2007)*

Both C Major and G Major Preludes appear in Pere Portabella's *Die Stille vor Bach*. Characteristically for this highly distinctive filmmaker, this film is episodic in design and surrealist in style, neither a biopic (though it hints at it) nor a documentary (though its episodic nature suggests that, too). I will pass over the scene of a young Johann Sebastian practicing the C Major Prelude—a somewhat clumsy segment that is of less interest than performances we will discuss in the later sections of this chapter—and consider instead the complete performance of the G Major Prelude by a group of twenty cellists riding a local transit train.

Figure 6.8. Johann Sebastian Bach, music of the C Major Prelude and G Major Prelude (Cello Suite No. 1) aligned through m. 17.

The C Major and G Major Preludes share not only a topic but also a basic formal design (see table 6.1). The relationship is closest at the beginning, as the G Major Prelude offers in simplified form the distinctive gesture of the C Major Prelude, $\hat{3}$–$\hat{4}$–$\hat{4}$–$\hat{3}$, at the top of similarly undulating arpeggios, but now over a tonic pedal (see figure 6.8). The texture is in three voices, not five, and the middle voice gives the purest form of a gesture missing altogether from the C Major Prelude: a rising stepwise counterpoint against the neighbor figure, or $\hat{5}$–$\hat{6}$–$\hat{7}$–$\hat{8}$. Part 2a is still aligned harmonically, but the figuration is now more complex than simple arpeggios. In part 2b, the parallel in harmony becomes more tenuous, but the basic goal of reaching a stable tonic is shared (although it takes several measures for that tonic to settle—see mm. 16–18). The cadence approach (part 3) is strangely distorted, though the arrival of the dominant pedal note in m. 25 is clear enough. Part 4a has the same dominant pedal point as in the C Major Pre-

Figure 6.9. *Die Stille vor Bach* (2007), four cellists. Screen still.

lude but is much longer; it takes on the character of a true virtuoso cadenza. The closing tonic, on the other hand, is reduced to a single measure and a single chord.

The twenty musicians concentrate intensely on their performance, never looking at the camera even by accident, though one does briefly break the spell with a slightly embarrassed smile at her counterpart across the aisle. No person speaks; we hear only the synchronized performances of the twenty cellists and environmental noise of the train running along the track. As with most contemporary cinema, it is impossible to tell if the sound was direct recorded: we can only say that the scene certainly achieves the effect of direct recording, as if a minimum number of just adequate microphones were positioned overhead to capture the ensemble of cellists but not in a way that would block out the sounds of the track as heard from the interior of the train car. The exterior noise is in fact quite loud in one or two places.

The effect of the sound track, in other words, is deliberately just a bit amateurish. We are, after all, hearing a group of students, skillful but not yet professional, probably the entire studio of the one older adult who appears late in the scene. The image corresponds: the performance itself is a single long take using a hand-held camera and a wandering style of framing. The basic trajectory of the scene is to begin with a few performers at one end of the train and gradually move down the line, showing a few more at a time, until we reach the near end of the train compartment and are given what in the classical model would most likely have been the last in a series of establishing shots: all the cellists in a row. Then, for no obvious reason, the camera movement reverses and simply stops partway down the aisle when the music stops.

Figure 6.10. *Die Stille vor Bach,* nine cellists. Screen still.

In a narrative sense, the scene is structured to reveal its agents gradually. At the beginning, we do see a view of the tracks from the front of the train as it comes out of the tunnel, followed by a shot of the side of the train passing an empty station platform. During this latter shot, music begins: a simple sound advance that leads us to expect the immanent appearance of the scene's agents. We are rewarded with a tight shot of four cellists playing—so tight, indeed, that the foreground pair are initially seen only as an arm, a bow, and half a cello each (see figure 6.9). If the "story" of this scene is that twenty cellists play music on an apparently otherwise empty train, it is only in the middle of the cadenza that we realize this. Since we are offered no larger narrative frame, the scene is confirmed as a "production number," where the aural and visual are closely coordinated in a single effect of design and expression.

By the end of part 1 (that is, in m. 4), the camera has started to pull back; we see more of the fourth cellist at the right and also the knee and arm of the fifth. (For the sake of my description, the odd-numbered players are at the left, even-numbered at the right.) Through part 2a, the camera continues to pull back slowly, revealing players 5 and 6, but then drifts to the right, so that at the end of part 2a (m. 10), we see only the three right-side cellists (or nos. 2, 4, and 6). The camera compensates by drifting to the left in the beginning of part 2b—certainly an appropriate parallelism with the music's design—but does not hold there. Instead it moves to the center again and continues down the line, so that in m. 19—the one clearly expressed G major triad between m. 4 and the end—we see nine cellists, four on the left and five on the right (see figure 6.10). (There would be ten, but player no. 1 is missing from the image, as he is completely obscured behind no. 3.) The camera drifts right again fairly quickly at the beginning of part 3, reaching a parallel shot to m. 10 at the fermata midway through m. 21: a line of six cellists at the right plus the bow and arm of a seventh (no. 14); no one can be seen at the left. The arrival on D2 in m. 25 is nearly the same: after a slight move in, the camera is back on the right side of the train, showing us seven cellists. The slight pause on D2 in m. 29—the last low D in the prelude—brings a straight-on view with fourteen players visible, including the older man, who is in the left foreground (he is player no. 13). Movement thereafter is straight and forward down the middle of the train, until the nineteenth and twentieth cellists are revealed (in m. 36) and we see the entire line. With the change of figuration in m. 37 (at a pedal D3), the camera moves back into the car, settling briefly on player no. 15, then no. 13, before moving into the center again for the final chord.

A final, brief crane shot of the train moving away and around a corner closes off the scene effectively, making the final connection between train and performance, machine and music. Like a painting in a frame, the G Major Prelude and its twenty cellists are separated out from the world for us to contemplate. The difference is that the frame, a moving train, heavily interprets the picture for us.

Between Étude and Pastoral

The Failed Étude and Silence in Ma saison préférée *(1993):*
Anne Plays the C Major Prelude

If, in *Allegro,* Bach's C Major Prelude served an essentially neutral role as underscore, and, in *The Silence before Bach,* the G Major Prelude became an expressively foregrounded aural and visual event, in André Téchiné's *Ma saison préférée* the C Major Prelude explores a third option, that of subjectivity or interiority. The music in this instance marks a young woman's attempt to express herself and win approval from her family, the disappointment of that hope, and symbolically the disappointed hopes of her life. As Roger Ebert (1996) succinctly put it, *My Favorite Season* is "about a family that is unhappy in so many different ways that death is not a defeat but an escape. It is about the way a hurt in childhood can bend and shape an adult life years later, and about the way guilt may make us regret being selfish, but is unlikely to make us generous."

The story is primarily about the relationship of a woman (Emilie, played by Catherine Deneuve) and her brother (Antoine, played by Daniel Auteuil) with their mother (Marthe Villalonga), but, in one of several secondary plots, the tensions in the two women's relationship are displaced onto Emilie and her daughter, Anne (Chiara Mastroianni). The telling moment that provokes this transferal involves the C Major Prelude. In the middle of a scene where the family is eating the traditional meal after Christmas midnight mass, Anne offers to play the piano (see the timeline below). The idea is hers, but performance by the daughter of the family also fits a long tradition of bourgeois domestic entertainment (just as *The Well-Tempered Clavier* as étude fits piano pedagogical traditions). As she plays, her uncle makes an encouraging comment, but her grandmother says,

"Isn't it a little loud?" and Anne stops abruptly, leaving the room with her brother and her friend Khadija, a guest. The music was not actually foregrounded (that is, high in the mix or distinguished by an unusual sound quality), so that attention drawn to it by the grandmother's question is all the more striking: the question is marked, not the music. Thus, the principle of clarity is respected, despite the layers in the sound track: it is precisely the point that the piano and the voice interfere with each other here. It should also be noted that anempathy is produced by the treatment of the voice, not the music.

ca. 19:00	meal after midnight mass
ca. 20:00	Antoine (Emilie's brother) talks about hospitals
20:45	discussion of food
20:55	Lucien (Emilie's son, Anne's brother) snickers at "sleep in"
21:10	Anne and Khadija (friend of the children, employee of Emilie) tease Lucien
21:25	toast
21:30	at the table, Anne says "Shall I play?" She goes to the piano, Khadija joins her, then Lucien: Khadija is at the left, Anne is in the middle at the piano, Lucien is leaning on the back of a couch at the right
21:43	music in
21:52	Bach, m. 4; Lucien says her music puts him to sleep; as if timed to the beginning of the measure
21:54	m. 5, second half; cut to the dinner table: Antoine is at the left, Emilie's mother is in the middle, Emilie is at the right, Bruno (Emilie's husband) is at the far right; Antoine says that Anne plays well, "not half bad"
22:00	m. 6, beat 3; Emilie's mother says, "Isn't it a little loud?"
22:03	m. 7, missing the last two notes; cut back to the piano and music out; Anne stops abruptly, as if it is a practiced response or something she expected (note that, once music is established as diegetic, it moves easily back and forth between on- and offscreen)
ca. 22:30	the children leave, and the rest talk about Khadija

In a later scene, Anne, who has been training to be a lawyer like her parents, announces that she has dropped out of school, thus disappointing her mother just as the latter had disappointed her own mother by following a professional path in the first place. When the old woman dies, Anne helps her mother prepare another traditional meal, a family gathering after the funeral. In the kitchen, Emilie breaks eggs (this is late in the film, or about 1:51:00). At one point in the preparations (beginning 1:53:58), Anne pauses in her task of setting the table to sit at the piano, humming and playing in shadow above the keys, through m. 3, note 4. Shortly thereafter (1:54:10), she tries again. This time she hums, with the piano cover closed, up to m. 2, note 8. No one is in the room for either performance. The emotional distancing is parallel to the earlier scene, down to the parallel (almost) silences of mother offscreen and daughter onscreen. But this time is worse, because not only is the mother silencing the daughter, but the daughter is also now silencing herself.

Even during the Christmas meal, Bach was more than a simple entertainment, one neutral choice from many possibilities. Through Lucien's deprecating comment and Antoine's encouraging remark (which suggests a patronizing obligation to assist a mediocre student), we are given to understand that Anne is either at the limit of somewhat meager abilities or that she has made a poor choice if her goal is to impress the audience with her skill. After the funeral, Bach—like Anne's professional career—is little more than a shadow. Here, Bach becomes a symbol of a tradition, both professional and familial, that Anne yearns to satisfy but cannot if she wants to maintain her individuality. The C Major Prelude, for Anne, becomes the sonic locus of those complexities and tensions, internalized in her own voice (humming) and body (moving fingers as if playing). Bach is both hope and guilt.

The Erotic Étude in The Pianist (2001): Dorota Plays the G Major Prelude, Szpilman Listens and Looks

The C Major Prelude does not appear in *The Pianist,* which documents the miraculous survival of the Jewish pianist Władysław Szpilman in Warsaw during World War II. But there is a moment in the film that is parallel to—if decidedly more powerful rhetorically than—Anne's shadow performance. In one of several apartments where Szpilman (Adrien Brody) is hidden by sympathetic Poles, there is a piano, but Szpilman dare not play it for fear that his hiding place might be discovered. The best he can do is to uncover the keys and play Chopin's Grande Polonaise, op. 22, in his imagination, with fingers an inch or two above the keys. We are hearing what Szpilman himself hears mentally. The music is thus like point-of-view speech—other terms are point-of-audition (Altman 1992, 251) and internal diegetic sound (Bordwell and Thompson 2003, 368). The obvious symbolism of the pianist reduced to shadowplay is treated motivically in the film, the most important dramatic outcome being Szpilman's performance of the piece with orchestra in the final scene (which continues to run behind credits to the very end).[18]

Only two minutes earlier, we do hear a few measures of a work by Bach. Dorota (Emilia Fox) is the wife of a couple who have aided Szpilman; she is a professional cellist and practices the G Major Prelude. The scene lasts about a minute, and the music runs continuously throughout, reaching m. 17 before a simple cut to the next scene (see the shot list and descriptions below). As the shot list below shows, the action, too, is simple—Szpilman awakes to the cello's sound, walks toward the room from which the sound is coming, and from outside the doorway looks at Dorota as she plays. The shot / reverse shot sequence with increasingly tight framing is a conventional way to emphasize Szpilman's reactions and emotions, which are both nostalgic and erotic. (The contrast of this scene with the

Figure 6.11. Johann Sebastian Bach, *The Well-Tempered Clavier,* Book I, Prelude in E Major.

next—Szpilman's imagining the Chopin polonaise—makes the desolation of his situation even more poignant.)[19]

1. music in; couch, Szpilman sleeping; wakes
2. cut at m. 4.5; point-of-view shot of the next room through a partly open door (G Major Prelude, section 1, end)
3. m. 5.5; Szpilman walks toward the room (section 2a)
4. m. 11 (not precise); Dorota seen through the door, side shot of her playing the cello (section 2b)
5. m. 13 (not precise); reverse to Szpilman in medium shot
6. m. 14.5 (not precise); reverse to Dorota medium close-up
7. m. 15.5; reverse to Szpilman in close-up; music out at m. 17, beat 1 (still in section 2b)

The Étude, Pedagogy, and the Pastoral: The Chronicle of Anna Magdalena Bach *(1968),* Entrapment *(1999),* Following Sean *(2005)*

In the opening minutes of *The Chronicle of Anna Magdalena Bach,* we watch a silent credits sequence, which is followed abruptly by Gustav Leonhardt's vigorous performance of the cadenza from Bach's Brandenburg Concerto No. 5, first movement, and then—via a brief sound advance—by the voice-over of Christina Lang as Bach's second wife. The voice-over continues as we look over the shoulder of a young Wilhelm Friedemann playing from his *Clavier-Büchlein.* This volume, assembled by his father for Friedemann's instruction, contains the earliest versions of the C Major Prelude (see again figure 6.3), but the child plays the opening measures of a different prelude from the *Clavier-Büchlein,* the one that became the E Major Prelude in Book I of *The Well-Tempered Clavier.* This piece represents a true pastoral topic, with its moderate to slow tempo, pedal point, and eighth-note triplet groups (see figure 6.11). The priority given the performance (stationary camera, no cutting) only increases the sense of contemplation or attention to the music's topical and expressive qualities, in contradistinction to the scenes from *My Favorite Season* and *The Pianist,* where editing put more attention on the performer and other agents than on the music.

Figure 6.12. Johann Sebastian Bach, Christmas Oratorio, Part II, Sinfonia.

The music in figure 6.11 would need only the slight alteration of dotted sixteenth notes to fit securely into the siciliano style of a slow pastorale, a type that Baroque composers, including Bach, often used in connection with that most traditional formation of the pastoral topic: the rural, shepherds, and flutes. Although it can, of course, be associated with the Arcadian, or the ancient pastoral, for Bach the siciliano-pastorale typically has a religious connection, as is the case with his sole entry in Becce and Erdmann's catalog (see figure 6.12). This Sinfonia opens part 2 of the Christmas Oratorio, BWV 248. Immediately after it, the Evangelist begins a recitative by intoning "Und es waren Hirten in derselben Gegend" (the familiar "And there were in the same country shepherds abiding in the field . . ."). Becce and Erdmann label this excerpt (no. 1,677) "Hirtenmusik" (Shepherds' music); it is the first entry in an eleven-item section "Pastorella alten Stils. Weihnachten" (Pastorale in the old style. Christmas).[20] Raymond Monelle reproduces the passage (2006, 232ex14.4) and says of it that "the connections of Virgil's Golden Age with the Christian heaven, [of] piping shepherds with the world of biblical pastoralism, are brought together in this kind of piece."

Although different in its repetitiveness and its shapes (but note the arpeggio in m. 1 of the E Major Prelude!), the C Major Prelude is easily understood in terms of the pastoral topic. Friedemann plays at a tempo of approximately quarter note = 60. If the C Major Prelude is played at that tempo per quarter beat, it easily achieves the leisurely movement of the pastoral, an effect made more prominent (that is, still more leisurely) by the slow rhythm of chord changes. Especially at moderate to slow tempi, the C Major Prelude becomes much more flexible—and more complex—in its topical potential. The C Major Prelude may take one or more of the other historical connotations of the pastoral, including nostalgia, utopian or religious feeling, the erotic (in its combination of repetitive figures and expressive peaks), or even—at very slow tempi—minimalistic trance (see again figure 6.0b).

We have already seen the combination of the pedagogical prelude and nostalgia (as loss) in *My Favorite Season* and the professional performance and the erotic (also figured as loss) in *The Pianist*. In *Entrapment* (1999), Sean Connery plays a highly skilled and experienced art thief whose operation is being pene-

Figure 6.13. *Following Sean* (2005), the director's mother plays the C Major Prelude.
Screen still.

trated by Catherine Zeta-Jones in the role of an undercover insurance agent; eventually, Zeta-Jones's Virginia abandons her assignment, and the two join forces. Connery's character realizes that Virginia has great natural ability as a gymnast and takes her on as an apprentice. They go to his Scottish castle (at about 25:10), where she practices to infiltrate a museum's laser protection system, and her sinuous moves provoke erotic feelings in her mentor (a reaction shot early on in the sequence makes this abundantly clear). After the laser practice (around 39:21), we hear a sound advance, then with a cut five seconds later we see her playing the C Major Prelude on what appears to be an antique piano. After mm. 1–2 and half of m. 3 (or, without completing the opening neighbor-note figure), she stops, and he enters the frame to put a box on the piano (at 39:34). The playing is a bit tentative and might indeed be Zeta-Jones's own; it is clearly not a professional recording. The tempo here is quarter note = ca. 62–64. The playing, brief as it is, has the effect of rereading her sexuality by reinstating the child-like "apprentice," who was insulted by her mentor's deprecating remarks after she successfully traversed the exceedingly complex maze. That the playing is essentially private is emphasized in the frame by the fact that she is half hidden behind the piano's music stand and assorted treasures piled on it and by the fact he gives no indication that he has heard her. He repairs—and equalizes—their relationship with the gift of the dress, which she will wear for their first heist. The result is a complex troping on the C Major Prelude as high art (she uses it to try to reach his level as highly cultured) and the pedagogical (the prelude as belonging to education, and, by extension, her youthfulness as opposed to his age). There is also an element of loss: Zeta-Jones's character behaves in this moment like a child who has lost the approval of a parent.

The C Major Prelude as loss linked to playing the piano is also an element in a poignant moment from *Following Sean* (2005), Ralph Arlyck's "what's he doing now?" film that looks at life thirty years later for a child he had filmed in the early 1970s as part of a "free spirit" family of hippies in San Francisco's Haight-Ashbury district. Interweaved with this account are scenes about changes in Arlyck's own family over the same time period. Nearing the end of the film (at about 1:15:00) Arlyck explains by voice-over to a series of snapshots that one of Sean's sisters refused to participate in the filming and that his own younger sister, Susan, who had cerebral palsy, had died. The C Major Prelude fades in (at 1:16:06) as he talks about her, beginning in the middle of m. 22, or shortly before the beginning of section 4a. Ten seconds later a cut returns to live action as we see his ninety-year-old mother playing her Steinway piano (figure 6.13). The camera is active and moves from a view from the end of the piano across the room to Arlyck's father sitting in a chair, then back to the inside of the piano before cutting to a side view of her playing (the cut comes on the tonic pedal, or m. 32). The voice-over is out for a few measures, entering again at m. 28. When she finishes, the voice-over stops, too, and she and Arlyck talk briefly; she has forgotten that she planned to give him the piano. The elderly couple are moving to an assisted living center, and the subsequent scene shows them leaving their house. Her playing is quite adequate, but the setting and the lowbrow edition of music on the stand—Schirmer's *59 Piano Solos*—emphasize the pedagogical/domestic. Still, the main topical implications are clear and direct: nostalgia as loss, in this case, the loss that comes with age. In the setting of this film, the C Major Prelude sounds even more forlorn, since it is the only piece of historical music we hear.

The neutral—that is to say, clearly defined and stable—pastoral topic of the E Major Prelude was combined with an equally clear topic of the pedagogical étude for Friedemann's performance in *The Chronicle of Anna Magdalena Bach*: a simple complementation of visual and aural that disturbed neither. The elderly mother's performance in *Following Sean* was more complicated in that the étude topic was not defined uniquely by the music but by the prelude combined with the presence in the image track of the old woman playing, of the *59 Piano Solos,* and of the lingering images of the piano's interior. Nor is the pastoral obvious: it depends heavily on narrative information we derive from the voice-over and the subsequent conversation. The troping of étude and pastoral is therefore relatively subtle: what appears to be merely a performance in aid of the narrative can be understood as suggesting the "hopeless motion" of nostalgia, of a loss one can in fact do nothing to undo. The brief performance in *Entrapment* is more complicated still. Its brevity is a problem, as it seems to be little more than a throwaway scene opening—the narratively significant event, the delivery of the gift, happens immediately afterward. The pedagogical étude, furthermore, is reinforced by both image and sound. But there are other clues in the image: as I noted above, Zeta-Jones is nearly hidden by the elaborate music stand, as the piano itself is nearly covered over by a pile of expensive rugs and figurines. The performance is brief and in that sense far more hidden than highlighted. The brevity, the hiddenness, and the tentative playing combine to swing the pendulum 180 degrees from the previous scene, which consisted of an extended, foregrounded, and extraordinarily confident gymnastic performance. We are given simultaneously to understand that she, too, has newly awakened erotic feelings and that she assumes the possibility of a relationship has been lost—or, as depicted here, what might be called a fantasy relationship of a younger woman with a wealthy older man. Thus, in a short and awkward performance, the pedagogical arpeggios of the C Major Prelude are asked to absorb an erotic utopia (Monelle refers to Arcadia as the "scene of lovers' yearnings" [2006, 271]).

We will see this trope of the erotic and the transcendent played out in different ways in later examples, but first we must consider a different sort of troping involving the transcendent: the religious pastoral.

Religious Pastoral:
Gounod's "Ave Maria" in Girl of the Golden West (1938)

Unless one is willing to assert that all of Bach's music, no matter its genre or intended performance venue, was theologically grounded, then the religious pastoral would be difficult to pair with the C Major Prelude (unlike the more general category of the utopian, which, as we have already seen, is easily brought out). I say "would be difficult" if it were not for Gounod's "Ave Maria," which uses the C Major Prelude as its accompaniment. Probably created sometime in 1852 during a session of improvisation, it was published for violin and piano (with obbligato organ and cello parts) as *Méditation sur le premier prélude de Bach* (1853). During the course of the piece the C Major Prelude is played twice. The vocal version appeared six years later and became at least as popular throughout the second half of the nineteenth century as Schubert's earlier setting of the same text.

Recalling J. A. Fuller-Maitland's sharp criticism of Gounod's "*eau sucrée*," we doubt that he would be at all mollified to hear that the great popularity of the *Méditation* embarrassed Gounod, who wanted above all to be recognized as a serious composer and who thought the thing a mere bauble, dashed off as it was in a few minutes. Yet, *pace* Fuller-Maitland, Gounod wrought better than he imagined: he introduces a melodic expressiveness that heightens qualities already implied in the original but that also prompts a wholly different way of conceiving the large-scale shapes of the upper parts. Considered in Schenkerian terms, the melody hangs on a newly imposed interruption of the *Urlinie* (see figure 6.14). This change brings five more bars into the realm of the dominant than in Bach's original and creates the effect, overall, of a sea of dominant expressive tension with three small islands of tonic repose (mm. 1–5, 19–21, and 32–35).

After the opening few measures, almost all the pitches are chosen from inner voices, not from the C Major Prelude's uppermost voice. But this suggestion of descant melody disappears by mm. 9 and following, as the new melody takes clear priority, and Bach's upper voice is relegated to the role of accompaniment. Figure 6.15 maps the course of Gounod's melody through the "continuo grid" of Bach's C Major Prelude, whose harmonies are transposed down a fourth to provide a more comfortable space for the voice. Nevertheless, and throughout,

Figure 6.14. François Gounod, *Méditation sur le premier prélude de Bach* ("Ave Maria"), voice-leading reading.

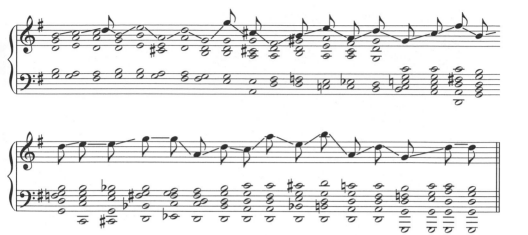

Figure 6.15. Gounod, *Méditation* / "Ave Maria," melody in the voice-leading grid of the C Major Prelude (which has been transposed to G major, the key of the first vocal edition of "Ave Maria").

Gounod exaggerates or draws out qualities already inherent in the C Major Prelude's melody or harmony. In the opening, for example, he reaches one note too far, as it were, by expanding the neighbor figure (C5) to D5 in m. 3. In addition to the expressive lift this note adds to the first phrase (coinciding with the accent in the word "Maria"), a gap is filled between the opening and the leap to E in m. 5 (B–C–D–E). In sections 2a and 2b, Gounod assigns the melody a cycle-of-fifths sequential pattern, although these are mostly fifths and not roots of the underlying chords in the longish "rule of the octave" progression. In mm. 13, 15, and 17, he does a remarkable job of maintaining tension by shifting the melody upward on a resolution chord, not its preceding dissonance (thus, A minor in m. 13, not the G#°⁷ in m. 12). In section 3 (which includes m. 22a, the Schwenke measure), the fairly small chromatic movements are mirrored in a compactly rising melody, but a sudden drop to A4 gives Gounod the beginning point for a dramatically expanded version of the stepwise rise and fall over the dominant—in this place Bach runs from A3 to D4 and back to B3, but Gounod flies from A4 up to B5 and then back to G4. In consequence, the melody resoundingly ends in m. 32, despite the C⁷ chord, and the cover-tone "Amen" not only provides an effective denouement but also effectively obliterates the significance of the coupled octaves in Schenker's familiar reading of the C Major Prelude.

Gounod produced several versions of the *Méditation* in quick succession (Hiemke 1999, 32). Thereafter, even into the early twentieth century, many different transcriptions were produced by a number of different arrangers. There is little to be said about most of them here because changes in instrumental colors had little effect compared with the initial trauma of the addition of the new melody itself. More important is that, according to Sven Hiemke, the *Méditation*

Figure 6.16. *Girl of the Golden West* (1938), Mary (Jeanette MacDonald) practices the "Ave Maria." Screen still.

and the "Ave Maria" in effect kick-started the far-reaching French Bach reception in the latter half of the nineteenth century (31, 32) and a minor industry in transcriptions and arrangements of Bach's compositions. Georg Feder (1969) documents these in exhaustive detail. The connection between Gounod and the Bach cult in Germany is Mendelssohn, who promoted the work of Bach during a Paris tour in 1831–32, met with Gounod several times in the early 1840s (Hiemke 1999, 40), and might even have inspired the composition of the *Méditation* through the original melodic elements he added to his own published arrangement of the Bach D Minor Chaconne (Feder cited in Hiemke, 44).

Gounod's setting was eventually put to good use by Herbert Stothart in *The Girl of the Golden West* (1938), a film that sentimentally evokes the period in which the "Ave Maria" was written, though in a very different place: the California of the 1849 Gold Rush. The fourth musical pairing of Jeanette MacDonald and Nelson Eddy, this film is by no means the best in the series. It is marred by a generally undistinguished score (despite eight original songs from Sigmund Romberg and Gus Kahn), by characters who embarrassingly represent ethnic stereotypes, and by an overly predictable story that greatly exaggerates Robin Hood–like qualities in the complex hero of David Belasco's famous play, with the result that "Ramerez" (Eddy) too closely resembles the B-film hero Zorro.[21] The

Figure 6.17. *Girl of the Golden West*, Mary sings, as seen from the congregation. Screen still.

two principals, on the other hand, are in fine voice, and thankfully there is a great deal of singing.

MacDonald (as Mary Robbins) renders Gounod's "Ave Maria" at a crucial moment, one not found in either stage or novel version of *The Girl of the Golden West*.[22] She has traveled from the gold fields, where she owns a thriving tavern, to Monterey in order to visit a friar who was kind to her in earlier years. By a ruse she was able to save a quantity of gold meant for the friar's church when Ramerez and his bandits intercepted the stagecoach en route—the first encounter between Ramerez and Mary. Now the priest tells Mary about the anonymous donor who leaves gold in the collection box every month to assist the work with indigent Native Americans. The priest then quickly turns the conversation to the next day's mass, which will be attended by the governor, who is visiting the city, and reminds Mary that they need to "practice our Ave Maria" (46:05). He sits at a small organ and plays mm. 1–4 of Gounod/Bach while advising Mary to "sing it for me," trying to soothe her, as she had expressed apprehension about performing for distinguished visitors. She begins (at 46:31) in m. 5 with the A minor $^6_4$ chord, a delightful choice by the arranger, as it combines metric security and a dramatic moment (a contextually dissonant chord and the highest note so far; see figure 6.16).[23] Similarly, the dominant arrival (m. 11) is the final bar of this extended shot (fifty-one seconds). The move to a C♯°⁷ chord (m. 12) coincides with a dissolve to the choir loft, as Mary, in medium long shot, continues to sing, backed by a boys' choir (at 47:00). Like MacDonald's voice, the organ sound is continuous, but the C Major Prelude's sixteenth notes disappear, replaced by block chords, and the organ's sound level drops slightly. There is, unfortunately, also an audible click in the sound track at this point, another instance of production weaknesses for this film. Despite all this, the sense of continuity is largely preserved, thanks mainly to MacDonald's voice and a simple image match on her face.

The camera does not hold her for long, however: it pans down to the altar (m. 14), then pulls back slowly to reveal the nave and the congregation. By m. 20, the choir loft is visible again in the upper right of the frame (at 47:28). The arrival on the final dominant (m. 24, at 47:45) is matched by a simple cut to the governor and his companions as they admire the singing. Then the camera tilts fairly quickly up to the choir loft, as if in the line of sight of the governor's party (see figure 6.17). These two shots (moving through the church, followed by the governor) last forty-five and sixteen seconds, respectively.

After this, the pace picks up, but the cutting still holds closely to the rhythms of the music: at m. 28 with an F♯ diminished chord over a pedal dominant, there is a cut to a close-up of the collection box in the entryway and a hand dropping in a bag of gold; the camera pans left and on the downbeat of the next measure reveals Ramerez (in medium shot). The next downbeat cuts to MacDonald singing. Two measures later, the arrival of the tonic brings a cut back to Ramerez and his companion as they recognize the young woman they had robbed only days before. On the cover-tone G (m. 34) there is a cut to a view of the nave from the back (with the choir loft visible, as if in Ramerez's line of sight). Then, four minutes after the point Mary entered the doorway of the priory room, a dissolve shifts us outdoors after the mass to a conversation in which the governor invites Mary to sing at a fiesta he is sponsoring in two nights' time.[24]

The fact that the cutting is timed to coincide in obvious ways with structural events in the music might have been awkward in a dramatic film, but it is by no means unusual in musicals; nor is the time-absorbing dissolve that makes us forget that this compact and perfect performance is actually a merging of two performances that take place over two days. In the simplest sense, the image track becomes instead an interpretation of the music. A link between historical classical music and purity is one of the underlying messages. The rules of melodrama transform Mary from a somewhat confused tomboy or virtuous tramp, impervious to the local sheriff's wooing, into a woman both respected and nubile, a transformation that takes place essentially in two stages involving her singing. In the first of these, a blind "professor" of music accompanies her while she sings "Liebestraum" for an audience of rough prospectors in her saloon. The second is the "Ave Maria" performance aided by the priest and approved by the governor. Both "Liebestraum" and "Ave Maria" are positioned as high culture, something above the everyday fare of song and dance, but it is the imprimatur of the leaders of church and state that confirms that status. Ramerez, who also hears and approves, then woos Mary in subsequent scenes (while masquerading as an army lieutenant). Following a standard formation-of-the-couple narrative, the rest of the film is concerned with Mary's eventual pairing with Ramerez.

Bach—and the church to which he is often assigned by convention but concretely by Gounod—is the cultural frame. Gounod's setting is its melodious and individualistic expression. The troping is layered: the C Major Prelude, with Gounod's melody, appears dramatically as the "Ave Maria" in a filmed performance. Remarkably, however, what one might expect could be an incoherent jumble is exactly the opposite, and reasons for the smooth merging of different elements are several. First, the long notes that open Gounod's melody make the rhythms of the accompaniment seem to move along faster by comparison, and they also encourage a moderate to faster tempo (here, quarter note = 66–68). Because the dynamic level of the C Major Prelude is also subdued compared to a solo keyboard performance, the result is a clear transformation into the pastoral, with effects of rippling water that suit a Romantic conception of the pastoral as a focus on nature (Monelle 2006, 244–45).[25] Gounod has succeeded in creating a masterful troping and blending of the old arpeggio prelude with the nineteenth-century *mélodie*. Second, by the early twentieth century, only an educated musician would even take notice of the C Major Prelude underneath Gounod's melody because the "Ave Maria" had long since become a clichéd example of occasional music, very much like the wedding marches of Mendelssohn and Wagner. In other words, by 1938, only the rarest of filmgoers would even notice there was a trope to be heard. Finally, the close synchronization in the editing of music and image minimizes any disjunctions. It is paradoxical—but not surprising—that a diegetic performance, which by its nature tends to interrupt narrative flow, can also provide examples of image/sound coordination that are as simple and direct as any "stand-and-deliver" conversation with a shot / reverse shot design and eyeline matches.

The Amateur Performer and the Prelude as High-Art Culture in Bagdad Café (1987): Sal Jr. Plays the C Major Prelude, and Everyone Listens

My last example of the C Major Prelude as diegetically performed is also by far the most complex. An extraordinary scene in *Bagdad Café* retraces aurally the early history and pedagogy of this prelude as a young man warms up for a practice session by condensing the arpeggiations into block chords and then plays through the piece as written while gradually accumulating an audience of family and neighbors. In effect, the scene recapitulates a century's worth of change from figured-bass improvisation to pedagogical étude to concert-worthy masterwork. This diegetic performance of the C Major Prelude must compete with an active image track, and it is connected to a second scene that includes a nearly complete, nondiegetic repetition that invites a point-of-view reading (I will argue that this cue sits in the "fantastical gap"). Taken together, the two scenes show opposing sides of the C Major Prelude and, ironically, flip a stereotype as the diegetic music is carefully synchronized to narrative events but the nondiegetic cue contributes little.

Not well known in the United States, *Bagdad Café* was one of the most successful films of the 1980s in Europe (Ebert 1988). It entices at the beginning with a play on a German New Wave road film in the manner of Wim Wenders, but we quickly learn that the road is short. After a German tourist, Jasmin Münchgstettner (played by Marianne Sägebrecht), takes her luggage and walks away from her husband's car following an argument, it's only a short distance down the desert road to Bagdad, California, where she stays and transforms a nearly derelict motel and restaurant. The film is a coming-to-terms romance, with an ultimately happy racial? romantic? as friends? reconciliation between white (Jasmin) and black (Brenda, the motel owner, played by CCH Pounder).

In her critical study of the film, Anahid Kassabian reads "romance" more literally than the archetype (after Northrop Frye) that I just invoked in the previous paragraph. Where I see *Bagdad Café* as having affinities with road films—typically, adventures featuring a quest—and its happy ending as affirming the community that is centered around the motel and restaurant, Kassabian focuses on the two leads, Jasmin and Brenda, and reads the film as chronicling "the development of their friendship, from mutual terror through cautious understanding to a centrality ordinarily only granted in films to heterosexual romantic relationships" (2001, 74). Kassabian foregrounds two motif-forming cues: "a kind of neo-Scott Joplin rag" (76) and a pop ballad, "I Am Calling You," written for the film by Bob Telson. Of the first, she says that it "signifies as a piece of music from a historically black genre that became popular internationally. . . . Its bright, cheerful (interracial) sound serves perfectly to represent the black, Native American, and white community of the cafe" (76). "I Am Calling You," on the other hand, is associated with the developing relationship of the two leads. Marked as a "love song, . . . [it] enables *Bagdad Cafe*'s audience to imagine female friendships in eroticized terms . . . , [even though finally] each woman repartners" with a man from the community (76).

This "imagining," which I find to be a plausible reading based on the song's lyrics and placement but which I will qualify below, is an example of what Kassabian calls an affiliating identification, or an audio-viewer's response to character agents in a way that sidesteps the constraints of the narrative presentation—in other words, it is a particular instance of reading against the grain. The term assimilating identification covers the conventional mode of synchronization and empathy as described in part 1. The opposition assimilating/affiliating is linked to a historical opposition between classical Hollywood and more recent compilation scores (the latter being underscore consisting largely or entirely of existing music, a method sometimes referred to as "score by Tower records" [Hubbert 2014, 300]). Further oppositions align with the pair assimilating/affiliating: classical Hollywood underscore versus post-1960s compilation scores based on pop songs, heterosexual versus LGBT, and patriarchal versus nonpatriarchal. This series is the interpretive background of all the book's readings of music in film.

The starkness of these clusters of oppositions—which Kassabian does nothing to undermine, despite the occasional disclaimer—directs the reading of *Bagdad Café* in a way that, in my view, misses some important features of the film's narrative and of music's work within that narrative. Most importantly, the analysis reads the treatment of "I Am Calling You" too narrowly. One of the distinguishing features of compilation scores, especially in the 1980s, was the frequent crudity of the music/image relation. Ballads were indeed used for love scenes and other scenes about romantic relationships, but they were also ubiquitous in the pop repertoire and therefore might well show up in situations that were not eroticized by other elements of sound or image. None of this takes away from the possibility that an audio-viewer might use the obtuseness of song placement in the compilation score associatively as an opportunity to read against the grain: narrative films, after all, coerce one, through synchresis, into forging connections between image and sound, but it follows that those connections will be the freest where the implications are least clear.

In this case, however, the song is not a piece of preexisting music dropped onto the film. There are several specific references in the lyrics, which mention the Nevada desert (close enough: Bagdad is in the northern Mojave Desert of California), a rundown café (which certainly is the film's physical setting), and a baby crying (we will encounter this baby in the scene to be discussed in detail below). The title line, "I Am Calling You," refers to Bagdad itself and to the exotic (for a staid European) California setting as represented by a dusty, rundown motel set next to a highway and the Santa Fe Railroad tracks. The song is heard in complete form twice, in the opening and end credits. In various abbreviated forms, it appears six additional times, always as nondiegetic underscore. The first complete presentation of the song follows the film's prologue, which is the argument between Jasmin and her husband. As she walks down the road and he drives away, the song and credits begin (2:58). A series of scenes then introduces life in the café and on the motel grounds. The only music we hear during this segment is from *The Well-Tempered Clavier*: the D Major Prelude from Book I, whose practice performances by Brenda's son, Sal Jr. (Darron Flagg), are repeatedly cut off. At 16:12, "I Am Calling You" fades in as Brenda sits outdoors following a parallel argument scene that ends with her husband driving off. The song, including its vocal style, is plainly associated with Brenda. It expresses what her look and posture, a combination of angry frustration and despair, cannot: a desire for hope or rescue that in effect "calls forth" Jasmin, who walks up shortly thereafter (appearing onscreen for the first time since the credits). The music goes out as they stare at one another, and the director, Percy Adlon, indulges in the first of many moments that combine a certain level of pathos with humor and a sense of magic (the exotic): the actors are placed on opposite sides of the screen as Brenda wipes away tears and Jasmin wipes away sweat from her face. Jasmin's "magical" appearance at the café transforms—literalizes itself—into a motif that is tied to a central theme of the film: as we later discover, Jasmin can perform magic tricks.

We hear the song again—the instrumental interlude and the voice's opening phrase of the second verse—at the end of the same day (48:20) in a slow montage for evening: Jasmin is in her room, Brenda is in the office, and a richly colored desert twilight settles on the long shot of the motel and its grounds. Music goes out at 49:32 with a simple cut to the restaurant the next day.

Here Kassabian's reading is at its strongest. Details of the image track clearly set Brenda and Jasmin in an attraction-of-opposites mode that could easily evolve into an eroticized relationship. The remainder of the film, however, continues to develop the trope of the mutually exotic: Jasmin's magical strangeness to Brenda, Brenda's "real-life" earthiness to Jasmin. For Brenda, it is the strange attraction of an unknown Europe; for Jasmin, it is the strange attraction of an unknown, under- and working-class America. When "I Am Calling You" is next heard (1:04:55), the slow introductory chords underscore the first part of an equally slow montage. Brenda's angry outburst (the last of many) is followed by an apology to Jasmin during which Brenda reveals that her husband has left her. Shots of the highway and the restaurant are followed by Jasmin's entrance and her first magic tricks. The music goes out at 1:05:50 but reappears about twenty seconds later to accompany a series of these tricks, which culminate with a rose that Jasmin gives to Brenda. The scene and music go out at 1:07:00.

We hear the song's intro again at 1:15:10; here it is ironic, as still another slow montage depicts the end of the magic, so to speak, since Jasmin is forced to leave because her tourist visa has expired. The montage continues up to and past Jasmin's return, at which point the music of the interlude and the voice's opening phrases of the second verse return as well (1:18:58; cut off at 1:20:40). Far from being affiliating or merely associative, the image track specifically links the song with a relationship between Brenda and Jasmin that not only is close in friendship but also carries the possibility of physical intimacy. Their greeting earlier in the sequence, on the other hand, is all about Europe and America, white and black, despite the fact that they hug each other warmly. In a long shot with the two positioned at the extremes of the screen—a parallel to a shot that I have already mentioned from early in the film—Jasmin is dressed in white, Brenda in a striped blouse of gray and black. The clothes remain visually prominent when they embrace. This happens in a single brief shot (at 1:20:30), a long shot in which the two are shown standing on open ground, slightly obscured by plants, and they place tiaras on each other's heads. The magic is still present (in the tiaras), but the strong sense of a mutual affection expressed in a private space is unique in the film.

By the end, then, when we hear the entire song again over the end credits, the two thematic threads have merged into an allegorical trope: the magical union of Europe and America, and the range of the potential of Brenda and Jasmin's relationship. That the former remains the overt, dominant theme of the film is clear from the "finale," a surreal, even absurd musical number in which the cue that Kassabian calls a "neo–Scott Joplin rag"—I prefer "honky-tonk"—is transformed into a song and dance in which the various members of the community (including the truck drivers) participate. The lyrics emphasize "magic." The whole film is thereby confirmed as a fantasy, a comedy-romance of wishful thinking that is elevated by the poignancy of the characterizations and by the strength of Sägebrecht's and Pounder's performances.[26]

That the film is, first of all, about clichéd visions of Europe and America is supported by the film's historical musics, which fit the category of "art music," or

Figure 6.18. *Bagdad Café* (1987), Sal Jr. (Darron Flagg) plays the opening of the C Major Prelude in block chords and triple meter. Transcription from the sound track.

preexisting concert works that Kassabian says function like pop music in a compilation score, that is, as another alternative to the traditional Hollywood symphonic underscore (2001, 72).[27] In this instance, however, the three preludes from *The Well-Tempered Clavier* that we hear during the course of the film are all presented diegetically, and one of them—the C Major Prelude—is foregrounded in a performance. It is this performance that suggests to me the overriding importance of the Europe/America theme.

The three preludes appear in succession, the D Major first (up to 18:30), the C Minor next (up to 50:25), and the C Major last. Sal Jr. is introduced by means of the music. We learn little else about him in the early minutes of the film except what we see—piano; open music scores; a metronome sitting on top of a book, *The Great Pianists*—and what we hear, which is several attempts to practice the D Major Prelude, twice cut off by Brenda yelling at him to stop. In the first instance (10:42), she denigrates it as "sewing machine music." The second time (at 18:30) comes after Jasmin arrives and goes into the motel office. In both instances, Sal Jr. is offscreen when Brenda calls out.

During the film's second act—after Jasmin takes a room and begins to work her way tentatively and reluctantly into the café community—the C Minor Prelude is equally tentative. We first "hear" it as air piano: the score is open as Sal Jr. plays silently outdoors on his soundless practice keyboard (23:40). Ten minutes later the prelude is heard again, in the background and very low in the mix; it comes up a bit after about thirty seconds, then fades. Considerably later (49:35), we see the restaurant and hear the C Minor Prelude, right hand only, offscreen, then the music, with both hands, restarting at the beginning. A cut to Sal Jr. at 50:15 is followed ten seconds later by Brenda yelling out "Cut it!"

The C Major Prelude is another matter, as it is directly tied to Jasmin's settling into the café community and her eventual acceptance by Brenda. Brenda's two children are the catalysts. First, Phyllis (Monica Calhoun) and Jasmin share laughs as the latter allows the fashion-conscious teenager to try on a pair of lederhosen. Then, at 55:25, Sal Jr. makes yet another attempt to practice: he plays the first several measures of the C Major Prelude in the form of block chords in triple time, echoing the manuscript forms of the piece (see figures 6.18 and 6.19a). He breaks off after ten seconds, but Jasmin enters and tells him to continue (figure 6.19b). Thus encouraged, he starts over again (55:59) with the arpeggio version;

Figure 6.19, a–b. *Bagdad Café,* Sal Jr. practices; Jasmin (Marianne Sägebrecht) enters. Screen stills.

his playing, however, is very fast and uneven, a failed attempt at a toccata rendering. At 56:13 he stops when he sees that Jasmin has sat down to listen (figure 16.20a), and he starts at the beginning of the prelude a third time, using both soft and sustaining pedals and playing more slowly and expressively.

Finally, Sal Jr. is able to offer a complete performance, though he just barely gets in the final chord before his mother again interrupts him. Figure 6.20a emphasizes the special character of this scene as a performance for an audience, and figure 6.20b—timed to the A minor^6 chord that starts part 2a—emphasizes the abstract (and therefore high-art) quality of the music with a sustained shot of the

Figure 6.20, a–f. *Bagdad Café,* Sal Jr. plays the C Major Prelude; Jasmin listens; Rudi (Jack Palance) enters. Screen stills.

restaurant devoid of people. The abstract, pictorial character of this shot is further emphasized by the fact that what it shows cannot be what would be visible to either Jasmin or Sal Jr., even if they had been looking. That the music has thoroughly engaged Jasmin is apparent when the G major triad shared by parts 2a and b arrives (figure 6.20c). It is this moment when the audio-viewer realizes that Jasmin is doing more than just listening to a pastoral bit of concert music. Instead, the C Major Prelude has extended the pastoral to the nostalgic, as it invokes memories of her homeland, which remains the benchmark against which the exoticism of her current situation is measured. More to the immediate point, when the tonic triad ending part 2b arrives, Sal Jr. looks over at her (figure 6.20d) and is clearly gratified that someone, finally, really understands his music (he says as much after his mother interrupts him). When the dissonances of part 3 ensue, Rudi (Jack Palance), a retired scene painter who lives in a trailer on the motel property, invades the restaurant shot (figure 6.20e). The remainder of the

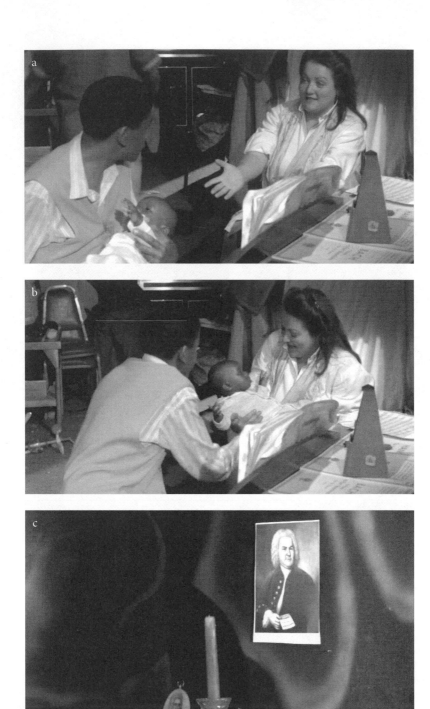

Figure 6.21, a–c. *Bagdad Café*, Jasmin holds the baby; "Bach." Screen stills.

scene cuts back and forth between the performance and Rudi's slow approach, which is noisy as he slides a chair across the floor—the association of dissonance with noise is telling. A perhaps unexpected expressive potential in the Schwenke measure is realized through all this as well, as the extra bar of dissonance brings out the change from minor chromatic sounds to the V^7 that begins part 4a—in this context the chord sounds very like an emerging triadic consonance and is appropriately matched to another shot of the rapt Jasmin (at 57:46; figure 6.20f). We see the same shot at the arrival of the tonic $^6_4$ chord (58:03). By this time, Rudi has advanced sufficiently that the view can be taken as a correct reaction shot: we see what he sees, not merely what the camera saw earlier. Brenda breaks the mood with a mean gesture: she brings in a baby, announces that it is Sal Jr.'s son, and drops the baby in his father's lap.

The scene is not finished, however, as Jasmin refuses to be disconcerted. She asks Sal Jr. to let her hold the baby (figure 6.21a–b) and then answers his query about where she is from with "Bavaria," then a couple of seconds later, "Germany," to which he somewhat unexpectedly responds "I knew it" and looks toward the wall behind the piano, where hangs a print of a familiar Bach portrait (figure 6.21c).[28] In this interaction is concentrated the sympathetic meeting of Europe and America on the terms the film wants to define it: Jasmin accepts the baby, and Sal Jr. acknowledges (enthusiastically) Jasmin's cultural ownership of a music that is manifestly of great importance to him. Brenda is left out for the moment. It will take one more outburst from her before she and Jasmin come to terms (in the scene mentioned above, during which "I Am Calling You" is heard beginning at 1:04:55).

From the enclosed space of the cluttered room with the piano, the next scene shifts abruptly outdoors at 59:20. At 59:44, the C Major Prelude begins again at a low level apparently intended to be the offscreen diegetic sound of Sal Jr. playing indoors. The slightly out-of-tune piano is the same, but the expressively neutral and correct performance, combined with a sweetened sound that resembles production for recording, leading to a very gradual fade, all compromise the presumed diegetic connection to the previous scene. This is a music that has wandered into the "fantastical gap." Bach is now the accompaniment to the formation of two new couples, but at the same time the music lends a hovering thematic presence that holds our attention on the transformation effected by Jasmin's encouragement of Sal Jr.'s performance in the preceding scene. The result is a mélange of personal narrative (in the couple formations), the diegetic, and the abstract nondiegetic. The couple we see with the cut is Phyllis and Eric (Alan Craig), a backpacking student who has set up his tent on the property and is now showing Phyllis how to throw a boomerang (thus adding the Australian exotic; see figure 6.22a). Jasmin joins them (figure 6.22b), but the bulk of the scene is a conversation between Rudi and her (figure 6.22c–d), during which he asks if he can paint her portrait. She is reluctant until he mentions Hollywood, which clearly fascinates her—and provides yet another exotic venue and another locus of "magic."

The C Major Prelude is heard three more times in the film, each as part of a trope that brings the prelude into alignment—indeed, a merger—with the other

Figure 6.22, a–d.
Bagdad Café, outdoors;
the C Major Prelude is
heard uncertainly as
underscore ("fantastical
gap"). Screen stills.

a
*original in G
Slowly
(guitar)

Figure 6.23, a–b. *Bagdad Café,* (a) guitar introduction to "I Am Calling You"; (b) merges with the C Major Prelude. Transcription by Joel Love from the sound track.

*original in B♭
Slowly

Figure 6.24. *Bagdad Café,* opening of the C Major Prelude transformed into the rhythms of the introduction to "I Am Calling You." Transcription by Joel Love from the sound track.

musics of the film. Sal Jr. hints at the "honky-tonk" theme as he plays a leisurely swung version of the prelude's mm. 4–14 at 1:07:32 while Jasmin exhibits another "magic trick" behind him—we can see that the café is now prospering, with tables and customers in the formerly cluttered space. At 1:16:00 the prelude and "I Am Calling You" are juxtaposed: the guitar intro (see figure 6.23a) merges with Sal Jr.'s barely completed first bar of the prelude as the café and its inhabitants are forlorn after Jasmin's departure (see figure 6.23b). This juxtaposition prepares the ground for a synthesis that gives us the opening of the prelude in the rhythms of the intro for "I Am Calling You" (at 1:16:45; out at 1:17:13), a parallel to the opening call but now explicit: a call for Jasmin/Bach/magic to return (see figure 6.24).

Over the course of the film, the three preludes accomplish a move from one side of the topical continuum to the other. The D Major, the C Minor, and Sal Jr.'s aborted fast performance of the C Major Prelude all lie squarely in the associative cluster of pedagogical/machine/fast: Sal Jr. as a student making mistakes in practice, the preludes with consistent repeated figuration highlighted by Brenda's sneering remark, and the exaggeratedly fast tempo of the abandoned performance. The juxtaposition with the pastoral is abrupt, directly generated by Jasmin seating herself to listen. Sal Jr. responds, and the associative cluster pastoral/nostalgic/slow promptly arises. And with this cluster comes the potential for the final step: from the nostalgic to the utopian. Jasmin looks in the direction of the camera when she answers Sal Jr. about her country of origin, he looks off to the right when he responds, and on the reaction shot Bach looks out at us.

It is only during this scene that the topical juxtaposition of the Bach preludes and the ballad begins to shift. The link in figuration between the C Major Prelude and "I Am Calling You" is obvious when the latter returns at 1:04:50, and we are not surprised when the two merge into one. If the C Major Prelude moved the topical expression from étude to pastoral and then to the utopian, the trope is exactly the blending of the opposites presented to us up to this point: Bach and ballad, white and black, European and American—exotic and magic.[29]

Conclusion

It would be easy for the reader to conclude from the mode of analysis in this chapter that the diegetic/nondiegetic distinction is aligned with pure performance / close synchronization: with an anempathetic "stopping" of narrative, in the first case, and empathetic support of narrative, in the second. These pairings, however, are correct only for the extreme cases: to diegetic and performance, an unknown musician playing onstage with a drapery backdrop in a single extended shot; to nondiegetic and empathy, original symphonic underscore in the highly detailed "mickey-mousing" manner that Max Steiner popularized in the 1930s. The G Major Prelude as played by twenty cellists in *The Silence before Bach* does comes close to the pure performance extreme in its framed presentation and single long take. Nevertheless, the train noise, amateurish camera work, and two *puncta*—the young woman's embarrassed smirk, the presence of one obviously older man—all contrive to offer potential narrative ties. The persistent train noise prevents the listener from concentrating on the performance alone: there is no concert hall quiet. The camera work suggests a "home-movie" capture of a somewhat unusual rehearsal, making us wonder who is doing the recording and why. And the two persons are singled out—though by no means emphatically—as potential agents. Is the young woman a lead or supporting character? Will the next scene show the older man leading his troupe across a plaza toward their salon performance before the king and queen of Spain?

Agents—which I define here as characters known to us or brought to our attention through the visual process Altman calls focusing—bring with them the persistent possibility of reinterpretation of any simultaneous music's presumably stable topical signification. "Reinterpretation" here, of course, means a greater or lesser effect of troping. The diegetic cues examined above for *My Favorite Season*, *The Pianist*, *The Chronicle of Anna Magdalena Bach*, *Entrapment*, *Following Sean*, and *Girl of the Golden West*, along with Sal Jr.'s performance in *Bagdad Café*, all function in this manner. A succinct way of putting it is that the agent (or agency) mediates between the sound (that is, the music) and the image.

In *Chronicle*, the music is at the fore, its presence anchored by a body seen only from behind and in which we take little interest, being offered almost nothing beyond the identity of the child as Wilhelm Friedemann. The irony of such pure performance is that, without any strong motivating tie binding narrative, actor-agent, and music, the piece in and of itself doesn't matter: the C Major Prelude would have been equally authentic, the more so as one of its versions is also in the *Clavier-Büchlein*. Similarly, in *The Pianist*, preludes from any of the other cello suites would have suited, but the scene lies a step away from pure performance: we are motivated to an empathetic response because Szpilman is shown to be interested in Dorota and her music. In both cases—*Chronicle* and *The Pianist*—the topic is more important than its individual instantiation, an indication of topical stability.

The status of the C Major Prelude is different in *My Favorite Season, Entrapment, Following Sean,* and *Bagdad Café.* In each of these, what we might call a minimal troping of the pastoral and the pedagogical is tied to a character and to a significant moment in the narrative. Uniquely among the preludes and fugues of *The Well-Tempered Clavier,* the C Major Prelude suits this combination of the nostalgic or utopian and modest means of performance. In other words, only the C Major Prelude is appropriate to the performances in these four films, as the amateur status of the players is central to our understanding of—and involvement in—these particular narrative moments. Despite its much heavier dose of troping, even *Girl of the Golden West* fits this model, in that the priest makes a point of emphasizing their need to practice and Mary responds with apprehension when told that the governor will be in attendance: "I don't mind singing for you and the people, but . . ." All this is a way of saying that the more the character means to us, the more the music does, too.

In terms of the vococentric cinema model, the hierarchy is guaranteed (one might equally say generated) by the agents as presented to us and by the empathy we audio-viewers feel in response. It is important to recall here that, for my purposes in this book, "voice" means human speech in the sound track. If a character sings—combines music and speech—the perfect synthesis of those sound track elements occurs, and also of image and sound, so long, that is, as the singing agent is onscreen. A fear of throwing the viewer off if the singer is not a significant character (as with Corinna Mura, who sings "La Passion" in *Casablanca,* for example), as well as a fear of the power of a sustained onscreen vocal performance, may well be behind frequent cutaways such as those that happen in *Casablanca* and also in the "Ave Maria" scene of *Girl of the Golden West.* On the other hand, if the character plays but does not speak, the sound track dialectic is in full play, and music challenges, possibly even substitutes for, the voice. The fragility of this attack on the voice's priority, however, is readily shown by the immediate deflation of music under speech that follows or interrupts a performance, as happens on a small scale in *Entrapment,* where the performance barely has time to begin, and on a larger scale in *Bagdad Café,* where the performance is denied an appropriate closure by Brenda's abrupt and noisy appearance with Sal Jr.'s baby.

Quite a different situation applies to nondiegetic music. As we shall see in the next chapter, the nondiegetic status of the music imposes a distance between agents and sound and in so doing shifts the burden of mediation to the underscore. That "distance" is the imposition of the level of the narrator. Underscore is always analogous to—occupies the same level as—the voice-over narrator. To put it another way, the underscore always substitutes for the voice-over narrator: it acquires something like the status of the narrator's voice. The most complex kind of cinema is the narrative feature film that combines the primary level of diegetic action and speech with the secondary level of the voice-over narrator.[30]

7 Underscore:
Four Studies of the C Major Prelude

The audiovisual combination inevitably involves a troping effect on preexisting music, since any film will change the music it incorporates simply by combining it with images. The character and effect of the troping, however, vary greatly, from minimal disturbance to a music's topical stability to much more far-reaching reinterpretations. As we saw in chapter 6, unless it is presented as something approaching pure performance (after Gorbman's pure musical code), a diegetic performance will always invite attention to agents' motivation and action. A nondiegetic cue, on the other hand, will tend to emphasize coincidences of design—in other words, sync points and matches in the audiovisual phrasing. Because of the cognitive habits of viewers—that is, because of synchresis—these coincidences will be present whether they are accidental or planned. Thus, for our purposes here, the stability of the topic or the clarity and extent of the troping will depend in significant part on the music's design. For that reason, the introductory section below examines the C Major Prelude from the standpoint of the familiar model of Schenkerian analysis.

Following from that work, the four readings of film scenes that constitute the bulk of the chapter emphasize the relation of image to harmony, the motif of the neighbor note, and the figure of register. The work begins with one of the simplest, most conventional filmic treatments of the C Major Prelude as underscore. Ironically, it occurs in a film noted for anything but the conventional: Peter Weir's *Picnic at Hanging Rock* (1975). I will argue that the contrast is very much to the point. Two very different takes on the prelude and the transcendent follow. *Thirty Two Short Films about Glenn Gould* (1993) juxtaposes a voice-over narrator's statement about Gould's legacy against the pianist's recording of the C Major Prelude, coming as close as anything I know to subverting the vococentric hierarchy through its idiosyncrasies in articulation that make music into the character's voice, the Romantic ideal of music as transcendent speech. Even there, however, the status of the music is problematized by our knowledge of it as a recording, as something that is simultaneously present and past, as Barthes (1981, 79) said of the photograph. *Je vous salue, Marie (Hail Mary;* 1985), which includes an improbable juxtaposition that puts the prelude in the context of a high school basketball game, is equally notable as the scene during which Mary has the first intimation of her special status as the mother of Christ: the kinetic is transformed into commentary on the transcendent. The chapter's final section is on a scene from *Lola* (1961), where the same move is played out with two preludes, a driving D Minor Prelude from Book I and a contemplative-transcendent C Major Prelude.

On Design-Based Readings of the C Major Prelude

Joel Lester takes the evidence of the preliminary and final versions of the C Major Prelude in a different direction from that of David Schulenberg and David Ledbetter (see again the first section of chapter 6). Where they emphasized the close connection between figured bass, continuo practice, improvisation, and composition, Lester is concerned with Bach as experienced composer and skillful constructor of texts. He identifies three compositional principles that Bach applies consistently across all his mature compositions: the material of a piece derives from the opening, recurrences of material introduce heightened tension (*Steigerung*) or activity, and sections are organized in parallel constructions (2001, 52–53). In the C Major Prelude, unity of material is all too obvious, but the other principles are represented as well. The large design is a single section—the scalar descent and dominant pedal, these being framed by the opening neighbor-note gesture and the final tonic pedal—but "parallelisms arise during both the descending bass scale and the dominant pedal. Each of these events is broken into two parallel halves, with the second portion presenting a heightened version of the first" (67). Lester notes (as we saw in figure 6.3) that Bach expands a dominant pedal of four bars in the *Clavier-Büchlein* version into eight bars in *The Well-Tempered Clavier,* the second four of which (mm. 28–31) introduce heightened tension. Similarly, the chordal variety of the scale harmonization in the earlier version becomes a strict set of parallelisms in the later one, with more intense chromaticism in the second part (68).[1]

Lester's account fits well with Heinrich Schenker's ideas of unity, synthesis, and foreground chromatic immediacy. Figure 7.1 gives a schematic version of Schenker's celebrated analysis of the C Major Prelude, a reading that is organized according to an *Urlinie* $\hat{3}$–$\hat{2}$–$\hat{1}$ in note-against-note counterpoint with a bass I–V–I.[2] In the upper system of figure 7.1, I have kept Schenker's two lower-order inner voices, even though their main purpose seems to be to generate a leading tone and the seventh in the dominant chord. The first middleground expansion of this *Urlinie* is managed primarily through coupling (middleground doubling) of the $\hat{3}$ downward and the $\hat{2}$ upward, as shown in the lower system of figure 7.1.

Even without its prominent position in the volume of *Five Graphic Music Analyses* (1969), Schenker's analysis would undoubtedly have secured its place in Schenkerian pedagogy, thanks to the elegance and clarity of the reading and its notation (which does not require verbal commentary), and thanks to the fact that it offers something of all the essential elements in Schenker's theory.[3] The three basic levels (background, middleground, foreground) are presented with their correct content and laid out on the page (with background at the top) so as

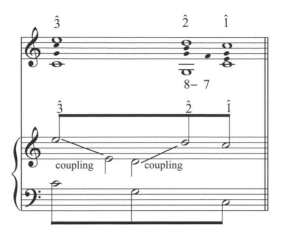

Figure 7.1. Johann Sebastian Bach, *The Well-Tempered Clavier,* Book I, Prelude in C Major, schematic version of Schenker's analysis.

to show that the *Ursatz*—the figure of the background—generates the content of the "later" levels. (My schematic version in figure 7.1 shows only the background level.) This *Ursatz* is the simplest of the three classes the theory offers—and the surest (one can always read from $\hat{3}$). The middleground elaboration by means of coupling (middleground doubling) is easily understood intuitively (unlike the somewhat fraught notion of interruption, for example), and Bach obligingly repeats the coupling. In so doing, he not only reinforces the figure with an additional instance but also solves the problem of obligatory register for the *Urlinie*—the requirement that the *Urlinie* proceed as a line in the same register.

The formal units suggested by the durations of the couplings correspond exactly with the two major distinct blocks of figuration in the piece: the long gesture of descent in the first half (parts 1, 2a, and 2b), and the slow-moving but intense arch shape of the second half (parts 3, 4a, and 4b). These are so obvious that contrary figures at the very beginning and the end can be explained readily as supporting events, the first four bars as establishing C major and $\hat{3}$ with a neighbor-note figure (the arch in miniature!) and the meandering but ultimately ascending arpeggios as enacting (or dramatizing) the octave shift required by the coupling, but which would be awkward to produce with the slowly shifting figures of the earlier measures.

In the foreground, the initial neighbor-note figure forms a neat, compact prolongational unit with components from elementary music theory: the neighbor note, the harmonic cycle (I–ii–V–I), and a suspension-like treatment of the seventh in the supertonic chord. Milton Babbitt's demonstration of this passage is captured in an anecdote by Arthur Komar, who was visiting a class with his friend David Lewin in the late 1950s: "Babbitt play[ed] the opening measures . . . , holding down the sustaining pedal to indicate the background primacy of

Part: (1)　　　　　　(2a)　　　　　　　　　(2b)

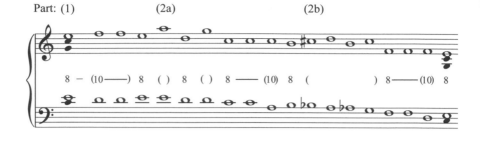

(3)　　　　　(4a)　　　　　　　　　　(4b)

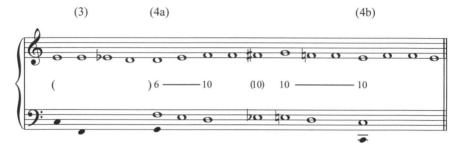

Figure 7.2. Johann Sebastian Bach, *The Well-Tempered Clavier,* Book I, Prelude in C Major, pattern of doubling E4–E5.

C major throughout. He explained that he was not rendering an actual performance of the passage, but merely trying to give an aural impression of its level structure" (1994, 23).

Schenker's reading certainly does get across graphically the nestings of the I–ii–V–I cycle. One may object, however, that although the *Ursatz* properly is in two parts (*Urlinie* and bass arpeggiation), he insists on four-part voice leading (as the top of figure 7.1 shows), even to the extent of including an 8–7 passing motion in the background level (to accommodate that seventh). One might make an allowance for constraints of presentation: with the inner voices, the background level is just a more schematic version of a first middleground. My real complaint, however, is that he ignores the piece's most obvious feature: the five-part voice leading that is readily apparent in his own foreground reduction. Schenker is hardly alone in this: so far as I can tell, no commentator has made a point of this texture (which, as it happens, is by no means unusual in Baroque arpeggio preludes). As one example, Allen Forte and Steven Gilbert (1982, 188–89) do mention five-part writing, but only as a practical problem for a reduction exercise; their reading quickly reverts not to four parts but to two.[4]

Figure 7.2 takes the odd property of the very first chord—its doubling of the third (E4, E5)—and follows the relevant voices through the prelude. Note that these voices return repeatedly to the octave, that they move the pairing down to E3 and E4 halfway through, and that only thereafter are the octave doublings

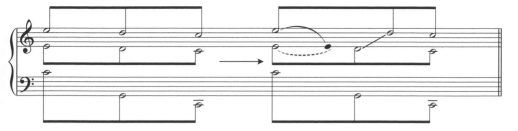

Figure 7.3. Johann Sebastian Bach, *The Well-Tempered Clavier*, Book I,
Prelude in C Major, reading in terms of doubling, not coupling.

abandoned for sixths and tenths. It seems reasonable, given that this voice pair
is a constant feature of the piece, to acknowledge its salience in the design of the
background. See figure 7.3, where true octave doubling is the form of the background (at the left). From this Schenker's coupling is derived as (in part) temporal
variation in the first middleground (at the right). I have marked the parts or gestures of the piece in the same way as in table 6.1: (1) the neighbor-note figure; (2a)
the descent to V; (2b) the descent to I; (3) the approach to V; (4a) the dominant
pedal point; (4b) the tonic pedal point. These line up fairly closely with Lester's
divisions except that I give a separate unit to the approach to V—my part 3—and
regard the dominant pedal point (part 4a) as a single arch gesture.

Doubling, I argue, is better as a description of the theme of the prelude than is
a descending line to $\hat{1}$. But doubling is not the only way we might treat this prelude productively. Schenker's notion of hidden repetition (the idea that the often
abstract patterns of the background and first middleground replicate themselves
at later, more immediate levels) suits the C Major Prelude very well, if one takes
as the starting point (that is, as the content of the background) a figure different from the simple descending *Urlinie*. Figure 7.4 uses the simple motive of the
opening, $\hat{3}$–$\hat{4}$–$\hat{3}$, and maps it at four levels (indicated by brackets in the example):
the opening as cited, the first half of the piece, the whole of the piece, and the final
tonic expansion. The tension introduced by this reading is typical of many: a tension between contrapuntal, motivic, and harmonic explanations. The linkage of
the harmonic with the motivic is a coincidence of this piece, but direct: we cannot have the neighbor note F4 without the expansion of the dominant that is one
of the most curious features of the prelude's first half. After bars 1–4, G is defined
as a key. Once the bass note G3 is reached, G is then promptly redefined as a harmony, as V in C major, but all in all, thirteen of the first eighteen bars are occupied with expressing the dominant.

I admire the elegance of Schenker's reading and even find appealing the notion of a nostalgic reference to the syncopes of the antique style (Snarrenberg
1997, 40),[5] but I find much more compelling a broader integration based on the
simple I–V–I harmonic frame of the seventeenth-century organ prelude. Recall that, as figure 6.3 showed, the early version of the C Major Prelude explic-
itly ends with the $\hat{3}$–$\hat{4}$–$\hat{4}$–$\hat{3}$ figure. Komar also proposed a reading based on the

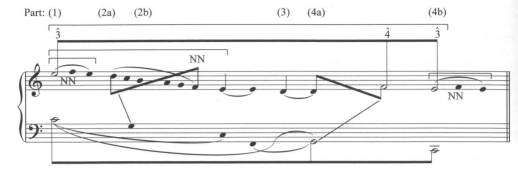

Figure 7.4. Johann Sebastian Bach, *The Well-Tempered Clavier,* Book I, Prelude in C Major, reading with neighbor note (3̂–4̂–3̂).

neighbor-note figure. His argument starts from a problem that I conveniently ignored in my appreciation of Schenker's analysis earlier:

> Another stickler arising from the study of this prelude concerns the resolution of the background soprano 2̂. Schenker claims that this happens in m. 32, although [D5] does not actually appear in the foreground until m. 34, resolving to [C5] in m. 35. . . . The difficulty here is that since mm. 32–35 represent the final tonic prolongation, the Ds in m. 34 must be thought of as being suspended from the background V which resolves in m. 32; yet the powerful C7 chord of that measure convincingly resolves . . . D to an implied [C3]. (1994, 28)

Komar did not regard this C3 as the concluding tone of the *Urlinie,* however, because of the parallelism between the closing bars and the opening four bars, where the Ds "belong to an inner voice, with 3̂–4̂–3̂ serving as the essential top line," and therefore "the soprano 4̂–3̂ motion in mm. 30–32 would seem to take precedence over 2̂–1̂" (1994, 29). He also suggests that Bach may have wanted to make a motivic connection between the end of the prelude and the subject of the ensuing fugue.

I find both the neighbor note and the doubling readings truer to the prelude than Schenker's and would set them side by side as the most plausible "background" candidates for this prelude.[6] Both are equally notable—each deals with a different aspect of the piece, and each traces a different theme through its pitches and its time. Therefore, I would not elevate one over the other. Their features can in fact be merged—although not without some visual opacity—in a middleground, from which the immediate features of the foreground can be derived easily (see figure 7.5).

The rich traditional texture of five voices intersects with the degree of motivic integration that was an almost necessary result of the Italianate concept of one affect (or mood) per movement, even in purely instrumental music. This counteracts the improvisation-like diversity of figures: the traditional counterpoint in the first third of the prelude, the chromatic and dissonant cadence in the second,

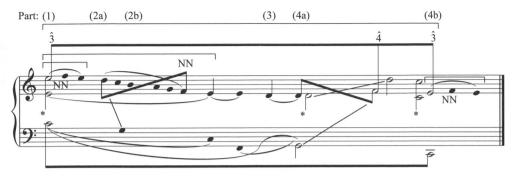

Figure 7.5. Johann Sebastian Bach, *The Well-Tempered Clavier,* Book I, Prelude in C Major, merger of doubling and neighbor-note readings.

and the final coda-cadenza that breaks the registral and figural patterns as an imaginative gesture of conclusion (though not one unusual in the organ prelude repertoire). Thus Bach can make reference to ancient and modern, and to vocal and instrumental (sixteenth-century motets and seventeenth-century organ preludes), in his mixing of styles, as found throughout *The Well-Tempered Clavier.*

High Art, High Culture

The Kinetic Étude, High Art, and Class Difference: Picnic at Hanging Rock *(1975)*

The C Major Prelude plays only a small and largely conventional role in Peter Weir's *Picnic at Hanging Rock* (1975), but it is of interest because it is specifically associated with machine motion. Although its treatment is effective in its place, the prelude cue lacks motivic significance and might easily have been replaced by something topically and expressively similar. Two other classical works—the second movements of Mozart's *Eine kleine Nachtmusik* and Beethoven's "Emperor" Concerto—are treated quite differently in the film: they are not only repeated but placed in much more prominent positions. The latter especially acquires strong narrative significance, as its nondiegetic cues are balanced against the diegetic string quartet performances of Mozart, on the one hand, and Gheorghe Zamfir's pan flute music, on the other hand. Thus, Beethoven becomes the mediator between the Victorian European world that white Australians are shown as being at great pains to develop and sustain, and the natural or Aboriginal world of the continent they have colonized.

A sumptuously photographed, widescreen art film, *Picnic at Hanging Rock* was an immediate success not only in Australia, where it spawned a whole genre of period films, but internationally as well. Jonathan Rayner describes it as "a methodologically rebellious film about individual rebellion, a nonconformist's view of conformity that succeeded ironically in pleasing the establishment of a traditionally conservative industry, the cinema" (2003, 86). Characteristic of its art-film ethos, the narrative is sometimes obscure and the plot remains un-resolved, but these are devices that in fact are central to the film's goal, which is to set up—but not resolve—a series of oppositions by developing the theme of the "notion of time as a human rather than natural construct" (Bliss 2000, 50).

On Valentine's Day in 1900 a group of students and their teachers go on a picnic. They come from a girls' school on rural property near a village; they travel to a nearby landmark, Hanging Rock, a volcanic formation that stands up five hundred feet from the surrounding land and is in the vicinity of a mountain con-sidered sacred by the Aborigines. Although warned against it, four of the girls climb the rock, ascending through its labyrinth of channels. Two, along with a teacher, disappear and are never found.

The oppositions posed in *Picnic at Hanging Rock* include at least these: civi-lization/nature, European/Aborigine, linear time / stasis (or out-of-time), Vic-torian repression / emerging sexuality, idealized sexual relations / actual sexual relations, any attempt to measure universal forces / the ungovernable power of the rock itself.[7] In this remarkable complex of associations, the C Major Prelude contributes to the expression of two pairs: upper class / lower class (here, as the school versus the village) and repression/sexuality. In addition, the film's first obvious bit of "methodological rebellion" uses the forward-moving character of the prelude to emphasize by contrast the flipping of elements in a classical es-tablishing sequence, thus pitting linear time and its reversal—hence, negation—against one another.

The film's opening nine minutes are occupied with an extended prologue dur-ing which the girls share their greeting cards of endearment with each other. Throughout, the viewer is confronted with strong but still enigmatic suggestions of idealized, potential, or actual sexualized relations among the girls. Only with the announcement of the picnic outing and the arrival of the carriage does the film "proper" begin. I will first consider the sequence from the standpoint of the music and its contribution to narrative and then look at the opposition between time of the music and time of the film.

The prelude cue is a professional piano recording (uncredited) at a moder-ate tempo with very consistent rhythms. It is clear—foregrounded but not un-duly loud. Against it we hear occasional noise of the carriage, horses, and chil-dren and one brief comment by Miss McCraw (Vivean Gray), the science teacher who will disappear along with two of the girls. The music begins just after the carriage draws forward to pick up the students and their chaperones at the front steps of the school (figure 7.6a) and cuts off on the tonic $^6_4$ chord in m. 29, just after the driver draws attention to Hanging Rock and their imminent arrival there (figure 7.6h).

The connection of the prelude to the kinetic is as direct, as simple, as one might want in the carriage and the journey. Within that frame, there are a few form-partitioning and expressive moments that rely on the prelude's design. The neighbor-note figure is buried in the clatter of the carriage's arrival on-screen—it will not be *that* characteristic motive but rather triads and dissonances

Figure 7.6, a–h. *Picnic at Hanging Rock* (1975), the trip from the school to the rock. Screen stills.

Figure 7.7, a–b. *Picnic at Hanging Rock,* Miranda and Sara. Screen stills.

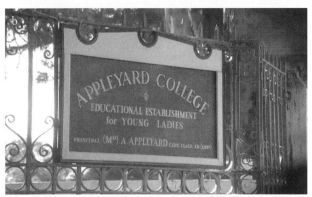

Figure 7.8, a–d. *Picnic at Hanging Rock,* the reversed establishing sequence embedded in the trip scene. Screen stills.

Table 7.1. *Picnic at Hanging Rock*, the trip from the school to Hanging Rock (events collated with the C Major Prelude in the underscore)

Part	1	2a	2b	3	4a	4b
Coupling/ doubling	E5 to —			— E4	D4	(D̶5̶)̶ C̶4̶/̶C̶5̶
Figures	nn; $\hat{3}$ — C	Am^6	— $\hat{7}$ — G C#$^{\circ 7}$	— $\hat{3}$ $\flat\hat{3}$ C	$\hat{2}$ G^7 C$^6_4$	
Image	Carriage arrives	Sara/Miranda	Miss McCraw speaks	Village: four girls at back	Girls remove gloves	Hanging Rock

Note: Dashes show the opening and closing of gestures. "nn" = neighbor note. Part 4b and its main melodic pitches are struck through here because the cue cuts off before we reach them.

Table 7.2. *Picnic at Hanging Rock,* the opening of the trip scene as an "inverted" establishing sequence (parts of the C Major Prelude noted against events as in the actual film)

Part	2b end	2b	2a end	2a	1 end	1 —
Image	Extreme long shot, landscape		Long shot, carriage leaves school grounds	CU sign	Group, carriage in background	Medium shot, Mrs. Appleyard

associated with the prelude's part boundaries that provide the linkage and help bring out the significance of specific shots. I have worked these out schematically in the following diagram, which should be read in conjunction with figure 7.6. Part 1 of the prelude is played out against the arrival of the carriage and horses (again, figure 7.6a). At the A minor[6] (m. 5), with its leap to A5—an expressive registral lift in this small context—a cutaway to the top of the school building shows one student, Sara (Margaret Nelson), who is being left behind (figure 7.6b). As an orphan possibly of mixed ethnic heritage and whose guardian is dilatory in financial support, she is the odd person out in the school, a status of which the principal, Mrs. Appleyard (Rachel Roberts), continuously reminds her. This image refers to a pair seen a minute or two earlier, shots that are rich in contrasts and contradictions (see figure 7.7a–b). The two girls, Sara and Miranda (Anne Lambert), are roommates and close friends. As they are also the first two persons we see at the beginning of the film, we expect them to have roles in the narrative that exceed those of most of the others. Miranda is shown here in medium close-up, Sara in extreme long shot. Miranda is in the open with others around her, whereas Sara appears alone, contained by the great bulk of the school building. What is not obvious is that the pair gives us a visual synopsis of the narrative trajectory for the two girls: by climbing Hanging Rock, Miranda literally disappears into an idealized (impossible) Aboriginal sexuality symbolized by Sara and the white sky behind her; Sara, on the other hand, cannot bear to leave the school after her guardian refuses to pay her tuition, and she commits suicide by leaping off the roof.

The carriage leaves the school grounds (figure 7.6c), and the prelude moves through parts 2a and 2b. At its stable (consonant) midpoint, the G major triad in m. 11, we see paired images reminding us of the school's (and its culture's) stable order: one of the teachers (figure 7.6d) and one of the younger students (figure 7.6e). Immediately afterward, at the $C\sharp^{o7}$ (m. 12), Miss McCraw, dressed conspicuously in drab black, undercuts the preceding by commenting sarcastically on one of Mrs. Appleyard's admonitions to the students before the trip began (figure 7.6f).

At the conclusion of part 2b, or the arrival on the tonic, we see the carriage from the back as young boys run after it down the village main street (figure 7.6g). Here again, cultural order is affirmed, and once again it is contradicted, but this time in a mild way that was already sanctioned by the principal: once they leave the town, the girls are allowed to remove their white gloves, which they begin doing on the V^7 arrival that starts part 4a. For most of them, this will be the extent of their rebellion on this day. As the treble line rises above the dominant pedal, the driver points out the rock, and in a reaction shot we see it (not the first time—it was the film's first image). The luminous and, in context, entirely consonant sounding tonic $^6_4$ chord sounds at that moment—but, unfortunately, it is only cut off prematurely; indeed, it had already started to fade out. Ending the cue here is appropriate, not just for the simple reason that by convention underscore cues most often fade out without decisive endings but more importantly here because, with the sight of the rock, the journey is over, and there is no longer a need for the machinery of carriage noise or arpeggio prelude. More prosaically, at this moment Miss McCraw begins a long exposition of the geological properties and history of Hanging Rock.

Hidden in the scene of a journey is its contradiction: the conventional pattern of an establishing sequence played out backward. An extreme long shot of the landscape (between school and village) (figure 7.8a) is "followed" by a more localized shot of the carriage and the school gate, along with an insert giving information about the school (figure 7.8b). Next in this reverse sequence we see a group of people (figure 7.8c), and finally we move in to a medium shot of one person, who then speaks (figure 7.8d).

Both linear and reversed time patterns are contained by a symmetrical formal frame: at either end, we see what I will call an inside/outside pairing tied to the opposition civilized/Aboriginal, but attention shifts literally from left to right. As the carriage leaves the school, its gate and manicured property at the left of the frame (recall figure 7.6c) are juxtaposed against open ground in dark tones and light tones, respectively. At the end of the sequence, a cut from the interior of the carriage to a view of the rock (figure 7.6h) replicates the dark/light pattern, but the monumentality of the school's gate (and by extension its buildings) is usurped by the rock in the near distance. The school is replaced by the rock, and what Bach and the carriage have done is get us from the one to the other.

In a small compass, this picnic trip realizes as a series of steps the characteristics of a Romantic conception of the pastoral as Robert Hatten (2004, 55–56) describes them. In the first of these steps, "an individual retreat[s] from a complex and less-euphoric reality." If most of the students are on a picnic, Miranda is on a journey, one that will shortly take her away from the school and the world as she has known it. The second step, "an attempt to regain lost simplicity, innocence, happiness, or the sublime—or to imagine a similarly euphoric present or future idealized state," is very nearly a summary of Miranda's apparent motivation for climbing the rock, which results in step 3, or "inhabiting an idealized space of reflection or serenity that emulates those envisioned qualities." Step 4 needs no explanation: "evoke[s] the monumentality of a landscape, with its poignant juxtapositions of geological time, historical time, and individual memory." The C Major Prelude, then, is the pastoral engine that enables the beginning of Miranda's journey.

The Abstract Étude and the Transcendent:
Thirty Two Short Films about Glenn Gould *(1993)*,
the Final Sequences

In François Girard's *Thirty Two Short Films about Glenn Gould,* a sympathetic yet by no means uncritical appreciation of the famous Canadian pianist, the two basic topical associations of étude and pastoral are combined and clearly audible in the music itself. Set loosely as a documentary biography, Girard's film also includes a simple framing device: the first and final sequences show an identical setting seen from opposing directions: a frozen, snow-covered lake. In the first, Gould (expertly portrayed by Colm Feore) walks at an excruciatingly slow pace toward the camera to a sound track with barely audible natural sounds (the whistling of a light wind).[8] Music begins extremely low at 0:17 and becomes gradually louder as he comes nearer (eventually it's recognizable as the theme of the Goldberg Variations). At the end we can hear his feet—music goes out at 2:18, but we hear a crunchy footfall after the music fades; the scene finishes at 2:24. In film no. 31 (the end credits are film no. 32), Gould/Feore slowly walks away from the camera into the distance to the accompaniment of the C Major Prelude and a voice-over narration. The latter is linked to—and explains—the immediately preceding sequence, which shows stock footage of a rocket launch seen close-up (in that case, to the accompaniment of one of the "small" preludes, BWV 926). Through the voice-over, we learn that Gould's recording of the C Major Prelude was included in the repository of data/messages sent with Voyager 1 and 2.[9]

The framing sequences are by no means the only design device in the film: patterns of recurring interview segments, recorded performances, and radio broadcasts by Gould; animation; and short narratives achieve both variety and a certain loose continuity. A narrative drive becomes more obvious in the latter half, where Gould is consistently shown as older (and aging), and the negative edge of his eccentricities is foregrounded. It is surely not coincidental that twentieth-century music appears in the sound track only at this point—among others, the music of Hindemith backs a narrated series of photos of the many prescription pills Gould took, and music by Schoenberg backs notations from Gould's diary on times to take the pills. All this reaches its low point when the pianist makes a phone call (phones and phone booths are recurring motifs) during which he recounts Schoenberg's morbid fascination with numerology, specifically a fear of years in which the digits in one's age add to 13 or are divisible by 13. Gould was forty-nine at the time, and he ends by saying, "Schoenberg's still talking to me." In the next segment, Gould's cousin Jessie Greig talks about the last week of his life. Then, "Leaving" gives a visual parallel to "49" as Gould's car draws up to a phone booth, and he asks the person he calls (perhaps Jessie) to listen to his recording of the sarabande from the French Suite in D Minor, which has just come on the radio. After a fade to black, the narrator announces Gould's death.

Thus, the final two segments are set off from the rest of the film as posthumous commentary. In this context, Gould's subdued performance of the C Major Pre-

Figure 7.9, a–b. *Thirty Two Short Films about Glenn Gould* (1993), early and late in the final film. Screen stills (widescreen images cropped).

lude and its relatively low level in the sound track are affectively appropriate, the simplicity of the work's texture and design bringing a sense of clarity or peace after the narrative push toward Gould's death—and easing the viewer/listener's path to finding the transcendental in Voyager's carrying Gould's music into "eternity." The music is no longer "inside" the notes, as it were, but outside, in this life after death that combines reproduced sound (a constant theme in Gould's life), fame, and the for-itself starkness of absolute music. Here it is texture and affect more than design devices in the notes (like lines, neighbor notes, and doubling) that are elements linking to these themes. For example, the voice-over narrator enters with the prominent A minor $^6_3$ chord in m. 5, separating the cleanly defined and stable opening phrase and the (contextually) dramatic moment that follows. Identification of the C Major Prelude and its recording, messages from Earth, and the Voyager launches all precede the completion of the first large I–V–I pattern, suggesting a division of the scene into two parts and a sense of resolution in the scene that correlates with the resolution of tension with the tonic arrival and the completion of the octave descent (part 2b, end). The second half murmurs along with Feore's increasing distance from the camera, but the final ascending arpeggiations have the unmistakable up-and-out effect of many conventional movie scores (although rendered far more subtly than usual because of the low volume). Here, the design of the sequence is matched to the recurrent, stable harmonic patterns and the motion through pitch register.[10]

What becomes thematic, then, is Gould's legacy. Properties of such a legacy—stability and transcendence—are registered in the music's harmonic progressions and its broad spatial motions, respectively: the narration is tied to the earthly—falling shape, intermediate tonal resolution ("intermediate" only in the sense that the uppermost voice reaches $\hat{3}$, not $\hat{1}$)—and the second half correlates with the "heavenly," as we hear Bach's broadly stretched out cadence with the (mostly) rising shapes above (when Colm Feore's body recedes in the distance, it literally moves higher in the frame; see figure 7.9). The distinctive combination of stability

Figure 7.10. Glenn Gould, recording of the C Major Prelude, articulation.

and transcendence is also registered in two other ways. First, the narrator ties the music track to space travel: the stability of earth's culture—in the messages—and the transcendence of Voyager's eventually passing out of the solar system into deep space. Second, the repetition of the framing scene itself lends shape to the film overall, imparting a sense of these thirty-two films as showing a coherent life, one that transcends any personal weaknesses to affect culture as a whole positively. The film's thesis is closely tied to this last: Gould is a genius whose cultural contributions give him a kind of eternal presence, and he (this posthumous self) thus achieves a salvation that he (as a living person) would certainly never have believed in, even as he struggled with the existential problem of a temptation to believe in the face of death. Here the C Major Prelude also achieves a level of modernist severity toward which one would expect Gould to turn at the last, rather than to the sentimentality implied in achieving a "legacy." The simplicity of the surface textures, however, is contravened by one final instance of Gould's eccentricity and thus his individuality. Though the articulation is essentially legato throughout, Gould applies varying degrees of staccato to the melody notes (E5 in bar 1, F5 in bar 2, etc.), thus effectively bringing out these pitches and entirely contradicting the usual temptation to apply a slight tenuto to them (see figure 7.10). The implication is that death and immortality are exemplified by this staccato as a letting go, rather than by a tenuto, which might imply a refusal to let go.[11] The complexity of Gould's life became apparent to us early on, in the "Lake Simcoe" segment about his childhood, where acoustic music (piano) and recorded music (radio) were juxtaposed. In the final sequence, that same juxtaposition is refined to represent the fundamental twentieth-century paradox that recorded sound (here, several layers thick) can be the medium of an individual's voice.

Here, finally, where we have reached what surely seems to be a space beyond the voice, the category of the voice and its priority remain nevertheless. This is hardly a surprising outcome, as music has been situated in Stilwell's "fantastical gap" in most of Girard's thirty-two films. If music's nondiegetic status is repeatedly compromised by alternating with or following directly from Gould's speech, as if the music were a continuation of—or substitute for—that speech, its diegetic status as performance is often compromised by the sense that it also represents point of view, perhaps in that Gould is hearing the music in his head, or perhaps in that we are hearing the music as an emblem of what he hears (a status high-lighted by opposing cases where Gould specifically draws attention to the music, as in the scene before his death mentioned earlier). In film no. 31, the sound of the nondiegetic narrator is layered above/onto Gould's personal musical voice (the C Major Prelude) and ironically is much closer to us, as if just offscreen. In the film, the greater irony is that the transcendental itself is also radically "offscreen," as allegorically represented by the Voyager 1 spacecraft, which is now beyond the solar system, in interstellar space (Jet Propulsion Laboratory 2013).[12]

The Erotic and the Transcendent

Étude/Athletics, Pastoral/Transcendence:
Je vous salue, Marie (Hail Mary; 1985), Basketball Scene

Though its method is strikingly different, Jean-Luc Godard's *Je vous salue, Marie*, a modernized, deliberately vulgarized biopic of the Annunciation, treats the C Major Prelude in a manner similar to that of *Picnic at Hanging Rock*: its kinetic qualities are contradicted by the utopian in a trope that maintains the force of its initial juxtaposition. In the two-minute scene to be discussed here, the prelude not only reaffirms music's potential to supplement or even take over acoustic nar-ration (as if that affirmation were needed for such a firmly entrenched conven-tion) but also actually competes with a voice-over, trying to draw the narrative back to the physical and away from the transcendent, as we shall see, but without success.

The film is presented not as one but as two. The first is *Le livre de Marie* and the second *Je vous salue, Marie*. *Le livre de Marie* tells young Marie's story, and its di-rectorial credits go to Godard's scriptwriter, Anne-Marie Miéville. *Je vous salue, Marie* is credited to Godard himself. Each film runs with its own set of opening and ending credits, and there is no overlap in the cast or in the music (Chopin and Mahler in *Le livre de Marie*, Bach and Dvořák in *Je vous salue, Marie*).

The music of Bach has a prominent place in the formal system of the latter, as it accompanies each significant dramatic stage: Marie's moment of existen-tial wonder during a basketball game (to be discussed below); the gynecological exam that confirms her pregnancy; the decisive confrontation with Joseph over their relationship; and a second basketball game, which she attends as a specta-tor but is forced to leave, since the Child is born shortly thereafter.[13] The only sig-nificant event where Bach's music is missing is the Annunciation itself, which fo-cuses on the rude and physically abrupt behavior of the angel Gabriel and his young companion more than on Marie herself. One might reasonably argue that Bach's music is thus reserved for Marie's personal experience of the transcen-dental mystery, not expanded to exemplify the transcendental itself. This is a cru-cial distinction that speaks directly to the general goals of Godard's highly dis-tinctive directorial style.

It is generally acknowledged that there is a close relationship between Go-dard's earlier film *Prénom Carmen* and *Je vous salue, Marie*. As Laura Mulvey states, "After *Passion* [1982], Godard made two films in succession that both deal directly with myths of feminine 'mystery' and the 'enigma' of the female body," but they seem to come at the issue from entirely different directions: "*Prénom Carmen* reworks, in its main narrative strand, Prosper Mérimée's 1845 story, whose heroine, due to the success of Bizet's 1875 opera, quickly became an icon of feminine seductiveness and infidelity, and of rampant, independent sexuality. The other, *Je vous salue, Marie,* daringly retells the myth of the Annunciation and the Virgin Birth and the story of Mary, the Christian culture's icon of feminine chastity, submission to the will of God, and spirituality. The two films polarize femininity into a binary opposition, the carnal and the spiritual." Mulvey does not leave it there, however, for "the simple fact of polarization always links, as well as opposes, and the attributes that separate Carmen and Marie, only superficially conceal the underlying 'fit' between them." The synthesis of terms in this binary pair is itself an expansion of the Janus-faced opposition of Carmen and Claire in *Prénom Carmen* to Carmen (in one film) and Marie (in the other). For Mulvey, this opposition is "a zero point for Godard," a foundational moment, where "the mystery of the feminine, profoundly destructive on one level, becomes a threshold to and signifier of other, more profound mysteries[—]a complex conflation between the enigmatic properties of femininity and the mystery of origins" (1992, 81).

Myriem Roussel, who played the principal supporting role in *Prénom Carmen* as a dreamy and somewhat hapless second violinist, is now the star, the Virgin herself. Godard's central conceit in both films is to take a historical narrative—the Mérimée/Bizet story in the one case, the biblical tale of the Annunciation in the other—and pull it rudely into the present. Carmen was a member of a gang of robbers, and Claire is a young woman still in high school who helps her father run a gas station and plays on the school's basketball team. Carmen's Joseph was a bank guard; the biblical Joseph drives a taxi. The author of the story *Prénom Carmen,* Claire, is a member of a professional string quartet; the author of *Je vous salue, Marie* is the preteen who is the protagonist of *Le livre de Marie.* Marie (Rebecca Hampton) is devastated both by her parents' divorce and by her inability to suppress her affection for each of them.

The essential bit of action in *Je vous salue, Marie,* as Roger Ebert (1986) succinctly describes it, is "an angel arrives by jet plane, is taken to the service station in Joseph's taxi and tells Mary that she will soon bear God's child." There is, however, a larger narrative context. The angel's companion—or accomplice (played by Manon Andersen)—remains unnamed but, not surprisingly, looks rather like the young Marie, who thus indirectly finds her way into the diegesis of the imagined story just as Claire did through the quartet's hotel performance in the finale of *Prénom Carmen.*[14] If, in that earlier film, the relationship of the film's "real-world" diegesis to the diegesis of the imagined story remains somewhat uncertain, in *Je vous salue, Marie* it is very clear. To a very considerable extent, *Je vous* makes sense because of *Le livre de Marie,* or, one might say, because of the formal frame established by the division into two films. The young Marie of *Le livre de Marie* is clearly traumatized at the outset as she reacts with loud denial to her mother's announcement that she wants a separation (and presumably divorce). In the film's final scene, after the divorce, Marie is left at the breakfast table in her mother's apartment (after her mother leaves with a man whose role is unspecified but not difficult to guess) and tries to bring order back into her world by imagining herself as the heroine of a story whose necessity she announces in her last line.

Le livre de Marie and *Je vous salue, Marie* abound in doublings, whether in the form of characters from the first film who find parallels in the second or in the form of opposed pairs within each film. I will mention only a few. The stark emotional opposition of the father and mother is obvious, but it translates into *Je vous salue, Marie* as the opposition of Marie and Joseph, whose relationship is always tense. The mother and Marie are obvious parallels, as the mother's first words are that she wants a separation; and early on (well before the Annunciation) Marie says that she intends to remain a virgin, to remain sexually separated from men (including Joseph). The pathological level of young Marie's unhappiness shows itself almost immediately in her reaction at the dinner table: rather than respond directly to her parents, she repeats a class lesson in a slightly too-loud formal voice, as if she were the teacher lecturing. In *Je vous salue, Marie*, Godard cuts between two quite different narratives (though they are apparently happening in the same general time frame). In one is the Annunciation and the events that follow from it—this is the "positive" story that young Marie imagines. In the other a schoolteacher leads a class talking about the origins of life. He later takes them on a field trip and has sex with one of the students, Eve (Anne Gauthier)—this narrative represents the pathological side of young Marie's reactions to her parents' divorce. Between the two narratives we might follow endless doublings of oppositions: miracle/science, Marie/Eve, virginity / sexual activity, to name but a few. For the present purpose, it is sufficient to point out that the oppositions and parallelisms extend to the music for the two films as well. In *Le livre de Marie*, a Chopin concerto represents music's place as entertainment and emotion in a "real world" (much of the scene depicting young Marie's weekend visit to her father's apartment is given over to their listening to a record), but Mahler is the deeper stratum of her relationship with her father (much more comfortable and affectionate than her relationship with her mother). As they are listening to Chopin, her father asks young Marie about a recording of Mahler that he cannot find. There is a cut to the mother's apartment and young Marie dancing with increasing energy and physically expressed anger to a Mahler excerpt from the "missing" record. Unexpectedly long, this scene shows us more clearly than anything else in *Le livre de Marie* her intense unhappiness over her parents' separation, and more than anything else it provides motivation for the equally intense reaction of her withdrawal into the imagined narrative of *Je vous salue, Marie*. Chopin morphs into the Dvořák Cello Concerto in the latter film—one concerto into another—and this new concerto also serves as typical dramatic underscore. More importantly for our purposes, of course, Bach replaces Mahler at the deeper stratum of young Marie's psychological struggle.

As David Sterritt puts it, "Godard's enthusiasm for fracturing words and images . . . disrupt[s] any intimidating or distracting powers they may appear to have, anchoring them in the here-and-now of real intellectual and emotional needs." In each of several films preceding *Je vous salue, Marie*, Godard "took art forms rooted in the physical world . . . and made them into a sort of aesthetic ballast, using their materiality to keep storytelling or psychology from whisking us into the Never-Never Land inhabited by most narrative films." It was music in *Prénom Carmen*, but in *Je vous salue, Marie* it is "historically freighted 'Catholic images and Protestant music,' as Godard describes them," that provide this same aesthetic ballast (Sterritt 1999, 169). In an interview, Godard discusses his choice further: "I knew that the only music that would work would be Bach. I tried to put in all sorts of Bach: violins, church music, piano, choral. The picture could be described also as a documentary on Bach's music." He then makes a direct connection between Bach and "Protestant music": "It couldn't have been Beethoven, or Mozart, because historically Bach was the music of Martin Luther. And as I was saying before, Martin Luther was attacking the Catholic church, specifically the way the Catholic church makes images" (Dieckman 1993, 121).

The first moment of contact between "Catholic images and Protestant music" comes in a high school basketball game, less than five minutes into the second film, but this moment has nothing of the starkness of the Bach overture that accompanies the gynecological exam confirming the Divine Mystery or the solo cello suite that accompanies Marie's realization that the Child is about to be born. Indeed, the anchoring described by Sterritt prevails, and the "freighted" meanings of image and music are almost entirely suppressed. Nevertheless, this is a crucial sequence in the film: "In the basketball scene, we discover Mary as the film's principal subject, and we see her begin to act, more strongly than anyone, as if she is the author of the film" (Warren 1993, 18).

As she sits on the team bench, Marie does not utter a prayer; instead, she expresses the existential kernel of all teenagers' thought: "I began to wonder if something would happen in my life" (shot 5 in the list below). Bach's C Major Prelude plays an important role: all but three bars (mm. 26b–29a) are heard, in correct sequence, but with several temporal gaps (see the aligned music and shot samples in figure 7.11). When the C Major Prelude enters (shot 3), it is trivialized as music for a fitness class warm-up (Charles Warren dubs it "God in the lightest of spirits" [1993, 18]): it does, however, refer back to *The Well-Tempered Clavier* as a common nineteenth-century source for exercise études. But we cannot miss the allusion to Charles Gounod's absent melody and its text, "Ave Maria" (Cavell 1993, xxiii), and, that being the case, it is crucially important that this is the first moment in the film when the camera focuses on Marie's body (as she jumps up from the bench). The music immediately becomes tied to her (athletic) physicality.

30:45   1. Basketball game, long shot in a line from the end of the team
        bench. Game sounds.
30:57   2. Recurring intertitle "en ce temps là."

31:03   3. Bench (as seen from on the court; fills the screen horizontally). Bach C Major Prelude (on piano) in at 31:08 as Marie loosens up to go into the game; music starts just after she gets up from the bench. The tempo is fast: quarter note = 104. We hear mm. 1–4, then the music is briefly out.

31:18   4. Game as seen from behind the bench. With the cut, m. 4b is repeated, and the music goes on. Room sounds briefly go out, and we hear only Bach with a basketball player's successful shot.

31:34   5. Medium close-up of Marie, side view. Inner speech at 32:05 (in m. 23): "I began to wonder if something would happen in my life"; 32:07, music out at m. 24.

32:07   6. Game as seen from a position near one end of the court. Music in with the cut: m. 25; out at 32:10, after m. 26a.

32:19   7. A player comes out; the two slap hands as Marie goes in to substitute (she goes offscreen to front left).

32:21   8. Moon in a dark, empty sky: no diegetic sound; music comes in at 32:23, in m. 29b.

32:28   9. Marie, in profile, prepares for a free throw. 32:29, inner speech begins again.

32:32   10. Cut back to the moon. Music out (the prelude ends, the final chord fades quickly) at 32:40. Brief game sounds.

32:53   Scene out (last phrase of the inner speech overlaps into the next scene).[15]

By shot 8, the game has receded abruptly (though we continue to hear some game sounds, and shot 9 shows Marie preparing for a free throw). As inner speech takes over, at 32:23 in shot 8, the music is bound to a cluster of figures: Marie's youthful vigor, her nascent sexuality, the potential for symbolic meanings (and transcendent events), and a narrative path. All this happens as the dramatic tonic $^6_4$ chord of m. 29 enters abruptly and the rest of the prelude plays out. Once it is done, Marie's inner speech continues, but it seems clear that she has already passed beyond the common question of a teenager to the realization that something will indeed happen in her life.

The prelude is pulled along Marie's own path from a simple, unexamined athleticism to a moment of epiphany,[16] a remarkable trajectory for a piece of music with such a radical lack of variety in its texture and figures. It does have a vocabulary of gestures, however, and Godard takes advantage of them to match image to music in surprising detail, an uncharacteristic strategy that may reflect his view of the importance of this scene. The closed neighbor-note figure of mm. 1–4 is set off from the following; its simple diatonic vigor fits Marie's warm-ups. The prelude's second gesture (part 2a, mm. 5–11) expands the idea of dissonance-settling-into-consonance and introduces chromaticism; with this expansion, the framing shifts outward to the action of the game. The third gesture (part 2b, mm. 12–19) is a variation of the second, starting high and chromatic and settling eventually to a cadence, the final five bars being identical to those in gesture

2 but transposed down from dominant to tonic level; throughout this, the game continues. With the darker chromaticism of gesture 4 (part 3, mm. 20–24), which leads to the dominant arrival, the image shifts abruptly to a close-up: it forces attention additionally by being both static and long. The chromaticism correlates closely to Marie's pensiveness.[17] Gesture 5 (part 4a, mm. 24–31) is the dominant prolongation that expands the neighbor-note figure of the opening to a rising-then-falling scale figure that goes through a perfect fourth and reaches the tonic $^6_4$ chord before relaxing to a dominant seventh chord in mm. 30–31. The return to a long shot of the court and action is abruptly undercut when the music goes out just as Marie finally enters the game, the signal for the transcendent, achieved, ironically, just when Marie by rights should be thinking about nothing else but the game. The final gesture is the tonic pedal of the last four bars, whose oddly tentative quality is exaggerated in the recording, a trait one can hear in Marie's voice as well. The music ends, but the inner monologue continues.

Whereas the young Marie's dance to Mahler places attention on the music (as a performance, it comes close to Gorbman's pure musical code), the basketball scene fractures the C Major Prelude to serve the narrative through recognizable cultural musical codes. First the prelude is tied through rhythm and tempo as dance-class music and then generalized from Marie warming up to the athletic activity of the game itself (in shot 3). When the prelude is abruptly cut off (in m. 24), it acts as a "reverse stinger" (or silence creating an unexpected, negative accent) for Marie's inner speech (shot 5). The prelude, nevertheless, contributes to formal unity by reappearing with the cut back to the game (shot 6), though Godard weakens this function when the music goes out again after only three seconds. Finally, the musical climax at m. 29 (shots 8–10) emphasizes the turn from the game to inner emotion.

It is crucial that the voice outlasts the music, no matter how well matched they are: it is the teenager's voice, Marie's voice, that abandons the physicality of the exercise. The voice-over is the device that achieves this, and it has consequences: Mary's voice "becomes very important . . . , almost making the action and images of the film seem generated by her intense concern about what is happening to her, her questionings about the relation of the spirit and the body" (Warren 1993, 18). I would therefore disagree with Ebert: if it is true that the Annunciation itself is the film's only strictly necessary action, the transcendent moment of revelation actually occurs here, in the inner monologue that distracts Marie from a basketball game.

It is a commonplace that Jean-Luc Godard highlights the constructedness of the sound track, forcing the audio-viewer's close attention by "fracturing words and images" (recall Sterritt) and thereby preventing the smooth alignment of image, sound, and narrative as presupposed by continuity editing and synchronization. At the same time, this highlighting demonstrates that the sound track—and not music, effects, or even speech itself—has ultimate priority: it is the sound track as a whole that is constructed, "designed," and that artifice is set before us—not hidden—throughout. The sound design, nevertheless, is clearly controlled by the voice: not only does Marie continue to speak after the music stops on its

(no music in the sound track) ━━━━━━━━━━━━━━━━━━━━━━━

10

(music continued) ━━

12   20

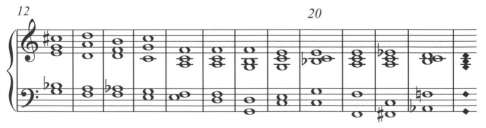

Above and facing. Figure 7.11. *Je vous salue, Marie* (1985), basketball game, music and images aligned. Smaller, diamond-shaped noteheads indicate a measure that either is cut off or enters midway through.

30

"like the reflection
of a water lily in a pond,"

(music continues)

Figure 7.13. *Lola*, carnival scene, Cécile's euphoria. Screen still.

ignominiously faded and shortened final chord, but the music is also mixed lower than the voice throughout (which is definitely not always true when Bach's music appears elsewhere in the film). The C Major Prelude begins as mimetic (warm-up music) but eventually becomes an aural analogue to Marie's inner monologue. It is also motivic (that is, Bach's music recurs) and perhaps thematic (if one accepts Godard's claim to have opposed Protestant music to Catholic images).

The Prelude in C Major and a Utopia of Erotic Innocence in Lola (1961)

As was the case with *Bagdad Café* in chapter 6, the final example in this chapter is also the most complex. The design is likewise in two parts and equally clear: whereas diegetic and nondiegetic status (and a change from interior to outdoors) separated the two parts in *Bagdad Café,* in *Lola* we hear all of one Bach prelude—the D Minor from *The Well-Tempered Clavier,* Book I—and then a slightly condensed version of the C Major Prelude.

The D Minor Prelude is a heavily registrated, full harpsichord performance (uncredited); the C Major Prelude is played on a piano. The D Minor Prelude is performed at a fast, even frenetic tempo in the manner of a virtuoso toccata; the C Major Prelude is played slowly (quarter note = 58), legato, and with pedal, and it plainly exemplifies the pastoral topic. The difficulty comes near the end of each of the preludes, where the affect seems to contradict the image. Cécile (Annie Dupéroux), a young teen, has become infatuated with an American sailor, Frankie (Alan Scott). He indulges her in a friendly way and agrees, on her suggestion, to go with her to a carnival for her birthday (1:03:36). The disparity between the two is obvious visually in their conversation (figure 7.12a) and in their first carnival ride (figure 7.12b), but equally obvious is her pleasure with his company during their second ride (figure 7.12c) and after he lifts her out (figure 7.12d). Only a few seconds later, however, he tells her good-bye—his ship is leaving port—and Cécile's mood promptly deflates (figure 7.12e).

Table 7.3. *Lola*, Cécile and Frankie at the carnival; he leaves (events collated with the C Major Prelude in the underscore)

Part	1	2a	2b		~~(3–4a)~~	4b		
Coupling/ doubling	E5 to —					— E4		~~(D5)-C4/C5~~
Figures	nn; $\hat{3}$ — C	Am⁶	— $\hat{7}$ — G	c♯°7	G⁷	— $\hat{3}$ C⁷		
Image	In slow motion; her hair floats	She looks at him; they run	They stop; he speaks, "Au revoir"	"Triste"	She says, "Good-bye, Frankie"	He walks away	She walks on the street	Opens door

Note: Dashes show the opening and closing of gestures. "nn" = neighbor note. Parts 3 and 4a are struck through because those measures were cut; what would have been the C major triad in m. 19 is instead the C7 chord that begins part 4b in m. 32.

Figure 7.14. Johann Sebastian Bach, *The Well-Tempered Clavier,* Book I, Prelude in D Minor, beginning.

The D Minor Prelude is the aural mimic of the carnival rides; the C Major Prelude begins immediately after (at 1:05:09), as Frankie lifts Cécile up and through the air, the contrast sharpened by slow motion and a moment of euphoria as her hair floats loose (figure 7.13). Once the two of them get into the bumper car and the D Minor Prelude begins, the remainder of the scene, including the beginning of the C Major Prelude, is silent except for the music: there are no effects, speech, or background sound until Frankie stops and suddenly tells Cécile "au revoir." His good-bye and her "good-bye, Frankie" (spoken in English) frame the C Major Prelude's part 2b (see table 7.3).

The difficulty in the two preludes—the complexity I alluded to earlier—comes with their respective endings, both of which seem to turn suddenly anempathetic, contradicting or ignoring the image. The D Minor Prelude is in two parts: its first page is continuous triplet figuration with a walking bass (see figure 7.14), and its second page is a prolonged tonic pedal point, over which the figuration continues and intensifies till it breaks into a short cadenza and a final cadence of four strongly punctuated chords. We hear the latter against Cécile's look of contentment and satisfaction (as in figure 7.12c). Here, the D Minor Prelude is an "overall mood" cue, where a general correlation with the experience of carnival rides is the point, not close synchronization. At the end, the machines have receded from view, but the mimicking prelude has not faded: it is the environment, the background we can barely see any longer. It is difficult for an audio-viewer to make the separation, because we are trained to assume that nondiegetic music, when paired with a close-up, as here, gives access to the character's psychology or emotions.

The abrupt ending of the carnival ride sequence in the four cadence chords has the effect of setting off by unusual contrast the remarkable moments that follow. As Mark Shivas, an early reviewer of *Lola,* describes it, "In a beautiful slow-motion sequence, Cécile and Frankie leap off the roundabout and through the crowds, as if in a dream. Her hair streams lazily on the air and her face shines with delight. The rhythm of the sequence lightly conveys the nostalgia that Cécile is already weaving into these moments, storing them for some future dream. They are at once the present and the future past" (1964, 50). What we see and hear is a tale of fantasized romance, of erotic innocence, all the more poignant because by this juncture we realize that young Cécile is reimagining what the film's principal protagonist experienced in real life: a romance years earlier with a man similar in looks to Frankie ended with his abandoning mother and child. As Shivas puts it, "Demy achieves not only a reflection of Lola's past infatuation, but also of the happy illusion she has treasured during the seven long years she has waited for [her lover's] return."

Raymond Monelle says, "The pastoral is about finding perfection in innocence, heaven in the uncorrupted, true morality in the irresponsible, the mystic vision of maturity in an allegory of youth and simplicity" (2006, 271). Here the C Major Prelude's figure of descent marks a descent from innocence and imagination to reality and time. If in *Je vous salue, Marie* the C Major Prelude went from the athletic to the transcendent, here it does nearly the reverse, going from the utopian to the mundane.

Conclusion

By the conventions that evolved out of its history, and by the preferences of its creators and their audiences, the sound cinema is centered on the images and actions of agents and by consequence is vococentric. If that status of the sound film was abundantly clear in the case of a classical film such as *Casablanca*, with the Bach preludes we might seem to have pushed the boundaries, perhaps even come to the cliff edge of the vococentric cinema. The impression, however, is a false one produced by part 3's concentrated dose of the analytical and interpretive act of close reading. It is important to recall that in every case, the scenes examined constitute a very small percentage of the runtime in feature films that range from 90 to more than 120 minutes in length. The sound film is still a medium rich in information, and the professional practices of filmmakers in the 1930s reflected the priority given to narrative clarity in the sound aesthetic they established. The vococentric cinema was the result.

As we have seen, however, none of this erases the significance of the creativity born out of the internal dialectic of the sound track, the play of voice, sound effects, and music. In the two chapters of part 3, we have encountered treatments of the C Major and G Major Preludes that run the gamut from complete diegetic performances, as in *The Silence before Bach* and *Bagdad Café* (though neither is wholly devoid of voice or effects); to scenes where the music, whether diegetic or nondiegetic, is dominated by voice-over narration, as in *Allegro, Following Sean, Thirty Two Short Films about Glenn Gould,* and *Je vous salue, Marie;* to fragments embedded in scenes otherwise without music, as in *Entrapment;* and to scenes where the music of Bach signifies as the presence of an absence—as missing sound—through the C Major Prelude in *My Favorite Season* and the C Minor Prelude in *Bagdad Café*. The variety of genres and narratives further suggests not only that a single musical cue may receive a multiplicity of specific treatments within the sound track but also, by a kind of reverse demonstration, that the music track has an omnivorous appetite—or, as I asserted in the third of the three principles in chapter 1, any music in film is by definition film music. Here, Bach is "any" music, and the C Major Prelude generates a broad range of topical statements and degrees of tropological effects. In *Picnic at Hanging Rock*, the C Major Prelude is the European conflation of high art and cultural status but also a vehicle of escape; in *Thirty Two Short Films about Glenn Gould*, it is the peculiar combination of transcendence and subjectivity in recorded sound; in *Je vous salue, Marie*, it morphs from arpeggio prelude into murmuring of consciousness in the inner monologue of Marie; and in *Lola*, it likewise morphs, but now out of a dream of love. What I would ask the reader to take away from these readings is the realization that the vococentric cinema, which historically was always rich with music, still is.

Notes

Preface

1. On the history of film theories in relation to sound and music, see Buhler (2013, 2014a, 2014b). Buhler isolates the distinction between realism (acoustic fidelity) and construction (sound montage or design) as central. Chion (2003, 237–46) calls these "real" and "rendered."

2. Some sources give 1942 as the release year for *Casablanca*. Because of the historical coincidence of the Allied capture of the Moroccan city, Warner Bros. rushed the premiere of the film: it was first shown in New York on 26 November 1942. The custom in the film literature, however, is to use the general release date for first-run theaters. That was 23 January 1943.

3. These unpublished papers were "The Unattainable Text?—on a Contemporary Film Music Studies," annual meeting of the American Musicological Society, Quebec, 3 November 2007; "Raymond Bellour and Film (Music) Studies: Music as the Unattainable Text," conference "Sound, Music and the Moving Image," University of London, 10 September 2007; "Musicology, Film Studies, Sound Studies," Congress of the International Musicological Society, Zurich, 11 July 2007; and "Music and Mediation with Images in Motion: Priorities and Method in the Study of Film Music," International Summer School for Semiotic and Structural Studies, Imatra, Finland, 12 June 2006.

1. Music in the Vococentric Cinema

1. The term "stand-alone sequel" used in this paragraph refers to a film that resembles a previously successful film in some obvious respects but is independent of it in story and characters. It is telling, of course, that this film's trailer announces Clifton Webb as "surpassing his triumph in *Laura*." The shot / reverse shot pair is one of the most common methods for conversation scenes: one person speaks while the other is either offscreen or seen over the shoulder. When the second person speaks, the image setup is flipped accordingly—and so on for as long as needed. Such scenes depend on an eyeline match: when we see one person, we presume he or she is looking directly at the other.

2. Not long after, a scene in a nightclub reproduces the design in surprising detail, including the pan across a roomful of dancers. This time the band leader, Eddie Heywood, is highlighted at the beginning, the pan is slower, and the couple the camera eventually settles on is a lower-class pair: a private detective and his secretary, who acts like a detective sidekick and also makes no secret of her intention to marry her boss. As a higher-budget film, *The Dark Corner* differs from the several *films noirs* Catherine

Haworth (2012) analyzes in detail for the ways music helps to forward—or limit—characterization. *The Dark Corner* also has relatively little music, and its treatment of gender relations is more complicated, due in large part to the acting credit hierarchy. Lucille Ball has top billing, but she plays the secretary of the private detective (Mark Stevens), who is fourth, behind William Bendix (who plays the heavy). Ball is active in the investigation from the beginning, and, if the result of the narrative fits the mold—as Haworth puts it, "the successful resolution of the female detective's 'case' . . . ensures that the leading man is exonerated, leading to a final shift into the role of love interest and its containment of investigative agency" (571)—that final containment may be said to be limited at best.

3. This general characterization of "voice" is sufficient for my purposes, but it should be noted that the term also includes other aspects to which Michel Chion draws attention and that we will discuss under Roland Barthes's term "grain" in chapter 3: "By what incomprehensible thoughtlessness can we . . . 'forget' the voice? Because we confuse it with speech. From the speech act we usually retain only the significations it bears, forgetting the medium of the voice itself" (Chion 1999, 1).

4. These three principles are also the foundation of our pedagogy in Buhler, Neumeyer, and Deemer (2010, esp. xxii–xxiii, 1–6, 7–10). I should add that all four of the principles (these three plus the "vococentric") assume not only the establishment of a classical model for the narrative feature film as it developed for the image track in the 1910s and 1920s and for the sound track in the 1930s but also the persistence of that model through later historical periods. On the early period, see Bordwell, Staiger, and Thompson (1985, 231–40; and on the persistence of the model, 367–77); see also Bordwell and Thompson (2011, 255); Lastra (2000, 10). On the ideological implications of stylistic plurality, especially for early twentieth-century musical modernism, see Neumeyer and Buhler (1994, 381–85); Smith (1998, 231–35); Franklin (2011, 138–67).

5. I prefer "music studies" as a general disciplinary label, analogous to "film studies" and "dance studies," fields in which I have also worked. I have not attempted to trace a history or establish priority for the term "music studies" and will only observe here that Anahid Kassabian (1997, 1) uses it in the same sense that I do, though with less optimism (9–10). The term seems to be better established in the United Kingdom, as see the title of Harper-Scott and Samson (2009): *An Introduction to Music Studies*.

6. The whole of Bordwell (1989) is devoted to filling out the argument presented in brief here. See also Ray (2001, 120–31) on the "norm of cinema" and academic writing on film; and Bordwell (2005, 32–42) on film style as central to creative strategies and to the audio-viewer's experience. Also see our brief summary and comment in Neumeyer and Buhler (1994, 367–68), where we refer to the literature of response and counterresponse provoked by the program of historical style studies promoted by Bordwell, Staiger, and Thompson (1985) and by the cognitivist theoretical model in Bordwell (1985). From that literature see particularly Robert Ray's "The Bordwell Regime and the Stakes of Knowledge" (originally published in 1988, reprinted in Ray 2001, 29–63) along with Dudley Andrews's response (1989). The exchanges as a whole are dated now in their ideological focus—and in any case were largely superseded by Bordwell (1989), which contains an extended analysis and critique of what the author calls "routine" interpretive practices in film studies. The opening essays in Bordwell and Carroll (1996) enlarge on this critique. I would also recommend Annette Davison's (2004, 12–23) succinct account of the dominant ideological mode of film criticism and Bordwell's challenge to it as well as comments in Price (2008, 38–40).

7. I give more extended versions of this account in Neumeyer (2009c, 2011). Berman (1988, 283–91) offers a particularly lucid summary of the shift from text to reader in the context of a critique of deconstruction, where the central argument is that deconstruction is an extension of the New Criticism rather than radically different, as it was usually portrayed by its advocates (even the clearest eyed among them; see Culler 1981, chap. 1; 1982, introduction and chap. 1).

8. Nattiez (1990, 116), on the other hand, criticizes Jakobson for favoring text-based analysis, represented by introversive in the introversive/extroversive pair. Nattiez argues that musicians also tend to favor introversive semiosis (118) but that the two types are in fact "inextricably mixed" and are to be distinguished only "for the sake of analytical clarity." His view does approach mine, however, in the assertion that "if there is an *essential being* of music defined from a semiological vantage point, I would locate that being in the *instability* of the two fundamental modes of musical referring" (118; emphasis in original).

9. Among the recent entries are Biancorosso (2009), Smith (2009), Winters (2010; 2012). In Neumeyer (1997, 46), I demoted the diegetic/nondiegetic to one of ten interacting pairs, the others being onscreen/offscreen; vocal/instrumental (performance forces); synchronized/not synchronized (rerecording); "realistic"/unrealistic (sound levels for diegetic music) and loud/soft (sound levels for nondiegetic music); musically continuous/discontinuous; musically closed/open; formal interaction of cutting and music, as yes/no; motivation, or narrative plausibility, as yes/no; "pure"/culturally or cinematically coded. I later decided that the new construct was too unwieldy to be useful for practical analysis, and, like Stilwell, I now argue in favor of maintaining diegetic/nondiegetic as a basic construct with the "fantastical gap" accounting for an ambiguous middleground (Neumeyer 2009a; see also chapter 2, below).

10. We discuss these three functions at length in Neumeyer and Buhler (2009). Here and elsewhere I use the term "motivic" rather than "leitmotivic" for two reasons: (1) to make it clear that I am making an analogy to the wide variety of literary uses of motifs; (2) to avoid entangling the discussion in the fraught question of the relationship between the Wagnerian leitmotif and classical-era film music practices. On this latter point, see Paulin (2000); Buhler (2010).

11. Peter Franklin (2011) takes the problem of historical narratives for music as a basic theme, in particular using the gendering of popular music as the key to a nuanced view of the variety of musics and their interrelations in the first half of the twentieth century.

12. On the complicated history of sound in the transition decade (1926–34), see Lastra (2000, esp. 154–215).

13. Cook (1998, 99) then proposes three fundamental types of intermedia relationships: a "consistent" relationship of *conformance,* a contradictory relationship of *contest,* and an intermediate relationship of *complementation.*

14. Granted, this is the default state of a commentative underscore in the narrative film. It does not rule out the possibility of an "operatic" mode wherein the underscore maintains its own continuity while still paired closely with the progress of the drama. Rare in Hollywood films of the 1930s but by no means unknown in European films of the time, this operatic mode appears in isolated if prominent instances in the 1940s (for example, in *Spellbound* [1945]), then somewhat more often after the 1950s.

15. For a careful exegesis of Barthes's argument in—and motivation for writing—*Camera Lucida,* see Allen (2003, 125–32).

16. The consequences of this opposition for film history are explored at length in Mulvey (2006), where the argument is developed out of the "direct contrast" between "the insubstantial and irretrievable passing of the celluloid film image" and "the photograph's stillness [that] allows time for the presence of time to emerge within the image" (66).

17. My distinction between static and moving in music bears some resemblance to Raymond Monelle's lyric time and progressive time, his terms for the familiar contrast between thematic and unstable or "developmental" passages in Classical period music (see Monelle 2010). I am grateful to James Buhler for making this connection.

18. This hardly resolves the mystery, but the mordent-*punctum* is found in the first edition (that is, the vocal setting) of Gounod's "Ave Maria," which appeared in 1863: see the figure below. It does not appear in the choral setting, the piano solo, or the violin and piano versions published between 1853 and 1858. The mordent was carried over into Georges Bizet's piano arrangement of the song (1867) and into subsequent nineteenth-century and early twentieth-century editions of the song itself.

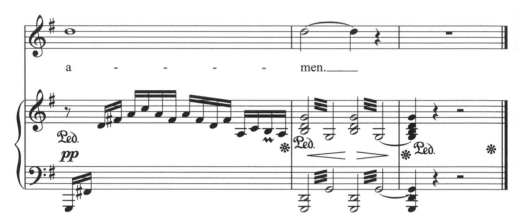

19. On the history of Newman's music for *Street Scene,* focusing on the *films noirs* reuses, see Malsky (2008).

20. The film has a checkered history in circulation—many corrupt versions were available until restorations were carried out in the late 1990s. Some of the earlier versions added the Grieg piece to main titles and end credits (these are mentioned in Kramer 2002, 180), but the cues were not in the original. The version I am using was released by Criterion in 2004. Goldmark, Kramer, and Leppert state that Grieg's tune is "the only music we hear in the whole film" (2007, 1). That is incorrect. In addition to the prominent hurdy-gurdy music, which is offered as diegetic performance, Inspector Lohmann whistles a tune during the police raid sequence.

21. In the Criterion restoration, Beckert never "covers his mouth in an attempt to stifle" the whistling (Goldmark, Kramer, and Leppert 2007, 1). And, in reference to "In the Hall of the Mountain King," the following claim is incorrect: "In narrative terms the Grieg tune is only a tic, the sign of Beckert's compulsion. . . . But any tune with a high degree of internal repetition could have served that purpose. The specific choice . . . transforms the genre of the film by associating it with narratives, and types of narrative, that are not represented in any other way. Without the music—and a bare scrap of music at that—*M* would be a different film" (6). Dozens of other grotesque *agitati* or *misteriosos*

would have worked just as well, and it is those—not some other narratives—that Lang knew his audience would associate with this tune.

22. Only one moment of whistling lies outside the film's first half. It occurs at 1:20:55 as a man whistles to signal to the members of the burglars collective that they should come out of the building in which Beckert has hidden.

23. Sirk did not include this departure resolution; it was added by the studio (Halliday 1997, 207).

24. "Sync point" is used here in relation to Chion's notion of "audiovisual phrasing," on which more in chapter 2. Chion defines sync point as "a salient moment of an audio-visual sequence during which a sound event and a visual event meet in synchrony. It is a point where the effect of synchresis is particularly prominent, rather like an accented chord in music" (1994, 58).

25. Ennio Morricone says very nearly the same thing, reflecting an approach that, in foregrounded underscore, often leads to anempathy or irony (Leinberger 2004, 18).

26. Gorbman asserts that "the story is more complex than [a continuity of conventions] would suggest" (1987, 42). Her argument, however, is based on the notion of a radical rejection of earlier practices during the first half-dozen years of the transition period (42–52). That story, too, has turned out to be much more complex. There is no question that David O. Selznick and others in the mid- to late 1930s, as they looked back specifically to the picture palace era for their model of the prestige film, included that era's high-quality music performance practices as part of their agenda.

27. I am grateful to James Buhler for this observation.

28. This is not to say that synchronization cannot be read in terms of containment, particularly containment of the female body and agency. See Stilwell (2002, 43); see also Lawrence (1991, 87–90, a section on music in an excellent, highly detailed analysis of a sequence from *Rain* [1932]).

29. The medieval "square of logical oppositions" was revived in the mid-twentieth century by the semiotician A. J. Greimas. An early paper that explains the construct with particular clarity is Greimas and Rastier (1968). Fredric Jameson made influential use of the square for literary analysis (see esp. 1981, 46–49, 82–83, 253–57, 275–77). See also Prince (1987, 85–86); Tarasti (1994); Simeon (1996); and the whimsical dialogue in Klein (2012). I have occasionally made use of the square myself (Neumeyer 1995, 1998, 2000b).

30. Here the large question of opera, filmed opera, and opera in film is relevant. I am not concerned with those repertoires and refer the reader to authors who have written extensively and authoritatively on them, particularly Citron (2000, 2010); Grover-Friedlander (2005, 2011); and contributors in Joe and Theresa (2002).

31. My interpretation of the square is rotational; that is, it contains oppositions on all four sides and therefore could be turned in order to make any one of the four terms into the initial one. According to Prince (1987, 85), Greimas understood the relations of the second and third terms and of the first and fourth terms to be complementary—alternatives rather than oppositions. Bal (2009, 211) uses "implication" rather than "complementarity." Tarasti (1994, 8, 19, 45, and passim) seems to downplay the oppositions graphically by removing the horizontal and vertical lines; he is in any case mainly concerned with either categories or instances represented by each of the four terms or with the narrative trajectories that can be traced across the terms.

32. Chion (1994, 95–98) sharply criticizes some French filmmakers' insistence on an aesthetic of direct sound recording, which he considers not only ineffective as a cinematic tool but also frequently not adhered to even by those who promote it.

33. For concise summaries of different approaches and attitudes, see Almén (2008, 11) and the review of that book by Arnold Whittall (2010). On the history of narrative theories of film in relation to the sound track and music, see Buhler (2014b). Among the most important of the recent narratological models for film are Chatman (1978, 1990); Bordwell (1985); Branigan (1984, 1992); Altman (2008); Verstraten (2009, based on Bal 2009).

34. At another level, Schoenberg does say of opera that "responsibility for the structural logic [may be put] upon the text and the drama," but he is uneasy about that: "It is difficult to believe that the sense of form, balance and logic of those masters who produced the great symphonies should have been renounced in controlling their dramatic structures" (1969, 191).

35. Among the most influential works are Genette (1980, 1982); Barthes (1968); Metz (1982, 1991); Bellour (2000); Chatman (1978, 1990); Gorbman (1987). For a history of film theory conceived in terms of "medium specificity" (distinguishing film from other media, positioning film as an art), see Price (2008). On different aspects of film as art, see Bordwell and Thompson (2011, 85–95).

36. As James Buhler notes, this is not to say that music is different from other representational registers of film as a means of filmic stylization. Music asserting its own properties should be understood as a figure of filmic excess, a principle of stylization that resists its subordination to the narrative system (private correspondence). On "excess," see Bordwell (1985, 53); Thompson (1991, 259–61).

37. David Bordwell (1985, 1–26) explicitly rejects Metz's semiotics-based enunciation theory, which is reflected in Scholes's model, but Bordwell nevertheless also places heavy emphasis on a viewer's active engagement with a film. Instead of assuming that the viewer works through a set of codes, constructing the story by a process of "decoding," Bordwell focuses on cognitive strategies that respond to genre and stylistic conventions (see also Bordwell 2005, 33–34). For attempts to combine a linguistics-based film semiotics and cognitive science, see Branigan (1992); Buckland (2000). Two more recent theoretical models of particular substance include one grounded in cognitive science and aesthetics (Plantinga 2009) and another based in cognitive and evolutionary psychology (Grodal 2009).

38. In this connection especially, see Gorbman (2011), a careful and perceptive discussion of "artless singing," a character's informal humming, whistling, or spontaneous singing that "lies somewhere between speech and music" (158).

39. Silverman (1988) and Lawrence (1991) are the classic psychoanalytically based feminist treatments (see also the comment in Buhler 2014a, 366–70). For semiotic models of the cinema voice, see Chion (1999) and the summary in Leeuwen (2009). On voice in a narratological model for film, see Verstraten (2009, 146–70).

40. To these, one might add *Confidential Agent* (1945), a less successful Bacall vehicle, and perhaps even Hitchcock's *Notorious* (1946), which brings back Ingrid Bergman as a woman trying to maneuver between two warring groups (in this case, spies), as represented by Cary Grant and Claude Rains. An actual sequel, continuing Rick's story but now in Algiers, was mooted in spring 1943 but never pursued seriously (Behlmer 1985, 219–20). For comments on these and other "clones," see Osborne (1997, 239–40). McCarthy (1997, 358–78) is a very accessible account of production for *To Have and Have Not*. Mast (1982, 245–69) contains a good descriptive analysis of the film as well but suffers from an auteurist viewpoint according to which Hawks could do no wrong. A succinct overview of early Hawks criticism is Poague (1982, 19–24).

41. For an extended description of music cue sheets, primarily in the studio era, see chapter 5 in Pool and Wright (2011).

42. Carolyn Abbate extends agency to music: "Music's *agency* upon bodies and objects ["music seeming to give impetus or animation to objects," Abbate states later in the same paragraph], is an under-appreciated and utilitarian technical reality in cinematic production from the silent era onwards" (2006, 607; emphasis in the original). She cites music played live during shooting and music prerecorded and shot to playback (routine for song performance and production numbers). I find this claim about music's agency dubious because it really refers to motion (rhythm and pacing), which is not a unique attribute of music. If anything, the rhythm and pacing of music implies and points to the movement of human agents.

43. For book-length treatments of this idea of the persistence of the classical model, see Thompson (1999); Bordwell (2006).

44. The influential structuralist narratologist Gérard Genette introduced a collection of specific terms relating to narrators and narrative levels, most of which end with "-diegetic." Despite the historical importance of his narrative theory to film studies, only a few of Genette's terms have been widely adopted. Gorbman offers his "metadiegetic" as "point of view," or sound heard "in a character's head," but she rarely uses the term after introducing it. I should also note here that "diegetic" as used generally in the film music literature is Genette's "intradiegetic" (1980, 228). His "extradiegetic" is the "nondiegetic." Intradiegetic and extradiegetic are used consistently in Verstraten (2009, see esp. 155 ff.).

45. For a summary of "native" music ideas in film and music studies, see Buhler (2014b, 208–13). In the main title cue of *To Have and Have Not,* the "native music" is uncharacteristic of Waxman and so poorly localized (given that the original site of Hemingway's story was Cuba, one might have expected Latin music) that I am led to wonder whether the composer was asked to write something that reminded the listener of the analogous "Africa" in the main title music for *Casablanca.*

46. For examples of these categories, see Rapée (1924, 1925).

47. On the usefulness—and limitations—of linear analysis and voice-leading reductions as applied to film music, see Neumeyer (1998).

48. On the flip side, the opening and ending of a film were frequently the last to be decided on, sometimes after previews, so that a composer would often end up writing several versions of the music. For one such case involving Waxman, see our study of *Rebecca:* small changes at the beginning that disrupted a harmonic progression and made an awkward gap in orchestration (Neumeyer and Platte 2012, 96–97), and for the film's finale—which David O. Selznick reworked and even refilmed—a request to write two versions of the music, from which one would be chosen (175).

49. Some of the text in this and the following paragraph is a revised version of a description in Buhler, Neumeyer, and Deemer (2010, 182).

50. One might go further to argue that the embodied singing voice is the best filmic instantiation of the voice in general. The singing voice is a voice where the audience is asked to attend to the spectacle of voice *qua* embodied voice, a voice that is not reducible to the meaning of the lyrics. I am grateful to James Buhler for this observation.

51. On the siren quality of a female lead singing, see Laing (2007, 101). On musical analysis of song numbers as a grounding for critique, see McDonnell (2014, 250–51), who cites Laing (2000, 10).

52. Andy Williams later claimed to have substituted for Lauren Bacall in both of her songs, but Howard Hawks denied this, saying that he dropped Williams after hearing Bacall sing during rehearsals (McBride 1982, 130). McCarthy corroborates this account,

saying that Williams's version was recorded and used for playback during filming, but, "as was customary, Bacall sang along while Carmichael tinkered along on the silent keyboard, and as she did, Hawks liked what he heard and told her to keep going" (1997, 377). Sudhalter (2002, 238) has the same account.

53. Cue 7b is credited in the cue sheet to William Lava, a second-tier arranger and composer at Warner Bros. who received a few assignments for feature films but mainly provided "additional composition" (usually one or two cues) to others. This *agitato* cue is generic enough that it might even have been stock or library music, although, if it was a reuse from an earlier film, the cue sheet, under normal circumstances, would have indicated the fact and named the source.

54. Fawell (1989) discusses the musicality of the script in *To Have and Have Not*. By "musicality" he means phrases and short sentences repeated in the manner of motifs. Helen Cox and I explore the music-like qualities of speech and effects more directly, with examples from Hitchcock (Cox and Neumeyer 1998).

55. On this history, see also Buhler and Neumeyer (2014). On acoustical fidelity versus narrative clarity, see chapter 2.

2. Tools for Analysis and Interpretation

1. On cognitive science and film music, see Cohen (2009, 2010, 2014; Tan 2013). See also Bordwell (2011, 96–102), a chapter meant as a brief introduction of film cognition using suspense as the example.

2. See his narrative of a class experiment with the opening of *La Dolce Vita* (1960) (Bordwell 2011, 192–98).

3. See also Chion (2009, 263–78, 469); Buhler, Neumeyer, and Deemer (2010, 137–40).

4. The obvious question is, Why would the normal pattern not be followed here? The answer requires context: the goal is to play up the contrast with William Bendix, on the other end of the line, using a hallway phone in a tenement house. This is the first direct connection between Bendix's character and Cathcart, and the contrast highlights a sleazy undercurrent in Cathcart's dealings.

5. One explanation might involve a certain doll-like stiffness in Mari's body, reflecting a common *noir* preoccupation with beautiful women and fashionable clothing styles, signifying "to-be-looked-at-ness" (Laura Mulvey quoted in Naremore 2008, 197). Naremore's is certainly the best historical-critical survey of *film noir* currently available.

6. Peter Larsen (2005, 110–22) discusses Bellour's analysis in detail, also noting that Bellour ignores the music and arguing that the scene is in fact thirteen shots: "The music continues after the final dissolve, thereby stating that the following image—where one sees the car come to a halt—is actually part of the same formal unit, that the segment, in other words, does not consist of twelve but of thirteen shots" (118).

7. It should be noted that speech (in its nonsemantic dimension) and effects can also be said to operate within these codes, but neither does so with anything like the frequency or the same level of influence on narrative as does music. The three codes are (1) pure codes (speech heard entirely as speech—not in relation to image; music heard as musical design and expression; sound effects heard purely as ambient sound—not in relation to image—as a kind of *musique concrète*); (2) cultural codes (conventional associations for speech, music, and effects); (3) cinematic codes (associations for speech, music, and effects as established within an individual film).

8. James Buhler notes (private correspondence) that there is no reaction shot of Marlowe in this sequence, a lack that points to a latent asymmetry contradicting the prevail-

ing symmetries. This asymmetry is systemic, rather than part of the asymmetries Bellour traces and uses to account for narrative propulsion. Following the dialogue, the "Love" theme seems to have a call-and-response quality, as I have noted in the main text, but the missing reaction shot means that the music seems to score Vivian more than the couple. This particular asymmetry is not at all surprising; it inscribes a basic gender imbalance where the scoring probes the woman's interiority at greater depth than the man's (see Laing 2007).

9. In the context of an extended analysis of the distinctive ways that plot manipulates story information in detective films, David Bordwell does observe that "Max Steiner's score for *The Big Sleep* signals whether Marlowe judges the scene to be menacing, comic, or romantic" (1985, 65). I first described the origins of Steiner's method of dialogue underscoring in Neumeyer (1995); I also discuss *The Big Sleep* in Neumeyer (2009b).

10. On the binary pair unmarked/marked and correlations of marked pairs, see Hatten (1994, 29–66; 2004, 11–16). Stilwell (2007) speaks to "multiple axes"—clearly meaning correlations—for diegetic/nondiegetic, empathy/anempathy, objectivity/subjectivity, and aural perspective, or there/here. The first two pairs are among the five binaries. Objectivity/subjectivity can be referred to the correlations of diegetic/nondiegetic and onscreen/offscreen as discussed here in a later section of chapter 2, aural perspective to the correlations of foreground/background and empathetic/anempathetic.

11. On clarity and fidelity, see also Chion (1994, 107 ff.). Gorbman's categories of silence are the following: diegetic musical silence (we expect music by convention, but there is none), nondiegetic silence (no sound at all), and structural silence (if music was present earlier in a parallel situation) (1987, 18–19). On silence in recent films, see Kulezic-Wilson (2009).

12. See Buhler (2014b, 193) for a summary and comment on Siegfried Kracauer's early disposition of synchronism/asynchronism and onscreen/offscreen. In this final sentence I use "easily" in the same sense as Bellour's "obvious": everything has been carefully arranged to meet the requirements of this conversation. One might not say the same a few seconds earlier, as an extra at the bar commits an egregious double error by looking toward the camera while standing in the background between the two principals.

13. The scene is DVD chapter 17 plus the beginning of 18 and runs from 46:22 to 52:12. Previn's "Muzak" begins immediately with the cut. Herrmann's "Love" theme enters at 49:55. The train whistle blows at 50:40, near the end of the silence (that is, period without speech) lasting from 50:21 to 50:45. For a synopsis of the film, evaluation, and annotated cue list, see Karlin (1994, 116–22).

14. Daubney (2000, 15–17) offers a selection of Steiner's comments, including the word "schmalzando" (16–17). Steiner uses several versions of the word, including the proper German word *schmalzig*, in marginal notes for his music to *Gone with the Wind*.

15. Marks reads this number as anempathetic: "The crowd sings 'we're unlucky'; and Sam tells them to 'knock on wood'; the jaunty music enables them to make light of their troubles, but the song's superstitious lyrics also anticipate impending turns of fortune's wheel: Ugarte's arrest, Ilsa's arrival" (2000, 173).

16. The music of Beethoven is a recurring figure in the films of Godard—Jürg Stenzl (2010, 107–60) devotes a chapter of his book on Godard to the filmmaker's use of Beethoven's music in seven films.

17. Annette Davison (2004, 78–79) gives a good summary of Musy's comments and places them in the context of Godard's anticonventional practices of the 1970s and 1980s. Marshall Leicester has written perceptively on filmed versions of Bizet's opera, as

well as its relation to Godard's film. He observes that "the exclusion of *Carmen*—of traditional opera . . . seems to produce an absence the characters themselves rush to fill." He then generalizes to the condition of opera in the contemporary world: "Godard's film, haunted as it is by the *Carmen* it alludes to yet withholds, turns out to be about the desire for *Carmen*, understood as the hunger for operatic directness and intensity embodied in characters who, in striving to compose the image-and-sound-track of their stories, also strive to find contemporary models for operatic lives" (1994, 253).

18. Sheer includes op. 132, first movement, in her table, but that is an error. For a listing of all the musical quotations, see Davison's (2004, 96–116) highly detailed timing table. The entrance times she gives are slightly different from mine at the point of the scene I will spot: the first entrance of op. 132, third movement, which I have marked as 30:07, is marked by Davison as 28:38.

19. Christopher Reynolds (2000, 160–61) comments on the role of op. 132, third movement, in *Prénom Carmen*. On the mingling of spiritual and carnal in music, see McClary (2000, 19–21).

20. For a different reading, one that finds a more empathetic treatment of the third movement in this sequence than I do, see Stenzl (2010, 146–48).

21. The opening of this section was developed from an unpublished draft text by James Buhler. The reading of *Rebecca* is based on Neumeyer and Platte (2012).

22. The final pair in figure 2.8, on the other hand, not only is relatively rare but also is not easily managed. The onscreen nondiegetic might be a cameo—usually head and shoulders in one corner of the screen—or a character's visualization of something in memory or imagination. The fact that both of these types occur most often in comedies suggests something of their awkwardness.

23. For readers who may be disturbed by the appearance here of a low-budget picture from one of the minor studios, I recommend Catherine Haworth's argument for her study of several 1940s B-films. Although she is speaking specifically of films with library scores (that is, compiled in part or whole from stock music), the general point holds: "The cheaper films and scores of B production units and minor studios are frequently less polished and subtle than their A picture counterparts, but this often means that they provide an even clearer indication of Hollywood's strategies and politics of representation" (2012, 572). This viewpoint is also entirely consistent with the project of Bordwell, Staiger, and Thompson (1985) and with similar arguments Bordwell has repeatedly made since, most consequentially in the first chapter of *Poetics of Cinema* (2008, 11–55).

24. Among familiar instances discussed by Chion are Dr. Mabuse, Claude Rains as the invisible man, and Norman Bates as his mother in *Psycho* (1994, 128–31; 1999, 15–29, 140–51).

25. On *Rebecca*, see Neumeyer and Platte (2012); on *Laura*, see Neumeyer (2014, 359–62).

26. See the list of changes from novel to film in Neumeyer and Platte (2012, 42–43).

27. For an account of Selznick's early career that contextualizes it in the Hollywood studio system, see Schatz (1988, 48–57, 69–81, 125–34, 176–98).

28. The story of *Rebecca*'s music is actually more complicated than described here. Selznick himself did major editing on the film and, following his habit with all his films, continued to make all manner of changes up to the last minute, but substantial final changes in the music could not be done by Waxman, who was already back at MGM working on other projects. Thus, the burden fell to Selznick's music producer, Lou Forbes. See the detailed account of this work in Neumeyer and Platte (2012, 47–80). On Waxman's work for *Young at Heart,* see Neumeyer and Platte (2012, 28–31).

29. Text in this and two subsequent paragraphs is a lightly edited version of text from Neumeyer and Platte (2012, 98, 100).

30. The cliff scene is not wholly without precedent in the novel. After Maxim and "I" have gotten to know one another and make a number of day trips in the areas around Monte Carlo, he suddenly decides one afternoon to drive up a narrow road to a summit, where he edges the car close enough to the cliff to frighten "I," who begins to wonder if he doesn't mean to drive off it. Later, after apologizing, he tells her that he and Rebecca had a particularly harsh confrontation at that place and that he had been tempted to kill her.

31. On Waxman's music notes, see Neumeyer and Platte (2012, 51–55; the transcription is on 149–54).

32. On the luncheon scene and its waltzes, see Neumeyer and Platte (2012, 57, 99–100). For a detailed discussion of the terrace scene, including a summary of the music, see Buhler, Neumeyer, and Deemer (2010, 218–21).

33. The reconstruction of figure 2.13 as figure 2.16 does lay bare the complexity—and therefore logical weaknesses—of this particular Greimassian square. Its four terms can generate sixteen possible combinations of onscreen/offscreen, diegetic/nondiegetic, bodied/bodiless, and voiced/mute. From these, I have chosen a subset as applicable to my analysis.

34. In the novel, Rebecca never loses her power because her husband did kill her, and that fact forced the permanent exile of Maxim and "I" from England.

3. Acoustic Stylization

1. The text in this paragraph is drawn from Buhler (2001, 51–56). The reader is also referred to the analysis of a scene from *Impromptu* (1990) that follows in Buhler's essay (56–58). Peter Wegele's *Max Steiner Composing, "Casablanca," and the Golden Age of Film Music* (Rowman & Littlefield, 2014) was published after production started on the present volume, and we were therefore unable to critique its narrative of the composer's place in film music history or its extended analysis of *Casablanca*.

2. See Nattiez (1990, 91–101) for a critique of Schaeffer's sound theory. Nattiez's primary objection is that "concentrated hearing" is in reality the mode of hearing unique to a composer and therefore lacks general applicability to music listening.

3. To clarify: dialogue is not "about" sense and meaning but about the means by which sense and meaning take form. One could argue that, technically, dialogue is a medium and words are the figures, but "dialogue" here serves as the collective figure of such figures.

4. For basic information on "As Time Goes By," Max Steiner, Dooley Wilson, and others associated with the music in *Casablanca*, see Harmetz (2002, 253–64); Miller (1992, 104–107, 137–38, 159–61).

5. Staiger (2008) notes the close relationship between *film noir* and melodrama, as does, from a different standpoint, Jancovich (2009). In its treatment of Rick, *Casablanca* resembles *film noir*, except that he is allowed to survive his fall into music.

6. For a recent critique along these lines, see Winters (2012, 45).

7. Anderson (2006, 511–13) argues convincingly that Sam's repeat performances of "As Time Goes By" put him in the position of functioning as a kind of "human jukebox" for Rick and Ilsa, provoking memory, desire, and regret in the way that hearing a recording of a favorite song might.

8. The scene certainly has the effect intended but would have been puzzling for a Nazi, as "Die Wacht am Rhein" was not accepted by them because of its associations with World War I. The problem for Warner Bros. was that the "Horst Wessel" *Lied,* the actual party anthem, was under copyright (see Harmetz 2002, 169; Miller 1992, 159). The best study of the political and war-historical contexts of the film is Raskin (1990). A good chronological summary of war actions during the period of the film's production and premiere is Anderson (2006, 488–95).

9. Studio records show that Frank Perkins, who was responsible for the band arrangements in the film, wrote the battle of the anthems as well—including the orchestral sweetening of "La Marseillaise" (Warner Bros. Collection, University of Southern California). Franklin's wish for significant expressive dissonance is fulfilled multiple times elsewhere in the film: see the discussion in chapters 4 and 5.

10. Experienced and astute a viewer as Steiner was, one cannot attribute all the effective spotting to him. According to Harmetz, Steiner "had written music for the first sequences in the gambling room. [Producer Hal] Wallis decided to have only the murmur of voices and the sound of the roulette wheel, with a little [diegetic] music seeping through from the main room every time the door was opened" (2002, 261). Wallis's judgment was certainly correct in this instance.

11. For a survey of classical theoretical models in film, including how they conceptualize sound and music, see Buhler (2014b).

12. See the discussion of *The Cabinet of Caligari* in Smith (2009, 4). We should note also that this stratification enables dramatic irony, as in a tropological narrative (see Almén and Hatten 2012, 71–72; and chapter 6).

13. Ben Winters has seemingly advanced a similar proposal in two recent articles (2010, 2012). We say "seemingly" because we are not quite certain what his final position is. On the one hand, he wants to offer an antirealist position similar to the one ascribed to him by Daniel Yacavone (2012, 22–24, 26). On the other hand, Winters seems reluctant to actually surrender the distinctions he labors so hard to undermine. (This is a particular problem in the 2010 article; see p. 243, where instead of dissolving the distinction between diegetic and nondiegetic or even really unsettling their boundary, he ends up simply offering a division of nondiegetic music. The "fallacy" of nondiegetic music apparently consists in an inadequate articulation!)

14. Marks interprets the first as a "pseudo-Arabian fragment," "a kind of Arabian source music, emanating from the city, even though no musicians are seen" (2000, 165–67, 171). The music in the Blue Parrot is simply listed as "source music" (see also Gorbman 1987, 83). The music heard in some of the intervening daytime scenes is a neutral "Arabic" ensemble for the Blue Parrot, music not only relatively quiet but also stylistically and motivically unconnected to anything else in the film—the recording was tracked in from Steiner's score for *The Garden of Allah* (1936).

15. Ben Winters's best examples in support of his antirealism all involve diegetic sound that is used in physically unrealistic ways, such as sound in space. Here, we have to believe either that the diegetic world differs from our own in substantive ways or that these sound effects, which really do seem to belong to the objects depicted, are in fact nondiegetic, that is, addressed to us as the audience rather than something perceived (or potentially perceived) by the characters. These impossible sounds are rather like certain impossible shots or impossible geometries that film occasionally indulges in.

16. For a summary of the musicological issues of Orientalism and postcolonial theory, see Head (2003) and a belated reply in Bellman (2011). For a discussion of topic theory and postcolonial theory, see Buhler (2014a).

17. On the structuring force of this oscillation between diegetic and nondiegetic music, see Neumeyer and Buhler (2001, 32–33).

18. See Howard Koch's account (1992, 11–20), which includes his assertion that only half the script was finished on the day production started and his claim that the director, Michael Curtiz, asked others in the studio for ad hoc assistance, dropped in changes without Koch's knowledge, and then told him not to worry about resulting inconsistencies because "I make it go so fast no one notices" (19). Curtiz's biographer confirms the latter but also downplays both script and production problems (Robertson 1993, 78–79). For more on the chronology of the scriptwriting, including interactions between Koch, the Epstein brothers (the initial writers), and the producer, Hal Wallis, see Harmetz (2002, 55–60). See also Lebo (1992, 97–103, 152–54); Miller (1992, 111–23, 138–50). Maltby (1996) thinks the stories of the script's chaotic state are overblown and have been repeated because it suits the film's mythology. He is particularly doubtful that there was ever any question about how the film was going to end.

19. Among the most egregious of the scheduling problems, Paul Henreid was not available to start work on *Casablanca* before 25 June, exactly a month after shooting began. Narrative accounts of the production may be found in Lebo (1992); Miller (1992); and Harmetz (2002). Miller (207–209) also provides a three-page timeline. As one detail worth noting here, Miller (123) states that production reports affirm that *Casablanca* was not shot in film order, as is frequently asserted in the literature. For example, on the first day of shooting, the scenes worked on were from the flashback (Harmetz 2002, 117; Miller 1992, 132). Harmetz (11) reproduces a camera report from the final day (3 August 1942), which shows that six of the ten scenes done during "clean-up" shooting were from the beginning of the film (the roundup of refugees by the police). Also see p. 234 for more on the last three weeks of shooting.

4. Music and Utopia

1. Harmetz (2002, 11), reproduces the camera report from the last day of shooting. On the New York premiere and the film's first run, see Harmetz (2002, 282–83); Osborne (1997, 216–22).

2. Wallis's memo as reproduced by Behlmer has "Lisa" rather than "Ilsa." Both were derived from "Lois," the name of the female lead in the original play. For a good synopsis of the play, along with commentary, see Miller (1992, 212–18). For the story synopsis by Stephen Karnot written up for the studio in early 1942, see Behlmer (1985, 194–95).

3. A detailed list of all the cues and songs in the film may be found in Marks (2000, 165–67).

4. On the solutions to the problem of Wilson's inability to play the piano, see Miller (1992, 137); Harmetz (2002, 128).

5. Marks (2000, 176) says that only the opening eight bars are used in the film, but that is clearly incorrect.

6. This list first appeared in Neumeyer and Buhler (2009, 51).

7. The timings are taken from Steiner's sketches (Max Steiner Collection, Brigham Young University) and studio piano/conductor scores.

8. The music production materials include copies of the published sheet music, which is in E♭, and dittos of a voice part in D♭ (Warner Bros. Collection, University of Southern California). Why the latter were created is a mystery. The most likely explanation, because there are multiple copies, is that they were simply prepared to be used if needed in the recording session.

9. For other analyses of the reunion scene, see Marks (2000, 174–76); Neumeyer and Buhler (2001, 21–22; 2009). See also Franklin (2011, 118–23); Buhler, Neumeyer, and Deemer (2010, 102–106).

10. This notion of chromatic deflation is hardly new. It is the expressive ground for the emergence of the Neapolitan sixth chord in seventeenth-century Roman opera, for example, and also for the borrowed chords (chords from the minor key imported into analogous positions in the major) so common in eighteenth- and nineteenth-century practice. David Lewin (2006, 193–200) discusses in detail a remarkable case in Wagner's *Parsifal* in the context of an account of enharmonicism as a hinge (or passage) between what he calls Stufen space (traditional functional harmony) and Riemann space (abstract third/fifth networks); see also Cohn (2012, 173–74).

11. I am grateful to Thomas Mathiesen for sharing this information. Kate Daubney (2000, 2) also quotes Steiner's own comments in his unpublished autobiography about the importance of improvisation in his early experience of music making.

12. In itself, this is hardly surprising. Steiner, according to his own account (Daubney 2000, 2), received a year's intensive training in the Vienna Conservatory (then called the Imperial Academy) in 1903–1904. Viennese fundamental bass theory was well established there through its originator, Simon Sechter, and followers, including most notably Anton Bruckner. In this harmonic theory, a diatonic basis is absolute, and chromatic chords are traced to alterations of diatonic chords; thus, it would have been natural (assuming he remembered specifics of his theory training, of course) for Steiner to treat A♭⁶ as a simple substitution for A minor⁶. Arnold Schoenberg (1969, 15–18, 35–43), whose tonal harmony model also lies in the Viennese fundamental bass tradition, offers succinct descriptions of such substitutions and "transformations," although he holds awkwardly to Sechter's notion of individual chromatic notes as originating in the church modes (see Bernstein 2002, 790–91). Schoenberg's (1978, 350–52) eminently practical explanation by means of a table of interval alterations, on the other hand, would certainly have appealed to Steiner.

13. The archetype of this cadence is the close of the first movement of Hindemith's Symphony "Mathis der Maler" (which is also the prelude of the eponymous opera): B♭ major–A minor–G major, all in root position with reinforcing fifths.

14. An oddity of the orchestral parts is that they reflect this pairing more directly. Most parts are written in notation for F major⁷–D♯ minor–C♯ major/minor. Only the harps, celeste, and piano are written as in the figure here. (Parts are in the Warner Bros. Collection, University of Southern California.)

15. On the casting of Dooley Wilson, see Lebo (1992, 86–88).

16. Music in fact is excluded from this portion of the scene in the French dubbed version (the audio track is included on the DVD released by Turner Entertainment in 1999). The earlier part of the scene includes new "mood" scoring (that is, nonsynchronized) based on "As Time Goes By." This version stops as Ilsa and Laszlo approach the table. The music picks up again as they leave, but Steiner's three-chord cadence suddenly emerges at the end.

17. Osborne has $2,500, but that was Robinson's weekly salary (already the highest among the studio's writers). According to a memo from Hal Wallis to the accounting department, Robinson was paid $3,000 for his time, over and above salary (Behlmer 1985, 213). See also Harmetz (2002, 172–73).

18. Excerpts from Robinson's memos are given in Behlmer (1985, 206–207). Given Robinson's essential role in improving the romance aspects of *Casablanca*, it is perhaps ironic that he was the principal writer for the "sequel" *Passage to Marseille*, in which the

couple-forming romance between Bogart's and Michelle Morgan's characters falls flat, in part because it was backgrounded.

19. A facsimile of the daily production report for 25 May 1942 is in Harmetz (2002, 116). Harmetz gives a detailed account of the first day's work (117–36). Unfortunately, the increased presence of the song didn't result in immediate gain. The song "stayed at No. 1 on the Hit Parade for four weeks in the spring of 1943," but Wilson could not make a commercial recording because of the ongoing musicians' strike. Instead, it was Rudy Vallee who benefited: his 1934 recording was recycled (260).

20. On Sam's need to "disappear from the world to Casablanca," see Anderson (2006, 485–86). Anderson also draws particular attention to "Sam's absence from the group performance of the 'Marseillaise.' . . . [That absence] casts an especially long shadow over the latter performance's confident expression of musical unisonance and international solidarity," which is limited to white Europeans. Sam becomes "the surrogate for other nonwhites in the world of Casablanca. [His] subsequent disappearance from the film signals the limit of the film's racial liberalism" (502).

21. Ray (1985, 88–112) provides an excellent overview of the contrast between Laszlo and Rick as archetypes of "official" hero and "outlaw" hero, respectively.

22. The "tinny piano in the parlor downstairs" and the quoted words are from Rick's speech to Ilsa during the first confrontation scene. "Brothel" comes from Eco's description of Rick's Café Américain and its habitués: "[Like] the Foreign Legion (each character has a different nationality and a different story to tell—as well as his own skeleton in the closet), Grand Hotel (people come and people go, and nothing ever happens), the Mississippi River Boat, the New Orleans Brothel (with the black piano player), the Inferno of Gambling in Macao or Singapore (with Chinese women), the Smugglers' Paradise, the Last Outpost on the Edge of the Desert. Rick's place is a magic circle where everything can happen" (1985, 8).

5. The Reunion Scene's Contexts

1. Marks (2000, 163) comments on this point and also describes the layout and notational style of Steiner's sketches. Another description of Steiner's scores and sketches may be found in Daubney (2000, 14–17).

2. These markings were for the convenience of both composer and orchestrator but were only useful in passages long enough that the relevant score material could be pulled out of the department library easily. Steiner did borrow some additional short passages from *Confession of a Nazi Spy* but wrote them out: four bars later in cue 5,3; five bars from two different places for cue 8,4; and five bars used in cue 9,3 and again in 11,1. One prominent reuse is not marked in the score, since it comes from a film Steiner had worked on for a different studio nearly ten years earlier: the theme labeled "Africa" in the main title comes from the main-title cue for *Lost Patrol* (1934), a film about a British patrol trapped by Arabian snipers (Marks 2000, 164).

3. Sometimes the piano/conductor score was dated. That information only tells us when the copyist did the work, but it is still a rough guide to composition order. In the case of *Casablanca,* neither the piano/conductor nor the orchestral score is dated.

4. The work here, and later in this chapter, touches *very* lightly on transformation theory (after David Lewin). For extended discussion of this theory (also called "neo-Riemannian theory") in connection with film music, see Lehman (2013a, 2013b); and Murphy (2014).

5. This page of the sketch is reproduced in Marks (2000, 170).

6. The chord also appears against the credit for the director, Michael Curtiz. Steiner is known to have engineered musical expressions of opinion into his main-title cues, and it is clear that he disliked Curtiz (who is given similar negative attention in the main-title cue for *Mildred Pierce*). Note the contrast with Steiner's credit and the producer, Hal Wallis's credit, both of which appear against triumphal notes of "La Marseillaise."

7. The only music heard in the intervening time is the backgrounded neutral music for the Blue Parrot café.

8. Reyland (2012, 64) says that Steiner's short score labels what we call the "Trouble" motive "doom." Steiner has no such label in his sketches, the word is not used in the studio cue sheet, nor does it appear on the first page of cue 5,4 in the piano/conductor score (one possible meaning of "short score"). A studio copyist would have prepared the piano/conductor score, although Steiner's sketches would have been the basis for it. Dittoes or lithograph copies of piano/conductor scores were used by multiple individuals involved in production and postproduction. Reyland appears to have taken the label from Marks (2000, 165–67), where the theme names are Marks's own.

9. This paragraph and figure 5.13 are taken from Neumeyer (2009b, 122, 124).

10. Given that cue 5,4 may have been among the first—or perhaps the first—written, the fact that "As Time Goes By" is initially quoted in E♭ major is very likely due to the fact that it is the key of the published sheet music. Several copies of that music remain among the music production documents.

11. Even if the director or producer had thought of it or desired it, however, retakes on this scale were not possible: the film was in fact closed out on 3 August 1942, two days late, in large part because Paramount wanted Bergman back immediately to begin production on *For Whom the Bell Tolls* (Sperber and Lax 1997, 206).

12. Steiner himself did not think of this as a solution, apparently. In a marginal note in the sketches, he refers crudely to a "sort of hysterical humping finish, hence the 'peculiar' last bar!" (Max Steiner Collection, Brigham Young University).

13. Reyland's analysis of the transformation of the style topic is excellent. However, the assertion that "Laszlo's theme underscores Rick and Louis' stroll from antiheroic ambivalence into glory" (2012, 66–67) is obviously incorrect. In the final segment, Laszlo's theme is heard in its string scoring under Rick telling Laszlo about Ilsa's visit and then in a brass chorale scoring when Renault accuses Rick of being a sentimentalist, distorted into an ominous minor when he tells Rick he will have to arrest him. That is its final appearance in the film.

14. Umberto Eco (1985, 7) appropriately dubs the plane a "magic horse" in his quick overview of the archetypal figures of the film.

Introduction to Part 3

1. On music in this historical moment, see Buhler (2010, 34–37). For period documents relating to this question, see Taylor, Katz, and Grajeda (2012, chapters in part 3); Wierzbicki, Platte, and Roust (2012, chapters in part 1); and Hubbert (2011, chapters in part 1). Hubbert's introduction (1–33) is an especially valuable survey and summary.

2. Long (2008, 51–53) makes two errors in connection with his reading of the Tchaikovsky theme in *The Jazz Singer*. First, he claims that "for audiences of the 1920s, [it] was not really representative of specifically highbrow symphonic musical style or culture, of 'art music'" (51), but instead was understood in terms of a cultural musical code as music for heightened emotion. The latter point might well be true, but the former is contradicted by the picture-palace environment and prestige-show ambitions that Warner

Bros. had for this film and for its predecessor, *Don Juan* (1926). Second, Long fails to take into account differences between European and American practices and so conflates the catalog placements of Becce and Erdmann with the choices made by Louis Silvers, *The Jazz Singer*'s music director. If Long's characterization of "the love theme [as gaining] its climax not in a moment of passionate excitement in the romantic sense but in the heated argument between Jack and the cantor" (52) is obvious enough, the path that required a deeroticizing of the theme was unnecessarily convoluted.

   3. "Drohende Gefahr," "Angst," "Katastrophe," respectively. On Schoenberg's op. 34, see Feisst (1999) and score and commentary in Schoenberg (1988).

   4. Still larger categories are "expressive genre" (Hatten 1994, 290), which refers to categories of expressive development across entire compositions, and the closely related "mode" (Hatten 2004, 53), which transforms a topic or a trope into an overarching thematic principle for a composition or group of compositions. Although the pastoral is important to both of these in Hatten's accounts (see 1994, 67–111; 2004, 53–67), neither "expressive genre" nor "mode" is directly relevant to the dimensions of single film scenes and individual music cues that I discuss in chapters 6 and 7. On topics and intertextuality, see Klein (2005, 62–76).

   5. The understanding of topic as stable, if historically contingent, has its source in the foundational work on the subject by Leonard Ratner (1980, 1992) and can still be plainly seen in, among others, Agawu (2009, esp. 41–50). For an excellent historical overview and critique of topic theory as applied to music by Ratner, Agawu, and Hatten, see McKay (2007).

   6. This latter usage is near to that of Lawrence Kramer's term "structural tropes" (1990, 10–12) and is at the core of the more general "expressive tropes" (1995, 33, 35). Eero Tarasti's (1994, 6–10) even more general term "isotopy," on the other hand, refers not to figures at all but to categories of structural articulations found in first listenings to a piece of music. Byron Almén (2008, 139–61) uses the isotopy as a segmentation criterion for an analysis of a Schubert sonata movement.

   7. This continuum construct is useful here because of the need for comparative evaluations ("Bach in film *x* is more firmly in the pastoral mode than it is in film *y*," etc.); see Hatten (2014) for a model based on relative ease or difficulty of interpretation. In chapter 1, on the other hand, I deliberately avoided a continuum in connection with the "fantastical gap," where a field construct was more useful: there it was a matter of being in the "gap" or not, clear or ambiguous with respect to diegetic/nondiegetic status, not a question of gradations.

   8. I am grateful to Alex Newton for the information about *Dr. Jekyll and Mr. Hyde*.

   9. Buhler, however, continues with "but at the cost of resorting to and reifying pernicious stereotypes." See his 2014b, 208–11, for more on this.

   10. Jeremy Barham has recently published a study (2011) of the cinematic appropriation of Schumann's "Träumerei" that is very similar in its basic design to part 3 here. Barham's goals, however, are different, as he is concerned with positioning the Schumann character piece in stylistic and reception history, whereas I am looking at varieties of music and image interaction and their effects on these two Bach preludes.

   11. Historical European music in the repertoire of the cinema occupies a small but by no means insignificant place in the critical writings of Lawrence Kramer, who uses his readings to argue that music is the equal of the image in film experience and that classical music is uniquely important in establishing and realizing character subjectivity (see, among others, Kramer 2002, 2007, 2014; Goldmark, Kramer, and Leppert 2007; the best critique of Kramer's hermeneutical method in general is Clarke 2011). The chapters

of part 3 here may be regarded as complementary to that work in the strict sense that I argue the opposite. Music is only rarely the equal of the image in a film's narrative or stylistic systems; and historical music, though it is what I focus on here, is not privileged among the possible musics of the sound track—that is to say, the wide variety of uses to which the two Bach preludes are put is evidence of their *typicality* as film music cues, not their uniqueness. In general, I think the richest rewards in the near future will come not from hermeneutics but from music-filmological style studies, the historical study of music and sound practices, patterns, and creativity in films, for which there can be no better foundation than Bordwell (1997, 2005, 2008), a trio of closely related volumes that lay out a system for the study of film style: as history (1997), as a case study of cinematic staging and style (2005), and in terms of theory and methodology (2008).

6. Performers Onscreen

1. David Schulenberg (1995) addresses these issues in much greater detail. Niedt is discussed along with Reincken (of whom more below) (7–9). The C Major Prelude is mentioned in connection with formulaic opening harmonic gestures (20–22). For a valuable discussion of Bach and his music as presented by eighteenth-century theorists (mainly his students), see Christensen (1998). And, of course, the tight connection between improvisation, composition, and figured bass links Bach closely to the Italian *partimento* tradition (see Gjerdingen 2007; Sanguinetti 2012).

2. It is instructive that one of the early connoisseurs of Bach's music should get this backward: in his biography, Johann Nikolaus Forkel ([1802] 1974, 144) reverses the chronology to claim that Bach's unerring musical sense obliged him to cut out "redundant" passages and reduce the length of the prelude "by one-half."

3. Bach maintains the five-part texture throughout the arpeggio opening section of the C♯ Major Prelude in Book II. This prelude, coincidentally, was originally in C Major and, according to Schulenberg (1992, 205), may originally have been intended to open the second volume of *The Well-Tempered Clavier*.

4. Robert Snarrenberg (1997, 40) provides an especially clear presentation of these suspension figures, with a graphic.

5. Audiences might even have heard the two pieces in the same program. As Janet Ritterman explains, the études "became the first pieces by Chopin to appear in many pianists' concert programs" in the later 1830s and 1840s (1992, 30), the period in which preludes and fugues from *The Well-Tempered Clavier* also came into the recital repertoire. Clara Schumann was among the prominent pianists who played both Chopin études and Bach by 1850 (31).

6. Ritterman (1992) explores the relationship of repertoire choices to changes in public concert life in the early nineteenth century. Bodo Bischoff (1997) discusses the contexts of Schumann's view of *The Well-Tempered Clavier* as a pedagogical document. A highly accessible, concise summary of Bach reception may be found in Finscher (1998). Kinderman (1998) is an equally approachable essay about Bach's influence. Simon Finlow (1992, 52–53) gives a list of the more important pedagogical collections. Claudia MacDonald (2002) gives a detailed account of Schumann's sometimes excruciating immersion in the pedagogical and étude repertoire in the early 1830s.

7. Some of Chopin's students, on the other hand, particularly recall the fugues: "He then prescribed . . . J. S. Bach's Suites and individual fugues from *The Well-Tempered Clavier*"; "Chopin held that Clementi's *Gradus ad Parnassum*, Bach's pianoforte Fugues,

and Hummel's compositions were the key to pianoforte-playing" (quoted in Eigeldinger 1986, 60–61).

8. On the practice of preludizing in the early nineteenth century, see also Temperley (2009). Multiple publications give examples of such improvised preludes. Some of the most extensive and instructive may be found in Czerny ([1829] 1983, [1833] n.d. [before 1840]), Knecht (1791–95), and Schumann (2001).

9. Bischoff gives many more details about Schumann's activities during these months (1997, 427–38, 442–43). Jensen (2001, 143–46) discusses Schumann's study of Bach during the early 1830s. Jensen (13) notes that Bach's name appears in Schumann's diaries as early as 1827. According to Bischoff (1997, 440), Robert and Clara played duets for house guests, on which occasion(s) Clara also gave solo performances of several of Bach's fugues.

10. According to Hans Joachim Köhler (1981, [27]), Schumann actually composed the beginning of the melody (it is found in a sketchbook, written down after Schumann heard Paganini play a concert in 1830). If that is true, he either contrived to let Clara think that it was hers or at least allowed her to finish the tune over his bass and then claim it as her own. On the significance of the notational symmetry, Köhler (1981, 28) speculates that, since Schumann is known to have associated "C" with Clara, "F" and "G" might well refer to "Florestan" and "Gustav," two Jean-Paul characters Schumann is also known to have associated with himself.

11. Kallberg (1992, 116–26) explores more serious implications of quotations during the period of Robert and Clara's clandestine engagement later in the decade. Finscher points to 1838 as a crucial intermediate point, the "beginning of a new stage of Bach reception in composition": "In March 1838 [Schumann] wrote to Clara that Bach was 'his daily bread,' and in the same year he prepared a copy of the *Art of Fugue*. In 1838 he also composed *Kinderszenen, Kreisleriana* (reflecting E. T. A. Hoffmann's Kapellmeister Kreisler, the Bach addict), and *Novelletten*." In Schumann's compositions after this point, "the whole style of writing is saturated with a Bach experience where the real music has been transformed into a poetic image even before the process of composing has begun" (1998, 17). Bischoff (1997, 446–51) gives further details about this period—especially appealing is the account of Robert and Clara's thorough study of *The Well-Tempered Clavier* shortly after their wedding (450).

12. Schulenberg (1992, 409n22) reminds us that there is no reason to assume Schwenke originated the measure that now carries his name. Müllemann (2012) is a particularly lucid and accessible account; see also Tomita (2008). Finally, I should note that, rather like the C Major Prelude score in his version, the spelling "Schwenke," although common in the literature, is not the preferred historical spelling of the family name, which is "Schwencke."

13. On the other hand, Schenker seems to have been concerned about the fact that the Schwenke measure turns thirty-five measures into thirty-six, or a series of nine four-measure "phrases," a regularity that might have been considered praiseworthy in the later eighteenth century. Schenker reads the source of the C Major Prelude's design in eight four-measure groups, or a total of thirty-two, but with the "proper" first bar expanded by the neighbor-note figure. On August Halm's critique of the Schwenke measure (he sees it as disrupting a dramatic progress toward the V), see Rothfarb (1996, 70–74).

14. No comprehensive catalog of music cues for the sound cinema exists. McCarty (1998), by far the most carefully documented work available, covers only the classical sound era, nondiegetic music, and composers working in the studio environment. Thus,

it could offer nothing in locating uses of the two preludes or Bach's music in general. Although based on internet sources, in particular IMDb (Internet Movie Database), the generalizations made here, I think, will stand. In any case, I am comfortable that the census of films relying mainly on IMDb produced a robust and varied list of titles adequate to the goals of the study in part 3.

15. The C Major Prelude is clearly treated as both pastoral and kinetic through an association with rippling water in *Dynamiter* (2011). With sharply increased volume, the G Major Prelude acquires an unexpectedly monumental character—though still associated with the exotic—as a British ship wandering the Pacific during the Napoleonic Wars approaches the Galápagos Islands in *Master and Commander: The Far Side of the World* (2003). Two recent films that either bury the preludes in the mix or even cut the cues out without changing the credits are *Tyler Perry's Good Deeds* (2012) and *Elysium* (2013). The finale of *The American* (2010), similarly, renders nearly inaudible a boys' choir's rendition of Gounod's "Ave Maria" through fragmented quotation and low volume.

16. An effect at the opposite extreme of the continuum—the C Major Prelude as trance—is achieved in *The Letter* (2010), a dismal psychological drama about a playwright who suffers what appears to be a nervous breakdown, the gradual onslaught of which she uses the film to describe. At the last moment, we find that her boyfriend, one of the secondary characters, has been drugging her, and he is about to start in on one of the female actors. He is psychotic, to be sure, but also unmemorable. The C Major Prelude enters early (1:53) as Martine (Wynona Rider) recounts a dream; the music is played so slowly that we only make it to m. 8 in a minute and forty seconds. The tempo is less than sixteenth note = 40, and the repetitions in the second half of each bar were cut. Unlike the film's villain, this treatment of the prelude *is* memorable, the more so when we hear a simplified triple-meter version of it, with deep bass pedal notes, a few minutes later. This music deserves to be in a better film.

17. The synchronization, nevertheless, does generate some level of attention to the music. Unsynchronized cues, sometimes referred to as "overall mood," are more likely to be neutral or unnoticed. Good examples may be found in the end credits of more recent films. One among these is the end-credits sequence for *In the Loop* (2009). It is in two parts, the first (at about 1:40:00) has the entire C Major Prelude (piano) along with postdenouement action in a montage design along with some fairly subdued speech and of course credits for the film's principals, the second a conventional end-credits sequence with music by the film's underscore composer, Adem Ilhan, and showing lists of production staff.

18. Unlike these moments in *The Pianist,* most diegetic performance sequences in films involving musicians are relatively simple—they signify performance and draw attention to agents and their motivations. Among films with the C Major Prelude, the G Major Prelude, or Gounod's "Ave Maria" are *Intouchables* (2011), *The Soloist* (2009), *The Secret Life of Bees* (2008), *Music of the Heart* (1999), and *Diva* (1981).

19. The G Major Prelude is also quoted in *Hilary and Jackie* (1998), but it effectively disappears among all the other quotes from the cello suites in this controversial biopic of Jacqueline du Pré. As with *Allegro* and *Picnic at Hanging Rock* (discussed in chapter 7), the sound track of *Hilary and Jackie* is dominated by other music, in particular du Pré's definitive, trademark performance of the Elgar Cello Concerto.

20. A humorous twist on the rural pastoral may be found in *Antonia's Line* (1995). The G Major Prelude appears unexpectedly—there is no other historical music—as we see a young girl on a swing that is tied to a tall tree. The angle is such that we see only the back half of the arc; a barn blocks the forward half. A sudden cry offscreen alerts us to the fact

she has fallen. Music continues through a brief "nursing" scene with adults and into another scene where we see the girl sitting on straw bales at a hayloft door and writing. Other than a kinetic imitation of the swing, the role of the G Major Prelude is unclear; we can take it for little more than an odd moment of the rural pastoral.

21. Herbert Stothart was the musical director and therefore acted as administrative manager and conductor of the orchestra. Despite the number of veteran staff arrangers and orchestrators who worked on the project, including Leo Arnaud, Murray Cutter, Paul Marquardt, and Leonid Raab, Stothart apparently did the arrangements and underscoring cues himself, as he is credited with them in studio business records (MGM Collection, University of Southern California). I might add that the sets are surprisingly claustrophobic (even if the film is viewed properly in theatrical format)—a low-budget look that is uncharacteristic for MGM, even in its actual "B" productions, which *Girl of the Golden West,* at a budget of $1,680,000, decidedly was not. For comparison, the prestige films *Captains Courageous* (1938) and *Wizard of Oz* (1939) cost $1,500,000 and $2,777,000, respectively, while the Mickey Rooney and Judy Garland musical *Babes in Arms* (1939), a midlevel programmer, cost $750,000 (Schatz 1988, 262, 267). Low-budget films typically had budgets of $500,000 or less (often much less).

22. "Mary Robbins" was invented for this movie. Belasco's heroine is usually referred to as "the Girl," though her name is given as "Minnie"—she is unsure of her last name. Sheriff Rance, Ramerez, and Richard Johnson (as Dick Johnson) do come from the play. Neither the priest nor the trip to Monterey appears in the original (stage) version of *The Girl of the Golden West* (premiered in 1905), nor in Puccini's opera (*La fanciulla del West,* 1910). The priest is also missing from the novelized version that appeared in 1911, but in chapter 1 "the Girl" is returning from Monterey—the only details we learn about her stay is that she saw a bullfight and noticed a handsome, mysterious man (Ramerez), who stops her on her way home to give her flowers, then rides off. The screenwriters stay true to the novel in the minimal sense that Monterey is the locale in which the lovers are first attracted to one another. Katharine D. Newman discusses other differences between the versions, including the several filmed versions, in her introduction to the reprint of the novel (1978, x–xiii). On Puccini's opera, see Leppert (2002, 2009).

23. McDonald actually sings in G major, the key of the original vocal edition, but I have referred to the positions in terms of those in the C Major Prelude in order to make comparison easier.

24. It is worth noting that, despite the skillful direction and editing of this scene, the film's director, Robert Z. Leonard, was initially not pleased to include the "Ave Maria." In an extended memo outlining suggested changes in the script, Leonard objects, quite reasonably, that it is implausible for an apparently uncouth character such as the one played by MacDonald to suddenly be featured as soloist in a church service, and, in any case, that the "Ave Maria" seems out of place. His preference is to forgo the service and use MacDonald's voice for descant roles during a Mexican folk celebration (interoffice memo, MGM, 25 August 1937). When or why Leonard changed his mind is unknown.

25. See Monelle (2006, 185–250) for an extended history of the pastoral topic. On the religious pastoral specifically, see 198–200.

26. Because the song and dance is so clearly "over the top," this conclusion about the film as fantasy is by no means undermined by the film's final moments, in which Jasmin's enigmatic response to a marriage proposal from Rudi is "I'll have to ask Miss Brenda." In this connection, it is telling that the three actual or potential heterosexual mates for the women at the café are literally at a distance for most of the film: Rudi in his

trailer, Eric in his tent, and Sal—Brenda's husband—in a truck somewhere off-property but close enough to spy on her with binoculars.

27. On compilation scores after the mid-1960s and their relation to readily available stereo recordings of concert music, see Hubbert (2014, 300–302).

28. This Bach portrait also appears in a scene from the teenage horror flick *Mortal Instruments: City of Bones* (2013). Here the pianist is an unstable mad scientist type who breaks up his performance with furious banging on the piano, then resumes playing with an emotionless precision.

29. The absurdity of the finale keeps us from taking all this too seriously, but even there one finds a complementary moment: Sal Jr. takes a solo in which he mingles "honky-tonk" and evocations of Baroque figures—and finally he gets to play fast.

30. I have reversed the usual ordering of levels of narration here (where primary would be the narrator, secondary the diegetic world) in order to put the emphasis on film viewing.

7. Underscore

1. Lester (1998) shows very similar methods at work in all four of the preludes from the *Clavier-Büchlein* that were elaborated and expanded for inclusion in *The Well-Tempered Clavier*, Book I (C Major, C Minor, D Major, and E Minor). Lester calls these a "mini-series" characterized by changes that show a steady process of increasing elaboration (1998, 33).

2. Drabkin (1985, 256) offers correspondence that "captures the moment of [Schenker's] inspiration" of his reading of the C Major Prelude.

3. Schenker's one "Nota bene" is a philological reference meant to explain why the added "Schwenke" measure is musically inappropriate. He uses stem direction on the F♯2 (up) and the A♭2 (down) to claim a bidirectional motion to G2. See Rothfarb (1996, 73), for a cogent rebuttal. Nicholas Cook (1987, 28–39, 42–47) devotes considerable space to a detailed pedagogical exegesis of Schenker's reading of the C Major Prelude.

4. Carl Schachter (1987, 290) subjects the opening measures of the C Major Prelude to a brief phenomenological analysis that recalls the manner of David Lewin. Lerdahl and Jackendoff (1983) also derive 3̂–1̂ in their prolongational reduction (though their premises and method are different, of course). Fred Lerdahl (2001, 40) does not contradict the essentials of that reading, but he does categorize the C Major Prelude as a (presumably) rare clear example of transformation (by register).

5. Lester (1998, 35) shows the details of the common harmonic pattern in a "mini-series" of preludes from *The Well-Tempered Clavier*, Book 1 (recall note 1 above). The 2–3 bass suspensions are readily apparent in all, but I would argue that only the C Major Prelude, with its qualities of a stately *alla breve* movement, invokes the older syncopes as Snarrenberg (1997) says.

6. An interesting reading that takes off in quite a different direction—to patterns of metric and accentual hierarchy—is given by Wallace Berry (1985, 25–28). The skeptical reader may also have noticed that the readings presented so far do not require the arpeggio figuration—they are all based on the five-part *alla breve* level voice-leading grid. I see no way to overcome that limitation, and indeed I find in it another confirmation of Schulenberg's and Ledbetter's claims about improvisation and composition in the Bach circle. For what it's worth, one influential historical observer, Carl Czerny, thought similarly. Dividing preludes into two types, either "slow, full chords" or in "more or less florid movement of the several parts" ([1848] 1979, 1:114), he gives the chord progression

of the C Major Prelude as his model for the former. He then comments, "Such a Prelude might either remain in this state, or be varied in numerous ways. Bach himself has varied the [progression] in the following manner" (115).

7. The last two pairs are from Bliss (2000, 51) and are quoted here in edited form.

8. The sequence titled "Solitude" (no. 17) also uses the frozen lake; this time Gould walks into the frame from the right edge, continues to the middle, and then turns toward the camera, as if onstage. He talks, as if answering questions from radio listeners. The sequence consists of five shots (films 1 and 32 consist of a single extended shot), displayed symmetrically: extra-long shot, medium-long shot, long shot, medium-long shot, extra-long shot.

9. The voice-over narrator says only that "a short prelude by Johann Sebastian Bach, as performed by Glenn Gould" was included. It is perhaps an insignificant point that, although we hear the C Major Prelude under study in this chapter, the piece is not in fact on the "Golden Record" placed in both Voyager spacecraft. Gould's recording of the C Major Prelude and Fugue from the *second* book of *The Well-Tempered Clavier* is there (http://voyager.jpl.nasa.gov/spacecraft/music.html). For the audio tracks of all the music on the Golden Record, see http://goldenrecord.org.

10. Quiet as it is, the wind does have a role to play in defining the physical space. The sound is apparently direct recorded and thus helps tie us to the space of the frozen lake even as Gould walks out of it. At the same time, the wind sound has a visible effect in the drifting snow; together wind and snow clearly suggest a larger physical world offscreen, but one that is tenuous, unanchored, and featureless.

11. I am grateful to James Buhler for this last observation.

12. The voice-over narrator says that the two ships left the solar system in the late 1980s, but that refers only to the planetary region, not the more distant regions that mark the true edge of the system. According to NASA, Voyager 1 left the solar system proper only in August 2012 (http://science.nasa.gov/science-news/science-at-nasa/2013/12sep_voyager1/). As reported by @Voyager2 via Twitter on 19 October 2014, Voyager 1 is "17 hrs 59 mins 42 secs of light-travel time from Earth (2014:292:120000:11.)."

13. Jürg Stenzl (2010, 218–21) gives a detailed listing of the music collated with action for one eighteen-minute segment. See also his text discussion of the music in the film, beginning on p. 214.

14. Vlada Petric says incorrectly that Juliette, one of the students in the parallel subplot, is "spontaneously perceive[d] . . . as the grown-up dark-haired Marie" from the first film (1993, 101).

15. A complete shot breakdown and script translation for the film are given in Locke and Warren (1993, 131–83).

16. Vlada Petric points out that the image of the moon, which first appears during Marie's inner dialogue at the end of the scene, "becomes emblematic of the entire film's point of view, [representing steadiness and the power of the universe]. . . . As events develop, the moon—and the sun—is directly associated with Mary's destiny, symbolically exemplifying her obsessive search for an answer to her extraordinary physical condition (her mysterious pregnancy)" (1993, 101–102).

17. I am grateful to Robert Hatten for pointing this out.

Bibliography

Abbate, Carolyn. 2004. "Music—Drastic or Gnostic?" *Critical Inquiry* 30:505–36.

———. 2006. "Wagner, Cinema, and Redemptive Glee." *Opera Quarterly* 21, no. 1:597–611.

Agawu, Kofi. 2009. *Music as Discourse: Semiotic Adventures in Romantic Music.* New York: Oxford University Press.

Allen, Graham. 2003. *Roland Barthes.* London: Routledge.

Almén, Byron. 2008. *A Theory of Musical Narrative.* Bloomington: Indiana University Press.

Almén, Byron, and Robert Hatten. 2012. "Narrative Engagement with 20th-Century Music: Possibilities and Limits." In *Music and Narrative since 1900,* edited by Michael L. Klein and Nicholas Reyland, 59–85. Bloomington: Indiana University Press.

Altman, Rick. 1987. *The American Film Musical.* Bloomington: Indiana University Press.

———. 1992. *Sound Theory / Sound Practice.* London: Routledge.

———. 2000. "Inventing the Cinema Soundtrack: Hollywood's Multiplane Sound System." With McGraw Jones and Sonia Tatroe. In *Music and Cinema,* edited by James Buhler, Caryl Flinn, and David Neumeyer, 339–59. Hanover, N.H.: University Press of New England.

———. 2008. *A Theory of Narrative.* New York: Columbia University Press.

Anderson, Paul Allen. 2006. "The World Heard: *Casablanca* and the Music of War." *Critical Inquiry* 32:482–515.

Andrews, Dudley. 1989. "The Limits of Delight: Robert Ray's Postmodern Film Studies." *Strategies* 2:157–58.

Bachmann, Gideon. 1998. "The Carrots Are Cooked: A Conversation with Jean-Luc Godard." In *Jean-Luc Godard: Interviews,* edited by David Sterritt, 128–39. Jackson: University Press of Mississippi.

Bal, Mieke. 2009. *Narratology: Introduction to the Theory of Narrative.* 3rd ed. Toronto: University of Toronto Press. The first edition was published in Dutch in 1978, in English in 1985. The second English edition appeared in 1997.

Baldick, Chris. 1990. *The Concise Oxford Dictionary of Literary Terms.* Oxford: Oxford University Press.

Barham, Jeremy. 2011. "Recurring Dreams and Moving Images: The Cinematic Appropriation of Schumann's Op. 15, No. 7." *19th-Century Music* 34, no. 3:271–301.

Barthes, Roland. 1968. *Elements of Semiology.* Translated by Annette Lavers and Colin Smith. New York: Hill & Wang.

———. 1972. *Mythologies.* Translated by Annette Lavers. New York: Hill & Wang. An expanded edition with additional translations by Richard Howard was published in 2012 under the title *Mythologies: The Complete Edition.*

———. 1975a. *The Pleasure of the Text.* Translated by Richard Miller. New York: Hill & Wang.

——. 1975b. *S/Z.* Translated by Richard Miller. New York: Hill & Wang.

——. 1977a. "The Grain of the Voice." In *Music—Image—Text,* translated by Stephen Heath, 179–89. New York: Noonday Press.

——. 1977b. "The Third Meaning." In *Music—Image—Text,* translated by Stephen Heath, 52–68. New York: Noonday Press.

——. 1981. *Camera Lucida: Reflections on Photography.* Translated by Richard Howard. New York: Hill & Wang.

——. 1990. *A Lover's Discourse.* Translated by Richard Howard. New York: Vintage Books.

Behlmer, Rudy. 1982. *America's Favorite Movies: Behind the Scenes.* New York: F. Ungar.

——. 1985. *Inside Warner Brothers, 1935–1951.* New York: Viking.

Bellman, Jonathan D. 2011. "Musical Voyages and Their Baggage: Orientalism in Music and Critical Musicology." *Musical Quarterly* 94, no. 3:417–38.

Bellour, Raymond. 1987. "The Pensive Spectator." Translated by Lynne Kirby. *Wide Angle* 9, no. 1:6–10.

——. 2000. "The Obvious and the Code." The French original was published in 1973.

Berman, Art. 1988. *From the New Criticism to Deconstruction: The Reception of Structuralism and Post-structuralism.* Urbana: University of Illinois Press.

Bernstein, David W. 2002. "Nineteenth-Century Harmonic Theory: The Austro-German Legacy." In *The Cambridge History of Western Music Theory,* edited by David Nicholls, 778–811. Cambridge: Cambridge University Press.

Berry, Wallace. 1985. "Metric and Rhythmic Articulation in Music." *Music Theory Spectrum* 7:7–33.

Biancorosso, Giorgio. 2009. "The Harpist in the Closet: Film Music as Epistemological Joke." *Music and the Moving Image* 2, no. 2:11–33.

Bischoff, Bodo. 1997. "Das Bach-Bild Robert Schumanns." In *Bach und die Nachwelt,* edited by Michael Heinemann and Hans-Joachim Hinrichsen, 1:421–99. Laaber: Laaber Verlag.

Bliss, Michael. 2000. *Dreams within a Dream: The Films of Peter Weir.* Carbondale: Southern Illinois University Press.

Bordwell, David. 1985. *Narration in the Fiction Film.* Madison: University of Wisconsin Press.

——. 1989. *Making Meaning: Inference and Rhetoric in the Interpretation of Cinema.* Cambridge, Mass.: Harvard University Press.

——. 1997. *On the History of Film Style.* Cambridge, Mass.: Harvard University Press.

——. 2005. *Figures Traced in Light: On Cinematic Staging.* Berkeley: University of California Press.

——. 2006. *The Way Hollywood Tells It: Story and Style in Modern Movies.* Berkeley: University of California Press.

——. 2008. *Poetics of Cinema.* New York: Routledge.

Bordwell, David, and Noel Carroll, eds. 1996. *Post-theory.* Madison: University of Wisconsin Press.

Bordwell, David, Janet Staiger, and Kristin Thompson. 1985. *The Classical Hollywood Cinema: Film Style and Mode of Production to 1960.* London: Routledge.

Bordwell, David, and Kristin Thompson. 2003. *Film Art: An Introduction.* 7th ed. New York: McGraw Hill.

——. 2011. *Minding Movies: Observations on the Art, Craft, and Business of Filmmaking.* Chicago: University of Chicago Press.

Branigan, Edward. 1984. *Point of View in the Cinema*. Berlin: Mouton Publishers.
———. 1992. *Narrative Comprehension and Film*. London: Routledge.
Brophy, Philip. 2004. *100 Modern Soundtracks*. BFI Screen Guides. London: BFI Publishing.
Brown, Royal S. 1994. *Overtones and Undertones: Reading Film Music*. Berkeley: University of California Press.
Buckland, Warren. 2000. *The Cognitive Semiotics of Film*. Cambridge: Cambridge University Press.
Buhler, James. 2001. "Analytical and Interpretive Approaches to Film Music (II): Analyzing the Music." In *Film Music: Critical Approaches,* edited by Kevin Donnelly, 39–61. Edinburgh: Edinburgh University Press.
———. 2010. "Wagnerian Motives: Narrative Integration and the Development of Silent Film Accompaniment, 1908–1913." In *Wagner & Cinema,* edited by Jeongwon Joe and Sander Gilman, 27–45. Bloomington: Indiana University Press.
———. 2013. "The Reception of British Exhibition Practices in Moving Picture World, 1907–1914." In *The Sounds of the Silents in Britain,* edited by Julie Brown and Annette Davison, 144–60. New York: Oxford University Press.
———. 2014a. "Gender, Sexuality, and the Soundtrack." In *The Oxford Handbook of Film Music Studies,* edited by David Neumeyer, 366–82. New York: Oxford University Press.
———. 2014b. "Ontological, Formal, and Critical Theories of Film Music and Sound." In *The Oxford Handbook of Film Music Studies,* edited by David Neumeyer, 188–225. New York: Oxford University Press.
Buhler, James, and David Neumeyer. 2014. "Music and the Ontology of the Sound Film: The Classical Hollywood System." In *The Oxford Handbook of Film Music Studies,* edited by David Neumeyer, 17–43. New York: Oxford University Press.
Buhler, James, David Neumeyer, and Rob Deemer. 2010. *Hearing the Movies: Music and Sound in Film History*. New York: Oxford University Press.
Bullivant, Roger. "Fugue." *Grove Music Online,* edited by L. Macy. http://80-www.grovemusic.com.content.lib.utexas.edu:2048.
Cavell, Stanley. 1993. "Foreword: Prénom: Marie." In *Jean-Luc Godard's "Hail Mary": Women and the Sacred in Film,* edited by Maryel Locke and Charles Warren, xvii–xxiii. Carbondale: Southern Illinois University Press.
Chatman, Seymour. 1978. *Story and Discourse: Narrative Structure in Fiction and Film*. Ithaca, N.Y.: Cornell University Press.
———. 1990. *Coming to Terms: The Rhetoric of Narrative in Fiction and Film*. Ithaca: Cornell University Press.
Chion, Michel. 1994. *Audio-Vision: Sound on Screen*. Translated by Claudia Gorbman. New York: Columbia University Press.
———. 1999. *The Voice in Cinema*. Translated by Claudia Gorbman. New York: Columbia University Press.
———. 2003. *The Films of Jacques Tati*. Translated by Antonio D'Alfonso. Toronto: Guernica Editions Inc.
———. 2009. *Film: A Sound Art*. Translated by Claudia Gorbman. New York: Columbia University Press.
Christensen, Thomas. 1998. "Bach among the Theorists." *Bach Perspectives* 3:23–46.
Citron, Marcia J. 2000. *Opera on Screen*. New Haven, Conn.: Yale University Press.
———. 2010. *When Opera Meets Film*. Cambridge: Cambridge University Press.

Clarke, David. 2011. "Between Hermeneutics and Formalism: The Lento from Tippett's Concerto for Orchestra (or: Music Analysis after Lawrence Kramer)." *Music Analysis* 30, nos. 2–3:309–59.

Cobley, Paul. 2008. "Communication and Verisimilitude in the Eighteenth Century." In *Communication in Eighteenth-Century Music,* edited by Danuta Mirka and Kofi Agawu, 13–33. Cambridge: Cambridge University Press.

Cohen, Annabel J. 2009. "Music in Performance Arts: Film, Theatre and Dance." In *The Oxford Handbook of Music Psychology,* edited by Susan Hallam, Ian Cross, and Michael Thaut, 441–51. New York: Oxford University Press.

———. 2010. "Music as a Source of Emotion in Film." In *The Oxford Handbook of Music and Emotion,* edited by Patrik Juslin and John Sloboda, 879–908. New York: Oxford University Press.

———. 2014. "Film Music from the Perspective of Cognitive Science." In *The Oxford Handbook of Film Music Studies,* edited by David Neumeyer, 96–130. New York: Oxford University Press.

Cohn, Richard. 2012. *Audacious Euphony: Chromatic Harmony and the Triad's Second Nature.* New York: Oxford University Press.

Cook, Nicholas. 1987. *A Guide to Musical Analysis.* New York: W. W. Norton.

———. 1998. *Analysing Musical Multimedia.* New York: Oxford University Press.

Copland, Aaron. 1957. *What to Listen For in Music.* 2nd ed. New York: McGraw-Hill.

Cox, Helen, and David Neumeyer. 1998. "The Musical Function of Sound in Three Films by Alfred Hitchcock." *Indiana Theory Review* 19:13–33.

Culler, Jonathan. 1981. *The Pursuit of Signs.* London: Routledge.

———. 1982. *On Deconstruction: Theory and Criticism after Structuralism.* Ithaca, N.Y.: Cornell University Press.

———. 1983. *Barthes: A Very Short Introduction.* New York: Oxford University Press.

Czerny, Carl. (1829) 1983. *A Systematic Introduction to Improvisation on the Pianoforte.* Translated and edited by Alice L. Mitchell. New York: Longman.

———. (1833) n.d. [before 1840]. *The Art of Preluding.* London: John Bishop.

———. (1848) 1979. *School of Practical Composition, Op. 600.* 3 vols. Translated by John Bishop. London: Cocks; New York: Da Capo.

Daubney, Kate. 2000. *Max Steiner's "Now, Voyager": A Film Score Guide.* New York: Greenwood Press.

Daverio, John. 1997. *Robert Schumann: Herald of a "New Poetic Age."* New York: Oxford University Press.

Davison, Annette. 2004. *Hollywood Theory, Non-Hollywood Practice: Cinema Soundtracks in the 1980s and 1990s.* Aldershot, Hants, England: Ashgate.

Dieckman, Katherine. 1993. "Godard in His 'Fifth Period': An Interview." In *Jean-Luc Godard's "Hail Mary": Women and the Sacred in Film,* edited by Maryel Locke and Charles Warren, 119–24. Carbondale: Southern Illinois University Press.

Doane, Mary Ann. 1987. *The Desire to Desire: The Woman's Film of the 1940s.* Bloomington: Indiana University Press.

———. 1991. *Femme Fatales: Feminism, Film Theory, Psychoanalysis.* New York: Routledge.

Drabkin, William. 1985. "A Lesson in Analysis from Heinrich Schenker: The C Major Prelude from Bach's *Well-Tempered Clavier,* Book I." *Music Analysis* 4, no. 3:241–58.

du Maurier, Daphne. 1938. *Rebecca.* London: Victor Gollancz.

Ebert, Roger. 1986. Review of *Je vous salue, Marie. Chicago Sun-Times,* April. http://
www.suntimes.com/ebert/ebert_reviews/1986/04/51797.html.

———. 1988. Review of *Bagdad Café.* RogerEbert.com. http://www.rogerebert.com
/reviews/bagdad-cafe-1988.

———. 1996. Review of *Ma saison préférée. Chicago Sun-Times,* June. http://www
.suntimes.com/ebert/ebert_reviews/1996/06/060703.html.

———. 2000. Review of *Holy Smoke.* RogerEbert.com. http://www.rogerebert.com
/reviews/holy-smoke-2000.

———. 2012. Review of *The Iron Lady.* RogerEbert.com. http://www.rogerebert.com
/reviews/the-iron-lady-2012.

Eco, Umberto. 1985. "*Casablanca:* Cult Movies and Intertextual Collage." *SubStance: A
Review of Theory and Literary Criticism* 14, no. 2:3–12.

Eigeldinger, Jean-Jacques. 1986. *Chopin, Pianist and Teacher: As Seen by His Pupils.* 3rd
ed. Translated by Naomi Shohet with Krysia Osostowicz and Roy Howat, edited
by Roy Howat. Cambridge: Cambridge University Press.

Erdmann, Hans, and Giuseppe Becce, with Ludwig Brav. 1927. *Allgemeines Handbuch
der Film Musik.* Leipzig: Schlesinger.

Fawell, John. 1989. "The Musicality of the Filmscript." *Film and Literature Quarterly* 17,
no. 1:44–49.

Feder, Georg. 1969. "Gounods 'Méditation' und ihre Folgen." In *Die Ausbreitung des His-
torismus über die Musik,* edited by Walter Wiora, 85–122. Regensburg: Bosse.

Feisst, Sabine M. 1999. "Arnold Schoenberg and the Cinematic Art." *Musical Quarterly*
83, no. 1:93–113.

Finlow, Simon. 1992. "The Twenty-Seven Etudes and Their Antecedents." In *The Cambridge Companion to Chopin,* edited by Jim Samson, 50–77. Cambridge: Cambridge University Press.

Finscher, Ludwig. 1998. "Bach's Posthumous Role in Music History." *Bach Perspectives*
3:1–21.

Flinn, Caryl. 1992. *Strains of Utopia: Gender, Nostalgia, and Hollywood Film Music.*
Princeton, N.J.: Princeton University Press, 1992.

Forkel, Johann Nikolaus. (1802) 1974. *Johann Sebastian Bach: His Life, Art, and Work.*
Translated and edited by Charles Sanford Terry. New York: Vienna House.
Original edition 1920.

Forte, Allen, and Steven Gilbert. 1982. *Introduction to Schenkerian Analysis.* New York:
W. W. Norton.

Franklin, Peter. 2011. *Seeing through Music: Gender and Modernism in Classic Hollywood Film Scores.* New York: Oxford University Press.

Fuller-Maitland, John A. (1925) 1970. *The "48": Bach's "Wohltemperirtes Clavier."* Vol. 1.
Freeport, N.Y.: Books for Libraries Press.

Genette, Gérard. 1980. *Narrative Discourse.* Translated by Jane E. Lewin. Ithaca, N.Y.:
Cornell University Press.

———. 1982. *Figures of Literary Discourse.* Translated by Alan Sheridan. New York: Columbia University Press.

Gjerdingen, Robert O. 2007. *Music in the Galant Style.* New York: Oxford University
Press.

Goldmark, Daniel, Lawrence Kramer, and Richard Leppert, eds. 2007. *Beyond the
Soundtrack: Representing Music in Cinema.* Berkeley: University of California
Press.

Gorbman, Claudia. 1987. *Unheard Melodies: Narrative Film Music.* Bloomington: Indiana University Press.

———. 2011. "Artless Singing." *Music, Sound, and the Moving Image* 5, no. 2:157–71.

Greimas, A. J., and F. Rastier. 1968. "The Interaction of Semiotic Constraints." *Yale French Studies* 41:86–105.

Grodal, Torben Kragh. 2009. *Embodied Visions: Evolution, Emotion, Culture, and Film.* Oxford: Oxford University Press.

Grover-Friedlander, Michal. 2005. *Vocal Apparitions: The Attraction of Cinema to Opera.* Princeton, N.J.: Princeton University Press.

———. 2011. *Operatic Afterlives.* New York: Zone Books.

Hall, Stuart. 1999. "Encoding, Decoding." In *Cultural Studies Reader,* edited by Simon During, 507–17. New York: Routledge.

Halliday, Jon. 1997. *Sirk on Sirk: Conversations with Jon Halliday.* London: Faber and Faber. Originally published in 1971.

Harmetz, Haljean. 2002. *The Making of "Casablanca": Bogart, Bergman, and World War II.* Originally published in 1992 as *Round Up the Usual Suspects: The Making of "Casablanca": Bogart, Bergman, and World War II.* New York: Hyperion.

Harper-Scott, J. P. E., and Jim Samson, eds. 2009. *An Introduction to Music Studies.* Cambridge: Cambridge University Press.

Hatten, Robert. 1991. "On Narrativity in Music: Expressive Genres and Levels of Discourse in Beethoven." *Indiana Theory Review* 12:75–98.

———. 1994. *Musical Meaning in Beethoven: Markedness, Correlation, and Interpretation.* Bloomington: Indiana University Press.

———. 2004. *Interpreting Musical Gestures, Topics, and Tropes: Mozart, Beethoven, Schubert.* Bloomington: Indiana University Press.

———. 2015. "The Troping of Topics in Mozart's Instrumental Works." In *The Oxford Handbook of Topic Theory,* edited by Danuta Mirka, 514–36. New York: Oxford University Press.

Haworth, Catherine. 2012. "Detective Agency? Scoring the Amateur Female Investigator in 1940s Hollywood." *Music & Letters* 93, no. 4:543–73.

Head, Matthew. 2003. "Musicology on Safari: Orientalism and the Spectre of Postcolonial Theory." *Music Analysis* 22.1, no. 2:211–30.

Herzog, Amy. 2010. *Dreams of Difference, Songs of the Same: The Musical Moment in Film.* Minneapolis: University of Minnesota Press.

Hiemke, Sven. 1999. "Aspekte der französischen Bach-Rezeption." In *Bach und die Nachwelt,* edited by Michael Heinemann and Hans-Joachim Hinrichsen, 2:31–83. Laaber: Laaber Verlag.

Hubbert, Julie, ed. 2011. *Celluloid Symphonies: Texts and Contexts in Film Music History.* Berkeley: University of California Press.

———. 2014. "The Compilation Soundtrack from the 1960s to the Present." In *The Oxford Handbook of Film Music Studies,* edited by David Neumeyer, 291–318. New York: Oxford University Press.

Jameson, Fredric. 1981. *The Political Unconscious: Narrative as a Socially Symbolic Act.* Ithaca, N.Y.: Cornell University Press.

Jancovich, Mark. 2009. "'Thrills and Chills': Horror, the Woman's Film, and the Origins of Film Noir." *New Review of Film and Television Studies* 7, no. 2:157–71.

Jensen, Eric Frederick. 2001. *Schumann.* New York: Oxford University Press.

Jet Propulsion Laboratory. 2013. "NASA Voyager Status Update on Voyager 1 Location." http://www.jpl.nasa.gov/news/news.php?release=2013-107.

Joe, Jeongwon, and Rose Theresa, eds. 2002. *Between Opera and Cinema*. New York: Routledge.

Kallberg, Jeffrey. 1992. "The Harmony of the Tea Table: Gender and Ideology in the Piano Nocturne." *Representations* 39:102–33.

Karlin, Fred. 1994. *Listening to Movies: The Film Lover's Guide to Film Music*. New York: Schirmer Books.

Kassabian, Anahid. 1997. "Introduction: Music, Disciplinarity, and Interdisciplinarity." In *Keeping Score: Music, Disciplinarity, Culture*, edited by David Schwarz, Anahid Kassabian, and Lawrence Siegel, 1–10. Charlottesville: University of Virginia Press.

———. 2001. *Hearing Film: Tracking Identifications in Contemporary Hollywood Film Music*. New York: Routledge.

Kinderman, William. 1998. "Bachian Affinities in Beethoven." *Bach Perspectives* 3:81–108.

Klein, Michael L. 2005. *Intertextuality in Western Art Music*. Bloomington: Indiana University Press.

———. 2012. "Musical Story." In *Music and Narrative since 1900*, edited by Michael L. Klein and Nicholas Reyland, 3–10. Bloomington: Indiana University Press.

Knecht, Justin Heinrich. 1791–95. *Neue Vollständige Sammlung aller Arten von Vor- und Nachspielen, Fantasien, Versetten, Fugetten und Fugen für geübtere und ungeübtere Klavier und Orgel Spieler*. 6 vols. Mainz: Schott.

Koch, Howard. 1992. *"Casablanca": Script and Legend*. Woodstock, New York: Overlook Press.

Köhler, Hans Joachim. 1981. "Concluding Remarks." In *Robert Schumann, Impromptus, Opus 5, für Klavier*. Leipzig: Peters, [27]–32.

Komar, Arthur. 1994. "Ruminating about Schenker: Personal Notes and Theoretical Revisions." In *Musical Transformation and Musical Intuition: Eleven Essays in Honor of David Lewin*, edited by Rafael Atlas and Michael Cherlin, 23–39. Dedham, Mass.: Ovenbird Press.

Kramer, Lawrence. 1990. *Culture and Musical Hermeneutics: The Salome Complex*. Cambridge: Cambridge University Press.

———. 1995. *Classical Music and Postmodern Knowledge*. Berkeley: University of California Press.

———. 2002. *Musical Meaning: Toward a Critical History*. Berkeley: University of California Press.

———. 2007. *Why Classical Music Still Matters*. Berkeley: University of California Press.

———. 2014. "Classical Music, Virtual Bodies, Narrative Film." In *The Oxford Handbook of Film Music Studies*, edited by David Neumeyer, 351–65. New York: Oxford University Press.

Kulezic-Wilson, Danjela. 2009. "The Music of Film Silence." *Music and the Moving Image* 2, no. 3:1–10.

Laing, Heather. 2000. "Emotion by Numbers: Music, Song and the Musical." In *Musicals: Hollywood & Beyond*, edited by Bill Marshall and Robynn Stilwell, 5–13. Portland, Ore.: Intellect.

———. 2007. *The Gendered Score: Music in 1940s Melodrama and the Woman's Film*. Aldershot, UK, and Burlington, Vt.: Ashgate.

Lapsley, Robert, and Michael Westlake. 1988. *Film Theory: An Introduction*. Manchester: Manchester University Press.

Larsen, Peter. 2005. *Film Music*. London: Reaktion Books.

Lastra, James. 2000. *Sound Technology and the American Cinema: Perception, Represen-tation, Modernity.* New York: Columbia University Press.

Lawrence, Amy. 1991. *Echo and Narcissus: Women's Voices in Classical Hollywood Cinema.* Berkeley: University of California Press.

Lebo, Harlan. 1992. *"Casablanca": Behind the Scenes.* New York: Simon & Schuster.

Ledbetter, David. 2002. *Bach's "Well-Tempered Clavier": The 48 Preludes and Fugues.* New Haven, Conn.: Yale University Press.

Leeuwen, Mary Stewart Van. 2009. *My Brother's Keeper: What the Social Sciences Do (and Don't) Tell Us about Masculinity.* Madison, Wis.: InterVarsity Press.

Lehman, Frank. 2013a. "Hollywood Cadences: Music and the Structure of Cinematic Expectation." *Music Theory Online* 19, no. 4.

———. 2013b. "Transformational Analysis and the Representation of Genius in Film Music." *Music Theory Spectrum* 35, no. 1:1–22.

Leicester, H. Marshall, Jr. 1994. "Discourse and the Film Text: Four Readings of 'Carmen.'" *Cambridge Opera Journal* 6, no. 3:245–82.

Leinberger, Charles. 2004. *Ennie Morricone's "The Good, the Bad and the Ugly": A Film Score Guide.* Lanham, Md.: Scarecrow Press.

Leppert, Richard. 2002. "Paradise, Nature, and Reconciliation: A Tentative Conversation with Wagner, Puccini, Adorno, and the Ronettes." *Echo: A Music-Centered Jour-nal* 4, no. 1 (online).

———. 2009. "The Civilizing Process: Music and the Aesthetics of Space-Time Relations in *The Girl of the Golden West.*" In *Musical Meaning and Human Values,* edited by Keith Chapin and Lawrence Kramer, 116–49. New York: Fordham Univer-sity Press.

Lerdahl, Fred. 2001. *Tonal Pitch Space.* New York: Oxford University Press.

Lerdahl, Fred, and Ray S. Jackendoff. 1983. *A Generative Theory of Tonal Music.* Cam-bridge, Mass.: MIT Press.

Lester, Joel. 1998. "J. S. Bach Teaches Us How to Compose: Four Pattern Preludes of the Well-Tempered Clavier." *College Music Symposium* 38:33–46.

———. 2001. "Heightening Levels of Activity and J. S. Bach's Parallel-Section Construc-tions." *Journal of the American Musicological Society* 54, no. 1:49–96.

Lewin, David. 1987. *Generalized Musical Intervals and Transformations.* New Haven, Conn.: Yale University Press.

———. 2006. *Studies in Music with Text.* New York: Oxford University Press.

Locke, Maryel, and Charles Warren, editors. 1993. *Jean-Luc Godard's "Hail Mary": Women and the Sacred in Film.* Carbondale: Southern Illinois University Press.

Long, Michael. 2008. *Beautiful Monsters: Imagining the Classic in Musical Media.* Berkeley: University of California Press.

MacDonald, Claudia. 2002. "Schumann's Piano Practice: Technical Mastery and Artistic Ideal." *Journal of Musicology* 19, no. 4:527–63.

Malsky, Matthew. 2008. "Sounds of the City: Alfred Newman's 'Street Scene' and Urban Modernity." In *Lowering the Boom: Critical Studies in Film Sound,* edited by Jay Beck and Tony Grajeda, 105–22. Urbana: University of Illinois Press.

Maltby, Richard. 1996. "A Brief Romantic Interlude: Dick and Jane Go to 3½ Seconds of the Classic Hollywood Cinema." In *Post-Theory,* edited by David Bordwell and Noel Carroll, 434–59. Madison: University of Wisconsin Press.

Marks, Martin M. 2000. "Music, Drama, Warner Brothers: The Cases of *Casablanca* and *The Maltese Falcon.*" In *Music and Cinema,* edited by James Buhler, Caryl Flinn, and David Neumeyer, 161–86. Hanover, N.H.: University Press of New England.

Mast, Gerald. 1982. *Howard Hawks, Storyteller.* New York: Oxford University Press.

McBride, Joseph. 1982. *Hawks on Hawks.* Berkeley: University of California Press.

McCarthy, Todd. 1997. *Howard Hawks: The Grey Fox of Hollywood.* New York: Grove Press.

McCarty, Clifford. 1998. *Film Composers in America: A Filmography (1911–1970).* New York: Oxford University Press.

McClary, Susan. 2000. *Conventional Wisdom: The Content of Musical Form.* Berkeley: University of California Press.

McDonnell, Cari. 2014. "Genre Theory and the Film Musical." In *The Oxford Handbook of Film Music Studies,* edited by David Neumeyer, 245–69. New York: Oxford University Press.

McKay, Nicholas. 2007. "On Topics Today." *Zeitschrift der Gesellschaft der Musiktheorie* 4, nos. 1–2. Online.

McLaughlin, Thomas. 1990. "Figurative Language." In *Critical Terms for Literary Study,* edited by Frank Lentricchia and Thomas McLaughlin, 80–90. Chicago: University of Chicago Press.

McLean, Adrienne. 1993. "'It's Only That I Do What I Love and Love What I Do': 'Film Noir' and the Musical Woman." *Cinema Journal* 33, no. 1:3–16.

Metz, Christian. 1982. *The Imaginary Signifier: Psychoanalysis and the Cinema.* Translated by Celia Britton and others. Bloomington: Indiana University Press.

——. 1991. *Film Language.* Chicago: University of Chicago Press.

Miller, Frank. 1992. *"Casablanca": As Time Goes By: 50th Anniversary Commemorative Edition.* Atlanta: Turner Publishing.

Mitry, Jean. (1963) 1990. *The Aesthetics and Psychology of the Cinema.* Translated by Christopher King. Bloomington: Indiana University Press.

Monelle, Raymond. 2006. *The Musical Topic: Hunt, Military, and Pastoral.* Bloomington: Indiana University Press.

——. 2010. *The Sense of Music: Semiotic Essays.* Princeton, N.J.: Princeton University Press.

Müllemann, Norbert. 2012. "On the Lookout for the Lost Measure: Bach's C-major Prelude from the Well-Tempered Clavier I." Post on the *Henle Blog,* 16 April 2012.

Mulvey, Laura. 1975. "Visual Pleasure and Narrative Cinema." *Screen* 16, no. 3:6–18.

——. 1992. "The Hole and the Zero: The Janus Face of the Feminine." In *Jean-Luc Godard, son + image 1974–1991,* edited by Raymond Bellour, 75–89. New York: Museum of Modern Art / Abrams.

——. 2006. *Death 24x a Second: Stillness and the Moving Image.* London: Reaktion Books.

Murphy, Scott. 2014. "Transformational Theory and the Analysis of Film Music." In *The Oxford Handbook of Film Music Studies,* edited by David Neumeyer, 471–99. New York: Oxford University Press.

Musy, François. 2000. "Recording Sound for Godard." In *Cinesonic: Cinema and the Sound of Music,* edited by Phil Brophy, 29–38. St. Leonards, New South Wales: Allen and Unwin.

Naremore, James. 2008. *More Than Night: Film Noir in Its Contexts.* Berkeley: University of California Press.

Nattiez, Jean-Jacques. 1990. *Music and Discourse: Toward a Semiology of Music.* Translated by Carolyn Abbate. Princeton, N.J.: Princeton University Press.

Neumeyer, David. 1995. "Melodrama as a Compositional Resource in Early Hollywood Sound Cinema." *Current Musicology* 57:61–94.

———. 1997. "Source Music, Background Music, Fantasy and Reality in Early Sound Film." *College Music Symposium* 37:13–20.

———. 1998. "Tonal Design and Narrative in Film Music: Bernard Herrmann's *A Portrait of Hitch* and *The Trouble with Harry*." *Indiana Theory Review* 19:87–123.

———. 2000a. Introduction to *Music and Cinema,* edited by James Buhler, Caryl Flinn, and David Neumeyer. Hanover, N.H.: University Press of New England.

———. 2000b. "Performances in Early Hollywood Sound Films: Source Music, Background Music, and the Integrated Sound Track." *Contemporary Music Review* 19, pt. 1:37–62.

———. 2009a. "Diegetic/Nondiegetic: A Theoretical Model." *Music and the Moving Image* 2, no. 1 (Spring 2009). Online.

———. 2009b. "The Resonances of Wagnerian Opera and Nineteenth-Century Melodrama in the Film Scores of Max Steiner." In *Wagner and Cinema,* edited by Jeongwon Joe and Sander Gilman, 111–30. Bloomington: Indiana University Press.

———. 2009c. "Thematic Reading, Proto-backgrounds, and Registral Transformations." *Music Theory Spectrum* 31, no. 2:284–324.

———. 2011. "Themes and Lines: On the Question of Hierarchy in the Practice of Linear Analysis." *Res musica* (Estonia) 3:9–29.

———. 2014. "Film II." In *Routledge Companion to Music and Visual Culture,* edited by Anne Leonard and Tim Shephard, 359–66. New York: Routledge.

Neumeyer, David, and James Buhler. 1994. A review-article on two books (Caryl Flinn, *Strains of Utopia,* and Kathryn Kalinak, *Settling the Score*). *Journal of the American Musicological Society* 47, no. 2:364–85.

———. 2001. "Analytical and Interpretive Approaches to Film Music (I): Analyzing the Music." In *Film Music: Critical Approaches,* edited by Kevin Donnelly, 16–38. Edinburgh: Edinburgh University Press.

———. 2005. "Music-Sound-Narrative: Analyzing *Casablanca*." In *Interdisciplinary Studies in Musicology 5,* edited by Maciej Jablonski and Michael Klein, 277–91. Poznan, Poland: Rhytmos.

———. 2008. "Composing for the Films, Modern Soundtrack Theory, and the Difficult Case of *A Scandal in Paris*." In *Eisler-Studien,* edited by Peter Schweinhardt, 3:123–41. Wiesbaden: Breitkopf und Härtel.

———. 2009. "Music in the Evolving Soundtrack." In *Sound and Music in Film and Visual Media: An Overview,* edited by Graeme Harper, Ruth Doughty, and Jochen Eisentraut, 42–57. London: Continuum.

Neumeyer, David, and Laura Neumeyer. "On Motion and Stasis: Photography, 'Moving Pictures,' Music." In *Music, Meaning and Media,* edited by Richard Littlefield, Erkki Pekkilä, and David Neumeyer, 11–33. Imatra/Helsinki: International Semiotics Institute, 2007.

Neumeyer, David, and Helen Cox. 1998. "The Musical Function of Sound in Three Films by Alfred Hitchcock." *Indiana Theory Review* 19:13–33.

Neumeyer, David, and Nathan Platte. 2012. *Franz Waxman's "Rebecca": A Film Score Guide.* Lanham, Md.: Scarecrow Press.

Newman, Katharine D. 1978. Introduction to reprint edition of David Belasco, *Girl of the Golden West.* Boston: Gregg Press.

Osborne, Richard E. 1997. *The "Casablanca" Companion: The Movie Classic and Its Place in History.* Indianapolis: Riebel-Roque.

Paulin, Scott D. 2000. "Richard Wagner and the Fantasy of Cinematic Unity: The Idea of the Gesamtkunstwerk in the History and Theory of Film Music." In *Music and Cinema*, edited by James Buhler, Caryl Flinn, and David Neumeyer, 58–84. Hanover, N.H.: University Press of New England.

Petric, Vlada, with Geraldine Bard. 1993. "Godard's Vision of the New Eve." In *Jean-Luc Godard's "Hail Mary": Women and the Sacred in Film*, edited by Maryel Locke and Charles Warren, 98–114. Carbondale: Southern Illinois University Press.

Plantinga, Carl R. 2009. *Moving Viewers: American Film and the Spectator's Experience.* Berkeley: University of California Press.

Poague, Leland A. 1982. *Howard Hawks.* Boston: Twayne.

Pool, Jeannie, and H. Stephen Wright. 2011. *A Research Guide to Film and Television Music in the United States.* Lanham, Md.: Rowman & Littlefield.

Price, Brian. 2008. "The Latest Laocoön: Medium Specificity and the History of Film Theory." In *The Oxford Handbook of Film and Media Studies*, edited by Robert Kolker, 38–82. New York: Oxford University Press.

Prince, Ellen. 1987. "Sarah Gorby, Yiddish Folksinger: A Case of Dialect Shift." *International Journal of the Sociology of Language* 67:83–116.

Prince, Gerald. 1987. *A Dictionary of Narratology.* Lincoln: University of Nebraska Press.

Rapée, Erno. (1924) 1970. *Motion Picture Moods, for Pianists and Organists.* New York: Schirmer. Reprint, New York: Arno Press.

———. (1925) 1970. *Encyclopedia of Music for Pictures.* New York: Belwin. Reprint, New York: Arno Press.

Raskin, Richard. 1990. "'Casablanca' and United States Foreign Policy." *Film History* 4, no. 2:153–64.

Ratner, Leonard. 1980. *Classic Music: Expression, Form, and Style.* New York: Schirmer Books.

———. 1992. *Romantic Music: Sound and Syntax.* New York: Schirmer Books.

Ray, Robert. 1985. *A Certain Tendency of the Hollywood Cinema, 1930–1980.* Princeton, N.J.: Princeton University Press.

———. 2001. *How a Film Theory Got Lost and Other Mysteries in Cultural Studies.* Bloomington: Indiana University Press.

———. 2008. *The ABCs of Classic Hollywood.* New York: Oxford University Press.

Rayner, Jonathan. 2003. *The Films of Peter Weir.* 2nd ed. New York: Continuum.

Reyland, Nicholas. 2012. "The Beginnings of a Beautiful Friendship? Music Narratology and Screen Music Studies." *Music, Sound, and the Moving Image* 6, no. 1:55–71.

Reynolds, Christopher. 2000. "From Berlioz's Fugitives to Godard's Terrorists: Artistic Responses to Beethoven's Late Quartets." *Beethoven Forum* 8, no. 1:147–63.

Rink, John. 1994. "Chopin's Ballades and the Dialectic: Analysis in Historical Perspective." *Music Analysis* 13, no. 1:99–115.

Ritterman, Janet. 1992. "Piano Music and the Public Concert, 1800–1850." In *The Cambridge Companion to Chopin*, edited by Jim Samson, 11–31. Cambridge: Cambridge University Press.

Robertson, James C. 1993. *The "Casablanca" Man: The Cinema of Michael Curtiz.* London: Routledge.

Rothfarb, Lee. 1996. "Beethoven's Formal Dynamics: August Halm's Phenomenological Perspective." *Beethoven Forum* 5:65–84.

Sanguinetti, Giorgio. 2012. *The Art of Partimento: History, Theory, and Practice.* New York: Oxford University Press.

Schachter, Carl. 1987. "Analysis by Key: Another Look at Modulation." *Music Analysis* 6, no. 3:289–318.

Schatz, Thomas. 1988. *The Genius of the System: Hollywood Filmmaking in the Studio Era*. New York: Pantheon.

———. 1997. *Boom and Bust: American Cinema in the 1940s*. Berkeley: University of California Press.

Schenker, Heinrich. 1969. *Five Graphic Music Analyses*. Edited by Felix Salzer. New York: Dover.

Schoenberg, Arnold. 1969. *Structural Functions of Harmony*. New York: W. W. Norton.

———. 1978. *Theory of Harmony*. Translated by Roy E. Carter. Berkeley: University of California Press.

———. 1988. *Arnold Schoenberg Self-Portrait: A Collection of Articles, Program Notes, and Letters by the Composer about His Own Works*. Edited by Nuria Schoenberg Nono. Pacific Palisades, Calif.: Belmont Music.

Scholes, Robert. 1982. *Semiotics and Interpretation*. New Haven, Conn.: Yale University Press.

———. 1985. *Textual Power*. New Haven, Conn.: Yale University Press, 1985.

Schulenberg, David. 1992. *The Keyboard Music of J. S. Bach*. New York: Schirmer.

———. 1995. "Composition and Improvisation in the School of J. S. Bach." *Bach Perspectives* 1:1–42.

Schumann, Clara. 2001. *Clara Schumann: Exercises, Preludes, and Fugues*. Edited by Valerie Woodring Goertzen. Bryn Mawr: Hildegard.

Sheer, Miriam. 2001. "The Godard/Beethoven Connection: On the Use of Beethoven's Quartets in Godard's Films." *Journal of Musicology* 18, no. 1:170–88.

Shivas, Mark. 1964. "Lola." *Film Quarterly* 18, no. 1:50.

Silverman, Kaja. 1988. *The Acoustic Mirror: The Female Voice in Psychoanalysis and Cinema*. Bloomington: Indiana University Press.

Simeon, Ennio. 1996. "Some Greimasian Concepts as Applied to the Analysis of Film Music." In *Musical Semiotics in Growth*, edited by Eero Tarasti, 347–56. Bloomington: Indiana University Press.

Smith, Jeff. 1998. *The Sounds of Commerce: Marketing Popular Film Music*. New York: Columbia University Press.

———. 2009. "Bridging the Gap: Reconsidering the Border between Diegetic and Nondiegetic Music." *Music and the Moving Image* 2, no. 1:1–25.

Snarrenberg, Robert. 1997. *Schenker's Interpretive Practice*. Cambridge: Cambridge University Press.

Sperber, Ann M., and Eric Lax. 1997. *Bogart*. New York: William Morrow and Company.

Staiger, Janet. 2008. "Film Noir as Male Melodrama: The Politics of Film Genre Labeling." In *The Shifting Definitions of Genre: Essays on Labeling Films, Television Shows and Media*, edited by Lincoln Geraghty and Mark Jancovich, 71–91. Jefferson, N.C.: McFarland.

Stenzl, Jürg. 2010. *Jean-Luc Godard—musicien: Musik in den Filmen von Jean-Luc Godard*. Munich: Edition et+k.

Sterritt, David, ed. 1998. *Jean-Luc Godard: Interviews*. Jackson: University Press of Mississippi.

———. 1999. *The Films of Jean-Luc Godard: Seeing the Invisible*. Cambridge: Cambridge University Press.

Stilwell, Robynn. 2002. "Music in Films: A Critical Review of Literature, 1980–1996." *Journal of Film Music* 1, no. 1:19–61.

———. 2007. "The Fantastical Gap between Diegetic and Nondiegetic." In *Beyond the Soundtrack: Representing Music in Cinema,* edited by Daniel Goldmark, Lawrence Kramer, and Richard Leppert, 184–204. Berkeley: University of California Press.

Sudhalter, Richard M. 2002. *Stardust Melody: The Life and Music of Hoagy Carmichael.* Oxford: Oxford University Press.

Tan, Siu Lan. 2013. "Why does this baby cry when her mother sings?" Oxford University Press Blog. http://blog.oup.com/2013/11/why-does-this-baby-cry-when-her -mother-sings-viral-video/.

Tarasti, Eero. 1994. *A Theory of Musical Semiotics.* Bloomington: Indiana University Press.

Taylor, Timothy D., Mark Katz, and Tony Grajeda, eds. 2012. *Music, Sound, and Technology in America: A Documentary History of Early Phonograph, Cinema, and Radio.* Durham, N.C.: Duke University Press.

Telotte, J. P. 1993. Review of Aljean Harmetz, *Round Up the Usual Suspects: The Making of "Casablanca." Film Quarterly* 47, no. 1:61–62.

Temperley, Nicholas. 2009. "Preluding at the Piano." In *Musical Improvisation: Art, Education, and Society,* edited by Gabriel Solis and Bruno Nettl, 323–41. Urbana: University of Illinois Press.

Thomas, Sarah. 2012. *Peter Lorre: Face Maker: Constructing Stardom and Performance in Hollywood and Europe.* New York: Berghahn Books.

Thompson, Kristin. 1986. "The Concept of Cinematic Excess." In *Narrative, Apparatus, Ideology,* edited by Philip Rosen, 130–42. New York: Columbia University Press.

———. 1991. *Breaking the Glass Armor: Neoformalist Film Analysis.* Princeton, N.J.: Princeton University Press.

———. 1999. *Storytelling in the New Hollywood: Understanding Classical Narrative Technique.* Cambridge, Mass.: Harvard University Press.

Thomson, Virgil. 1933. "A Little about Movie Music." *Modern Music* 10, no. 4:188–91.

———. 1981. *A Virgil Thomson Reader.* Boston: Houghton Mifflin.

Tomita, Yo. 2008. "The Simrock Edition of the *Well-Tempered Clavier* II." On the author's website, http://www.mu.qub.ac.uk/tomita/essay/simrock/.

Verstraten, Peter. 2009. *Film Narratology.* Translated by Stefan van der Lecq. Toronto: University of Toronto Press.

Warren, Charles. 1993. "Whim, God, and the Screen." In *Jean-Luc Godard's "Hail Mary": Women and the Sacred in Film,* edited by Maryel Locke and Charles Warren, 10–26. Carbondale: Southern Illinois University Press.

Wason, Robert W. 2002. "Two Bach Preludes / Two Chopin Etudes, or 'Toujours travailler Bach—ce sera votre meilleur moyen de progresser.'" *Music Theory Spectrum* 24, no. 1:103–20.

Wegele, Peter. 2014. *Max Steiner: Composing, "Casablanca," and the Golden Age of Film Music.* Lanham, Md.: Rowman & Littlefield.

Wexman, Virginia Wright. 1993. *Creating the Couple: Love, Marriage, and Hollywood Performance.* Princeton, N.J.: Princeton University Press.

Whittall, Arnold. 2010. Review of Byron Almén, *A Theory of Musical Narrative. Music & Letters* 91, no. 2:299–303.

Wierzbicki, James, Nathan Platte, and Colin Roust. 2012. *The Routledge Film Music Sourcebook.* New York: Routledge.

Winters, Ben. 2010. "The Non-diegetic Fallacy: Film, Music, and Narrative Space." *Music & Letters* 91, no. 2:224–44.

——. 2012. "Musical Wallpaper? Towards an Appreciation of Non-narrating Music in Film." *Music, Sound, and the Moving Image* 6, no. 1:39–54.

Yacavone, Daniel. 2012. "Spaces, Gaps, and Levels: From the Diegetic to the Aesthetic in Film Theory." *Music, Sound, and the Moving Image* 6, no. 1:21–37.

Yale Film Studies. 2002. "Film Analysis Web Site 2.0." http://classes.yale.edu/film-analysis/.

Index

mickey-mousing in, 74; second car scene from *The Big Sleep* and, 60; in *To Have and Have Not*'s style and, 39; underscoring rules in, 63; *Written on the Wind*'s title song and, 18

classical music, 11–12, 186, 220, 283n11

Clavier-Büchlein vor Wilhelm Friedemann Bach: Bach's C Major Prelude in, 191, 200, 233, 236, 288n1; in *The Chronicle of Anna Magdalena Bach*, 201, 211, 233

Clementi, Muzio, 195, 284n7

closed/open binary, realistic/unrealistic binary and, 269n9

codes: Gorbman on musical, 60, 63, 185, 186, 235, 257; visual and aural, 54–63

cognitivist models, 6

comparison of sound and image, 52–54; in *The Big Sleep*, 57–60

compilation scores, 222, 223

comprehension: interpretation versus, 7; narrative, 11, 16

Concerto in F Minor, BWV 1056 (Bach), 203

Cone, Edward T., 13

connotation, 101–102, 151

Conspirators, The (1944), 32

continuity editing, 29, 30, 76

continuous/discontinuous binary, realistic/unrealistic binary and, 269n9

Cook, Nicholas, 204, 269n13

Copland, Aaron, 23

counterpoint: versus spectacle, 26–27. *See also* synchronization/counterpoint binary

Couperin, François, 192–93

Cox, Helen, 274n54

Cramer, Johann Baptist, 195

credit music, 8, 36, 184

Crosby, Bing, 20

Curtiz, Michael, 279n18, 282n6

Czerny, Carl, 198, 288n6

D Major Prelude (Bach, *The Well-Tempered Clavier*, Book I), 223, 225, 232

D Minor Chaconne (Bach), 218

D Minor Prelude (Bach, *The Well-Tempered Clavier*, Book I), 236, 261, 263

Dark Corner, The (1946): deferral of sync point in, 83; diegetic music in, 8, 12, 32; evening party scene, 3, *4*, 8, 25–26, 52–54, 78, 79, 185; exterior offscreen diegetic in, 81; gender relations in, 268n2; *I Wake Up Screaming* compared with, 16; main-title music in, 17; nightclub scene, *64*, 267n2

Dark Victory (1939), 144, 178

Davison, Annette, 75–76, 275n17, 276n18

deconstruction, 6, 269n7

Deemer, Rob, xi, 268n4

Demy, Jacques, 201

denotation, 100–102, 151

Designing Woman (1957), 65, 66

"Deutschland über alles" (anthem), 126, 134, 142, 154, 165, 166

dialogue. *See* speech

Diamond, Neil, 8, 184

Dieckman, Katherine, 255

diegetic/nondiegetic binary, x; and acoustic stylization, 107–12; agency and diegesis, 95, 233; in *Allegro*, 201; in *Bagdad Café*, 221, 233; in *The Big Sleep*, 55; in *Casablanca*, 36, 69–71, 103–104, 107–12, 122, 126, 129–31, 133–34, 136, 137, 140, 142, 144, 148, 175, 179; coincidences of design and nondiegetic cues, 233; as complex in its effects, 77; criticism of, 7; in *The Dark Corner*, 8, 12, 32; defined, 38; description of, 63; diegetic music and pure performance, 60; diegetic performances in films involving musicians, 286n18; distance between agent and sound in nondiegetic music, 184, 234; in *film noir*, 152; first term of, 65; in *Girl of the Golden West*, 221, 233; in *Holy Smoke*, 8, 10; intersection with onscreen/offscreen binary, 77–85, 95, 269n9; narrative intrusion and nondiegetic music, 30–31; in *North by Northwest*, 65, 68; among other interacting pairs, 269n9; in *The Pianist*, 210, 233; and pure performance/close synchronization binary, 232; realism and, 23; in *Rebecca*, 89, 91; role for nondiegetic music, 24; in *Die Stille vor Bach*, 201; and Stilwell's multiple axes, 275n10; in *To Have and Have Not*, 36, 38, 41

direct recording of a conversation, 25, 27

Diva (1981), 286n18

Doane, Mary Ann, 149, 151

Dr. Jekyll and Mr. Hyde (1931), 186

Don Juan (1926), 283n2

Drabkin, William, 288n2

Dubois, Madame, 195

Dvořák, Antonin, 252, 254

Dynamiter (2011), 286n15

E Major Prelude (Bach, *The Well-Tempered Clavier*, Book I), 211–12, 214

Ebert, Roger, 10, 16, 208, 222, 253, 257

Eco, Umberto, 153–54, 281n22, 282n14

editing, continuity, 29, 30, 76

Eigeldinger, Jean-Jacques, 195

Eine kleine Nachtmusik (Mozart), 241

Eisler, Hanns, 26

Sabaneev, Leonid, 12–13
Salter, Hans, 184
scale matching, 12
Schachter, Carl, 288n4
Schaeffer, Pierre, 100, 277n2
Schatz, Thomas, 32
Schenker, Heinrich: analysis of Bach's C Major
    Prelude, 204, 215, 217, 235, 236–37, 238, 239,
    240; *Five Graphic Music Analyses,* 236; on ge-
    nius versus hack, 199; on hidden repetition,
    239; on Schwenke measure, 198, 288n3
schmaltz, 68, 275n14
Schoenberg, Arnold: on absolute versus pro-
    gram music, 27–28; expressionism of, 183–
    84; on opera, 272n34; and *Thirty Two Short
    Films about Glenn Gould,* 249; tonal har-
    mony model of, 280n12
Scholes, Robert, 29–30, 50, 186, 190, 272n37
Schulenberg, David: on Bach's C Major Prelude,
    236; on composition by variation, 190, 191,
    284n1, 288n6; on Schwenke measure, 285n13
Schumann, Clara, 196, 197, 198, 285n9, 285n10,
    285n11
Schumann, Robert, 195; on Bach's *The Well-
    Tempered Clavier,* 195, 196–98, 285n9,
    285n11; *Impromptus on a Theme by Clara
    Wieck,* op. 5, 196, 197–98, 285n10
Schwenke measure, 198–99, 285n12, 285n13,
    288n3
"score by Tower records," 222
Sechter, Simon, 280n12
Secret Life of Bees, The (2008), 286n18
Selznick, David O.: *Gone with the Wind,* 87; on
    prestige film, 87, 175, 271n26; *Rebecca,* 86, 87,
    92, 273n48, 276n28
Sheer, Miriam, 72–73, 75, 276n18
Shivas, Mark, 263–64
siciliano style, 212
Silence before Bach, The (2007). See *Die Stille vor
    Bach* (2007)
silent film, 23, 24, 100, 183–84
singing: artless, 272n38; *femme fatale* as singer,
    147; in reunion scene from *Casablanca,* 143–
    47; singing cowboys, 25; spectacle of singer's
    body, 25, 143, 148; speech and music com-
    bined in, 234; topics in song, 186; voice, 43,
    102–3, 141, 148, 273n50
Sirk, Douglas, 18, 22
Skinner, Frank, 20, 22–23
Soloist, The (2009), 286n18
sonatas, 27, 74
Sons of the Pioneers (1942), 82
sound: background, 24, 53, 62, 263; compar-
    ing image and, 52–54, 59–60; as component

of film, ix; design, 11, 12, 17; direct-recorded,
    18, 27, 271n32; distance between agent and
    sound in nondiegetic music, 234; excessive
    troping occurs between image and, 185; and
    image affect one another, xi, 12, 13, 48; im-
    age-sound dialectic, ix; music as structuring
    of sound in time, 100; music as stylized
    mode of representing sound world, 109; and
    physical space, 77; symbolic relation of image
    and, 25; synchronized, 38, 77–78, 83; visual
    and aural codes in second car scene of *The
    Big Sleep,* 54–63, 55. *See also* acoustic styli-
    zation; music; sound effects; sound track;
    speech; voice
sound design, 11, 12, 17
sound effects: in *Casablanca,* 107, 112–16, 143,
    178, 179–80; codes operating in car scene
    from *The Big Sleep,* 57, 274n7; in *The Dark
    Corner,* 53; "gags," 56; and narrative, 28–29;
    in sound design, 12; in sound track hierarchy,
    3, 264; in *Die Stille vor Bach,* 232–33; in *Writ-
    ten on the Wind,* 20
sound track: abstracting film music from, 103;
    agency in, 5, 13; audio dissolves, 104, 107,
    116; in *Casablanca,* 71, 99–117, 122, 130, 142,
    143–44, 146, 170–71; as composed, x, 3, 99–
    100, 257; continuous-level, 12, 24, 178; in *The
    Dark Corner,* 54; dialectic among elements
    in, 5, 48, 50–51, 99, 264; give-and-take with
    image track, 183; hierarchy in, ix, 3, 5, 12,
    25, 31, 48, 50–51, 100; music as one element
    in, 11; music track distinguished from, ix; as
    musical composition, x; narrative potential
    of, 31; in principle of vococentrism, 101; pri-
    ority of, x, 3, 5; speech takes priority in, ix; in
    Die Stille vor Bach, 206; stylization of, 109;
    in *To Have and Have Not,* 41–42, 46, 50; at
    Warner Bros., 178; in *Written on the Wind,*
    20. *See also mise-en-bande* (integrated sound
    track); music track; underscores
"Speak to Me of Love," 69–70
spectacle: action and speech give rise to, 5; for-
    warding narrative with, 49; realism versus,
    23–27; of singer's body, 25, 143, 148; in *To
    Have and Have Not,* 48
speech: background, 27; in *The Big Sleep,* 56; in
    Casablanca, 112, 116, 178; codes operating in
    car scene from *The Big Sleep,* 57, 274n7; dia-
    logue operates at level of denotation, 100–
    101; in *M,* 18; mediates for music, 24; music
    as transcendent, 235; point-of-view, 210; pri-
    ority of, ix; speaking voice, 25, 102; synchro-
    nized, 30, 38, 48; takes priority in sound
    track, ix, 3, 5; in *To Have and Have Not,* 39,

23; in *The Big Sleep,* 58, 61–62, 275n9; in
Casablanca, 36, 69, 99, 103, 108, 116, 118, 122,
126, 130, 137, 141, 142, 157, 160, 164, 171, 175;
connotation through, 151; dramatic presence
achieved by, 24; Gorbman's rules for underscoring, 63; in *Laura,* 84; offscreen nondiegetic as site for, 80; in *Rebecca,* 87; symphonic, 3, 11; in *To Have and Have Not,* 36,
43, 48; in *Written on the Wind,* 20, 22–23, 24
unmarked/marked binary, 275n10
utopias: Bach's C Major Prelude and utopia-
nism, 215, 233; and first confrontation scene
from *Casablanca,* 168; nondiegetic world
and, 104, 133, 136; reunion scene from *Casablanca* traces opening of, 140–43; Rick's
journey from, 100; Sam and personal utopia
of Rick and Ilsa, 130–31, 143

Vallee, Rudy, 69, 281n19
Vertigo (1958), 68
vocal/instrumental binary, diegetic/nondiegetic
binary and, 269n9
vococentric cinema, 12–23; on analysis always
taking account of the voice, 170; Bordwell
and, 202; *Casablanca* as, 102; grain as opposing principle to vococentrism, 102; music in,
3–49; narrative sound film as vococentric,
3, 5; principle of vococentrism, 101; reunion
scene from *Casablanca* and, 140–43; singing voice in, 148; underscore's supplementary
function of connotation in, 151; "vococentric" defined, 12; vococentrism's basis in human perception and cognition, 100
voice: attention by habit goes to, 43; in *The
Big Sleep,* 56; bodiless, 84, 93–95; in *Casablanca,* 141, 142, 143–47; categories of voice
in cinema, 31; in *The Dark Corner,* 52–53, 83;
of the dead, 83–84; in diegetic and narrative spaces, 77–85; embodied, 84; in field of
meaning, 142; film and music studies meet
in, ix; film music begins as performance but
leads to, 3; hierarchizes everything, 12; in hierarchy of perception, 50; ideology of the,
62–63; "in the ear," 31; music mimics, 11, 30,
31; music needs, 24; in *Prénom Carmen,* 76;
in principle of vococentrism, 101; priority of,
12, 31, 234, 251; in *Rebecca,* 77; singing, 43,
102–3, 141, 148, 273n50; speaking, 25, 102;
as speech, 234; speech distinguished from,
268n3; in *Written on the Wind,* 20. *See also*
speech; vococentric cinema; voice leading;
voice-over narration

voice leading: in Bach's C Major Prelude, 238,
288n6; in *Casablanca,* 138, 139–40; in *Girl of
the Golden West,* 216
voice-over narration: acousmêtre distinguished
from, 83, 85; in *Allegro,* 202, 264; in *The Big
Sleep,* 59; in *Casablanca,* 104, 112; in *The
Chronicle of Anna Magdalena Bach,* 211; in
Following Sean, 214, 264; in narrative feature films, 234, 288n30; as narrative intrusion, 30–31; nondiegetic music combined
with, 84; offscreen nondiegetic as site for, 80;
in *Prénom Carmen,* 76; in *Rebecca,* 89, 91, 94;
in *Thirty Two Short Films about Glenn Gould,*
235, 249, 264, 289n9, 289n12

"Wacht am Rhein, Die" 106, 144, 278n8
Wagner, Richard, 23, 221, 269n10, 280n10
Wallis, Hal, 106, 118, 127, 144, 278n10, 279n2,
280n17
warm/cold binary, 59, 61
Warren, Charles, 255, 257
Wason, Robert, 194
Waxman, Franz: "At Sea," 34, 43–48; *Laura,* 84;
Rebecca, 87, 89, 91, 92, 93, 185; "To Have and
Have Not" (cue), 33, 39, 40–41
wedding marches, 221
Wegele, Peter, 277n1
Weir, Peter, 235, 241
Well-Tempered Clavier, The (Bach): in *Allegro,*
203; in *Bagdad Café,* 223, 225; C Minor Prelude, 195–96, 199, 225, 232, 265; Chopin in-
fluenced by, 194–95, 284n7; in concert repertoire in Paris, 196; D Major Prelude, 223, 225,
232; D Minor Prelude, 236, 261, 263; E Major
Prelude, 211–12, 214; evolution of pieces in,
190; in German keyboard practice tradition,
192; in keyboard pedagogy, 195, 208, 255;
mixing of styles in, 241; Schumann on, 195,
196–98, 285n9, 285n11; Schwenke measure
in, 198; transformed into work of heroic perfection, 199; in twentieth-century films, 201.
See also C Major Prelude (Bach, *The Well-
Tempered Clavier,* Book I)
Wenders, Wim, 222
Westlake, Michael, 54
Wexman, Virginia Wright, 32
Wild Strawberries (1958), 201
Williams, Andy, 273n52
Winters, Ben, 278n13, 278n15
Wizard of Oz, The (1939), 17, 83, 178, 287n21
Written on the Wind (1957), 18–23; images as-
sociated with theme song, *21;* stingers in, 22;

"Temptation," 20, 23, 26; underscore in, 20, 22–23, 24

Wuthering Heights (1939), 178

Yacavone, Daniel, 278n13

Young, Victor, 20

Young at Heart (1938), 87

Zamfir, Gheorghe, 241

DAVID NEUMEYER is Marlene and Morton Meyerson Professor of Music in the Sarah and Ernest Butler School of Music, The University of Texas at Austin. He is editor of *The Oxford Handbook of Film Music Studies* (2014) and coauthor of the textbook *Hearing the Movies: Music and Sound in Film History* (©2010; second edition forthcoming, 2015).

JAMES BUHLER is Associate Professor of Music Theory in the Sarah and Ernest Butler School of Music, The University of Texas at Austin. He is the author of *Theories of the Soundtrack* (forthcoming, 2016) and coauthor of the textbook *Hearing the Movies: Music and Sound in Film History* (©2010; second edition forthcoming, 2015).